AA

Explorer
Spain

Adam Hopkins
and
Gabrielle Macphedran

AA Publishing

Cover (front a): costumed couple riding horse at a fair
Cover (front b): windmills of La Mancha
Cover (front c): matador in all his resplendent finery
Cover (front d): roof of Gaudí's sinuous Casa Batlló
Page 3: view of towers and rooftops from archway in Antequera's castle wall
Page 4: window of Gaudí's Casa Batlló
Page 5 (a): an oasis of waterfalls, Monasterio de Piedra
Page 5 (b): tiling on a shop, Calle Mayor, Madrid
Page 6 (a): the Mezquita, Córdoba
Page 7 (a): countryside near Granada
Page 7 (b): architectural detail from eastern Spain
Page 8 (a): typically pretty Spanish balcony, Torrox
Page 9: a classic view of a white town, Casares
Cover (back): Capilla de Nuestra Señora de la Visitación, San Roque
Cover (spine): the flamenco dancer, a cultural icon

Written by Adam Hopkins and Gabrielle Macphedran
Additional writing and research by Tony Evans, Nick Inman, and Clara Villanueva.
Updated by Nick Inman, Clara Villanueva, and Jo Hodgson.

Published by AA Publishing, a trading name of Automobile Association Developments Limited, whose registered office is Millstream, Maidenhead Road, Windsor, Berkshire SL4 5GD. Registered number 1878835.

ISBN 0 7495 3580 6

The contents of this publication are believed correct at the time of printing. Nevertheless, AA Publishing accept no responsibility for errors, omissions or changes in the details given, or for the consequences of readers' reliance on this information. This does not affect your statutory rights. Assessments of the attractions, hotels and restaurants are based upon the author's own experience, and contain subjective opinions that may not reflect the publisher's opinion or a reader's experience. We have tried to ensure accuracy, but things do change, so please let us know if you have any comments or corrections.

A CIP catalogue record for this book is available from the British Library

Colour separation by Fotographics Ltd
Printed and bound in Italy by Printer Trento srl

Find out more about AA Publishing and the wide range of travel publications and services the AA provides by visiting our website at www.theAA.com/bookshop

Revised sixth edition 2003. Reprinted 2004
First published 1993

Titles in the Explorer series:
Australia • Boston & New England • Britain • Brittany • California Canada • Caribbean • China • Costa Rica • Crete • Cuba • Cyprus Egypt • Florence & Tuscany • Florida • France • Germany Greek Islands • Hawaii • India • Ireland • Italy • Japan • London Mallorca • Mexico • New York • New Zealand • Paris • Portugal Provence • Rome • San Francisco • Scotland • South Africa Spain • Thailand • Turkey • Venice • Vietnam

A02226

How to use this book

ORGANIZATION

Spain Is, Spain Was
Discusses aspects of life and culture in contemporary Spain and explores significant periods in its history.

A–Z
Breaks down the country into regional chapters, and covers places to visit, including walks and drives. In addition, Focus On articles consider a variety of topics in greater detail.

Travel Facts
Contains the strictly practical information that is vital for a successful trip.

Hotels and Restaurants
Lists recommended establishments throughout Spain, giving a brief summary of their attractions.

ABOUT THE RATINGS
Most places described in this book have been given a separate rating. These are as follows:

▶▶▶   **Do not miss**

▶▶   **Highly recommended**

▶   **Worth seeing**

MAP REFERENCES
To make the location of a particular place easier to find, every main entry in this book is given a map reference, such as 176B3. The first number (176) indicates the page on which the map can be found; the letter (B) and the second number (3) pinpoint the square in which the main entry is located. The maps on the inside front cover and inside back cover are referred to as IFC and IBC respectively. A red square denotes a place of interest.

Contents

6

Adam Hopkins and Gabrielle Macphedran spend much of their lives either in Spain or working on Spanish topics. Adam is the author of several books on Spain, he also writes about Spanish subjects for various British newspapers. Gabrielle writes for magazines and newspapers. Jointly and individually, they have also written numerous guidebooks.

Our Spain

In 1977, after years of talking about it, we walked the Pilgrims' Way, the Camino Francés, from Orreaga in the Pyrenees to Santiago de Compostela in the northwest of Spain. It was a journey of one month, 805km (500mi) and many blisters, along the route taken over the centuries by thousands and thousands of European pilgrims, and now by those from other continents as well. There were forests and mountains and immense, lonely plains, country villages denuded of their people, as elsewhere in Europe, and grand historic towns as nowhere else; among them Burgos, León, and Santiago itself. What makes the Spanish towns so different is their assertive beauty after such wide and empty spaces.

As well as our fellow pilgrims, along the way we encountered, east to west, the loud, blunt Navarrese, Basques of independent spirit, cannier Castilians, and finally those bagpipe-playing Galicians of the far west: different languages, different food, different hopes and manners.

In a way, though a northerly journey, this was a shorthand for all of Spain, for what you notice most of all here are the differences. Andalucía in the south, with its flamenco music and fried fish, and solid, sophisticated, international Catalonia in the east, are a world away from one another. Moving between them, as between other parts of Spain, is a stimulus and a delight. So too is the weather, which is very welcome to those from countries farther north!

We have our differences. Gabrielle gives her allegiance to Barcelona; Adam, who lived in Madrid when younger, cannot abandon his local patriotism. But as we travel, on a journey that we hope will never finish, we are continually enriched by the unknown and unexpected; so deep and complex is the society, so awesome its historic roots. All of our favourite things are here, or almost all, but above all we hope the reader will pick up something of the atmosphere of a people who are generous, passionate, fiery, ready to be amused, with life coursing through every vein. It is they who are the real reason for getting to know Spain a little better.

Adam Hopkins and Gabrielle Macphedran

Spain Is
Spain Was

Spain Is
Spain Was

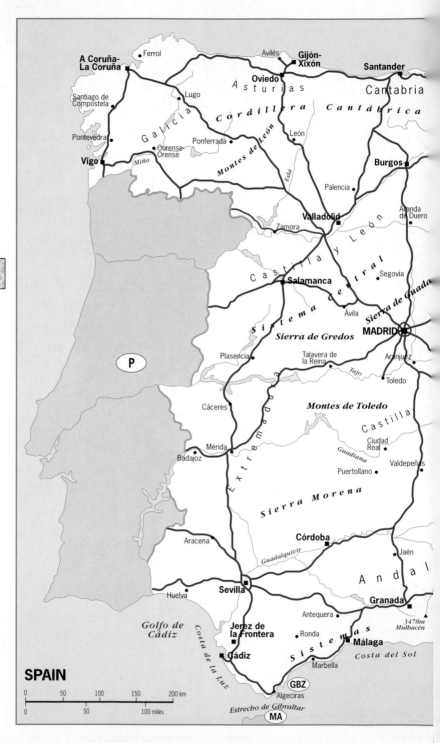

SPAIN

0   50   100   150   200 km

0   50   100 miles

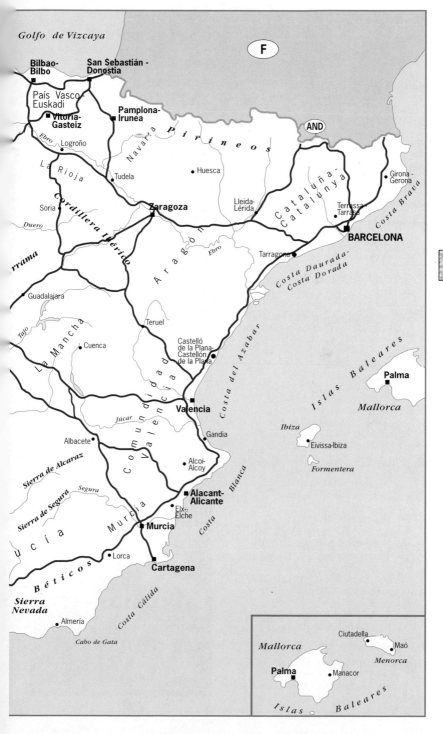

More than most countries, Spain manages to both live up to its stereotypes and defy them at the same time. This is still the land of the guitar, flamenco dance, and the carnation; of beaches, tapas, and red wine; where bulls run through city streets and hooded penitents go in procession during Easter Week. But Spain is also a developed modern country of enterprising and hard working people who have kept their roots while proclaiming their identity as mainstream Europeans.

From the visitor's point of view, the first attraction may well be the climate and the sea, in which case Spain's Mediterranean coast will be the target. This is where the postwar package tour boom took place in the late 1950s and '60s, with heavy overbuilding and the start of the Concrete Costas, so much discussed and criticized. In the last two decades the Costas have gradually tidied themselves up, with better facilities, clean beaches, and safe drinking water. Visiting them can be a crowded, cheerful, good-fun kind of experience, not by any means "real Spain," but something, nevertheless, that many will still find unbeatable for a holiday. There are some places on the Costas, as visitors and readers of this book will soon discover, which do remain remarkably attractive.

THE REAL THING Behind, in the mountains that line the coast, "real Spain" breaks out almost instantly. It is the cities, villages, and landscapes of the interior, and of the North Atlantic coast , which make up the vast bulk of this book, reflecting the depth of interest and historical richness of Spain-behind-the-Costas. Often you will see sights and encounter attitudes that seem to belong to a distant past. Often it is modernity that most impresses. Spaniards tend to prefer the latter version, because the former sounds like backwardness. But the

differences between Spain and other countries, long symbolized by the barrier of the Pyrenees, are somehow preserved in the midst of the great progress the country has made since the demise of Franco.

❑ "Spain…the best-known and the least-known of the major European nations." John Hooper, *The New Spaniards* ❑

Flamenco, one of the many and varied faces of Spain

IMPORTANCE OF PLACE Modern Spain can only be understood in terms of its regional diversity, which Franco tried to suppress and which democracy has addressed by granting huge powers of devolution. It can not be overstated that Spain is a large country which stretches from the Atlantic to the Mediterranean. Geography, climate, history, and economics have produced many peoples who live in many different ways. Gallegos (Galicians), Catalans, and Andaluces may all be Spanish as well, but their ways of working the land, their cuisine, festivities, even outlook on life are to a large part determined by the characteristics of the regions they inhabit. What unites all Spaniards is their attachment to their places of origin. Regions, districts, even suburbs and villages, exert strong ties of loyalty and belonging on the individual.

SPANISH ANIMATION Always a large part of the Spanish experience, this is perhaps most obvious in the world of high fashion and the glitzy, all-night hullabaloo of nightclubbers in Madrid and Barcelona. But that is only a beginning. The arts are burgeoning. New books are being published at a great rate. You cannot miss the snappy design of posters and other graphic art, or the confident liveliness of street life. Spain, with all the immensity of its up-and-down history behind it, is on the move. It is as exhilarating for its present as it is remarkable for its age-old survivals.

A CHANGING SPAIN Uniting so many different peoples in one country, and establishing a fair and prosperous democracy after centuries of instability, has not been free of problems. Spaniards are learning to live with a reduced bureaucracy, which they have historically both resented and relied on. An increasingly free-market economy provides more opportunities of employment but much less security for the employee. Meanwhile, the Basque separatist group ETA fights on. However, these problems are rarely perceived by the visitor who will find a country at once coping like any other in the modern world but also guarding its traditions, its exuberance, even brilliance, that has made it always such a fascinating place to visit.

13

The Mezquita mosque in Córdoba, a magnificent reminder of Spain's Moorish past

Spain is a big country, and most of its people are gathered in the cities. This means that much of the interior is sparsely populated. The landscape is often hard and challenging, green in spring but sun-hammered by summer. Yet there are zones of fertility. Valencia luxuriates in fruit and vegetables, while gardens and fruit trees line the valleys of the southern rivers, the Guadiana and the Guadalquivir. And, along the north Atlantic coast, the countryside is intensely, lushly green.

Cuenca in its majestic surroundings, a memorable Spanish landscape

MOUNTAINS AND PLAINS The central fact is that the gaunter inland parts are high, and Spain is more mountainous than any European country except Switzerland. Madrid is one of the highest capitals of the continent. The land climbs quickly up from the narrow strip of the north coast (except for Galicia, a plateau in the northwest corner). Across the northern mountains, or Cordillera Cantábrica, the open plains begin. This high level country is known as the *meseta*. Rivers criss-cross it, running considerable distances. The Ebro, starting towards the northwest, flows right across the country to the Mediterranean east, providing fertile ground along its length, which includes the vineyard country of the Rioja. The next river down is the Duero (Douro in Portuguese and, often, English), accompanied by vines and wheat. Now, working southwards to the River Tagus (Tajo), the countryside, still *meseta*, grows rougher and more rugged, broken by a series of inland mountain ranges, the sierras of Cuenca, Guadarrama, magnificent Gredos, and other, lesser outcrops. Last of all, dividing the southern region of Andalucía from the sea, comes the Sierra Morena.

Of all this countryside, only 10 percent is truly fertile. Some 40 percent is "moderately arable." Another 40 percent can be used for agriculture only with difficulty. And 10 percent is absolutely useless for farming.

TOWNS AND CITIES Within this challenging terrain, the Spaniards and the Moors, an Islamic people who held much of the peninsula for centuries (see pages 30–31), have managed to construct an extraordinary range of villages, towns, and cities.

Start in the warm south with Andalucía, and the romantic images are true: the cobbled streets with whitewashed houses, black grilles over windows, and a tumble of geraniums. Castles abound, the legacy of centuries of contention. Of the cities the great stars are Córdoba, Sevilla, and Granada.

Move on to the central *meseta*, where the climate is punishingly hot in summer and cold in winter. The villages are low and often poor, many built of adobe, clay bricks, and clustered round a dominant, stone-built church. The cities here are sturdily heroic, each with a historic centre or *casco viejo*. Often the major buildings are heraldically emblazoned; often there will be a Gothic cathedral. Around the *casco viejo*, 20th-century apartment blocks rise in depressing array.

The most beautiful cities of the middle are Toledo, Ávila, Segovia, Salamanca, and Cuenca, with Burgos and León a little farther north. The capital, Madrid, also falls into this zone. Much of it is 17th century or later, with a huge 20th-century extension. Although arguably short of memorable buildings, it is one of the most exciting places in Europe, with a large concentration of art.

Barcelona falls into the northern band but is a Mediterranean city, the most confident and lively of any in Spain, enriched by the extraordinary phenomenon of Modernista architecture, with the genius Gaudí as chief exponent. Farther down the east coast is Valencia, Spain's third largest city and growing in interest and importance. Of north coast cities, San Sebastián is most memorable at one end, and at the other is Santiago de Compostela, goal of pilgrims. And to all this, of course, must naturally be added those tourist honey-pots, the Costas.

The limestone massif of northern Spain's dramatic Picos de Europa

Democracy has sunk deep roots in Spain and modernity has touched almost every corner of national life. Regional identity is now promoted with pride; the Church and military have declined in importance. The power of the extended family threatens to follow suit as consumerism and leisure time become more appealing than bringing up a family. A slimmed down State and boosted private enterprise economy have meant less job security but also opportunities for those able to exploit them.

16

Rural Spain may still be characterized by a young woman in jeans strolling arm in arm down a village street with her grandmother; but in big cities, like those across Europe, young people are more likely to be found evading the pressures of home life.

Urban Spain is now urban western Europe. A Spaniard with a steady job is likely to be a practised consumer and enjoy regular foreign holidays, which was unheard of a generation ago when travel abroad meant migrant work for all but the rich. Some things do not change, however.

Dressing up for a wedding

Spaniards, in general, are direct in speech, to a degree which can seem like anger or rudeness to the unwary visitor. They express their emotions by the rich language of gestures to be observed in any public place.

WORK AND PLAY Spanish hours may be a puzzle at first. The day often starts early, with offices (not shops) opening at 8AM and carrying on till 2 or 3PM, at which point the working day for some people is over. Some enterprises (including all shops) have an afternoon session, starting about 5PM. In either case, where possible, Spaniards take a long, late lunch.

Lunch-time television news, for instance, is at 3PM. This system is breaking down somewhat in Madrid and Barcelona, due to the impact of international business and the EU, but it will be many decades before it disappears completely. In the evening, people have a coffee or a drink in a bar or café and eat a light dinner at any time from 9 till 11.

FAMILY BONDS In all of this, even in industrial cities, the family is the key, with mutual bonds extremely strong, mutual support freely given, and the mother at the heart within a rather "macho" society. The family is often celebrated over long Sunday lunches, usually in restaurants with children joining in from an early age.

However, Spain is suffering from a much reduced birthrate and the family of the future is likely to be based on a different model.

THE CHURCH Church attendance may have declined, but the Catholic Church still plays a key role in community life, especially as the focus for numerous religious festivals.

However, the number of atheists and agnostics is increasing steadily. Many hundreds of priests have left the church over the marriage issue and basic questions of reform versus conservatism.

❏ It used to be compulsory for Spanish boys to be named after saints and girls to be named after manifestations of the Virgin Mary (eg Virgin of the Immaculate Conception, abbreviated to Inma). The older generations still bear such religiously inspired names; but nowadays Spaniards are more likely to choose secular names for their children. ❏

THE MONARCHY The importance of the monarchy remains to some degree an open question. Brought to the throne after the death of Franco (see page 49), King Juan Carlos has not only defended democracy, but behaved with a prudent modesty and lack of ostentation which contrasts with the attitude of the political classes. Neither he nor his queen, Sofía of Greece, have much time for the old aristocracy. They keep no court, have no courtiers, and have brought up three civically minded children, now adults. Nevertheless, the monarchy itself appears to lack strong roots, thanks to its history during the 19th and early 20th centuries. The roles of the police and army have also changed. Where once the army dominated much of civilian life, now soldiers are largely invisible and compulsory military service has ended. The police, once feared, have re-emerged, in general, as public servants, symbolized by the fact that the Civil Guard or Guardia Civil, a paramilitary brigade has abandoned their famous patent-leather tricorn hats for workaday forage caps.

Spaniards know how to relax during the heat of the day

In Spain as elsewhere, television is the great pastime, with blaring TV sets a fixture in inexpensive restaurants, and game shows plentiful. Television also shows soccer, the nation's number one passion, although it has recently been challenged by a TV quest to catapult an unknown to pop stardom. Real Madrid and Barcelona dominate a league whose smallest quivers send shock waves through the nation. Sporting papers are eagerly read and supporters work themselves into a frenzy of enthusiasm.

Children take over the arena after a wood-chopping contest in San Sebastián, one of the traditional sports enjoyed by the Basques

Cycling is another major Spanish sport and even in the hottest weather motorists may encounter posses of brightly and tightly clad cyclists, heads bent down over handlebars, whizzing through remote and hostile territory.

Mountaineering and mountain walking are also popular, especially in the north and most of all in the Basque Country. Visitors are the main walkers in southern sierras, mainly in the Alpujarras south of Granada and the lovely, if steep, countryside around the White Towns in the provinces of Málaga and Cádiz.

Horse-riding and the management of horses is another Spanish passion, particularly in Andalucía, and visitors tap into this as well, with increasing numbers of trekking holidays now on offer, often amidst wild scenery.

Though attacked from abroad on grounds of cruelty, bullfighting (see pages 240–241) remains almost as important as soccer, with indications that young people are attending in greater numbers. Spaniards will tell you that it is not a sport but an ancient ritual, with a strong aesthetic content, and that it raises issues of life and death for man as well as bull.

Either way, like it or loathe it, it is there in Spanish society; not reported on newspaper sports pages, but reviewed on the arts pages along with literature and music.

SILVER SCREEN The cinema remains exceptionally well attended, with foreign films, largely American, dubbed into Spanish. For the original language, you need to look to specialist cinema houses. Quite a few Spanish films are made and a number of Spanish directors, such as Carlos Saura and Pedro Almodóvar, in lighter mode, have gained international reputations. With Luis Buñuel among their forebears, there is certainly inspiration available.

A MUSICAL NATION In music as well as dance, intensely local styles survive. The northwest, for example, is strongly attached to bagpipes. In Aragón they dance (and sing) the *jota*, with wonderfully rhythmic movement. In Catalonia, by contrast, the key dance is the *sardana*, very much a community affair, with ceremonious dancing in a ring, hands joined. People drop in and out; all ages circle round together in a relaxed sharing of experience.

Though it is thought of by outsiders as at the heart of the national stage, flamenco is also originally a local form: the music of the Andalucian south and especially of the gypsies. Its hypnotic singing style and dramatic dancing expresses a highly individual, sexually charged ethos, compulsively romantic and easy to subvert into the unchallenging form frequently offered to visitors. The names of the rhythms are often based on places: Malagueñas from Málaga, for instance; Sevillanas from Sevilla, of course; and Trianeras from that once-gypsy quarter of Sevilla, Triana, across the river from the city.

FESTIVALS AND DRESS Another aspect of Spanish life is based upon processions and dressing up. Early in the year, extravagant Carnival parades herald the end of winter and the onset of Lent. Forty days later, the Easter processions in Seville combine intense religious passion with a great deal of secular fun (see pages 140–141).

Less solemn ceremonies and feast days feature an assortment of men on stilts invisible inside vast costumes, and roly-poly figures dressed as human heads, making their way through the cheerful throng. The battles of the Moors and Christians are evoked in annual re-enactments. The best is at Alcoi, near Alicante, where the Moors give as good as they get and one dreads to think how much the costumes have cost.

The Fiestas de San Fermín, the bull-running festival in Pamplona, is world famous. Cartagena lays on a lively Romans-and-Carthaginians contest, with toga-swathed locals bearing a dashing line in swords and shields.

Every village in Spain has its own feast day, or even week of festival. Stumbling across one and joining in can be one of the great pleasures of a visit.

19

Festivals mean frills and finery

Each region of Spain makes its own dishes, based on the best locally available ingredients and served with regional wines or other distinctive drinks. The sum of them all is an extraordinarily varied national cuisine. Hotels catering for foreign visitors, however, are more likely to serve international food. For a quick bite, Spanish fast food restaurants are springing up in competition with the familiar American chains along the coasts and in the cities.

Essentially, the country has four broad culinary divisions. There is a band along the northern coast where seafood and bean dishes dominate; on the eastern seaboard, Catalonia has rich and subtle mixtures such as meat cooked in a fruit sauce; the interior (mainly "Old Castile" north of Madrid and "New Castile" to the south) goes in for meat, cooked in wood-fired ovens; Andalucía is the place for salad, fish, and fruit. There are local drinks like sherry in the south or alcoholic cider in the north. Many areas produce good cheese, once again highly distinctive in character. Excellent mineral waters abound, from Vichy Catalán in the

Outdoor eating in Valencia

Costa Brava, to Lanjarón from the springs of the Alpujarra mountains south of Granada. Madrid has a great range of regional and foreign restaurants, with some very good dishes of its own.

SWEETMEATS AND SNACKS
Desserts are less distinguished, except where they have Arab origins. But bar snacks are a vital part of Spanish eating. They are known as *pinchos* when they consist of a mere morsel alongside a drink, tapas when they are a little more substantial, which is the most common and most delicious form of bar snack, and *raciones* or rations when they amount to something the size of a restaurant dish. They come in huge varieties, ranging from mussels in vinaigrette, through Russian salad and kidneys in sherry to the wilder shores of fried pig's ear or snails and garlic.

THE NORTH San Sebastián in the Basque Country has arguably the best food in Spain. *Merluza en salsa verde* (hake in a green parsley sauce) is one of the dishes most praised. Asturias, in the middle of the coast, specializes in cider and *fabada*, a bean-and-sausage stew served as a first course. Galicia has a great feast of shellfish: spider crabs, oysters, scallops (*vieiras*). Some humbler dishes are also excellent: *caldo gallego*, a soup/stew with greens and meat, and *lacón con grelos*, pork hock with turnip tops. Wines are drunk young, often from little white china cups on pedestals.

CATALONIA AND VALENCIA

CATALONIA AND VALENCIA Catalonia yields such surprises as goose with pears, and the *mar i muntanya* dishes, literally "sea and mountain," mixing meat with fish and shellfish. Game is also good. The Raimat wine region produces some of Spain's best (still) white wines. *Cava*, a sparkling white made by the *méthode champenoise*, comes mostly from the Penedès district. Valencia is the home of paella, a dish of saffron rice, chicken, rabbit, or shellfish, made to order in great iron pans.

CASTILE AND THE CENTRE

CASTILE AND THE CENTRE *Cochinillo* and *cordero asado*, roast suckling pig and lamb respectively, crisp outside and tender within, leave space for little else. Vegetables are scarce, except in La Mancha, south of Madrid, where *pisto manchego* is close to ratatouille. La Rioja, in the

You can eat well and relatively cheaply at the counter in a tapas bar

northeast, produces Spain's best-known red wines. The best of all, however, come from the Ribera del Duero in the northwest, with a vast and less spectacular production from the area round Valdepeñas in La Mancha. Madrid's most famous dish is *cocido Madrileño*, a broth with chick peas, ham, and chicken, served in successive stages.

ANDALUCIA AND THE SOUTH

ANDALUCIA AND THE SOUTH Olives and olive oil are among the hallmarks of Andalucian cooking. The region's best-known dish is *gazpacho*, a cold soup of crushed tomatoes, cucumbers, and peppers. Restaurants on the coasts serve delicious grilled fish and in the mountains some of the best hams in Spain are cured. Sherry, and particularly the *fino* variety, is the thing to drink here. Fried fish, light and varied, is called *fritura mixta*, or, in the case of tiny fish, *pescaíto frito*. Asparagus and artichokes are wonderful.

21

The landscapes that Spaniards inhabit and the food they eat are pointers to Spain's diversity. Their language is an even deeper indication. There are four separate languages and numerous dialects. The language we call Spanish, variants of which are spoken by millions in Latin America, is really Castilian and known as such by speakers of Spain's minority languages. This is the language of Old Castile, a Romance or Latin-derived tongue that also contains thousands of Arabic words.

Two of Spain's other languages are also Latin-derived. Catalan is spoken and written not just in Catalonia but also in slightly differing forms which locals claim as distinct languages, right down the Valencian seaboard and as far as the Balearic Islands. Galicia has preserved a distinct Romance tongue akin to Portuguese, now, after some falling off (during the Franco government), once again widely spoken in this northwesterly region.

ANCIENT TONGUE The fourth language, completely separate, is Basque, which has no firm connection with any other language (though it does have some affinities with Georgian in the former Soviet Union). It is believed to be extremely ancient, certainly from before the times of literacy, though, like Castilian or any language, it contains many later borrowings and adaptations. The fact that the Basque word for "knife" derives from the word for "stone" is taken as an indication that it may really be a language with elements surviving from the neolithic period.

CONFLICT There is some mutual hostility between the languages. Road signs and place names are now almost all in the local languages, but, where they are not, campaigning enthusiasts still paint out the Castilian names. The history of each of these peoples is touched upon in the next chapter. Today, each of the regions retains its own character and many people feel a keen sense of regional pride.

A flamenco show in Sevilla involves exuberant performances coupled with bright costumes

CASTILIANS AND ARAGONESE
Historically, the Castilians have seen themselves as the "purest" Spaniards, speaking the true language and keeping the various unruly factions in order since the unification of Spain in 1492. The harsh, dry landscape of Castile is reflected in the solid stone buildings, the heavy food and wine, and a reputation for religious and political conservatism, although in these more tolerant, post-Franco days, many Castilians would resent the suggestion that they represent the serious side of Spain.

BASQUES The Basques have been described as Europe's aboriginal people, their language steeped in mystery, and their origins lost. They have a long tradition of fishing and seafaring, exemplified by Juan Sebastián Elcano, the first man to sail around the world (returning in 1522 to Spain). These days the Basque Country is industrial as well as rural, though rural life is celebrated by feats of strength such as wood-chopping at highland fairs. Although most Basques are happy to accept autonomy within the Spanish state, the terrorist group ETA has waged a campaign for many years. It believes in separation from Spain and the creation of a Basque homeland incorporating Navarra and parts of modern-day France.

CATALANS Thanks to industry and tourism, Catalonia is the wealthiest region of Spain. Its capital, Barcelona, has a youthful sense of exuberance. Throughout its history, Catalonia has looked outwards to Europe as much as in to the Iberian peninsula. The Catalan language has undergone a huge revival, but there is little sign of separatism and the Catalan politicians prefer to fight for concessions rather than outright independence.

GALICIANS (GALLEGOS) Galicia is Spain's Celtic fringe, a cold, wet region on the edge of the Atlantic famed for its seafood, wistful poetry, and haunting bagpipe music. This is one of the poorest region of Spain, and many Gallegos (among them the father of Cuban president Fidel Castro) have been forced to emigrate to Latin America to seek their fortune. As in Catalonia, despite a revival of the language in recent years, there is little enthusiasm for independence.

Village line-up in the rugged Picos de Europa region

Spain has changed almost beyond recognition since the demise of Franco's dictatorship and the restoration of democracy. And when it entered the EU in 1986 it fully cast in its lot with Europe. Progress continues apace with high-speed railways improving communications and cities being transformed by bold, innovative building projects. The tourist industry has switched from offering quantity to quality. Progress and prosperity have not, however, been evenly spread and problems of decline and depopulation in the countryside are having to be faced.

24

THE PROBLEMS Spain has endured relatively high levels of unemployment in the last decade, although the tradition of a black economy obscures the true picture. The country's once strong agricultural base, meanwhile, has suffered from depressed prices and the drift of the rural population to the cities, leaving some villages abandoned.

Despite its economic problems, Spain was an enthusiastic early

Rural Andalucía, a harsh land from which to scrape a living

entrant of European Monetary Union, and the peseta has been replaced by the euro.

A more intractable problem is that of Basque terrorism at the hands of ETA, a militant group whose name stands for "Basque Land and Liberty." ETA ended its 14-month-long cease-fire at the end of 1999 and immediately resumed its campaign of assassinations, kidnappings, and bombings designed to force the Madrid government to grant independence to the Basque Country.

Another serious issue is illegal immigration from across the Straits of Gibraltar. For many North Africans Spain is seen as the alluring gateway to Europe and a more prosperous way of life.

ENVIRONMENT The environment is another area of concern and has a direct bearing on visitors. Here, too, one must start with the positive, for Spain has more wild and untamed space, more mountain and forest than anywhere else in Europe. Flora and fauna are splendid, ranging from high Pyrenean to lowland Mediterranean species, and with such fine "extras" as the Ebro delta and especially the wetlands of the Coto de Doñana at the mouth of the Guadalquivir.

Against this, it must be said that environmental consciousness has been particularly slow to develop in Spain.

Individuals have a tendancy to dump litter indiscriminately, especially plastic. Agriculturalists show little awareness of the consequences of overusing pesticides and fertilizers. As elsewhere, an increase in traffic adds to existing industrial pollution.

Solutions are often being attempted to all these problems. The tourist trade wishes to smarten up its image and has made considerable improvements along the Mediterranean coast and in the Balearics.

The network of National Parks is being increased and regional governments are passing measures to protect large areas of their territories whose habitats are at risk.

THE FUTURE OF TOURISM Package tours and large resorts were and remain the staples of Spain's coastal tourism. Independent travel has always existed side by side with the tours, though on a far smaller scale. During the past 10 years, however, more and more people, Spaniards and visitors alike, have become aware of the beauties and pleasures of inland Spain. Roads have improved in general, historic towns have been restored, and areas of countryside protected as nature reserves and provided with marked hiking routes. To cater to the new "green" tourism, charming hotels, family-run bed-and-breakfasts, and rustic houses for rent have mushroomed in many parts of the country. So far supply has outstripped demand. Certainly if you can travel mid-week and off-season you will find a good choice of attractive, affordable places to stay in some of the most picturesque parts of the country.

Back in the 1920s, Spain invented a unique feature, which was later copied by Portugal. This was to turn some of its ancient buildings, of which there are so many that any use for them is an act of rescue rather than appropriation, into a chain of state-run hotels. These are the paradors, in Spanish *paradores*.

25

Entrance to Pedro the Cruel's castle at Carmona, near Sevilla, now a luxurious parador

From a history dogged by misfortune, Spain has delivered itself into a vibrant present at first enthusiastically received by its European partners and now achieving something like an international "normality." An impressive feat, considering the dark days of the 20th-century Civil War and the long period of military dictatorship that followed.

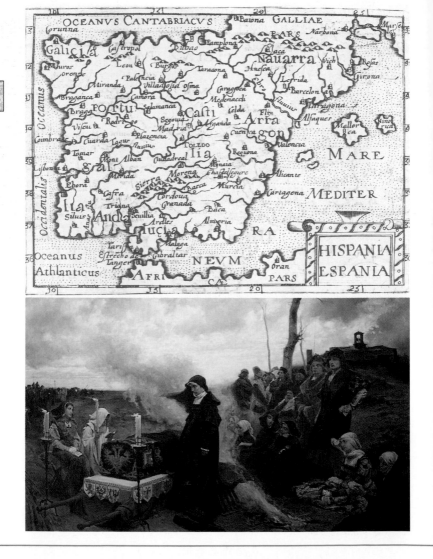

The White Town of Casares, inland from the Costa del Sol, topped by a Moorish castle

Behind the phenomenon of the present, there looms a long history. Spain's castles, cathedrals, churches, pretty arcaded squares, and streets stand as evidence of this past, a glorious architectural accumulation. While collapse and decay have also played their part, the magnificent and sometimes jagged edges of Spanish art and sculpture form an electric part of the country's long inheritance, sufficient reason in itself to visit Spain.

The work of Francisco Pradilla, one of Spain's last masters of 19th-century history painting. This depicts Juana la Loca accompanying the body of her husband, Philip the Fair

THE SPANISH STORY The Romans ruled for four centuries, then the Visigoths, and then, through most of the peninsula, the Moors. The Christians slowly pushed them back again. By the 16th century, Spain was the engine of an empire stretching over much of Europe and Latin America. In the 17th century, with the nation nearly bankrupt, Spain was producing its greatest works of art and literature in a profuse Golden Age. However, the empire was lost during the 19th century. From 1936 to 1939 Spain tore herself to pieces in a Civil War won by the right-wing Nationalists under General Franco. He died in 1975, to be succeeded by democracy and King Juan Carlos.

The first inhabitants of the peninsula included the palaeolithic cave-dwellers of northern Spain, responsible for, among many other works, the extraordinary painted bison of Altamira (around 13,000 BC). There are other interesting but less spectacular palaeolithic caves and rock shelters in eastern and southern Spain. The neolithic period left quite a wide range of dolmens, including huge burial chambers, with beautifully cut stone, at Antequera in the south, dating from about 2500 BC.

In the second millennium BC, from Africa and points east, there arrived the tribal peoples known to the Greeks as the Iberians. They were joined by a wave of Celts, creating a warlike people now called the Celtiberians. They left behind them, especially round Ávila, scores of sculpted bulls or boars, mysterious, sad-looking creatures. The round foundations of Celtic homes, and some that survive as inhabited structures, may still be encountered in Galicia. The most advanced populations were in the east, close to the Mediterranean. This area produced the stone-carved female bust, probably 5th century BC, known as *La Dama de Elche.*

TALES OF THE PAST Somewhere along the southern Atlantic coast, according to legend, lay the kingdom of Tartessos, famed for the wealth of its mines. Hercules killed its king while performing one of his 12 labours. He also set the rock of Gibraltar on one side of the exit of the Mediterranean and Ceuta on the other. The main site has not been discovered, but it is clear that a society like Tartessos existed in some form.

NEWCOMERS The Phoenicians began to arrive as traders in about 1000 BC. In due course, as Tyre collapsed, they shifted to Carthage, in Tunisia, and were known henceforth as Carthaginians. They founded a city on the site of modern Cádiz and traded with the Iberian settlements along the Spanish coast. They were joined in due course by Greek traders, moving into such sites as Empúries in modern Catalonia and Denia, on the Costa Blanca.

Above: megalith monument in the Sierra de l'Albera, on the border between Catalonia and France. Below: the dolmen of Menga at Antequera in Andalucía dates back 4,500 years

After losing the First Punic War, the Carthaginians fell back on the Spanish coast, founding the city of New Carthage, modern Cartagena. In 219 BC their leader, Hannibal, attacked the Roman ally Sagunto, starting the Second Punic War. He won, but only after the mass suicide of the inhabitants, and moved north against the Greek settlements. However, the Greeks allied themselves with the Romans, who subdued Spain with great difficulty. The Roman conquest ended in 19 BC.

soaring aqueduct of Segovia was used until modern times; the Roman bridge over the Tagus at Alcántara is 80m (262ft) high; Tarragona has a huge number of Roman remnants; and there are substantial remains at Itálica, near Sevilla. The greatest concentration of all is at Mérida in Extremadura, the former Augustus Emerita. Theatre, amphitheatre, and temples survive. Roman Spain produced grain, wine, and olive oil for export to Rome. Spanish-born emperors included Trajan, Hadrian, and Marcus Aurelius. Writers and poets Lucan, Martial, and the two Senecas were all born in Spain.

The Roman amphitheatre of Itálica was one of the largest of its kind in the Roman Empire

The country they took over was less sophisticated, raising cattle and sheep rather than crops. It also had a powerful military aristocracy. The Romans contributed social order and a uniform system of justice, widespread irrigation, and, importantly, roads. They divided the peninsula into three provinces: Lusitania, approximately Galicia and modern Portugal; Baetica, more or less modern Andalucía; and Tarraconensis, with Tarragona as capital and controlling much of the rest of Spain. They met constant resistance along the Cantabrian coast, especially from the Basques.

Above: Roman remains at the Greco-Roman city of Empúries. Below: traces of the old streets in the ruins of Itálica

TRACES OF AN EMPIRE Numerous Roman ruins remain, and some still-functional pieces of architecture. The

The Visigoths followed the Romans, and ruled for three centuries. They built small churches with horseshoe arches; their carved stonework can be seen at the National Archaeological Museum in Madrid. In AD 711 and AD 712, Berber troops came from North Africa under Arab leadership. These people, and their successors, united only in Islam, are usually referred to as the Moors. They captured the Visigothic capital, Toledo, and within four years had taken most of the rest of Spain.

Moorish castle, Vélez Málaga

Córdoba, on the Guadalquivir River, became the Moors' capital and prospered to an extraordinary degree. In 785, the territory of the Moors declared itself an emirate, under Abd al-Rahman I, the last surviving member of the Umayyad dynasty, who had escaped from a coup in Baghdad. Abd al-Rahman founded the Mezquita mosque in Córdoba, using ancient capitals and columns and constructing over them a double tier of horseshoe arches, brilliant in red and white segments. The city was by now the largest in Europe,

specializing in silks, leather, and luxury goods. The Moors had brought with them rice, citrus fruit, cotton, saffron, and a huge collection of useful plants. They developed the Roman irrigation system into a complex network still intensely admired.

BUILDING POWER Maintaining central control was always a problem. The reign of Abd al-Rahman III (912–961) was marked by the pacification of the country. He enlarged the Mezquita as a place of worship for a swelling population, and for himself he built the splendid palace of Medina Azahara, 8km (5mi) from Córdoba.

This has been described as a period of *convivencia* or mutual toleration in which the three civilizations of Islam, Christianity, and Judaism all lived together fairly peaceably. Córdoba had great libraries and nurtured philosophers, doctors, and mathematicians.

Soon, however, power passed to a military dictator, al-Mansur (in Spanish Almanzor), who launched devastating raids against the Christian north and built the last extension of the Mezquita, giving it a capacity of 25,000 worshippers.

DECLINE AND FALL Following Almanzor, at the start of the 11th century, the caliphate (empire) collapsed in sudden chaos, from which there emerged some 30 petty kingdoms, called the *taifas*. Sevilla and Zaragoza were the greatest. Soon, however, the Christians were pressing

hard, and the *taifas* summoned help from the North African Almoravids who simply took over tottering al-Andalus (Moorish Spain). Another group from Africa, the Almohads, followed. In Sevilla, their Spanish capital, they built a great tower for the mosque, the Giralda. Sevilla's famous Torre del Oro, or Golden Tower, is also their work.

Even the Almohads, however, could not hold off the Christians. Sevilla was lost in 1248 and then only the kingdom of Granada survived. It endured in artistic brilliance, creating the Alhambra palace and other splendours, till finally defeated in 1492. Granada's capture brought to an end one of the most brilliant civilizations ever seen in Europe.

The much restored Torre del Oro, Sevilla, on the banks of the Guadalquivir River

Elegant pillars and arches fill the prayer hall of the great mosque at Córdoba

MOORISH ARCHITECTURE Moorish building depended on delicacy, elaboration, and brilliant colour, with horseshoe arches, patios, paired windows divided by a single slender column (*ajimez/ajimeces*), and hanging ceilings of extraordinary complexity that look like wasps' or swallows' nests (*muqarnas*).

Decoration was in abstract plaster patterning, again amazingly complex, and often used with Koranic script. Bright wall tiles, or *azulejos*, were another major feature. They remain so in Spain today.

The *alcazaba* was the principal Moorish fortress, whereas the *alcázar* was a fortified palace. Both of these were among the many Arabic terms adopted by the Spaniards and have entered architectural language.

Some time in the 720s, starting at Covadonga in Asturias, the small, surviving pockets of Christians began to expand their territory. In the 8th and 9th centuries, the Asturians built themselves tiny but accomplished churches and palaces in Oviedo and the surrounding area, and then expanded south to León, only to be overwhelmed by Almanzor in 996. In Santiago, a tomb claimed as that of the Apostle James was discovered in the early 9th century. Almanzor devastated Santiago, too, sparing the tomb but stealing the cathedral bells.

Alfonso VI of Castile, conqueror of Moorish Toledo

EXPANSION Undaunted, the Christians once again began their expansion, now extending south and east into an area they filled with castles and called Castilla. In the mid-10th century, it proclaimed its own independence and from that point on dominated both the nearby Christians and the advance into central Spain. To the south of Castile and León lay a wild frontier area, only lightly inhabited but always dangerous. To cope with this, the Castilians developed an extraordinary mixture of spirituality and military might, two qualities with which future Spain was infused.

Meanwhile, over in the east, Barcelona and the Catalan region had been won from the Moors by the Carolingian kings of France, giving the area a quite different beginning. Barcelona became an independent territory in 878 under the rule of Wilfred the Hairy. Aragón and Navarra had also become tiny independent kingdoms, joining in the general southern movement.

The difficulty facing the Christian expansion was the lack of people to resettle conquered areas. When Alfonso VI of Castile recaptured Toledo in 1085, he was taking on an awesome responsibility. Moorish villagers and townspeople frequently remained as labourers, while the Christians, often unable to press on further, instead exacted tribute from the weakened *taifa* kingdoms. There was a great deal of coming and going across the lines. Christian kings often had Moorish wives and Moorish leaders Christian wives. The Christian hero El Cid (1026–1099) fought for years as a mercenary for Moorish Zaragoza. The Moors supplied the Christian aristocracy with silks and luxuries. Their learning was much admired and, as far as possible, absorbed. Meanwhile the Christian kingdoms welcomed French pilgrims and settlers.

NEW HOSTILITY In the 12th and 13th centuries both sides hardened up, the Moors now throwing Christians out of their territories, the Christians aiming for total reconquest under the banner of St. James the Moorslayer (the form into which St. James the Apostle had been transmuted). The Christians, though less sophisticated, were by now stronger, and slowly, over the centuries, accomplished their goal. The key Christian victory was at Navas de Tolosa near Jaén in 1212. Jaume I of Aragón-Catalonia pushed down the eastern seaboard in the 13th century, recapturing Valencia, earlier El Cid's private fief. Fernando III of Castile, who became a saint, retook almost all of Andalucía. Now Christians controlled all of Spain except Granada.

ART AND ARCHITECTURE French influence soon combined with Spanish taste to usher in a Romanesque period. Its key is the use of the round arch, in which the Romans had specialized. The ground plan of churches took on the form of the cross, with transepts and a rounded apse. Another great feature of Spanish Romanesque, which spread along the Pilgrims' Way and through the territories first reconquered, was its wonderfully

elaborate and often good-humoured sculpture. There was also fine Romanesque painting, especially in Catalonia and León. Gothic architecture, characterized by height, pointed arches, and tall windows, came in, again from France, by the 13th century. This was the style of Spain's great cathedrals and was extensively used in the later territories of the Reconquest.

Two other important styles originated in the south. In the early centuries, Christians moving north out of al-Andalus brought Moorish building habits, returning the horseshoe arch borrowed long before from the Visigoths. These were the Mozarabs, their style Mozarabic. As the Reconquest progressed, many Moorish craftsmen continued to work in a style called Mudéjar, creating some of Spain's most characteristic buildings. Mudéjar towers are patterned in raised brick and ceramics (Aragón is the best place for these, especially Teruel). Their other trademark was the *artesonado*, or coffered wooden ceiling, often star-patterned and with elaborate pendants. The Mudéjar style is almost as important to Spain as Romanesque or Gothic.

33

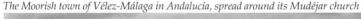

The Moorish town of Vélez-Málaga in Andalucía, spread around its Mudéjar church

Aragón absorbed Catalonia and the two of them established a empire which included, with historic consequences, Sardinia, Sicily, and Naples and even, for a century or so, Athens and much of mainland Greece. Nevertheless, the King of Aragón was in deep trouble with his nobles when his son Ferdinand, still a teenager, journeyed to Valladolid in 1469 to be married secretly to Isabella of Castile, one of two future claimants to the Castilian throne.

34

This marriage of Ferdinand and Isabella, which united two historic Spanish kingdoms, proved the making of the Spain we know today. Ferdinand and his father won their civil war at home; Isabella overcame her rival, known as La Beltraneja, in another civil war, sealed by a victory at Toro in 1474. It was a ruthless progress to the throne, and though the two monarchs represented separate kingdoms and were careful to maintain the constitutional difference, the alliance created a formidable power block which later evolved into a single nation-state.

❏ *Tanto monta, monta tanto* was the motto of Ferdinand and Isabella, meaning roughly "However high one climbs, so high climbs the other." Castile, however, was the dominant partner and Castilian the dominant language. ❏

Isabella of Castile. No woman had a stronger influence on Spanish history than this queen

FORMIDABLE TEAM Ferdinand and Isabella were an extraordinary couple. Ferdinand was a military leader and crafty diplomat, much praised by Machiavelli. The apparently simpler Isabella, rather plain in looks and resentful of her husband's many *amores*, was an administrator of extraordinary gifts, a "conviction monarch" who fought fiercely for her own vision of Castile and Catholic expansion. Together they imposed civic order through a vicious local police force, the Santa Hermandad or Holy Brotherhood, and tamed the hitherto warring nobles, forbidding them to build more castles. Though themselves of middle-brow tastes, at least in reading, they promoted sculpture, architecture, and painting to an extraordinary degree. They governed by itineration, that is to say, continual movement about their kingdoms, rather than ruling from a fixed capital. In their own day they were best known for the 1492 conquest of Granada, Spain's last Moorish kingdom, which fell after a

10-year war. Meanwhile, they had embarked upon the Spanish Inquisition. Its targets were those members of Spain's half-million strong Jewish community who were accused of false conversions to Christianity. These *conversos* were mercilessly harried with burning, imprisonment, and seizure of property.

EXPULSION AND EXPANSION With the defeat of Islam, the Catholic Monarchs (they received this title from the Pope) now banished the Jews from Spain. At the same time, they acceded to the pleas of the Genoese navigator Christopher Columbus to carry Christianity to the Far East. Columbus was convinced that Japan lay on the far side of the Atlantic. He wanted to keep one tenth of all his discoveries and demanded the hereditary title of Lord High Admiral. A disagreeable man of extraordinary courage and tenacity, he sailed with his three tiny caravels from Palos de la Frontera near Huelva on 3 August, 1492, but it was not till his third voyage that he passed right through the Caribbean islands (without realizing it) to reach the continent of South America. The Catholic Monarchs, as it happened, never kept their side of the bargain and Columbus died surrounded by acrimony. Isabella died in 1504, Ferdinand in 1516.

ART AND ARCHITECTURE The reign of Ferdinand and Isabella coincided with a new form of Gothic architecture, full of sweeping curves, with thrilling tracery and vaulting, in which style the Catholic Monarchs commissioned many buildings. Their shields, monograms, and other emblems contributed to the effect of Isabelline Gothic, as it is known. There are major royal buildings in Toledo and Granada. Finest of all in this style is the Chapel of the Constables in Burgos Cathedral. Isabella commissioned some of the most elaborate Gothic sculpture ever carved (see Burgos, Cartuja de Miraflores, pages 156–157).

Another style, named Plateresque from silversmithery, involved the shallow carving of facades in extraordinary, sinuous elaboration, often carrying messages connected with the Humanist movement, now arriving from Italy. Plateresque facades could be married to either Gothic or Renaissance buildings. Key examples are the University facade in Salamanca, and the Colegio de San Gregorio in Valladolid.

35

Ferdinand II of Aragón. His marriage to Isabella of Castile united two great kingdoms and instigated a period of conquest, discovery...and oppression

The epoch of the Spanish Habsburgs was even more extraordinary than that of the Catholic Monarchs. For within three years of the death of Ferdinand, Spain and its territories had become the biggest, most feared force on earth. Another 100 years and all was near collapse. But as national fortunes ebbed, so Spain produced the writers and painters of its Golden Age. Their brilliance remains astonishing.

Emperor Charles V, grandson of Ferdinand and Isabella

EMPEROR, KINGS, AND HAPPENINGS Charles I of Spain, Charles V of the Holy Roman Empire, was born at the start of the 16th century. He came to the Spanish throne in 1516, acquiring by inheritance not only Spain, its Italian possessions, and Flanders, but all the vast colonial spaces now opening out in South and Central America except for Brazil. He became Emperor in 1519, bringing in most of Germany and Eastern Europe. Nothing on this scale had ever been seen before, unless perhaps the empires of Alexander the Great and Tamburlaine. Yet when this grandson of Ferdinand and Isabella was called to the Spanish throne his language was Flemish, his experience foreign. He spent the greater part of his reign travelling and fighting in distant territories and ruled more from Brussels than from any Spanish point. Nevertheless, he learned good Spanish, became hispanicized to a surprising degree, and was in the end much loved by the Spanish people, retiring from empire in 1556 to live a monastic life in Extremadura.

In 1521, right at the beginning, the Spanish towns had erupted against him in the revolt of the Comuneros, which was successfully suppressed. From that point, Charles' life as emperor was overshadowed by the Reformation and the rise of Protestantism, which to him was heresy, in Germany and the Low Countries. He extended the Inquisition to Flanders and became involved in an unwinnable war there. This sucked in resources from the rest of the empire, first Italy and then Castile, which was easier to tax than Aragón for constitutional reasons. This meant that just as Castile achieved its peak as a wool-rearing and trading kingdom, it began to be devastated economically for reasons that were non-Spanish.

MIXED LEGACY Charles conducted other ruinous wars, fighting the French in Italy and at one point even sacking Rome. When he retired to Yuste, passing the Spanish (but not the imperial) throne to his son Philip II, Philip was obliged almost at once to declare bankruptcy. Even so, Spain

remained the superpower of the western world, with American gold and silver bullion entering in huge quantities (though often passing straight through to foreign creditors). Philip fought the Turks in the Mediterranean, stopping their up-to-now remorseless advance in the great sea battle of Lepanto in 1571 (his half-brother, Don John of Austria, was admiral). Married briefly to Mary Tudor of England (among four wives), he fought bitterly against her Protestant successor, Queen Elizabeth, unleashing the Invincible Armada in 1588. Devastated mainly by storm and the skill of Sir Francis Drake, this proved a self-defeating enterprise.

Philip established Madrid as Spain's first fixed capital, and ruled by an infinity of written memoranda, largely from the monastery of El Escorial in the Guadarrama mountains and for two years from Lisbon; Portugal was under Spanish rule from 1580 to 1640. Nothing was stronger than his sense of duty and his self-control was iron.

This dedication skipped a generation in the case of his son, Philip III, who frittered away 23 years, removing the capital to Valladolid and back again to Madrid. Spain, and especially Castile, continued to helter-skelter towards financial ruin. In 1609, the Moriscos, the remaining Moorish population, were expelled under cruel circumstances, with devastating consequences to Spanish agriculture, which they had sustained with their skills and hard work.

Philip III's successor, Philip IV, grave and sombre in his many portraits by Velázquez, fought more expensive wars, further impoverishing the country. A 10-year secession by Catalonia had disastrous consequences for that region. Moreover, Philip married his daughter María Teresa to Louis XIV of France, with fateful results. When the Spanish crown fell vacant in 1700, after a long reign under the ailing Charles II, the French were ready and waiting.

Philip II, whose reign saw much warfare and religious intolerance

Cervantes in literature, Velázquez in painting; two names synonymous with Spain's Golden Age, an ill-defined period with its first intimations under Ferdinand and Isabella, some slight consolidation under Charles V, a deepening and intensification under Philip II, and then, from the start of the 17th century, a flood of almost unbelievable achievement.

Early signs of glory to come appeared under Ferdinand and Isabella, when Plateresque facades were laid on Renaissance buildings. The Catholic Monarchs also imported some of the finest paintings from the Low Countries (such as van der Weyden's *Nativity* and *Pietà*, and Memling's *Descent from the Cross*), introducing a grave note of realism.

In the world of ideas, the Golden Age began with the arrival of Renaissance humanism to add a softening layer to the Castilian cocktail of mysticism and military might. The works of Erasmus, written in the Spanish Netherlands, became hugely popular, and the Spanish writer, Bartolomé de las Casas, shocked at the way millions of Indians were

Court painter Velázquez, whose own paintings scorn flattery

dying in Spain's colonies in the Americas as a result of Spanish actions, indicted his country in a volume of protest which rings down the centuries. With the best painters in the world at his command, Charles V employed the Italian Titian as his court painter, starting up a memorable tradition of royal portraiture.

EL ESCORIAL Philip II made his own massive contribution when he used the architect Herrera to build the huge monastery of El Escorial in a bare unornamented style, or *desornamentado*, to express the grand sobriety of the Spanish monarchy. This was the other side of the coin to the exuberantly decorative elements of Spanish style, and both were to endure as permanent currents.

Philip's court painters were now Spanish, with Sánchez Coello dominating. Outside the court, Renaissance models had now given way to the elongations and contortions of Mannerism.

❏ Luis Morales, El Divino, a painter from Badajoz, was an early Mannerist. The greatest was the learned Cretan, El Greco, who settled in Toledo, failed to find work with the court, and painted an unbroken flow of searing, saintly images. Meanwhile, St. Teresa of Ávila and St. John of the Cross were living out their spiritual ecstasies, expressing them in literature which used the erotic as a metaphor for the divine. ❏

San Lorenzo del Escorial, the great monastery and mausoleum built by Philip II, a gloomy memorial to the Habsburg dynasty in Spain

MIGUEL CERVANTES SAAVEDRA

(1547–1616) is the great figure who spans the junction of the centuries. Cervantes lost the use of an arm at the Battle of Lepanto, was captured at sea and held as a slave in North Africa, and finally ransomed, to resume a literary career which only brought rewards near the end of his life. In his great creation *Don Quixote*, he poked fun at the somewhat strangulated values of Spain and used the earthy squire Sancho Panza as a coarser, comic version of humanity to contrast with the lofty follies of his master.

ARTISTIC FLOWERING

Now Spain's greatest literature came in a torrent: Lope de Vega, who wrote more than 1,800 plays, and Calderón de la Barca, the other great classic playwright; Tirso de Molina, who created Don Juan; the poet Quevedo, who denounced the errors of his age and was imprisoned by the state; and Góngora, who struck a note of sonorous splendour.

Historically, this was the era of the Counter-Reformation, with Catholicism actively wishing to put forward a clearer imagery. This coincided with the clarifying spirit of early baroque. In Spain it ran along with the prodigious new wealth of Sevilla, which enjoyed a trade monopoly with America. Sevilla and Andalucía produced a multitude of painters and sculptors.

VELÁZQUEZ

(1599–1660) moved from his Sevillian beginnings as a realist, whose works were full of contrasting light and darkness, to become the greatest of Spanish court painters, with an all-seeing eye. He followed two very fine non-Andalucian Spanish painters, Ribalta in Valencia and Ribera in Naples.

SOUTHERN MASTERS

The greatest after Velázquez was Zurbarán, grave painter of monks and their white robes. Extremaduran-born, he worked in Sevilla. Juan Martínez Montañés was slightly older, a sculptor known to his own age as *el dios de madera*, the god of woodcarving. Alonso Cano, feckless and disorganized, produced painting and sculpture, combining a simple strength with delicate purity. Among the last in this line was the good-tempered Sevillian, Bartolomé Esteban Murillo, painter of smiling street children, soft doves, and scores of angels ascending in clusters. When he died in 1682, the Golden Age was coming to a close.

With the death in 1700 of Charles II of Spain, last of the Habsburgs, Louis XIV of France remarked that now there were no more Pyrenees. By this he meant that with France under his rule and Spain under that of his grandson, the Bourbon Philip of Anjou, they would be effectively a single realm. This horrified much of the rest of Europe, and the War of the Spanish Succession now began. By the end of it, Spain had lost Flanders, Naples, Milan, Gibraltar, and Menorca. But Philip of Anjou was now Philip V of Spain.

The siege of Barcelona in the War of the Spanish Succession

It was the misfortune of Barcelona, Valencia, and the Catalan-speaking east that they had backed the losing side in the war. Adopting the vigorous centralizing policies of France, Philip V subjected them to fierce repression, pulling down a chunk of Barcelona to build a fortress in its midst and closing the Catalan universities. Reaction to this was the start of the long drive towards separate Catalan status. The Basques, however, had been allies to the Bourbons and remained untouched for the moment.

TOWARDS A MODERN AGE Philip V reigned from 1700 to 1746, interrupted in 1724 when he passed the throne to his son Luis, who promptly died. His second son, Ferdinand VI, reigned from 1746 to 1759, but it was Phillip V's third son, Charles III, by his later marriage to Isabella Farnese, whose reign from 1759 to 1788 proved to be the most decisive for Spain. Charles III was the very model of a modernizing monarch. Though centralist and authoritarian, he gave an enthusiastic welcome to the more practical, project-orientated side of the 18th-century Enlightenment (in Spanish, *La Ilustración*).

Communications and harbours improved considerably. Charles established royal ceramics and glass factories (in Madrid and La Granja) and gave a boost to the royal tapestry factory founded by his brother Ferdinand VI (in Madrid and still existing). Under his sponsorship, the flora and fauna of Spain and its empire were collected and classified, and he moved his brother's botanical gardens to a site beside the Prado Museum, a building he himself initiated. It was intended as a natural history museum, not as the great picture gallery it has now become.

Charles was succeeded in 1788 by simple-looking Charles IV and his

❏ So many were Charles III's improvements to the capital that he was nicknamed the Mayor of Madrid. ❏

dominant but frumpish wife, María Luisa (familiar from Goya portraits) just in time for the hot breath of the French Revolution to reach Spain. María Luisa was enamoured of a young guards officer named Manuel Godoy, and he was soon propelled into control of the government. This curious trio took measures to respond to French aggression, but in the end, after a popular revolution had all but swept them away, they were neatly displaced by Napoleon, who needed the Iberian peninsula in order to pursue his sea blockade of Britain, and installed his brother Joseph on the throne. Spain now continued without the Bourbons.

18TH-CENTURY ART AND ARCHITECTURE The Bourbons were great palace-builders and restorers. The Royal Palace in Madrid burned down in 1734 and was rebuilt in a classic palatial style to the taste, finally, of Charles III. Another major palace was at Aranjuez, south of Madrid, beside the Tagus, and yet another, north of Madrid and easily the most charming, at La Granja de San Ildefonso. Baroque had given way now to rococo, which is most evident at La Granja and in the palace interiors.

The doorway of the palace of the Marqués de Dos Aguas in Valencia and the churches in Priego de Córdoba in Andalucía are examples of wonderfully extravagant rococo. The name of the Churriguera dynasty of architects has been fastened on the wildest instances, but they were not always so extravagant, as demonstrated by the ordered beauty of their Plaza Mayor (main square) in Salamanca.

Francisco de Goya y Lucientes, known as Goya, was a late developer in art, but made his way slowly towards its heart from his early beginnings in Zaragoza as a religious painter.

Summoned to Madrid, he and his brother-in-law Francisco Bayeu became extremely accomplished painters of vivid cartoons for the royal tapestry factory. He was soon painting portraits of leading Enlightenment figures, then of the aristocracy, and eventually, as court painter, of the royal family.

By the time of the Bourbon abdication in 1808, he had already produced the teasing, enigmatic, bitter etchings of his *Caprichos* series and was ready to move on again to document Spain's great tragedies of war.

War of the Spanish Succession: Anglo-Dutch victory at Vigo, 12 October, 1702

On 2 May, 1808, the populace of Madrid rose against the French, dragging Murat's Mameluke troops from their horses in the Puerta del Sol. By 3 May, it was over and the firing squads were in action. Goya was later to paint the central happenings. The thwarted rising signalled the start of the first modern war of independence, with Spain fighting against France in an unofficial, undercover struggle that coined the word guerrilla *or little war. A liberal, not to say revolutionary, constitution was promulgated in unconquered Cádiz.*

42

With Napoleon's eventual defeat, the Bourbons regained the crown when Ferdinand VII became the ruling monarch. However, ungrateful to the *guerrilleros*, Ferdinand began a repression which was to amount to an official terror. Meanwhile, almost without realizing it, Spain lost virtually all her American possessions to the continent's supposed liberators.

A wry look at Isabella II, whose succession began the Carlist Wars

THE CARLIST WARS After a reign in which he was at times ascendant and at times on the defensive, Ferdinand was succeeded by his infant daughter Isabella II, whose reign began with a long regency by her mother, Cristina. In bitter dispute over the legality of royal inheritance through the female line, Ferdinand's brother Carlos María Isidro unleashed the First Carlist War (1833–1839). Though restricted mainly to the north, and with the Carlists based in Navarra and the Basque Country, these sanguinary contests were a great setback to Spain. The Carlists remained a political force until at least the 1960s.

Isabella, whose reign officially lasted from 1833 to 1868, proved a frivolous monarch and Spanish politics became a to-and-fro contest between conservatives and liberals, with a sequence of military coups. The century included a military dictatorship (under Baldomero Espartero, who vigorously repressed the Basques), a short-lived First Republic (1873–1874), and the Second Carlist War (1874–1885).

Throughout this period, the Basque Country and Catalonia experienced an industrial revolution. One result of this was increasing wealth among the bourgeoisie, who became great cultural patrons, especially in Catalonia. Another was the rapid growth of a strong workforce movement, with radicalized trade unions and a strong anarchist movement.

Anarchist atrocities were met by government atrocities, which punctuated the last years of the century. In 1898, Spain found itself pitched against the young United States in an attempt to preserve Cuba as the last of its major colonies. Cuba was lost along with the Spanish fleet, the bulk of the Spanish army, and the last shred of national dignity. It was one of the nadirs in Spain's long history.

ART AND ARCHITECTURE Goya's dark vision was a beam of light to prove that Spain's artistic brilliance was not lost. He painted great wartime canvases and documented the detail in his infinitely painful, almost grotesque etchings, *The Disasters of War*. He died in exile in France, in 1828.

Queen Isabella gave her name to a new "Isabelline" style, a parallel to British mid-Victorian, with heavy furniture and profuse decoration. From now on, much Spanish art was *costumbrista*, literally "about customs," and devoted to evoking regional and folklore scenes. It paralleled a surge of romantic writing about Spain by foreigners, including Prosper Mérimée with *Carmen*. This helped to create the dagger-and-carnations image of Spain. By mid-century, Catalan language and literature were on the upturn, in what is known as the Catalan *Renaixença* or Renaissance. Its quick successor was Modernista architecture.

This style, the most exciting artistic phenomenon in 19th-century Spain and overlapping well into the 20th century, was an amalgam of northern European Arts and Crafts, art nouveau, and Jugendstil, with a recovery of Moorish and, especially, Catalan motifs of earlier centuries. Its greatest figures were Antoní Gaudí, Domènech i Montaner, and Puig i Cadafalch; its best known building Gaudí's extraordinary Sagrada Família in Barcelona.

43

Gaudí extravaganza in Barcelona's Parc Güell, good hunting ground for aficionados of Modernista style

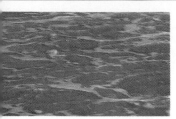

After the loss of Cuba, the cry was for national regeneration. It was uttered by both politicians and a new group of writers, whose work seemed to promise if not another Golden Age, at least a silver one. These writers were the "Generation of '98." But serious trouble was to strike again within a decade.

The flashpoint was North Africa. When Spanish interests came under threat in Morocco, the government attempted a military call-up. The Catalans refused to report for service in a national army they saw as Castilian. In Barcelona, the workers took to the streets. Churches and convents were ransacked and over 100 people died at the barricades. The year was 1909 and this was the Semana Trágica, the Tragic Week of Barcelona. It was a grim augury for the future.

THE GREAT WAR Ironically, World War I provided some relief, for though the political system came close to collapse, Spain managed both to protect its own neutrality, and to export goods and particularly food to a hungry Europe. Yet Morocco, now a protectorate, soon brought fresh troubles. A humiliating military defeat there by rebel tribesmen led to a downward spiral in Spanish political life and, in 1923, to take-over by a military dictator, Miguel Primo de Rivera. The Bourbon monarch of the day, the young Alfonso XIII, put up with this equably, even describing Primo as "my Mussolini." Primo's rule was, in fact, a much gentler affair, now often referred to as *la dictadura blanda*, the soft dictatorship. Meanwhile, under the surface, antimonarchical, republican sentiment was growing, along with Catalan separatism.

Primo resigned in 1930, and in the next year republican socialists combined with Catalans to win Spain's major cities in the local elections. Alfonso XIII knew his hour had come and simply left the country. Spain's Second Republic now began. Few recognized that it already contained its doom within it, in the fierce but so far submerged opposition between a long-suffering, anticlerical left and a right wing wedded to military values and traditional Catholicism. These forces were soon to polarize into a revolutionary movement on one hand, confronting a Spanish version of Fascism on the other.

44

Miguel Primo de Rivera, dictator from 1923 to 1930

The life of the Republic began quietly enough, with balanced budgets and respectable intentions among the new Socialist rulers. But traditionalists were deeply offended when Catalonia was granted autonomy within Spain, and by attempts at land reform, designed to alleviate shocking rural poverty.

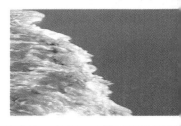

Nationalists "liberating" Toledo during the Civil War, an important symbolic act by General Franco

A right-wing government was returned in 1933. In 1934, in Asturias, in northern Spain, the coal miners and their industrial allies declared a soviet. Back in Madrid, one General Francisco Franco Bahamonde was called on to suppress the rebellion, which he did, with great loss of life. Primo de Rivera's son, José Antonio (known in Spain simply by his first names) had founded a diluted Fascist party called the Falange in 1933. The hard left won national elections in February 1936 and soon Falangists were murdering government allies and government hit-squads were murdering right-wing leaders. Some generals rebelled ostensibly to restore order.

ART AND LITERATURE The Generation of '98 included a number of writers who achieved an international reputation, among them the Basque-born philosopher and essayist Miguel de Unamuno (1864–1936), the intellectual and political theorist José Ortega y Gasset (1883–1955), and Salvador de Madariaga (1886–1978), who finally became a postwar voice for Spain's intellectuals in exile. Other writers include the poet Antonio Machado (1875–1939), Juan Ramón Jiménez, who won the Nobel Prize for literature in 1956, and Federico García Lorca (1898–1936), who produced a stunning effect with his lyrical poetry and symbolic drama. Spain had meanwhile given the world Pablo Picasso (1881–1973), Salvador Dalí (1904–1989), and Joan Miró (1893–1983). By the mid-1930s, the work of all three had become a prophecy of war.

Generals Franco and Mola repudiated the Republic on 18 July, 1936 and began a conflict that was to shatter Spain and lead to 36 years of military dictatorship. So passionately fought was the war and so burning the issues within it, that it became a representative conflict for the wider world of the 1930s, rather as Vietnam did in the 1960s and '70s. It too sucked in the great powers; but Spain's Civil War helped draw up the battle-lines for a World War which started immediately at its end.

The rebel generals had resolved at the outset that if they could not take over the country in what would in effect have been a protracted coup, then they would fight till they won, however long it took. This is exactly

General Franco, whose repressive rule spanned nearly 40 years

what happened. Far from falling into the generals' hands, the country divided itself into two zones, one Republican, one Nationalist (this was what the generals called themselves). The Republicans held Madrid and the middle of the country, Barcelona, Valencia, and the east. Very importantly, they held the Basque iron industry and the coalfields of Asturias on the north coast. The Nationalists held the rural west and an inland band across the north. They won Sevilla by a clever ruse involving General Queipo de Llano on the first day. The navy split down the middle, but the Nationalists' main asset was their command of the greater part of the regular army.

FOREIGN INVOLVEMENT Successfully transferring experienced, well-trained Spanish troops stationed in Morocco to the south of Spain, Franco raced towards Madrid and, to the astonishment of all involved, was unable to take the city, which was brilliantly defended by an improvized resistance. The war now settled down long enough for foreign countries to become involved. Nazi Germany and Mussolini's Italy sent men and war materials to Franco. The Republicans received material aid from Stalin's Russia and came increasingly, though secretly, under Russian political control. France and Britain, wary of Germany and trying to appease her, declared a policy of nonintervention. But they allowed

their citizens, along with a good many leftist Americans, to join a series of International Brigades and so to fight on the Republican side. As the battle spread round Madrid in 1936, all of these various forces were involved.

POLITICAL DEVELOPMENTS

Convulsive events were also occurring behind the lines. On both sides, in roughly equal proportions, slaughter was taking place. In the Republican zone, some 5,000 members of the clergy were murdered. The Nationalists more methodically eliminated the Left. Politically, Franco emerged as strongest of the Nationalist leaders and was nominated head of state. Lacking any obvious ideology, he adopted the Falangist party as his main vehicle. José Antonio had been shot by the Republicans in Alacant (Alicante in Castilian) jail and Franco was able to dominate the party easily. Meanwhile, on the Republican side, a genuine revolution was now taking place. Barcelona became a proletarian city. In rural Aragón, anarchist collectives were formed. They cultivated their lands success-fully until suppressed by their supposed allies, the Communists.

DEATH OF THE REPUBLIC The course of the war now slowly flowed against the Republicans. They held Madrid but as the war moved to the north, German assistance in the air helped the Nationalists take Bilbao. Meanwhile, the civilian population of the Basque town of Gernika (Guernica) was systematically bombed, the first time this had happened in Europe. By late 1937, the north was in Franco's hands, and the main struggle was now in the east. Some of the most fearful battles, marked by subzero temperatures, were fought for Teruel. By now, however, Stalin was pulling back from the war, convinced of the need for an alliance with Hitler, allowing German help to Franco to become decisive.

As the war moved into its final phase and Franco remorselessly pushed eastwards, his forces were met by the Republic's last throw: a counter-attack across the Ebro, with-out air cover. The long-running Battle of the Ebro became one simply of attrition and by the time it was over the Republic was lost. Franco entered Barcelona in triumph; Madrid collapsed upon itself, and with its fall on 27 March, 1939, the Civil War was effectively over.

INTELLECTUALS IN EXILE Picasso had painted his great work *Guernica* as a protest during the war. By the end of the war, the poets Lorca and Machado were dead, one murdered, one collapsing as he reached exile. Now most of the rest of Spain's surviving artists and intellectuals were also forced into exile, leaving a country denuded of its best minds for several decades.

Franco's main goals were order and the maintenance of his own authority. He began his postwar career by executing more than 40,000 of his former opponents. Many others remained in prison for long periods of time. Meanwhile, as World War II raged all around, Spain came close to starving. But though Franco sent volunteer troops to fight on the Eastern Front, he refused to open Spain to his former ally, Hitler. What animated him, at the deepest level, was his own view of patriotism.

Falangists on the march

After World War II, as the only surviving state that could be described (if rather inaccurately) as Fascist, Spain was profoundly isolated. Most countries withdrew their ambassadors. But soon the Americans discovered they needed Franco for their anti-Communist alliance and offered dollars in exchange for bases. From here onwards the tide began to turn. Spain joined the United Nations in 1953 and the OECD (Organization for Economic Cooperation and Development) in 1961. Vitally needed foreign investment began to flow in and it slowly became possible to reconstruct Spain's devastated industrial base. Catalonia and the Basque Country acquired the lion's share, though Franco also industrialized such places as Burgos and Madrid. Above all, he was a centralist, determined not to let Spain's peripheries off their short leash. The Basque and Catalan languages were repressed, along with any political opposition anywhere.

RURAL DEPOPULATION One thing that Franco could not stem was the rural exodus. Unable to earn a living in the countryside, millions decamped to the cities, settling in shanty towns that were eventually replaced by jerry-built apartment blocks. Countless thousands more migrated to northern Europe, becoming part of West Germany's earliest immigrant workers. Nevertheless, it is astonishing how much of modern Spain was taking shape in the Franco period.

NEW SPAIN Where only lately Spain had been poor, in the 1960s the economy came quite suddenly to life, helping create a large new middle class, a stabilizing factor Spain had always lacked. This was partly a result of the money sent home by migrant workers and partly due to foreign investment. Even more importantly, wealth came from tourism. Adopting what now seems a questionable course, Spain went in for mass tourism on its Mediterranean coast in a huge way. Success was almost instant. As foreign currency

King Juan Carlos, who brought in democratic rule after Franco's death

poured in, so did new ideas and new ways of behaviour.

The old dictator died a lingering death in 1975. His designated successor was Prince Juan Carlos de Borbón y Borbón, grandson of Alfonso XIII and sworn to uphold the Franco state. Once crowned king, however, Juan Carlos moved swiftly, with his chosen Prime Minister Adolfo Suárez, to install democracy. By manoeuvring within the system rather than challenging it from outside, he was able to comply, in form at least, with his previous promises, thus avoiding the risk of army intervention. Spain now began a hectic time of transition.

All nearly came unstuck in February 1981 when Antonio Tejero, lieutenant colonel of the paramilitary Civil Guard, entered the parliament with a troop of armed men and simply took its members captive, all in front of television cameras. It was the king, once more, who saved the day,

ordering back to their barracks the handful of generals who stood ready to rebel. The following year it was possible for Spain, without real fear of army intervention, to elect a moderate Socialist government under the Andalucian lawyer Felipe González. The only dark shadows were growing unemployment and the presence of the Basque terrorist movement ETA.

In 1986 Spain joined the then European Community, a symbolic return to a continent from which it had long been spiritually absent. In 1992 the Olympic Games were held in Barcelona and Expo 92 in Sevilla. The general election of 1996 resulted in a close victory for José Maria Aznar, leader of the centre right Partido Popular, advocating free-market economic policies and a hard-line stance against Basque terrorism. Aznar increased his majority in the March 2000 election.

CENTRAL MADRID

Museo de América

CALLE DE SAN VICENTE
CALLE DE FERRER

Parque del Oeste
Templo de Debod
Ermita de San Antonio de la Florida
Jardines Ferraz
Parque da la Montaña

San Marcos
REYES
PLAZA CONDE TORENO
S.Placido

PLAZA DE ESPAÑA
CALLE DE LA PRINCESA
CALLE VENTURA RODRIGUEZ
CALLE DE LA MADERA
CALLE DE FUENCARRAL

Estación del Norte
PASEO DEL REY
C DE CADARSO
SAN VICENTE
GRAN VIA
CALLE DE SILVIA
CALLE DE LA LUNA
CALLE DE SAN ROQUE

Palacio del Senado
PLAZA MARINA ESPAÑOLA
PLAZA SANTO DOMINGO
S Martín
CALLE DE SILVA

Jardines de Sabatini
Convento de la Encarnación
C. DE LA BOLA
CIA STO DOMINGO
JACOME TREZO
PLAZA DEL CALLAO
GRAN VIA
RED DE SAN LUIS

Casa de Campo
Jardines Cabo Noval
CARRETA
CALLE
PLAZA CARMEN

Campo del Moro
Palacio Real o de Oriente
PLAZA DE ORIENTE
Teatro Real
PLAZA ISABEL II
Convento de las Descalzas Reales
CALLE DE PRECIADOS
Real Academia de Bellas Artes de San Fernando

PLAZA DE LA ARMERIA
CALLE DE BAILEN
Santiago
CALLE DEL ARENAL
PUERTA DEL SOL
PLAZA CANALEJAS

Catedral Nuestra Señora de la Almudena
CUESTA DE LA VEGA
San Nicolás
PLAZA SANTIAGO
Torre de los Lujanes
PLAZA C MORENAS
MAYOR
Policia
CARRERA
PLAZA DEL ANGEL

Ayuntamiento
Casa de Cisneros
PLAZA DE LA VILLA
Mercado de San Miguel
PLAZA MAYOR
CALLE DE CARRETAS
NUÑEZ DE ARCE
CALLE DE ECHEGARAY

Plazuela del Cordón
C SACRAMENTO
Iglesia de San Miguel
PLAZA PROVINCIA
BOLSA
PLAZA JACINTO BENAVENTE

CALLE DE SEGOVIA
San Pedro
SEGOVIA NUEVA
Sta Cruz
PLAZA SANTA ANA

Jardines de las Vistillas
PL GABRIEL MIRO
REDONDILLA
San Andrés y Capilla del Obispo
CONCEPCION JERONIMA
CONDE ROMANONES
DOCTOR CORTEZO
PLAZA ANTON MARTIN

Catedral San Isidro
PL TIRSO DE MOLINA
CALLE DE LA MAGDALENA

CALLE DE SEGOVIA
CALLE DON PEDRO
HUMILLADERO
Mercado de la Cebada
DUQUE DE ALBA
CALLE DE LAVAPIES

PLAZA SAN FRANCISCO
GRAN VIA DE SAN FRANCISCO
CALLE DE AGUILA
TABERNILLAS
HUMILLADERO
SAN MILLAN
PLAZA DE CASCORRO
San Cayetano
PLAZA LAVAPIES

San Francisco el Grande
RONDA DE SEGOVIA
CALLE SANTA ANA
El Rastro
RIBERA DE CURTIDORES
MESON DE
CALLE
CALLE FE

PASEO IMPERIAL
RONDA DE SEGOVIA
MIRA EL RIO ALTA
CALLE RODAS
EMBAJADORES
CALLE MIGUEL SERVET

0 ____ 200 m
0 ____ 200 yards
CALLE ARGANZUELA
GLORIETA PUERTA DE TOLEDO
CALLE MIRA
CALLE DEL CASINO
CALLE DE VALENCIA

A   B   C

CALLE DE SEGOVIA

51

▶▶▶ CITY HIGHLIGHTS

Centro de Arte Reina Sofia *page 54*

Museo del Prado *page 55*

Palacio Real *page 56*

Palacio Villahermosa/ Thyssen-Bornemisza collection *page 54*

Plaza Mayor *page 64*

Warner Brothers Movie World *page 65*

THE PLAZA MAYOR

Madrid's main square used to be the scene of bullfights, public executions, and extravagant ceremonies to welcome Spanish and foreign potentates. The grandest welcome was probably that for Charles III, arriving from Italy to take up the throne in 1759. The most celebrated execution was that of Rodrigo Calderón in 1621. Though he was the hated servant of a corrupt minister, his bearing was so noble that his name has entered the language in the phrase "proud as Rodrigo on the scaffold."

The Plaza Mayor, built in 1619 by the Habsburg King Philip III

MADRID CHANGES If Madrid has few memorable monuments or architectural assemblages, it more than makes up for this with its great art galleries, museums (most famously the Prado), and the energetic life which fills its streets, cafés, and bars.

Set on a dour plain, Madrid still reflects the artificiality of choice that made it Philip II's capital in 1561. Starting life as Majerit, a tiny Moorish town around a fortress on the trickle of the Río Manzanares, it was chosen because of its position in the middle of the country. The court drew nobles, ecclesiastics, and their retinues, as well as adventurers and a vibrant low-life populace. The city's labyrinthine 17th-century quarter survives; in the 18th century, the Bourbons laid out avenues, installed fountains, and built the present day Royal Palace. After rebelling against the Napoleonic occupation, Madrid grew quickly, acquiring some lovely 19th-century districts. Trauma came in the 20th century when Republican Madrid was besieged by Franco. Madrid held its own until the bitter end of the war, after a three-year struggle. For almost 40 years, the city endured Franco's punitive rule. Following his death in 1975, it burst onto the modern European scene with unbridled enthusiasm.

FINDING YOUR WAY AROUND A broad artery formed by the Paseo del Prado, Paseo de Recoletos, and, to the north, the Paseo de la Castellana slices north to south through the heart of Madrid between the city's two main railway stations, Atocha and Chamartin. From the landmark Plaza de Cibeles, the Calle de Alcalá leads west into the old town which includes three important squares: the Plaza de la Villa (the oldest part of the city), the handsome Plaza Mayor, and the bustling Puerta del Sol. The Calle de Alcalá comes to an abrupt end at the Palacio Real. To get the real taste of old Madrid, you will need to explore the

maze of little streets south of Calle de Alcalá and Plaza Mayor. This is the best area to look for places to eat and drink (see page 67). In particular look out for the *tabernas*, bars which are often delightfully ornamented and which are typical of Madrid.

To the east, the old town merges into the 18th-century Bourbon-built districts wherein the Prado and other great museums and monuments are found. This side of the city is bordered by El Retiro Park. The elegant Salamanca district, north of the park, is a good place to shop.

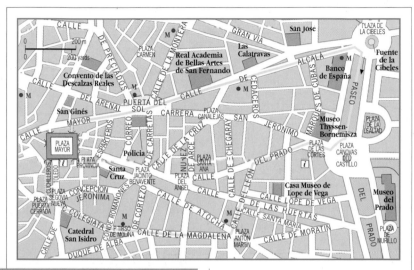

53

Walk

Through the Old Town

From Banco de España metro station, take Paseo del Prado exit and walk south down the central reservation. Turn right immediately after the Thyssen-Bornemisza collection onto Plaza de las Cortes.
The rather small Parliament building, or Cortes, is on your right.

Bear left along Calle del Prado.
There are antique shops here.

Take a left turn down Calle del León to the metro at Plaza de Antón Martín.
Here you enter a friendly blue-collar area.

Cross the square and bear right onto Calle de la Magdalena.
The wig shop on the left stocks false beards and moustaches. Continue to Plaza de Tirso de Molina.
There are cheap restaurants and a metro station here.

Go up Calle Colegiata past San Isidro cathedral. Cross Plaza de Segovia Nueva. Turn right up Cuchilleros (restaurants, see page 67), and enter the Plaza Mayor. Walk diagonally across and down Calle de Postas to the Puerta del Sol. Cut diagonally across and go down Calle de Alcalá.
The Real Academia de Bellas Artes de San Fernando is on your left.

Continue downhill to the Banco de España metro, your starting point.
Welcome views of the post office and Alcalá Gate greet you at the end.

Madrid

Picasso's Guernica, *inspired by the Civil War, is displayed as the centrepiece of the Reina Sofía Art Centre. This impressive canvas is a great attraction to visitors*

ART CAPITAL
Madrid has one of the finest concentrations of art of any city in the world. The Museo del Prado offers a complete review of the art of Spain and its European empire. Excellence in Spain after the empire can be explored via the fine 20th-century collection of the Centro de Arte Reina Sofía, which houses Picasso's *Guernica*, returned from New York to newly democratic Spain in 1981. The full international gamut is provided by the Thyssen-Bornemisza collection, with its German expressionists, Russian constructivists, and American pop artists, not to mention its magnificent medieval and Renaissance works. The Prado, Thyssen, and Reina Sofía collections are all within a short distance of one another, forming a spectacular "arts triangle." Other exceptional galleries such as the Royal Academy of San Fernando are not far away.

►►► Centro de Arte Reina Sofía 51D1
Calle Santa Isabel 52 (tel: 914 67 50 62)
www.museoreinasofia.mcu.es
Metro: Atocha
Open: Mon, Wed–Sat 10–9, Sun 10–2.30
Admission charge; free Sat afternoon and Sun morning
A major repository of art, the Reina Sofía has an outstanding collection of 20th-century Spanish art and hosts international exhibitions. Its crowning glory is Picasso's *Guernica*. There are works by Dalí, Juan Gris, Miró, Tàpies, and the Basque sculptor Chillida.

►►► Museo del Prado see page 55

►►► Palacio Real see pages 56–57

►►► Palacio Villahermosa/ 51D2
Thyssen-Bornemisza collection
Paseo del Prado 8 (tel: 913 69 01 51)
www.offcampus.es/museo.thyssen-bornemisza
Metro: Banco de España, Atocha
Open: Tue–Sun 10–7
Some 800 paintings of the highest quality, spanning eight centuries, are exhibited alongside sculpture and works of decorative art at the Villahermosa palace.

►► Puerta del Sol 50C3
Transport and pedestrians converges on this semicicular square at the heart of the city. A plaque on the ground marks the point from which all road distances in the country are measured. The headquarters of Madrid's regional government is here, and was formerly Franco's despised Ministry of the Interior. The statue of a bear guzzling the fruit of a strawberry tree is the symbol of the city.

►► Real Academia de Bellas Artes 50C3
de San Fernando
Calle de Alcalá 13 (tel: 915 24 08 64)
Metro: Sevilla, Puerta del Sol
Open: Tue–Fri 9–7, Sat–Mon 10–2. Admission charge
This 18th-century foundation, of which Goya was president, features a fine collection of his works. There are also magnificent works by Zurbarán, and good Murillos.

▶▶▶ Museo del Prado   51D2

Paseo del Prado (tel: 913 30 28 00)
http://museoprado.mcu.es
Metro: Banco de España, Atocha
Open: Tue–Sat 9–7, Sun 9–2. Admission charge

The Prado is one of the most spectacular picture galleries in the world. The power of the Spanish crown meant that the monarchs, on whose collection the Prado is founded, bought in the best of paintings from their dominions and from countries closely involved with Spain, including the Low Countries of Hieronymus Bosch and Rubens, and the Italy of Titian and Tintoretto.

At home, both Velázquez and Goya were court painters for most of their careers. El Greco was always at odds with the court but his works were bought in after his death. Quantities of the finest religious painting, representing the whole course of Spanish art, arrived after the disestablishment of the monasteries in the 19th century. A full range of all these works, including many masterpieces of world importance, is displayed in the Prado.

It is a huge gallery with over 2,000 paintings arranged on three floors, with a notable collection of sculptures, so it cannot comfortably be taken in on one visit. The following are suggestions on how to approach your visit.

On a first trip, you could concentrate on the main Spanish masters: El Greco (ground floor), Velázquez (first floor), and Goya (mainly on second floor) in historically correct order. A second visit could take in other Spanish masters: Zurbarán, Ribalta, Ribera, Alonso Cano, Murillo (ground and first floor), and Italian masters, especially Titian (ground floor). The French paintings on this floor are also very fine. A third visit might allow time to concentrate on earlier works (kept downstairs), mostly from the Low Countries. Bosch is the star here for many visitors, but the Rogier van der Weyden contribution is also magnificent.

Early Spanish paintings are less impressive but the country's individual strengths start to emerge with such Renaissance painters as Pedro Berruguete.

THE GREAT GOYA
The life of artist Francisco de Goya (1746–1828) was changed irretrievably by an illness which led to total deafness. It struck him when on a visit to Andalucía to stay with the Duchess of Alba, with whom he was in love. He painted her many times, but she is not "La Maja" in his two famous paintings of that name, a woman shown both dressed and naked in the same luxuriant pose. It was after the onset of his deafness that Goya's tormented inner life began to make itself manifest in fantastical and sombre works.

55

One of the world's great art galleries: the Prado. A visit to this museum, with its outstanding collection of paintings and sculptures, is a highlight of any stay in Madrid

Bourbon grandeur, the Palacio Real. The Changing of the Guard takes place in the Plaza de la Armería at midday every first Wednesday of the month and is worth watching

THE FORMER PALACE
The Arab fortress, or *alcázar*, in Madrid, was replaced by a Gothic palace, renovated and redecorated under the direction of Velázquez. This in its turn burned down, destroying many of Velázquez's own paintings.

►►► **Palacio Real** 50A3

Calle de Bailén (tel: 915 42 00 59; for information on the Changing of the Guard tel: 914 54 88 00)
Metro: Ópera, Plaza de España
Open: Mon–Sat 9.30–5, Sun 9–2; closed occasionally for state functions. Admission charge

The neoclassical Palacio Real (Royal Palace), stately home of the Bourbon dynasty from the 18th to the 20th centuries, contains 2,800 rooms, and is also known as the Palacio de Oriente, from the square on its eastern flank. The Bourbons preferred to live outside Madrid, but the palace which they used to act out the imperial role was erected by Philip V from 1734, on the site of the old Arab *alcázar* in Madrid.

The new palace was built by two Italian architects, Juvara and Sacchetti. They worked in a regal style, further sobered by Charles III. The result is an impressive building constructed of granite from the nearby Guadarrama mountains, combined with white Colmenar stone. Within, however, all is sumptuousness, for this remained the palace of the Bourbons up to the abdication of Alfonso XIII in 1931. The present king, Juan Carlos, lives in domesticity in the Zarzuela Palace outside Madrid. The Palacio de Oriente is used for state functions.

Visitors enter by the courtyard on the southern front and purchase their tickets on the right-hand side for a guided tour (in English as well as Spanish). Highlights include: the marble staircase at the start, with painted ceiling; Goya portraits of Queen María Luisa and Charles IV; the Salón de Gasparini, with oriental stucco ceiling; the Sala de Porcelana, its walls clad in porcelain plaques made at the Buen Retiro; the huge state dining room; and a sumptuous throne room with ceiling by Tiepolo.

There are several museums in the palace precincts, for which extra tickets are required. The **Biblioteca** (library) has 400,000 volumes. The **Armería Real** contains the suits of armour worn by the Spanish kings, their children, and horses. The **Museo de Carruajes** (Museum of Carriages) is reached via the adjacent park, the **Campo del Moro**.

Walk

Circuit of the Palacio Real

From Ópera metro in Plaza Isabel II, skirt round Teatro Real (the opera house) onto Plaza de Oriente. Turn left on Bailén, passing the Royal Palace.

Divert across the forecourt between the palace and the Almudena cathedral for views of the **Casa de Campo** (a park).

To the south of the cathedral there are some excavations of Moorish ruins.

Continue steeply downhill from the cathedral to Paseo Virgen del Puerto and turn right.

Here you can enter (towards the far end) the fine **Campo del Moro** park.

Go out the same way, turn right, and follow the road round the park for a steep climb up Cuesta de San Vicente along the side of another pleasant garden, **Jardines de**

Sanatini. Then turn left at Plaza de España along Ferraz to **Templo de Debod** in Parque de la Montaña.

Go back to Ferraz, cross it, and take Calle Ventura Rodriguez, then right down Martín de los Heros for Plaza de España. Start up the Gran Vía then turn right up Isabel la Católica.

This dingy street is redeemed by the ceramics shop **Casa Antigua de Talavera**.

Now pick your way downhill back to Ópera metro.

Madrid

Glimpses of the past in the Museo Arqueológico. With its rich and varied collection of art, ranging from prehistoric to medieval times, it is rated as one of Madrid's most important museums

Museums and galleries

▶ Casa-Museo de Lope de Vega   *51D2*

Calle de Cervantes 11 (tel: 914 29 92 16)
Metro: Antón Martín
Open: Tue–Fri 9.30–2, Sat 10–1.30. Admission charge
Reconstructed in period style and now converted to a study centre (open only briefly to the public), this house evokes its former inhabitant, the heroic playwright of the Golden Age and author of over 1,800 plays.

▶▶ Estudio y Museo de Sorolla   *51E4*

Paseo General Martínez Campos 37 (tel: 913 10 15 84)
www.mcu.es/nmuseos/sorolla
Metro: Rubén Darío
Currently closed for refurbishment
The Sorolla Museum, in the artist's home-cum-studio some way north of the old town, displays the works of the Valencian painter Joaquín Sorolla (1863–1923), full of the charm and radiant light of the Levante.

▶ Museo de América   *50B4*

Reyes Católicos 6 (tel: 915 49 26 41)
Metro: Moncloa
Open: Tue–Sat 10–3, Sun 10–2.30
Admission charge; free Sat afternoon and Sun
An impressive museum that celebrates the popular art of pre-Columbian Latin America and of the Philippines, with Mayan parchments and famous golden treasures.

▶▶ Museo Arqueológico Nacional   *51E4*

Calle de Serrano 13 (tel: 915 77 79 12)
Metro: Serrano
Open: Tue–Sat 9.30–8.30, Sun 9.30–2.30
Admission charge
This huge museum, founded by Queen Isabella II in 1867 and installed later in its current premises, contains an outstanding collection of art, from prehistoric to medieval times. Key exhibits and collections include: a replica of the Altamira caves on the Cantabrian coast (see pages 88–89); the 6,000-year-old painted and sculpted bust from Elx in the province of Murcia, known as La Dama de Elche; Roman material; Moorish exhibits and fine displays of Visigothic material rarely encountered elsewhere.

DIEGO VELÁZQUEZ
Diego Rodriguez de Silva y Velázquez (1599–1660) was more than a simple painter. Throughout his career he climbed steadily up the rungs of the court ladder, finally becoming a knight of Santiago. He is wearing the insignia in *Las Meninas*, his most famous painting. His job as courtier included long expeditions to Italy to buy paintings for the crown. He also decorated the now lost palace of the Retiro. Many of his greatest works hung in the earlier palace on the site of the old Palacio Real, destroyed by fire in 1734.

▶▶ Museo del Ejército   *51E2*

Calle Méndez Núñez 1 (tel: 915 22 89 77)
Metro: Retiro
Open: Tue–Sun 10–2. Admission charge
Housed in a surviving building from the Buen Retiro royal palace, the Army Museum contains all kinds of weapons and insignia.

▶▶ Museo Lázaro Galdiano   *51E4*

Calle de Serrano 122 (tel: 915 61 60 84)
www.flg.es
Metro: República Argentina
Currently closed; due to open end of 2003
The Lázaro Galdiano museum is named after the private collector who assembled it, and it provides an intriguing account of the Middle Ages in a variety of art forms. The second and third floors house notable paintings. Among the Spanish school are works by Coello, Goya, El Greco, Murillo, Zurbarán, and Velázquez. English painters are represented by Constable, Gainsborough, and Turner.

▶ Museo Nacional de Artes Decorativas   *51E3*

Calle de Montalbán 12 (tel: 915 32 64 99)
Metro: Banco de España, Retiro
Open: Tue–Fri 9.30–3, Sat and Sun 10–2
Admission charge; free Sun
With its display of Spanish furniture, fittings, domestic decorations, and many other comforts, ranging from the 15th to 19th centuries, this museum has it all, from Moorish *artesonado* ceilings to ceramics, leatherwork, clothing, and kitchens.

LA TERTULIA
Café society in Old Madrid revolved around *la tertulia*, a meeting of friends for formal discussion of intellectual and literary topics, rather like a French *salon*, but far less grand and far more public. Each *tertulia* would be a regular or semi-regular event, focused around some leading artist or thinker. One of the most famous of the 20th century was La Tertulia del Café de Pombo, shown in a painting by José Gutiérrez Solana in the Centro de Arte Reina Sofía. Its key figure was the artist Ramón Gómez de la Serna, whose study, rich in collages, is reassembled in the city's Municipal Museum. Gómez de la Serna died in exile after the Civil War; the *tertulia*, alas, is all but dead today.

59

THE SWORD OF BOABDIL
The Sword of Boabdil, who was the last king of Granada (displayed in the Museo del Ejército), was stolen by Napoleon and returned by Hitler as a gift to Franco, after the German conquest of Paris in World War II.

Decorative entrance to the Municipal Museum, where the history of the city can be traced. Pedro Ribera's fine baroque doorway livens up the plain façade of the old Hospicio de San Fernando, which houses the museum

Madrid's cathedral, Nuestra Señora de la Almudena, is a hybrid of styles: neoclassical on the outside, neogothic within

MADRID'S "RIVER"
In a continent whose capitals are built on great rivers such as the Danube and the Seine, the Río Manzanares has always seemed a joke, even to Madrileños. Its feeble trickle has been proverbial for centuries.

Religious buildings

While scores of major ecclesiastical monuments adorn the cities of Castile, Madrid is low on this element of its historic legacy. One or two set pieces are excellent, however, and others, though less impressive in themselves, form a familiar part of the cityscape.

▶ **Catedral Nuestra Señora de la Almudena**   50A2
Calle Bailén s/n
Metro: Ópera
Open: daily 9–9
Opposite the main entrance of the Palacio Real, this chilly white construction languished as a half-built shell for many decades, a symbol of a paralysis of will. It finally opened in 1993, revealing an austere interior, its vistas blocked by heavy columns. Round behind the apse, down the Calle Mayor extension, are excavations with remains of the Moorish city.

▶ **Catedral San Isidro and its neighbours**   50B2
Calle de Toledo (tel: 913 69 20 37)
Metro: La Latina
Down beneath the Plaza Mayor in the Old City, there are a number of churches to use as a focus while strolling. **San Isidro**, also called Parroquia del Buen Consejo, a twin-towered, 17th-century building, has long done temporary duty as a cathedral. **San Pedro** has a 14th-century Mudéjar tower. **San Miguel** dates from the 18th century and the **Capilla del Obispo** has interesting tombs.

▶▶ **Convento de las Descalzas Reales**   50B3
Plaza de las Descalzas, Reales 3, Arenal (tel: 914 54 88 00)
Metro: Sol, Ópera
Open: Tue–Thu, Sat 10.30–12.30, 4–5.30, Fri 10.30–12.45, Sun 11–1.30. Admission charge; free Wed afternoon
This convent-museum of the Barefoot Sisters, in this case royal ones (the order itself had been founded at a marginally humbler level by St. Teresa), was established in the 16th century by Juana de Austria, daughter of Charles V. It became a retreat for noble ladies, lavishly endowed by their families (see also Burgos, page 156). Along with its many chapels and grand baroque stairway (with frescoes by the court painter Claudio Coello), it has a fine collection of tapestries, sculptures, and paintings. There are works by Titian, Rubens, and other imported artists; Spanish painters and sculptors are represented by Alonso Cano, Zurbarán, Luisa Roldán, and others. Guided tours only, conducted at speed, in Spanish.

▶ **Convento de la Encarnación**   50B3
Plaza Encarnación (tel: 915 47 05 10)
Metro: Ópera, Santo Domingo
Open: Tue–Sat 10.30–12.30, 4–5.30, Fri and Sun 10.30–12.30
A Habsburg foundation like the Descalzas Reales, this convent was founded in 1611 by Margaret of Austria, and specializes in Spanish art. The sculptures by Gregorio Fernández are noteworthy, as is the work by Francisco Bayeu in the church.

►► Ermita de San Antonio de la Florida (Panteón de Goya)   *50A4*

Paseo de la Florida
Metro: Principe Pio
Open: Tue–Fri 10–2, 4–8, Sat and Sun 10–2, closed at weekends Jul and Aug. Admission charge; free Wed after 4

Goya's final resting place (he died in Bordeaux in 1828) is in a little church, now deconsecrated, close to the Río Manzanares. It is down behind the Estación del Norte, and reaching it requires a taxi or a little effort. He decorated it himself, to royal order, finishing in 1798. The fresco in the dome, the *Miracle of St. Anthony*, is Goya in genial mode, painting his own people with relish.

► San Francisco el Grande   *50A1*

Plaza San Francisco (tel: 913 65 38 00)
South from Royal Palace on Calle Bailén. Bus: 3, 60, 148
Open: Tue–Sat 11–12.30, 4–6

On down Calle Bailén from the Royal Palace and past the Almudena Cathedral, this large neoclassical church of the 18th century remains a considerable landmark. One chapel features a Goya scene. There is remarkable monastic woodwork. Tours are available.

► San Jerónimo el Real   *51E2*

Calle de Moreto
Metro: Banco de España
Open: Oct–Jun, daily 9–1.30, 5.30–7.30; Jul–Sep, 9–1, 6–8

A tall, rather gaunt building dominating the hillside above the Prado and beneath the Retiro park, San Jerónimo is all that survives of a former Hieronymite monastery. The church is famous for society weddings and royal associations. The present king, Juan Carlos, although married in Greece, was crowned here at San Jerónimo.

61

San Jerónimo el Real, church of Spain's élite, holds a commanding position above the Prado Museum

Other sights

▶▶ Campo del Moro   50A3

Metro: Norte
A rather formal park, the "Field of the Moor" climbs
steeply up from the Río Manzanares towards the Royal
Palace. There is a fine view upwards.

▶ Casa de Campo   50A3

Metro: Norte, Lago, Batán
A huge green lung on the west side of Madrid, accessible
by cable car from Paseo del Pintor Rosales on the edge of
Parque del Oeste, the Casa de Campo (once a royal
hunting ground) is a relatively natural tract of wooded
countryside with a zoo and an amusement park.

▶ Estadio Bernabéu   51E4

Metro: Nuevos Ministerios, Lima
Real Madrid, most glamorous of Spanish soccer clubs, is
based at the Bernabéu stadium, quite far north along the
Castellana. You are likely to see a great match if you can
get a ticket.

▶ Jardín Botánico   51E1

Plaza de Murillo 2 (tel: 914 20 30 17)
Metro: Atocha
Open: daily 10–6. Admission charge
The Botanical Gardens embody one of the strongest
themes of the Spanish Enlightenment in the 18th century,
the commitment to the description and classification of
the flora not only of Spain but of Latin America and the
Philippines. Initiated by Ferdinand VI and moved to their
present site beside the Prado by Charles III, the gardens,
with their methodical planting of trees, medicinal herbs,
and so on, make an interesting visit.
   The Prado building here was itself another
Enlightenment phenomenon, intended originally as a
natural history museum.

In Madrid's 200-year-old Botanical Gardens

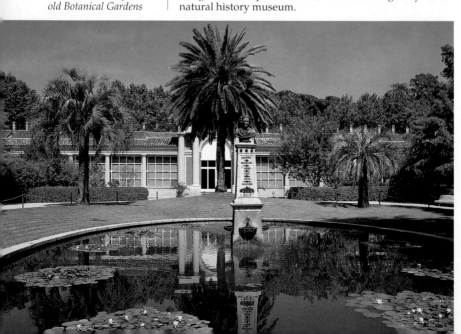

▶▶ Parque Biológico de Madrid　　*off 51E1*

Avenida de la Democracia 50 (tel: 913 01 62 10)
www.parque-biologico.com
Metro: Valdebernardo
Open: Sat–Sun 10.30–8, Mon–Fri 10.30–7. Admission charge
A nature theme park in the outskirts of Madrid exploring
the diverse ecosystems of the planet. It houses some 720
animal species, plus it puts on sound and light shows,
using fibre optic cables and hi tech special effects.

▶ Parque del Oeste　　*50A4*

Metro: Ventura Rodriguez
This green and relaxing area, set mostly on a slope above
the Río Manzanares, is the site of the incongruous but
marvellous 4th-century BC Temple of Debod, a gift from
Egypt reassembled here in recognition of Spanish engi-
neers' work on the Aswan Dam.

▶▶ Parque del Retiro　　*51E2*

Metro: Retiro, Atocha
Madrid is fortunate to have this stylish park right at its
heart. It was the garden of Philip IV's now-vanished Buen
Retiro Palace. There are flower-beds, a boating lake, and
plentiful trees to offer shade in summer. The Palacio de
Cristal (Crystal Palace) and Palacio de Velázquez are both
used for cultural activities. It is a gathering place for all:
Fortune-tellers, actors, bands, and puppeteers all perform
on Sundays. (See also **Walk** on page 64.)

▶ Plaza Canovas del Castillo　　*51D2*

Metro: Banco de España
This square, named after a 19th-century prime minister,
was adorned by Charles III with a fountain and statue of
Neptune (known to locals as "Neptuno"). Close to the
Prado, it has the Ritz Hotel on one corner and the equally
famous Palace Hotel almost diagonally opposite.

▶▶ Plaza de la Cibeles　　*51D3*

Metro: Banco de España
The fountain of the goddess Cibeles, her chariot drawn by
lions, is perhaps the most familiar image of Madrid for
Spaniards. It stands at the key intersection of Madrid,
where the Calle de Alcalá meets the lower part of the
Castellana, here called the Paseo del Prado (south of
Cibeles) and the Paseo de Recoletos (north).

▶ Plaza de España　　*50A4*

Metro: Plaza de España
Across Madrid from Plaza de la Cibeles and at the far end
of the Gran Vía, the Plaza de España acts as another of the
city's pivots. The area contains statues of Don Quixote
and Sancho Panza, and some of Cervantes, their creator.

▶▶ Plaza de Oriente and Teatro Real　　*50B3*

Metro: Ópera
The Plaza de Oriente, across Calle de Bailén from the
Palacio Real, is a most appealing pedestrian space, with
statues of the Visigothic and Spanish kings surrounding
it; the equestrian statue is of Philip IV. On the far side is
the revamped **Teatro Real**, Madrid's historic opera house.

Neptune all aglow in the
Plaza Canovas del
Castillo

63

ELEGANT MADRID
The Barrio de Salamanca,
a smart bourgeois district
north of the Parque del
Retiro and based on the
Calle de Goya, was built
as a real-estate specula-
tion by the Marquis of
Salamanca in the 19th
century. Incredibly, considering how central it seems
today, the well-to-do of the
period were reluctant to
live there, so far did it
seem from the Plaza
Mayor.

ACCOMPLISHED ART
The statue of Philip IV
in the Plaza de Oriente
(see page 63) represents
the height of 17th-century
achievement.
Commissioned by the
Count of Olivares, it was
modelled by the Italian
master, Pietro Tacca.
It is claimed as the first
bronze statue of a rearing
horse ever to stand
unsupported on its hind
legs. The monarch's face
is based on a portrait by
Velázquez.

▶▶ Plaza de la Villa 50B2

Metro: Ópera, Sol

This square on the Calle Mayor, leading down from the
Puerta del Sol towards the Almudena cathedral, contains
a cluster of Madrid's finest buildings. The 17th-century
ayuntamiento, or town hall (*Open* for free guided tours on
Mon at 5PM, prior booking tel: 915 88 29 06), on the west
side is flanked by the 16th-century **Casa de Cisneros**.
Opposite is the medieval **Torre de los Lujanes**. Beside this
stands the elegant building called the **Hemeroteca**.

▶▶▶ Plaza Mayor 50C3

Metro: Sol

This 17th-century square is the work of the architect
Gómez de Mora; the equestrian statue is of Philip III. It
has one particularly grand side, known as La Panadería
after a bakery that once stood on the premises. The best
exit is the southwest corner, into Calle Cuchilleros. Exit
southeast, and you will find the Foreign
Office in the Palacio de Santa Cruz.

Walk

Parque del Retiro

Start on Calle Felipe IV between the
Prado and the back of the Ritz hotel.
Walk up to the Prado annexe (Casón
del Buen Retiro) immediately ahead.
Cross Calle de Alfonso XII, turn left
and enter the Retiro park.

At the end of the Paseo de la
Argentina, lined with handless statues, lies the Estanque (lake with
boats for hire) and the monument to
Alfonso XII.

Go left and around the lake. Cross
the Paseo de Venezuela to the blue-
domed Palacio de Velázquez and
the Palacio de Cristal.

The latter is a huge conservatory,
with lake and fountains.

Continue in the same direction to
the rose garden by the Glorieta
(arbour) del Angel Caido on Paseo
de Uruguay. Turn right at the
glorieta and leave the park, cross
Alfonso XII and continue down
Claudio Moyano (with second-hand
bookstalls) to Paseo del Prado. Turn
right, keeping the Jardín Botánico
on your right and thus returning to
the Prado Museum.

*Monument to Alfonso XII in the
Parque del Retiro, once the garden
of a royal palace*

The Puerta de Alcalá,
a triple-arched classical
gateway not far
from Plaza de la Cibeles.
It was erected in honour
of Charles III

THE TALLEST
SKYSCRAPERS
Torre Picasso and Torre
Europa are Madrid's two
highest skyscrapers.
They rise high up Paseo
de la Castellana near the
Bernabéu stadium, at
the heart of Madrid's new
high-rise "downtown."
Their presence here
exemplifies the city's
northwards-shifting
pattern.

▶▶ El Rastro 50D1

Metro: La Latina, Embajadores
Running downhill from the area of La Latina metro on
Sunday mornings, the Rastro is Madrid's flea market.
Stalls in Ribera de Curtidores tend to sell Toledo table-
cloths and Talavera pottery. Regular shops sell army
surplus, wicker furniture, and antiques.

▶ Real Fábrica de Tapices 51E1

Calle Fuenterrasia 2 (tel: 914 34 05 51)
Metro: Menéndez Pelayo
Open: Mon–Fri 9–12.30; closed Aug. Admission charge
Tapestries are still woven by hand in this 19th-century
descendant of the 18th-century royal factory. Designs by
Goya and his brother-in-law, Bayeu, are still in use.

▶ Las Ventas (Plaza de Toros) and 51E3
Museo Taurino

Calle de Alcalá 237
Metro: Ventas
Las Ventas is Madrid's enormous bullring, built in 20th-
century mock-Mudéjar. There is a small bullfighting
museum attached.

▶▶▶ Warner Brothers Movie World off 51D1

Off NIV, San Martin de la Vega (tel: 918 21 12 34)
www.ayto-sanmartinvega.es/TimeWarner; for opening times
telephone ahead or check website
Renfe train direct from Atocha
A cinema theme park built around five areas: Hollywood
Boulevard, Cartoon Village, The Wild West, DC
Superheroes World, and Warner Brothers Studios. The 25
attractions include five roller-coasters (the fastest reaching 100kph/62mph), three water rides, seven shows, and
the highest freefall tower in Europe, the Venganza del
Enigma, a drop of 100m (328ft), accelerating passengers to
2 negative G.

HOW SPAIN SQUARES UP
Madrid's Plaza Mayor is
one of the most famous
squares in Spain and
almost every town and
village in the country is
similarly built around just
such a public space.
Usually much less preten-
tious, the typical *plaza*
mayor is a good place to
get your bearings when
arriving in a strange town.
On it stands the church,
town hall, shops, bars, and
usually an aristocratic
mansion or two. The
square itself is an open
place to stroll or sit in the
sun or shade. It may also
be used for a weekly
market or an annual fiesta.

The smart Galería del Prado shopping centre, on Plaza de Canovas del Castillo

BEWARE THE WIND!
Ready for a break from shopping? Beware as you sit outdoors at your café table, delightful as it may be. It is said that the wind of Madrid "can kill a man without snuffing out a candle."

Shopping

TRADITIONAL SHOPS Family-run small shops still thrive here, particularly around the historic part of the city. Shops selling similar merchandise will often share the same street. (Calle Esparteros for cutlery, Marqués Viuda de Pontejos for haberdashers, Zaragoza and Bordadores for religious items, and so on.) **Felix Manzarnero** at Calle Santa Ana 12 has been making guitars for 50 years, while exquisite hand embroidered shawls are the tradition at famous **Casa Jiménez**, Calle Preciados 42. A hat for every occasion can be found at **La Favorita**, Plaza Mayor 25, and the city's wonderfully historic espadrille shop is **Antigua Casa Crespo** on Calle Divino Pastor 29.

There are curiosities like **Bisutería Otero**, Calle Mayor 28, which specializes in bright plastic beads, and **La Violeta** on the Canalejas roundabout selling only sweets scented or decorated with violets. **Casa Mira**, at Carrera de San Jerónimo 30, is a wonderful nougat shop while nearby Calle del Prado is, appropriately, home to some fine art and antique shops.

The quintessential expression of the area is the **Rastro** market (see page 65). In contrast are the chic shopping malls, like **ABC Serrano**, housed in a five-level neo-Mudéjar building. Just north of Puerta del Sol are the inner-city branches of the main department store, **El Corte Inglés**.

FASHION The best place for fashion is Calle Serrano and the surrounding Salamanca area. Traditional Spanish designer, **Adolfo Domínguez** has premises at Serrano 96 and Ortega y Gasset 4. **Sybilla**, Calle Jorge Juan 12, specializes in striking women's fashion.

Behind the Café Gijon, the charming 19th-century Paseo de Recoletos is a focus for designers. For more affordable high-street fashion, head for Calle Princesa where you find the popular **Zara** and **Mango** clothing chains. For leather, **Loewe** at Calle Serrano 26 and 34, and Gran Vía 8 is still the top Spanish name.

ART AND BOOKS For quality art books check out the gift shops at the three top art museums; the Prado, Reina Sofia, and Thyssen-Bornemisza. For more general books there are three branches of **Casa del Libros**, the largest at Gran Via 29.

Food and drink See also page 281

There are more bars and restaurants packed in here than in any other city in Europe. Traditional cuisine, regional delicacies, and international dishes are available at a vast number of restaurants, while the city's elegant cafés serve wonderful cakes and coffee to accompany that after dinner coñac.

TAPEANDO IN MADRID The Madrileñan *tasca*, or "bar," home of delicious tapas (see page 20), is one of the city's institutions and at its best in the area around Plaza Mayor (down Cuchilleros and the Plaza de Puerta Cerrada). Other good areas include Calle Echegaray, Plaza Santa Ana, and the upper end of the Rastro. Be guided by eye and nose; try everything from *pimientos de Padrón* (hottish green peppers from Galicia) to *cecina* (raw, air-cured beef from León and Castile sliced thinly like Italian *prosciutto)*. Tapas are available all over the rest of the city, though in less concentration, served at the counter in cafés and in the street-facing bars of many smaller restaurants.

RESTAURANTS AND CAFÉS Restaurants vary from the modest diner to some of the finest establishments in the country. For Basque cuisine, **Zalacaín** at Calle Alvarez de Baena 4 is one of the best, while **Viridiana**, Calle Juan de Mena 14 is excellent for international, inventive cuisine. Try **Botín**, serving the thoroughly Castilian roast suck-ling-pig, on Cuchilleros, or **Casa Lucio** on Cava Baja. Vegetarians need not despair. There are several restau-rants, including **Esqui**, Buenavista 18, which has an excel-lent self-service buffet. Cafés built in 19th century, like the **Café Gijón** on Recoletos or the **Nuevo Café Barbieri** on Calle Ave Maria 45, have always been popular in Madrid.

LIFE'S PRIORITIES
"Ah what a place Madrid is, all show!...Facade, nothing but facade. These people have no idea of comfort in their own houses. They live in the streets and so that they can dress well and go to the theatre, some families eat nothing but potato omelettes all year round." Benito Pérez Galdos, *La de Bringas*

67

Tempting tapas served up for your delight

Madrid nightlife goes on right through until dawn

WEEKEND ITINERARY
Friday evening: Stroll to the Plaza Mayor; relax in a bar or restaurant on Calle Cuchilleros or the Plaza Puerta Cerrada.
Saturday: Visit the Prado today (you may have to queue on Sunday). Leave time for a daytime stroll through the Retiro Park and a wander along elegant Serrano for window-shopping.
Sunday: Start with chocolate and *churros* before a trip to the Rastro. Have lunchtime tapas in one of the bars at the top end of the market. If you want to see a bullfight, it has to be Sunday afternoon; Las Ventas is usually booked out, so you may have to go as part of an expensive city tour. End the day with a simple meal at the Brasserie de Lista, Ortega y Gasset 6.

Nightlife and entertainment

Nightlife in Madrid is fast, furious, and late. For the more staid, there are good venues for plays, operas, and films. Check the listings in *El Pais* newspaper or in the monthly leisure magazine *Guía del Ocio*.

THEATRE AND FILM Madrid's main theatre for drama is the **Teatro de la Comedia**, Calle Príncipe 14 (tel: 915 21 49 31). Opera and ballet performances take place at the **Teatro Real**, Plaza de Oriente (tel: 915 16 06 06). Cinemas abound in the Gran Vía area and increasingly show films in their original version with Spanish subtitles.

FLAMENCO Many of Spain's best flamenco artists gravitate to Madrid. **Sala Caracol** (Calle Bernadino Obregón 18) often plays host to them. **Corral de la Morería**, Calle Moreria 17 remains popular, but is expensive; the **Café de Chinitas** (Torija 7) is less so. **Corral de la Pachera** (Calle Juan Ramón Jiménez 26) features well-known flamenco artists.

THE LATE-NIGHT THRASH They say there are more people on the street at midnight than midday in Madrid. Consult *Guía del Ocio* for the latest clubbing news. The area around Plaza Santa Ana and Plaza Mayor provide plenty of choice. Serious disco die-hards should check out **Pachá** on Barceló. For a more sophisticated scene, stop by the former 19th-century palace **Palacio de Gaviria**, Arenal 9 with its luscious baroque interior and choice of sound. Another well-known nightspot is **Joy Eslava**, Calle Arenal 11 which attracts a slightly older crowd with its musical mix of latino and disco.

For those who prefer to sit down with a drink, people watch, and enjoy some conversation, **Bar Cock**, Calle de la Reina 16 is a Madrid institution and always entertaining. For ultra-elegance **El Salón del Prado**, Calle del Prado 4 is superb and hosts weekly chamber music concerts.

Accommodation See also page 274

Madrid has two wonderful, old-world hotels to rival anything in London or Paris, including their high prices. One or two modern imitations are also worth considering. Then come the smart international hotels, comfortable, clean, and anonymous. The city's older hotels and pensions in the middle and inexpensive range are more varied, but choice is made easier by the fact that each of these types tend to be confined to a single area. The difficulty occurs in the inexpensive range because of the variation of standards.

EXPENSIVE The two flagship hotels are the **Ritz** and **Palace**, 200m (655ft) from one another across the Paseo del Prado. The Ritz was built in 1910 for the guests of King Alfonso XIII. It retains its original grandeur along with the smartest of modern additions. The Palace, too, has been refurbished but retains, despite all the shops downstairs, an air of gravity and elegance at a lesser price than the Ritz.

To these should be added the modern but old-world-gracious **Villa Magna** at the nearer end of the Castellana, the newer and slightly less successful imitator, **Villa Real**, close to the Palace, and the older **Wellington**, elegant and rather grand, near the Parque del Retiro. The chain and commonplace modern hotels are mostly to be found going up the Castellana. In the north, near the "downtown" area, the expensively anonymous and efficient **Eurobuilding** is the leading example.

INEXPENSIVE The older hotels cluster around the middle of town, lying in an approximate fan shape, with its base in the Puerta del Sol, its left-hand edge by the Plaza de España, and the right-hand by Atocha station.

For good-value, comfortable hotels, the **Hotel Santander**, Calle Echegaray 1 is excellent, as well as the nearby, marginally smarter, **Hotel Inglés** at number 8. There are numerous hotels along the noisy Gran Vía, but ask for an internal room if you want peace and quiet. This area, as well as the Puerta del Sol, is a very good base for the major sights.

WEEK'S ITINERARY
Sunday: Visit the Rastro flea market; take in a bullfight in the afternoon, see Weekend Itinerary, page 68, or stroll in the old town. For dinner, fry your own steak at El Schotis, Cava Baja 11 (tel: 912 65 32 30).
Monday: Shopping day, as museums and public buildings are closed.
Tuesday: Make your first visit to the Prado, then take in the Thyssen-Bornemisza collection.
Wednesday: Time for an excursion to Toledo, Segovia, or Ávila.
Thursday: Morning visit to the Centro de Arte Reina Sofía and/or Academy of San Fernando. An afternoon walk and an early evening drink at the Café Gijón in Recoletos.
Friday: Time for another excursion (see Wednesday).
Saturday: Don't miss the Lázaro Galdiano museum. After last-minute shopping, blow your remaining cash on dinner at atmospheric, old-fashioned Lhardy.

69

Plaza de Colón (Columbus Square), where traditional mansions have given way in part to tower blocks and new developments

Madrid's red buses are a popular way of getting about

EXCURSIONS

There is a tremendous range of one-day destinations around Madrid (many described on pages 190–207). Toledo, Segovia, and Ávila are all quintessential Castilian cities. The monastery palace of El Escorial, whether you like it or loathe it, is a top European sight and combines well with a visit to the disturbing Valle de los Caídos (Valley of the Fallen). The delightfully positioned royal palace of Aranjuez is about an hour south of Madrid.

Practical points

GETTING AROUND

Metro The Metro is both the quickest way of getting around and the easiest for those with little or no Spanish. Stations are marked with diamond-shaped signs, with red borders, and with the name written in the middle. Tickets are bought in the station either from machines or manned *guichets*. There is one flat fare for a journey of any distance, but the 10-journey ticket is far better value. Route maps are clear (lines are numbered 1 to 10 with one short line marked "R"). Inter-line connections are simple to make. Look at the map before a journey, remember the line number and final destination on that line, then follow the signs. Trains run daily 6AM–1.30AM.

Bus Mastering the whole of the bus network is quite a business, but it is well worth the effort to identify one or two main lines; No. 12, for example, runs all along the Castellana from the Santiago Bernabéu stadium to the Prado. There is also a useful circular bus route which is just as good for sightseeing as any costly tour. Buy single tickets on the bus (valid for any distance) or a 10-ride *bonobus* ticket, which is highly recommended and available from kiosks and *estancos* (the most central spots are Cibeles and Puerta del Sol). On entry to the bus, insert the ticket into the machine by the door. A free bus map (*Plano de los Transportes de Madrid*) is available at bus kiosks.

Taxis Taxis are metered, safe, and plentiful. A green light shows when they are free. They are good value at night when streets are clear, less so during the day in busy areas of town. Madrid is often a fearful snarl-up of traffic, which is another good reason for using the Metro.

Trains Chamartín, way up north beyond the Plaza de Castilla, is the terminus for northern destinations. It is linked by a through line with Atocha, the old southerly station, now rebuilt, at the bottom end of the Botanical

Gardens. Atocha handles southern and eastern traffic. (There is also a Metro link, No. 8, Chamartín to Plaza de Castilla, then take No. 1 to Atocha RENFE.) The train may pass through both stations. Ensure you take it at the point of first departure, though, at weekends and during holidays. *Cercanías* refers to local and suburban trains, *largo recorrido* to intercity and long-distance trains.

EATING HOURS

Madrid not only stays up later than other Spanish cities; it also takes its meals appreciably later. Add maybe half an hour to each phase of the normal Spanish day (see pages 16–17) to stay in step. If you can adjust to this rhythm you will enjoy your stay much more than by arriving first at every restaurant.

SECURITY

Madrid is no more or no less safe than any other western European capital city. Normal precautions are in order (see page 258); and while there are no strictly "no-go" areas, it is wise to walk with care, especially at night, in the area south of the Plaza Mayor. Take care also around Atocha, the Plaza Santa Ana, and Echegaray (though the last two areas are said to have been "cleaned up"). In crowded places, be aware of opportunist pickpockets and do not carry large amounts of money with you. If you can, take advantage of hotel safes.

TOURIST INFORMATION

At Barajas airport, there is a desk on the departure level (tel: 913 05 86 56 or 902 10 00 07). Hotel reservations are also made here. In town, there are tourist offices at Plaza Mayor 3 (tel: 913 66 54 77); Chamartín railway station (tel: 913 15 99 76); Calle Duque de Medinaceli 2, beside the Palace Hotel; and Puerta de Toledo (tel: 902 10 00 07 for both). Also visit www.comadrid.es for more information.

A Madrid backstreet shows another side of the town: the medieval Madrid of dark, shady streets, and alleyways, steps and tiny squares, graced by many fine facades

---

NIGHT-WATCHMEN OF OLD
Until the early 1970s, Madrid had *serenos*. These were night-watchmen, who carried leaded sticks which they banged on the ground to indicate they were near and you were therefore safe. Coming home at night, people would stand by their apartment block door and clap their hands to summon the *sereno*. He would then unlock the door with a key from the mighty bundle at his waist.

MAY CELEBRATIONS
Processions in the Plaza Dos de Mayo on 2 May mark the events portrayed in Goya's famous paintings under the title *Dos de Mayo* (*Second of May*), the date in 1808 of a popular rising and, on the following day, executions by firing squad. The day of San Isidro, 15 May, Madrid's patron saint is celebrated throughout the city but particularly in the Plaza Mayor, with open-air concerts. There are bullfights at Las Ventas every day for a fortnight.

71

Galicia

Galician farms are characterized by the granite maize stores on legs called hórreos

TOURIST INFORMATION

A Coruña: Dársena
de la Marina
(tel: 981 22 18 22).
Ferrol: Plaza de España
(tel: 981 31 11 79).
Lugo: Praza Maior 27
(tel: 982 23 13 61).
Ourense: Edificio Caseta
do Legoeiro, Ponte
Romano, Ourense
(tel: 988 37 20 20).
Pontevedra: Calle
General Gutierrez Mellado
1 (tel: 986 85 08 14).
Santiago de Compostela:
Rúa do Vilar 43
(tel: 981 58 40 81).
Vigo: Avenida Cánovas
del Castillo 22
(tel: 986 43 05 77).

72

GALICIA

0   20   40   60 km

0   20   40 miles

Cabo Ortegal

Punta da Estaca de Bares

Cedeira

Ortigueira

Viveiro

Cabo Prior

Ferrol

Foz

Tapia

Navia

As Pontes de García Rodríguez

Costa da Morte

A Coruña-La Coruña

Foxas-Fene

Pontedeume

Ribadeo

Castropol

Malpica

A55

Betanzos

Mondoñedo

Vegadeo-A Veiga

Taramundi

Laxe

Carballo

Guitiriz

Villalba

Meira

Camariñas

Ordes-Ordenes

A9

Cabo Vilán

Muxia

Santa Comba

Rábade

Fisterra-Finisterre

Cee

Negreira

Friol

A Fonsagrada

Cabo Fisterra

Carnota

Santiago de Compostela

Melide

Lugo

Pobra - Navia de Suarna

Muros

Noia

G A L I C I A

Becerreá

Porto de Pedrafita

Fabero

Porto do Son

Padrón

Monterroso

Sarria

O Cebreiro

Boiro de Arriba

Rianxo

A Estrada

Lalín

Embalse de Belesar

Chantada

Santa Eugenia-Ribeira

Vilagarcía de Arousa

Cerdedo

Monforte de Lemos

Ponferrada

Cambados

A9

Oseira

Sil

O Grove

Marín

Pontevedra

A Rúa

Las Médulas

O Carballiño

Embalse de San Esteban

O Barco

VIGO

Redondela

Ribadavia

Ourense-Orense

Baiona

Ponteareas

A Caniza

Allariz

1707m

Viana do Bolo

Tui

O Porriño

Celanova

Xinzo de Limia-Ginzo de Limia

A Gudiña

Sierra Segundera

Dia

Miño

Embalse das Conchas

Verín

Puebla de Sanabria

A Guarda-La Guardia

P

see Drive page 82

GREEN AND GREY are the colours of Galicia. The green stands for the meadows and eucalyptus forests of this gently rainy northwest corner of the peninsula. Grey is for the granite of great headlands which rear up skywards or tilt down gently to an Atlantic fierce in winter, often suave in summer.

The landscape is melancholy, expressed in a folk music of drums, bagpipes, and the harp, and in centuries of plangent poetry in the local language, Gallego (Galician), a Romance dialect not far removed from medieval Portuguese.

The coastline is exceptionally lovely, deeply indented by long inlets called *rías*. These are wild in places, in others cultivated to the water's edge. They have many of Spain's best and least developed beaches. They are also rich in shellfish. There are good Galician wines, the sharp Ribeiros and Albariños, and *caldo gallego*, soups and stews with kale or turnip greens and local ham. The elements help to combine to make a distinctive and surprising cuisine.

The problem is and always has been poverty, however. Tiny, uneconomic allotments, endlessly divided by inheritance, have led to emigration on a huge scale, with Vigo and A Coruña as the ports for departing liners. So many are the emigrants that, in some parts of South America, the word "Gallego" is used as a substitute for "Spaniard." Even today, displaced Gallegos are found all over Spain, often working in the construction trade or as unskilled workers.

Galicia above all is Celtic country. The Celts arrived in about 1000 BC and constructed their round-house settlements mostly on hilltops. The Romans built bridges and the huge city walls of Lugo.

The Moors came and stayed only briefly. Soon after their departure, locals discovered a tomb that they claimed was that of St. James the Apostle ("Sant Iago"), thus starting off a pilgrimage that was one of the great features of the European Middle Ages and remains, with the *rías* and Galicia's unchanging country ways, among the chief reasons for visiting this most atypical and seductive region of Spain.

73

A wild shore under a grey sky, both typical of rainy Galicia

A Coruña's harbour is one of the city's main attractions

ST. JAMES IN MUXIA
Legend has it that the Apostle James (Sant Iago) preached in Muxia, arriving in a stone boat rowed by angels. The belief is associated with a far more ancient practice: the visiting of the sacred stones on the promontory. People crawl under one of them to restore their health and particularly to protect their kidneys. Large numbers rock the other stone while standing on it, believing it to be the sail of Santiago's boat. The festival in September draws penitents, as well as sick people hoping for a cure.

EARTH MAGIC
Since the 8th century, Christian pilgrims from all over Europe have made their way to the great Christian shrine of Santiago or St. James. Some believe the route is even more ancient, leading in pagan times to Cabo Fisterra (Castilian Finisterre, in English "World's End"), once the most westerly point of the known world. The area is steeped in Celtic lore and tales of earth magic.

In the gazetteer entries below, Castilian place-names appear in brackets after the Galician.

▶ **Allariz**   72B1
A rustic little town rising from the River Arnoia south of Ourense, Allariz offers a delightful main square and some attractive churches.

▶▶ **Baiona (Bayona)**   72A1
It was to Baiona, on the southern extreme of the Ría de Vigo, that the *Pinta* first brought word of the New World in 7 March, 1493. The charming little town is still guarded by a fortified peninsula, with 16th-century walls, a modern parador within them, and yachts moored beneath. The excellent beach of Praia de América is across the bay.

▶ **Betanzos**   72B3
Betanzos, at the head of the main *ría* dividing A Coruña from Ferrol, is set on a steep hill contained within a wider valley. The hilltop is crowned with an old main square, 18th-century town hall, and the guild church of Santiago, an odd and pleasing complex. A little lower down is the equally irregular and pleasing 14th- to 15th-century church of Santa María del Azogue (literally "of the market") and just opposite, the graceful, Gothic monastery church of San Francisco, a fine fusion of form and decoration. Note especially the wild boar and bear supporting the tomb of the founder, Count Fernán Pérez de Andrade.

▶▶ **Camariñas and Muxia**   72A3/72A2
These little fishing harbours, lively in summer, and with a tradition of lace-making, are tucked inside the mouth of the Ría de Camariñas (see **Costa da Morte**, page 76). On the Muxia cape is a sanctuary and two large rocks believed to have powerful healing properties. On Cabo Vilán opposite, there are, by contrast, modern electricity-generating wind turbines.

▶ **Cebreiro**   72C2
The pass of Pedrafita de Cebreiro is the climax of the pilgrims' climb up the final barrier that faced them, 200km (125mi) from Santiago, which is the forested slopes of the hills of the Bierzo region. There is a sanctuary above the present road, plus a radio mast.

▶ **Celanova**   72B1
This pretty little town, assembled round the Benedictine monastery of San Salvador, lies in sweeping, wooded country southwest of Ourense. The baroque monastery church contains a 10th-century Mozarabic shrine.

▶▶ **A Coruña (La Coruña)**   72B3
A Coruña, though dismal on entry, nevertheless has much of interest within. An old town lies on an isthmus with a harbour on one side and a beach on the other. Beyond, on the near-island to which the isthmus leads, is La Ciudad, the City, with a Roman-founded lighthouse and ramparts that have figured large in history.

A Coruña was the final departure point of the disastrous Armada sent by Philip II of Spain against England in 1588. A year later, during an English attack, local heroine María Pita gave the alarm and saved the day for Spain. In the Peninsular Wars of 1808–1813, a British expeditionary force was decisively defeated here by the French. It remains a garrison town. Spaniards, and especially Galicians, remember it and Vigo as the departure point for liners bearing emigrants to the New World.

THE SIGHTS It is natural for a visitor to begin on the isthmus, where beautiful glass balconies overlook the modern fishing harbour. At the far end of the isthmus, just before it rises to La Ciudad, a left turn takes you onto the grandiloquent if rather barren square named after María Pita. The town beach beckons over the ridge, though you could press onto the wilder beaches of the Costa da Morte (see page 76). La Ciudad is the original town. On its eastern side, confined within ramparts, is the Jardín de San Carlos, where Sir John Moore is buried (see panel). Leave by the archway behind the gardens for the pretty square of Santa Barbara, which is backed by a monastery of the same name. Angle up through the square for the Calle Herrerías and the house of María Pita, No. 28 (marked with plaques). Take the turning that was to your left as you first entered the square of Santa Barbara, looping back among granite and white Galician houses, for the Romanesque church of Santa María. Beneath is the gracious Plaza del General Azcarragas and, in the far corner from this approach, the Romanesque church of Santiago, with St. James himself on the main facade, at full gallop in a bowler hat. It is only a step down again to the Avenida Marítima on the isthmus. The famous lighthouse, Torre de Hércules, is a long hike or bus ride to the northern tip of the peninsula.

The peace and quiet of a lonely beach on the beautiful Ría de Camariñas

THE BURIAL OF SIR JOHN MOORE
"We buried him darkly at dead of night…"
The Burial of Sir John Moore at Corunna, written by the Reverend Charles Wolfe, mourns the loss of the general who commanded Britain's expeditionary force to Spain's Peninsular Wars. Forced back towards Galicia, Moore died while his beaten army was embarking at A Coruña. His tomb is in the garden on the San Carlos ramparts, where lines from Wolfe's poem, and others by the Galician poet Rosalía de Castro, are inscribed on a little *mirador* (lookout point).

75

RÍAS OF GALICIA

Studded with lovely beaches, Galicia's famous *rías* (sea inlets) are the region's chief delight. The Rías Altas lie on the north coast, wild, exhilarating, but sometimes rather exposed. The Rías Baixas lie on the western coast, south of Fisterra. The farther south you go, the more densely populated they are. Though Galicia is generally rainy, the Rías are a good deal drier than inland districts. (See also page 80 and Drive on page 82.)

GRACEFUL *ALAMEDAS*

Alameda is technically translated as a poplar grove but really refers to a tree-shaded public walkway, avenue, or square. Many Spanish towns are graced with one. In the best, the spreading branches of low trees are grafted together to form a single leafy canopy.

A deserted stretch of the Costa da Morte (coast of death). This wild coast, which leads to Fisterra, has claimed the life of many a fisherman and sailor

▶▶ Costa da Morte (Costa de la Muerte)   72A3

This is the fierce coast from A Coruña to Fisterra (Finisterre). Many fishermen are drowned here each year, often while trying to make the difficult harbours strung along the coast. Malpica and Laxe are examples of towns which lack elegance but whose beaches are both lively and lovely in summer. The *ría* entering the coast between Camariñas and Muxia may be the most beautiful part of the whole Spanish coast. The hinterland is deeply rural, with a profusion of stone crosses and stone-built *hórreos* (see panel on page 80).

▶ Ferrol (El Ferrol)   72B3

With a naval base and major naval dockyard to rival Cartagena (in Murcia), Ferrol was the birthplace of General Franco and once known as El Ferrol del Caudillo. The dictator holidayed nearby at Sada, making Ferrol/A Coruña the summer capital of Spain. Earlier, Ferrol had been extended under Charles III, and at its heart is a grid reminiscent of 18th-century Lisbon.

▶▶ Lugo   72C2

A small city buried deep in the countryside of northeastern Galicia, present-day Lugo offers an agreeable animation. The Romans left a wall of slate-like slabs laid sideways. Many times restored, these are now 10m (32ft) high and with 85 bastions. They still entirely ring the inner city, providing the route for a 2km (1mi) walk.

A little way downhill from the airy Praza Maior, the stone of the cathedral dourly confronts the stone of the bishop's palace. But the cathedral itself, a stopping point on one version of the Pilgrims' Way, is a gem, tiny inside and with an air of holiness, Romanesque running into Gothic into baroque, with baroque towers and facade in rough imitation of Santiago. In the nave, note the charming, round-arched galleries for pilgrims. The Gothic church of San Pedro has given its cloister to the adjoining **Museo Provincial** (tel: 982 24 21 12; *Open* Mon–Sat 11–2, 5–8, Sun 11–2. *Admission charge*), which has a good art and archaeological collection.

Solid pillars support the plain granite buildings of Pontevedra

▶▶ Mondoñedo 72C3

A small but charming cathedral town, with winding streets, houses of white rendering with granite trim, and glassed-in balconies. It has been a literary and religious focus for centuries. The cathedral, with baroque facade, abuts on a delightful square, watched over by a seated statue of the writer Alvaro Cunqueiro.

▶ Oseira (Osera) Monastery 72B2

Described as the Escorial of Galicia (tel: 988 28 20 04; *Open* Mon–Sat 9.30–12.30, 3.30–5.30. *Admission charge*), this vast Cistercian foundation has a fine carved facade from 1709, three excellent cloisters, a 12th- to 13th-century church, and a sacristy, with fine Gothic ribbing.

▶ Ourense (Orense) 72B1

Provincial capital and home of the singer Julio Iglesias, as well as Fidel Castro's family, Ourense sprawls across the Miño Valley. It is approached from the north by an interesting medley of road and rail bridges, including the wonderful 13th-century "Roman" bridge. The *casco viejo* (old town), high on the southern side, has lively bars, thermal springs, and a succession of attractive squares tumbling down round the cathedral. The archaeological museum lies behind a handsome heraldic facade.

▶ Pontedeume 72B3

The little town pitches itself downhill through arcaded streets to the site of the famous bridge built across the River Eume by the once-powerful counts of Andrade.

▶▶ Pontevedra 72A2

Until its river silted centuries ago, Pontevedra was the major port of the area. The almost circular white and granite church of the Peregrina stands above the three-sided Plaza de la Herrería. From here, take Calle Odriozala down through Plaza de la Leña (beautiful home of the provincial museum), then Plaza de Mugartegui. Calle Princesa off Plaza de Teucro is full of bars. Turn left at the T-junction here (bars galore) and climb to Santa María la Mayor, with its fine baroque facade.

LOCAL WRITERS
Galician has always been a language of literature, from the Middle Ages, when it was a vehicle for courtly poetry, right up to modern times. Alfonso X, the Learned, wrote verses in Galician. The most famous Galician writer is the poet Rosalía de Castro (1847–1885) from the little town of Padrón, where her house is now a museum. Her poetry, melancholic in tone, is often compared with that of the American poet Emily Dickinson. Galicia's most recent literary hero is Alvaro Cunqueiro (1912–1981), born in Mondoñedo. Locals are convinced that only death robbed him of the Nobel Prize.

The great cathedral of St. James in Compostela was the goal of and reward for the hardships of Europe's most celebrated pilgrimage, whose great days came in the 11th and 12th centuries. It stands below the crest of a hill in a city that is itself almost entirely a devotional work in stone.

ANCIENT PILGRIMS
Palmeros were pilgrims to Jerusalem; *Romeros* to Rome; *Peregrinos* and *Jacobitos* to Santiago.

78

The high altar of the great pilgrimage cathedral of Santiago de Compostela

The strong, grey granite of Galicia, glistening with mica in sunlight, smoothly shiny in the more customary rain, characterizes the attractive city of Santiago, which was once the capital of the kingdom of Galicia. From many points, you can look out of the city to green hills beyond.

Approaching the cathedral Pilgrims came in through the Porto do Camiño (the Galician language is generally predominant in signs here) and up over the hilltop, passing churches and monasteries, some small and Romanesque, others huge and classically baroque. The route leads on, most impressively, down Rúa Azevachería to the north transept of the cathedral.

Modern visitors still enter on foot but usually by a different route (the centre is mainly pedestrianized), taking any

one of three parallel granite streets that lead from the east towards the cathedral. Rúa Nueva is highest on the gentle hillside, then comes Rúa do Vilar, the traditional main street. Both of these have heavy arches and arcades, and vibrant shopping. The lowest, Rúa do Franco (with its side-streets), is packed with bars, restaurants, and lively students, and ends with the beautiful Palacio de Fonseca, a university building with a Renaissance facade, a Mudéjar-ceilinged lecture/exhibition hall to the left, and a two-storeyed cloister.

These two contrasting approaches to the sanctuary of the cathedral, one liturgical, the other abundant with life, make a fitting preparation for a building that is intensely dramatic in religious terms but full, too, of a sense of welcome and good humour.

Goal of the pilgrimage
The baroque facade of the cathedral on the Praza do

Obradoiro (*Open* daily 7AM–9PM), with its elaborate twin towers, dominates the large square bearing the same name. Rising from the entrance to the Romanesque crypt beneath (now part of the cathedral museum) is a gloriously baroque, intertwined, double ramp stairway.

Once in through the cathedral door, however, you are back in the old cathedral of the pilgrims (mostly 12th century) and on the site of earlier buildings destroyed by Almanzor at the end of the 10th century.

First comes the original (now cloaked) portal, the Pórtico de la Gloria, carved by Master Mateo from 1168. Christ sits in the middle showing his wounded hands, St. James below him in intercessionary position. The central column of the Tree of Jesse beneath bears the shapes of thumbs and fingers worn by the millions of right hands of pilgrims placed there. On the other side of the column kneels a figure believed to be Master Mateo; visitors bump their heads against his hoping to gain some of his wisdom. There are almost 200 figures in the full assemblage, including the 24 elders of the Apocalypse, the prophet Daniel (middle left, smiling broadly), and scenes of hell.

A high gallery runs round the cathedral, including the transepts. Above the altar is the image of St. James. His alleged remains are kept in a casket in a crypt. You may climb up behind the saint to kiss the shell on the back of his gown, which is the final "amen" of the pilgrimage.

The cathedral museum (tel: 981 56 15 27; *Open* winter, Mon–Sat 11–1, 4–6, Sun 11–1; summer, Mon–Sat 10–1.30, 4–7.30, Sun 10–1.30. *Admission charge*), divided into several parts in different places, is an extra to the cathedral visit. The best part is the sequence of tapestry galleries.

THE *BOTAFUMEIRO*
The cathedral's museum contains the famous *Botafumeiro*. This huge incense-burner is brought out for major festivals, when it is hung from the transept dome and swung from one end to the other, with eight men, known as *tiraboleiros*, attached to it by ropes, providing the propulsion.

79

Traditional trade is concentrated around the cathedral of Santiago de Compostela. Items include silverware, along with wood carving, wrought iron, ceramics, candles, and dolls

LOCAL CHINA

The most beautiful china in Spain, often in dashing shades of blue, is made at Sargadelos, not far from Ribadeo. The factory was set up in the late 18th century by Antonio Raimundo Ibañez, first Marquis of Sargadelos, to provide local employment. The subject of a Goya portrait, Ibañez was killed in mob violence after the French invasion of 1808. His offence: being too open to French ideas.

GALICIAN *HÓRREOS*

Galicia is rich in granite-built granaries called *hórreos*. These are raised off the ground on stone legs, so protecting the contents from the notoriously damp Galician climate. With pitched roofs and slatted sides, they resemble country chapels. Some are tiny. The biggest, at Lira near Carnota, hidden above the village and the sea, extends to a full 30m (98ft) and looks like a petrified railway carriage. Galicia also has many stone crosses standing in out-of-the-way country spots.

ROUNDING UP THE HORSES

Horses range free in some parts of Galicia. They are described as wild, but have owners. You are most likely to see them along the coast south of Baiona. In spring and early summer, there are festive round-ups for branding, known as *curros*.

View from Tui across the Miño to Portugal, connected by a modern road bridge and an older iron bridge designed by Eiffel

▶▶▶ Rías Baixas   72A1–A2

The Rías Baixas are the prettiest stretch of Galicia's coastline. Highlights include the two islands, Illa de Arousa and A Toxa; Cambados, with its handsome square, the Praza de Fefiñans; and Combarro, which has picturesque *hórreos* creeping down to the water's edge. (See panel on page 76.)

▶ Ribadeo   72C3

Ribadeo lies on the Galician side of the mouth of the Eo estuary and has scenic views over the *ría*. The town hall is the former mansion of Antonio Raimundo Ibañez, founder of the outstanding ceramics works nearby at Sargadelos.

▶ San Esteban Dam   72C1

The winding Río Sil is dammed in many spots as it makes its way to join the Miño. The biggest and best-loved dam is San Esteban, just west of Ourense. Northeast, at the heart of a circular plain, lies the excellent little town of Monforte de Lemos, which has both a castle and monastery.

▶▶▶ Santiago de Compostela   72B2

See pages 78–79

▶▶ Tui (Túy)   72A1

The fortified cathedral at Tui (*Open* daily 9.30–1.30, 4–7), rising above the Río Miño as guardian of the Spanish border, has a stout tower, pinnacles, and crenellations. Inside, it is tiny, mostly Gothic with Romanesque traces and Mozarabic horseshoe arches, reflecting the town's varied roots. The old stone-built town gathered round it on the hilltop is charming, with several notable churches and a broad main street.

▶ Verín   72C1

This small, modern town of decayed spas and excellent mineral waters (including Fontenova, found nationwide) lies in a broad valley. Nearby is Monterrey, an isolated hill topped by the most amazing castle-and-church complex in Galicia, once the refuge of Pedro I, the Cruel. The castle and tower (tel: 988 41 00 00; *Open* Wed–Sun 10.30–1.30, 4–7. *Admission free*) provide great views.

▶ Vigo   72A1

Spain's leading fishing port, this city of 300,000 dominates its *ría*, with traffic and apartment blocks. But the old town has serene old stone and wrought-iron balconies painted. A neoclassical cathedral replaces the earlier version, burned down in a raid by Francis Drake. The market of A Pedra (La Piedra) sells tobacco, trinkets, and oysters.

Drive/Walk

Reserva Nacional Dos Ancares

This is a one-day excursion from Becerreá, on the NV1 between Lugo and Ponferrada, involving three to four hours' hard driving, and with several possibilities for walks. It takes the visitor from deeply rustic farmland right up into wild but not very high mountains and finally to Piornedo. This village is much restored and popular, but in all essentials a pure, Celtic survivor, quite thrilling in its mere existence. It consists in large part of *pallozas* (Celtic round houses).

From **Becerreá**, follow the signs for Navia de Suarna, north on LU722. Ignore the first turn at Liber (9km/6mi), but 500m (1,640ft) farther on, turn right for Dos Ancares and San Román. Continue on the high ridge road (but not when cloud is low).

At **Sete Caballos**, there is a possible walk (of about an hour there and back) to **Quindos**.

Continue to **Degrada**.
From here car passengers could have a lovely 6km (3mi) downhill walk, and be picked up later by their kindly driver.

Go up again to Donis and 1km (0.5mi) farther to **Piornedo**.
Visit the round houses, and explore local paths and trackways here.

Return first to Degrada, go back to Liber/Puente de Galín via Doiras, making the trip effectively a triangle.

81

Walk

Exploring Vigo

This walk, uphill then down again, could begin or end at any one of three points, depending on energy.

Fit walkers should start at the Piscina Nautico and climb up Calle Carral to the Puerta del Sol.
Note the elaborate turn-of-the-19th-century buildings and a strange statue of a siren on a tall column.

Semi-fit people may join here in Puerta del Sol. Climb up the steps (Baixada a Principe), leaving Vigo's main shopping street, the pedestrian Calle del Principe, to the left.
At the top of the steps, the decayed red-light district lies to the right, unthreatening in daylight.

Turn left, however, up Paseo de Granada, past the town hall, and cross the main road.

The least energetic should start here, at the town hall.

Take the steps up towards the cross a short way above, turn right, and follow the gently climbing lane, with a park to the left (Parque do Castro).
You soon pass the round hut foundations of a Celtic settlement.

Continue on the lane through municipal nurseries, then go up left through the park, and left again along a few metres of road to the castle entrance.
The Castillo del Castro (*Open* 10AM–dusk) gives climbers a great reward; a gentle garden within the ramparts and splendid views of city, *ría*, and environs. (The least fit of all can drive right up to the castle.)

Galician shepherdess

The Rías Baixas of Galicia's coast

Drive

From the Miño to Cabo Fisterra

See map on page 72.

This is a drive northwards from the mouth of the Río Miño on the border with Portugal, following the complicated indentations of the Rías Baixas with Cabo Fisterra (Cabo Finisterre) as its climax. Allow three to four days for a leisurely trip.

Start at the summit of Monte Tecla above A Garda (La Guardia), self-proclaimed Capital of the Lobster.
   The road passes through a major Romano-Celtic camp.

Follow the road north to Baiona.
   A left turn just after the bridge at Ramallosa brings you to the popular but rewarding **Praia América** and, after 20km (12mi), to **Vigo**.

Crossing the Ría de Vigo by bridge, either cut off the next peninsula by proceeding directly overland to Pontevedra, or follow it round to complete the Ría de Vigo and continue to Ría de Pontevedra.
   Taking the peninsula road, you will notice fleets of *bateas*, low platforms for nurturing shellfish.

After Pontevedra, head west along the northern bank of the *ría* to the popular resort of O Grove (El Grove) and the island-resort of A Toxa (La Toja). Continue round the next *ría* (Arousa or Arosa).
   The whole *ría* varies between rurality and overdevelopment. It was at **Padrón**, at the head of the estuary, that the boat from the Mediterranean, bearing the body of St. James, is said to have come ashore.

Continue to Ría de Muros y Noia.
   This is suddenly far wilder. Bizarre headstones in the churchyard of **Noia's** Santa María a Nova record the professions of the deceased from the 9th to 19th centuries. **Muros** on the north shore has an arcaded front and tiny, steep alleyways leading up to fishermen's cottages.

Follow the road north from Muros.
   From here, views of Fisterra and the beautiful beach of Carnota emerge. At **Cabo Fisterra** itself, there is a real sense of being at the Land's End of Europe, the point at which, until 1492, known land stopped.

NORTHERN SPAIN'S ENCOUNTER with the Atlantic is a verdant affair, with lush meadows tilting down from the deep green of pine forests and the more varied hues of deciduous woods.

Where land meets sea there are rocks, cliffs, and scores of sandy beaches, ranging from super-smart town beaches to wild and little-visited corners. The coastal towns themselves are hugely varied: elegant San Sebastián and Bilbao (both Basque cities); Santander, university city and capital of the Cantabria region; and Oviedo, capital of Asturias. You will not reach Oviedo without passing by the Picos de Europa, to many the most thrilling mountains in Spain. This coast is green, of course, because it rains here, not all the time but enough to make this region totally different from Spain's Mediterranean costas.

In the following entries, where both Castilian and Basque place-names are given, the Basque appears in brackets after the Castilian.

▶▶ Bilbao (Bilbo) 85D1

Once Castile's great wool port and later Spain's steel and chemicals manufacturer, Bilbao has managed to reinvent itself since the decline of its heavy industry. This is largely due to the **Museo Guggenheim Bilbao** (Abandoibarra Etorbidea 2; tel: 944 35 90 80; *Open* Tue–Sun 10–8. *Admission charge*). The titanium, limestone, and glass building was designed by the American architect Frank O. Gehry. This museum is now Bilbao's most notable structure, providing an exciting venue for exhibitions and works from the Guggenheim Foundation's permanent collection of modern art.

The **Museo de Bellas Artes** (Plaza del Museo 2; tel: 944 39 60 60; *Open* Tue–Sun 10–8. *Admission charge*) is considered to be one of Spain's better regional galleries. The 1890s Teatro de Arriaga is 19th-century fake rococo. The streets beside it lead into the old town of Bilbao, the Casco Viejo, which focuses around the bar-lined Plaza Nueva (if you are looking for good places to eat, try Café Bilbao or Víctor Montes for tapas) and the Gothic Catedral de Santiago, which has a large porch on one side of it.

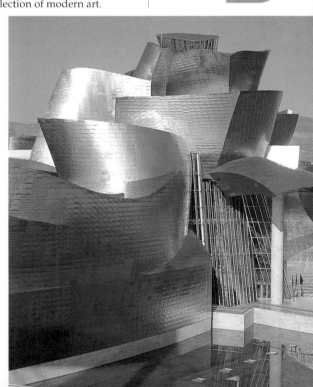

The ultra-modern Guggenheim Museum has changed the fortunes of the old industrial city of Bilbao

The North Coast

84

BASQUE NAVIGATORS
The Basque navigator Juan Sebastián Elcano of Getaria set sail with Magellan in 1521. After Magellan's death in the Philippines, Elcano took charge, becoming the first circumnavigator of the world on the *Victoria*.

▶▶▶ **Altamira**   see pages 88–99   *84C2*

▶▶ **Costa de Cantabria**   *85D2*

The soft green land behind the sea is dairy country, with pine-clothed hills and mountains and a few outbreaks of fierce grey rock. The coast has good, popular, sandy beaches. Though wave-pounded in bad weather, this is the least daunting stretch of Spain's north coast.

RESORTS

Castro-Urdiales is a busy little town, though its maritime promenade is calm and charming. It ends in a raised rock where the castle wraps itself round a lighthouse.

The little old town of **Laredo**, with its cobbled streets and 13th-century church of La Asunción, has sprouted a mini-Miami along the sand-spit that points at Santoña opposite. With an excellent beach, it's a lively resort where holiday apartments continue to go up. The old town is full of bars and discos.

Santoña has a narrow beach, a fort with an impressive number of gun emplacements, the revered 13th-century church of Santa María del Puerto, and a large, brightly painted fishing fleet. Its hilltop castle has good views.

Noja's curving golden beach, with hills behind and strange-shaped rocks, is a delight. The village of **Bareyo**, inland, has a restored Romanesque church.

Pretty **Comillas** is dominated by buildings in the Barcelona Modernista style, erected in the late 19th century when King Alfonso XII came here to relax. Biggest of these is the hilltop seminary by Domènech i Montaner. The summer palace of the Marquis of Comillas is by Joan Martorell, and a ceramic-laden folly, El Capricho (now a restaurant), is by Gaudí.

The pleasing estuarine fishing port of **San Vicente de la Barquera** is approached from the east by a long, low bridge. The old town is dominated by the church of Nuestra Señora de los Angeles, Gothic with Romanesque portals, which stands on a hill above it, along with a restored castle.

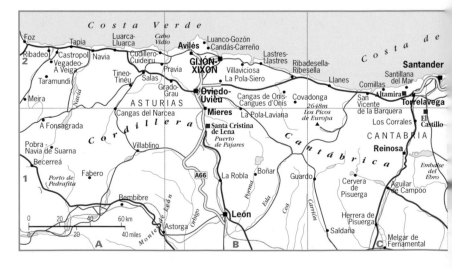

►► Costa Vasca 85E2

The "Basque coast" has cliffs and headlands and rivers that wind down through pine-covered mountains, each with a fishing port where it meets the sea. Except for San Sebastián and Fuenterrabía (separate entries), this coastline is used mainly by Basques and not visitors.

RESORTS

Bakio has a good wide beach but many apartment blocks. Continuing eastwards, the coastal scenery between Bakio and Bermeo is magnificent, with access to the rock sanctuary of San Juan de Gaztelugatxe.

Bermeo, a major fishing port, is one of the four towns (along with Guernica, Larrabezúa, and Vitoria) where Spanish kings swore to uphold Basque rights. The ceremony took place in the church of Santa Eufemia above the harbour. There is a fisherman's museum in the "Tower of Ercilla." Basque fishing boats in primary colours are brilliant en masse.

The fishing village of **Elantxobe** lies thrillingly under the rock face of a tall cape. The upper road offers views of harbour and trawlers far below.

A huge rock called El Ratón ("the mouse") stands off **Getaria**, joined to it by an isthmus with a fishing harbour. The steep little town sizzles with grilled fish.

Lekeitio is a river-mouth fishing port, with painted boats, houses with glass balconies, and a pinnacled and buttressed church. A pine-clad island stands in the river mouth with an excellent beach beyond. The tortuous but lovely coast between Lekeitio and Ondarroa has high capes, bracken, pine, and eucalyptus.

At **Ondarroa**, the river winds round an arrow-point of land, where church and old town rise dramatically. Glass balconies and half-timbered houses abound.

The stately resort of **Zarautz**, popular with the élite of Madrid in the 19th century, has a wide beach, a pair of historic palaces, and an attractive main square. It was in the boatyards that the first ship to circumnavigate the world, the *Victoria*, was built.

TOURIST INFORMATION
Altamira Caves: Avenida Jesús Otero 22, Santillana del Mar (tel: 942 81 82 51).
Bilbao: Paseo del Arenal 1 (tel: 944 79 57 60).
Costa de Cantabria: Plaza de Velarde 5, Santander (tel: 942 31 07 08).
Costa Vasca: Nafarroa Kalea, Zarautz (tel: 943 83 09 90).
Gijón: Calle Marqués de San Esteban 1 (tel: 985 34 60 46).
Oviedo: Plaza de Alfonso II El Casto 6, Oviedo (tel: 985 21 33 85).
San Sebastián: Calle Reina Regente (tel: 943 48 11 66).
Santander, El Sardinero: Jardines de Pereda s/n (tel: 942 21 61 20).

85

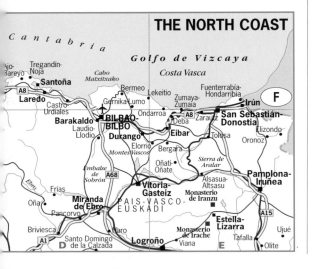

THE NORTH COAST

THE SPORTIVE BASQUES
The Basques are great sportsmen and, to a lesser extent, sportswomen. Competitive team rowing, town versus town, is very popular, heading straight out into the fearsome Bay of Biscay, around a buoy, and home again, regardless of the weather. Other sports involve chopping logs, shifting enormous weights with teams of oxen (and human assistance) and, especially, *frontón* and *pelota*, which are ball games played in a walled court. In the former, the ball is struck with the bare hands, which often bleed. In *pelota*, said to be the fastest game on earth, a curved basket is used to hit the ball.

▶▶ Costa Verde 84B2

The "Green Coast" is no misnomer for Atlantic Asturias, despite one or two large industrial towns like steel-making Avilés and, especially, Gijón. East of Gijón, the beautiful Picos de Europa rise high behind a friendly coastline. Westwards the shore becomes wilder and rockier. There are great beaches all along.

RESORTS AND SIGHTS FROM WEST TO EAST

In the Eo estuary in the far west, **Castropol** has a lovely, boaty feel to it. **Figueras**, closer to the Eo's mouth, is a good spot for food and a bed, and has Atlantic-facing beaches. East towards **Luarca** lies a series of unspoiled fishing villages, white with black slates; among them Viayelez, Ortigueira, and Vega.

Midway along the western coast, **Cabo Vidio**, with its lighthouse, has a grand view of cliffs and inset beaches. Hawks hang over the cliff edge; autumn crocuses flower here; winter winds rock parked cars. The best beaches are **El Aguilar** and **Concha de Artedo**.

At **Cudillero**, the road winds down a tight valley with just a row or two of cottages on either side, leading to a substantial fishing port cheerful with fish restaurants.

Luanco, on the cape north of Gijón, is tops for Asturian fish dinners. The road winds through a defile of fishermen's cottages, to a harbour, bars, and restaurants.

Lastres, east of Gijón, is another fishing port. A little inland the Mirador de Fitos offers fine rural views.

Ribadesella is a town on a pretty rivermouth with a good beach and the cave of **Tito Bustillo** (see panel on page 89). It makes a great base for exploring the Picos de Europa. From Villanueva, nearby, there is low tide access to the sea caves of **Cuevas del Mar**. There are pretty coves at **Celorio** as well as many good beaches.

The grey but friendly little town of **Llanes**, with its crenallated towers and little squares, is another excellent base for exploring the Picos de Europa.

Costa Verde fisherman with his catch

(see panel on page 89)

RACING RIVER
Ribadesella is the destination of the world's largest canoe race in late August, the Descent of the River Sella. Around 1,400 canoeists from over 20 countries race for their canoes during the spectacular start at Arriondas. The winner takes just over an hour to cover the 19km (12mi) downstream to the finish line. Except on the day of the race and after heavy rain, you can hire a canoe from Arriondas and follow the course at a more leisurely pace, stopping for a picnic on the riverbank.

A corner of Veigas, an 18th-century time capsule in a grey-green landscape

Walk

Taramundi

Taramundi is a deeply rural area of hills and valleys, woods and meadows just within the western limits of Asturias and south of the delightful Eo estuary. Historically it has been desperately poor. In the mid-1980s, the local community decided, against the odds, to open their forgotten countryside to visitors. They built a small hotel in the old rectory, provided a few rooms to rent, and put up wooden signboards to steer their visitors around a network of paths and lanes.

Another age-old feature of the area, throughout history, has been the production of handmade steel blades, tools and, especially, clasp-knives in tiny forges worked in individual homes and one-man workshops. Power for flour-milling was, and still is, provided by small streams pelting down the valley bottoms. The little mills, in the last half century, have also produced a faltering supply of electricity, replaced only in the 1980s and '90s by the mains.

All these peculiarities combine with a sense of nature abundant on all sides to make this one of Spain's most pleasing areas for walks or strolls. No skills are needed, since it is virtually impossible to get lost.

The most obvious walking circuit is to drop down from the village of Taramundi on its hillside, cross the little river of La Salgueira, and ascend to the right. Take a left-hand turn for Esquios and ascend for about 3km (2mi) to the knife workshop of Manuel Lombardia. Now follow the path straight along the wooded valleyside, clothed with oak, birch, and chestnut, as far as Veigas.

Veigas is an almost perfectly preserved 18th-century hamlet, without plastic or concrete, but now almost entirely empty.

Should you return by the same route, you will be rewarded with beautiful and markedly different perspectives. Most walkers, however, continue the walk by taking the track on to Texois.

Texois is a remarkable combination of flour mill, generator, and forge. Far larger than most, the forge has a water-powered oak-beam hammer, on record since the 17th century. The site is believed by locals to have been in use since Roman times.

Now return by lane to Taramundi, as signposted.

The whole walk takes 4–5 hours, or 3 hours if you are just walking to Veigas and back.

> *Northern Spain possesses an extraordinary and wonderful phenomenon: scores of painted caves, decorated by their palaeolithic inhabitants, between 25,000 and 10,000 years ago, with a brilliant array of naturalistic animals.*

One of the famous Altamira bison, part of a whole herd of animals painted in red ochre in various positions, which covers the ceiling of a large gallery

88

DISCOVERY OF THE CAVES

Altamira was discovered in 1868 by a local man following his dog. He told the Santander lawyer and antiquarian Marcelino Sanz de Sautuola. Ten years later, Sautuola came to investigate, eyes fixed firmly on the ground in the manner of the ardent excavator. It was his bored daughter María, waving the lantern about, who first saw the great painted ceiling.

ANCIENT AND MODERN THEORIES

Early theory held that the cave paintings were a form of sympathetic magic as an aid to hunting. It is now known, however, that the animals most frequently hunted were not those most frequently painted. Present speculation suggests that the paintings were somehow connected with fertility—particular animals, regardless of their gender, possibly repesenting male and female. There are certainly painted signs and even depictions of parts of the human body which have explicit sexual reference.

Altamira is the most celebrated site. This is the series of caverns near Santillana del Mar where a herd of bison painted in red ochre dating from around 12,000 BC was discovered in 1879. Despite the painstaking presentation of the first analysis of the paintings by Marcelino Sanz de Sautuola, many of Europe's scholars promptly declared them a fake. Their authenticity has now been long established and more than 80 other painted caves have been discovered right across the Basque Country, Cantabria, and Asturias. The observation and sure technique displayed in the paintings remain astonishing, but their meaning, or at least the intention of the painters, remains elusive.

Most of the paintings are of animals, with bison predominating, and horses, deer, and wild goats in lesser numbers. There are also representations of wild boar, aurochs, elk, and wolves. Bones and utensils found in the first cave suggest the earlier inhabitants may have lived here, near the light.

The gallery of the bison, once part of the main entrance cave but now shielded by a specially built rock wall, is one of the most staggering sights in Spain. Up to 2m (6ft) long, moving, mooing, curled up, and even looking at their own tails, the red beasts spread over the ceiling, accompanied by a few animals of other species. The painter or painters used bosses and protrusions in the rock surface to gain effects of realism and animation, and the ceiling gives the strong impression of being a single composition. The galleries beyond contain large numbers of line paintings, engravings, and signs, and in a recess not shown to visitors, a weird human mask.

Atmosphere changes caused by visitors began to threaten the paintings and the cave was closed in 1977. It reopened in 1982, but now admits only 20 visitors a day, depending on the conditions. Write at least a year in advance to: **Centro de Investigación de Altamira**, Santillana del Mar, Santander (tel: 942 81 80 05; www.mcu.es/nmuseos/altamira). To cater to the tens of thousands of visitors who descend each year hoping to see the famous paintings the **Museo de Altamira** (tel: 942 81 88 15; *Open* summer, Tue–Sat 9.30–7.30, Sun 9.30–5; winter, Tue–Sun 9.30–5. *Admission charge*) on the same site includes a replica, the Neocueva.

Puente Viesgo The caves of El Castillo and Las Monedas (*Open* guided tours only: summer, Tue–Sun 9.30–12, 3.15–6.30; winter, Wed–Sun 9–2. *Admission charge*), south of Torrelavega and near Puente Viesgo (300 visitors maximum each day, first come, first admitted), make the liveliest substitute for Altamira. There are striking representations of animals and human hands, and shapes or signs, which may stand for women or for female sexual organs.

Pindal This magically sited cave (*Open* summer, Wed–Sun 9.30–1.30, 3–4.45; winter, Wed–Sun 10–2, 3.15–4.15) runs inwards from a cleft above the sea, and is full of early primroses and violets in spring, blackberries in summer. The main painted surface, with three clear animals, one arguably a wild boar, and a row of strange signs which may be hunting implements or human figures, lies some 260m (853ft) deep into the cave. There is also the rarity of a painted fish, not shown to visitors for conservation reasons.

TITO BUSTILLO CAVE
Tito Bustillo Cave at Ribadesella in Asturias, discovered in the late 1960s, may disappoint some since many of the paintings are faint. There is, however, a great variety of animals, including two fine horses, one in bold head and shoulders outline. Multiple images are curiously superimposed, and there is a set of red ochre signs, or drawings, generally accepted as representing the human vulva (*Open* Easter–early Sep, Wed–Sun 10–5; 360 visitors maximum each day; first come, first admitted).

89

The hand of palaeolithic man on a cave wall is an illustration of the important prehistoric art found in the region

90

Palacio de Revillagigedo in Gijón. Two solid towers dominate this handsome 15th-century structure, which stands squarely on the Plazuela Marqués, near the harbour

▶ Durango 85D1

Durango is a busy main road town with pretty corners, important as an access point to the mountains of the Duranguesado Massif. There is an attractive drive south to the pass and shrine of Urkiola. Elorrio, to the southeast, has many heraldically emblazoned mansions.

▶▶ Fuenterrabía (Hondarribia) 85E2

Looking into France at the mouth of the Río Bidasoa, Fuenterrabía is a charming spot. La Marina, the lower town, is based around the *alameda* in Calle de San Pedro. Above is the dominating castle of Charles V, now a luxurious parador. Noble houses line the hill; the Calle Mayor, running away down the far side with wide eaves and stone houses, is even more attractive. The beach faces the river mouth and can get very busy in summer.

▶▶ Guernica (Gernika) 85D2

A market town near a lovely estuary, Gernika, to give it its Basque name, was one of four sacred places where Spanish monarchs swore to uphold Basque rights. On 26 April, 1937, Franco's German allies attacked Gernika from the air in Europe's first mass air attack on a civilian target. The remains of the sacred tree, beneath which the Basque parliament used to meet, are under a cupola beside the **Casa de Juntas** or Batzar-Etxea (open to the public), where the Basque parliament holds occasional meetings. Note in particular the large stained-glass ceiling depicting the Basque people.

▶ Navia, Valle de 84A2

The ascent of the Navia Valley from the coast leads into deep Asturias (follow the western bank). Shortly beyond Coaña, the ruins of a Celtic settlement cover a conical

A carving in Oviedo cathedral. Built between the 14th and 16th centuries, the cathedral is typical of the Flamboyant Gothic period. Its high altar-piece has fine wooden carvings depicting scenes from the life of Christ

green hill. Soon the hills climb sharply. The river is mostly dark reservoir, and the hamlets are white or grey.

▶ Oñati (Oñate) 85E1

Oñati is massively monumental, with the former Basque university (16th century), the baroque church of San Miguel and its tombs, the town hall, and old town. Once headquarters of the Carlist pretender, modern Oñati is deeply committed to Basque separatism.

▶▶ Oviedo (Uviéu) 84B2

Despite its initial greyness, the Asturian capital has a fine old town. The **cathedral** has 14th-century cloisters. The building itself is mainly Flamboyant Gothic, but contains the early Asturian "Cámara Santa," whose rich treasury includes the cross supposedly carried by Pelayo at the Battle of Covadonga (see page 92). From the cathedral, take La Rua and Cimadevilla towards the town hall. One street before the arch, the fish market is on the left, surrounded by restaurants. Through the arch and down to the right is Fontán, a fruit and vegetable market set around an old arcaded square. The **archaeological museum** (tel: 985 21 54 05; *Open* Tue–Sat 10–1.30, 4–6; Sun 11–1. *Admission free*) has early Asturian carved stonework. The **Museo de Bellas Artes** (tel: 985 21 20 61; *Open* winter, Tue–Fri 10.30–2, 4.30–8.30, Sat 11.30–2, 5–8, Sun 11.30–2.30; summer, Tue–Sat 11–2.30, 5–9, Sun 11–2.30. *Admission free*) exhibits 19th- as well as 20th-century Asturian painting. On a hillside above Oviedo stand two exquisite churches, Santa María del Naranco and San Miguel de Lillo (both *open* Tue–Sat 9.30–1, 3–7, Sun–Mon 9.30–1). See panel on page 86.

▶ Pasajes (Pasaia) 85E2

Effectively the industrial port of San Sebastián, this one-time whaling community has three villages with different saints' days and an equally festive disposition, along with pretty views across the river. The French writer Victor Hugo lived in the village of San Juan (right on the water, with great fish restaurants), while in exile in 1843.

IGNACIO DE LOYOLA
The Basque Ignacio de Loyola (1491–1556), future saint and founder of the Jesuits, was born Iñigo López Recalde in the family mansion of Loyola just by Azpeitia to the south of San Sebastián. As a young soldier, he received a near-fatal wound in a battle at Pamplona. While recuperating, he devised the spiritual exercises that were to be so important both for the Jesuit Order and the future of Catholicism. The large monastery at Loyola incorporates the room of the older house in which the saint was born.

91

OVIEDO
Oviedo was the springboard for the recapture of León in the Middle Ages, and so for the emergence of the kingdom of Castile. In 1934, as centre of the Asturian coalfield, it was the site of a miners' revolution, bloodily suppressed by the young General Francisco Franco. Now recovering from the decline of coal, Oviedo is finding a new post-industrial identity.

The Picos de Europa rise close to the north Atlantic coast. Essentially a limestone massif divided into three by a series of gorges and rivers, the mountains culminate in great stone spires which rise to 2,640m (8,660ft), far more impressive than their mere height suggests.

The medieval stone bridge at Cangas de Onís

The peaks are harsh and exposed, but the deep valleys are calm and sheltered, harbouring Mediterranean plants and a local architecture of stone and tile that looks as if it has grown from the green meadows. Some of the finest parts of the range are protected by the Picos de Europa National Park.

The national flora is magnificent and a prodigious amount of butterflies inhabit the mountians.

The trouble with the Picos is that it rains or snows here half the days of the year. Mists linger for weeks.

Covadonga Back in the 8th century, only one small area and one people held out against the Moors: the stout Asturians, under their leader Pelayo, in the Picos valley of Covadonga in the northwest corner of the range. Here, the final refuge was a shallow cave. The story is that Pelayo and his men, assisted by the Holy Cross and the Virgin of Battles, trounced 20,000 Moors sent after them in about AD 724. Pelayo became king; and the Christian Reconquest, or Reconquista, now began.

As well as the cave and Virgin, there is a huge basilica, a choir school, a Civil Guards barracks, and considerable numbers of souvenir shops. The road past the shrine continues to two mountain lakes (Enol and Ercina). The views are wonderful.

A round tour of the peaks
The tour includes some walking suggestions. Four-wheel drive vehicles may be hired for the high terrain.

Cangas de Onís Begin here, before the mountains start, in the northwest corner (easily reached from Oviedo or Ribadesella). There is a medieval bridge and a chance to buy *cabrales*, the fierce cheese of the region. Covadonga is 7km (4mi) into the base of the mountains.

Arenas de Cabrales Eastwards from Cangas, the soft valley soon narrows for a first real glimpse of rock. Just past Carreño, the Mirador del Pozo de la Oración offers views of Naranjo de Bulnes (2,519m/8,262ft), the majestic column of rock on which the Picos centre.

Arenas is not so special, but the road south leads to the **Cares Gorge**, dividing eastern and western massifs.

There is a tremendous walk here from Poncebos through the gorge to Caín and on to Posada de Valdeón, with a high path and bridges across the cleft. Allow a day for this.

Panes Continuing east from Arenas, follow the Cares River to Panes, another point of entry to the Picos.

The green valleys of the Picos de Europa provide good grazing

Desfiladero de la Hermida From Panes, a twisting limestone gorge climbs slowly south, while eagles and vultures wheel above. Tucked away by Lebeña is the interesting 10th-century Mozarabic church of Santa María, with Byzantine-style roof and Moorish-style horseshoe arches on its belfry.

Potes Before Potes, the road enters the beautiful and wide Liébana valley with views up to the eastern Picos massif. (Coming from the other direction, from central Spain, there is a fine drive northwards to Potes, through the Cordillera Cantábrica from Cervera de Pisuerga.) Potes has a castle, and holiday charm.

Fuente Dé From Potes, drive up northwest to Fuente Dé, where a parador stands under a vast rock wall and a cable car ascends. There is a 1.5-hour walk up from the higher cable-car station (taxing in its second half) through pure limestone to the Verónica refuge. Before the refuge, up round the corner to the right, there are some stunning views of Naranjo de Bulnes and its mountain cirque.

San Glorio Pass/Collado de Llesba Returning to Potes, ascend the ravishing San Glorio pass to the west.

At the top, take the dirt road right to Collado de Llesba (1km/0.5mi), where you will find a sad-faced "Monument to the Bear," views of the central Picos, and the Cordillera Cantábrica behind you.

Posada de Valdeón Continuing west, turn north at Portilla de la Reina. From the Pandetrave pass, there are more views of the central massif and at last a clear sight of the rock spires of the western group.

Drop down into the valley of Valdeón, continuing to Caín for the southern entry to the Cares Gorge (see page 92).

Panderruedas Pass On the way up and west from Valdeón, this is another great viewing point for the western massif (climb for five minutes up to the right).

Desfiladero de los Beyos (Beyos Gorge) This limestone slit descends to Cangas, and marks the western limits of the Picos.

San Sebastián was patronized in the past by the Spanish royal family. Its beautiful beach and attractive setting serve to retain its reputation as an elegant summer resort

WILDLIFE IN THE CORDILLERA

The Iberian brown bear is a dwindling and desperately threatened species. The few survivors live almost exclusively in the Reserva Nacional de Somiedo, southwest of Oviedo. The reserve, which includes both the crest of the Cantabrian Cordillera and the deep lake of Salienca, also has a population of wolves and golden eagles.

SAN SEBASTIÁN FIESTAS

San Sebastián is mad on festivals and sports, with rowing regattas (September), jazz festival (July), film festival (September), wood-chopping contests (any time), and bands composed of children, all smartly dressed in Napoleonic uniforms. The latter feature in the famous San Sebastián *tamborada* (January). Find out what's happening in the useful monthly guide available from the tourist office.

▶▶▶ San Sebastián (Donostia)   *85E1*

San Sebastián is a fashionable seaside city, the leading resort on the north coast. Its greatest asset is its setting: a near-perfect circle of bay, the entrance guarded on either side by a single steep hill, and with the pretty little island of Santa Clara right in the middle. An old town and fishing harbour are tucked in behind Monte Urgull, the guardian hill on the eastern side, surmounted by castle remnants and a gigantic statue of Christ.

A ROYAL PAST Round the rest of the bay, a classic Belle Epoque resort grew up in the late 19th century. This was above all thanks to Queen Isabella II, who began to come here from 1845, when her doctors recommended sea bathing to cure a skin complaint. By 1893, Queen María Cristina had built the royal palace of Miramar right in the heart of the bay, in brick and tile and with half-timbered gables, using English architect Seldon Wornum to achieve a Queen Anne "cottage" effect (nowadays it is used as a summer university). A casino went up in 1887, elaborate in brownish stone, but is now the town hall. Visitors included Bismarck and Napoleon III, Sarah Bernhardt, and King Leopold of Belgium. The Spanish court came here each summer.

FASHION AND FOOD San Sebastián is still elegant, with well-dressed citizens, its own designers, and scores of small fashion shops, mostly on Urbieto, the Boulevard (Alameda del Boulevard), and Avenida (the Avenida de la Libertad). Apart from its summer beach life, the other great feature of San Sebastián is the food. Bars serve elaborate tapas and the restaurants, some of which are the most exclusive in Spain, offer cuisine largely based on fish. Behind this lies a unique Basque phenomenon; more than 120 men-only gastronomic clubs, whose members meet to cook each other elaborate meals, play cards, and generally socialize. The setting for these clubs is rather like a restaurant, but one where all members are free to enter the kitchen.

CHURCHES Santa María, close to the fishing harbour, has a fine, elaborate Churrigueresque facade. Gothic **San Vicente**, deep in the old town, holds services in Basque.

MUSEUMS The provincial museum occupies the former Dominican monastery of **San Telmo** (tel: 943 42 49 70; *Open* Tue–Sat 10.30–1.30, 4–8, Sun 10.30–2); the permanent cloister exhibition is of Basque life and painting. The **Palacio del Mar** (Palace of the Sea, tel: 943 44 00 99; *Open* daily 10–8), above the fishing harbour, has an aquarium.

SANTA CLARA ISLAND
Boats leave for the tiny (five-minute) hop to the island of Santa Clara from just beneath the information kiosk in San Sebastián's harbour (100m/328ft) from the town hall). It's the top spot for Sunday afternoons in summer.

Walk

San Sebastián: around the bay

Start facing the town hall, and go left along the front.

You soon pass the **Hotel de Londres y de Inglaterra**, marking the early arrival of the British in the resort and now with a casino.

On your right all the way are the sands of the beach of **La Concha**, crowded but lively in summer, with cafés and changing rooms tucked in beneath the road. This is interrupted by a spit of land, site of the royal palace of Miramar, and the rest of the beach is known as Ondarreta. Better for swimming, **Ondarreta** is preferred by

San Sebastián's picturesque Bahía de la Concha

the locals to La Concha.

After the beach, to the left behind the tennis courts, there is a funicular railway to Monte Igueldo.

On this western peak guarding the bay are viewing points and a fun fair.

Continuing at sea level, the walk ends at **El Peine de los Vientos** (the Comb of the Winds).

This consists of iron sculptures like alphabet spaghetti, by the distinguished Basque artist Eduardo Chillida.

95

Walk

Monte Urgull

A road runs above the waves all the way around the base of Monte Urgull but the 180m (590ft) hill can only be ascended from the side looking out over the bay. Starting from the *Ayuntamiento* (town hall) go around

the fishing harbour, past the aquarium, and follow the road along the shore until a ramp sets off up the hill to your right. Various diverging paths lead among the trees and past an overgrown monument to British soldiers who died in a battle here in 1813.

Eventually you should reach the Castillo de la Mota on the top, underneath the statue of Christ, from which there are good views of the town.

A series of paths and steps takes a more direct way back down either to the fishing harbour or to the aquarium.

Drive

Alto Campoo

Just beneath the mountains in the deep south of Cantabria, west of Reinosa, take the C628 into the Alto Campoo (High Country).

At 5km (3mi) is the sleepy village of **Fontibre**, with the source of the Ebro in a poplar-filled dip to the left. You can park and walk down. The river runs out under loose stones into pools of milky blue.

Continuing, the road leads up past the skiing station of Braña Vieja towards the final watershed (a short walk from Fuente de Chico parking area). Rivers descend from here in three magnificent directions: to the Atlantic north coast, to the Atlantic west (the Duero system), and to the Mediterranean (the Ebro system).

PRIVILEGES OF THE NOBLES
One of the advantages of being a Spanish aristocrat in the past was that you were exempt from all taxes. The inhabitants of the north coast sought to make an unfair system fairer by spreading noble titles as widely as they could. In some places, the entire population was simply declared noble; a tax dodge to beat all others. Heraldry and aristocratic emblems are perhaps even more common here than elsewhere in Spain and Santillana del Mar is a case in point.

SEX AND THE ROMANESQUE
Romanesque stone carving, one of the glories of medieval Spain, is open, frank, humorous, and often sexually explicit. This is made evident by the carvings on the exterior of the handsome collegiate church of Cervatos, today no more than a tiny village, 5km (3mi) south of Reinosa.

►► Santander   84C2

Santander lies at the mouth of a wide bay. Rebuilt after a fire in 1941, the city has fashionable beaches (such as El Sardinero), and the agreeable feel of a port, seaside, and university town. Out on the promontory, in public gardens, is La Magdalena, the summer palace of King Alfonso XIII. You can visit the home of the great conservative scholar Marcelino Menéndez y Pelayo (1856–1912), opposite his 42,000-volume library and the **Museo de Bellas Artes** (tel: 942 23 94 85; *Open* summer, Mon–Fri 10.30–1, 5.30–8, Sat 10.30–1; winter, Mon–Fri 10–1, 5–8, Sat 10.30–1. *Admission charge*). The much remodelled Gothic cathedral is built over a 13th-century crypt. The International Music Festival is held here every August.

Beach, resort, and suburb of Santander, **El Sardinero** has 19th-century mansions, modern apartments, hotels, restaurants, and a casino. The beach is deservedly popular and it has good nightlife in summer.

►►► Santillana del Mar   84C2

This beautiful village is full of stone-built mansions, dripping with heraldic emblems. Look for the home of the Marquis of Santillana and the Casa de los Hombrones. The Romanesque collegiate church of **Santa Juliana** (*Open* Thu–Tue 10–1, 4–6.30; closed Feb. *Admission charge*) has magnificent carved capitals in the cloister. Use the same ticket for entry to the museum of religious art in the **Convento de Regina Coeli** across the main road.

Balconied old houses in Santillana del Mar

Bridge in the "High Country," Alto Campoo, which is a winter ski area

▶ Villaviciosa   84B2

Villaviciosa is a surprisingly monumental little town tucked into beautiful Asturian countryside behind Tazones on the coast. This is where Charles V landed by mistake in 1517 on his first arrival in Spain, as he had intended to dock at Santander. The house in which the future emperor stayed is Calle del Agua 31. The Romanesque church of Santa María is notable. So too is the early Asturian church of **Valdediós**, set in rural tranquillity 10km (6mi) south.

▶▶ Vitoria (Gasteiz)   85D1

As home of the tumultuous Basque parliament since the 1980s, Vitoria is often on Spanish TV screens. The modern town is surprisingly calm in appearance. The old town, on a hill above, is striking.

In the **new town** are the pleasing Parque de la Florida and the neoclassical new cathedral, the Basque parliament, and the broad, arcaded 18th-century Plaza de España, built to accommodate the town hall. From here, the Plaza de la Virgen Blanca ascends the hill.

Once you are in the **old town**, steps lead up to the church of San Miguel, with a large portico and carved tympanum. The Virgen Blanca (White Virgin) stands outside in a kind of sentry box of black marble and tinted glass. To the right, an arcaded walking street, Los Arquillos, passes through the middle levels of a Renaissance building on the hillside. Behind it, and beneath the hilltop church of San Vicente, is the historic Plaza del Machete. The hilltop has two palaces, and it ends with the agreeable old Gothic cathedral of Santa María. Dropping down steeply on the far side of the hill are several restored medieval mansions, among them El Portalón. There are antique shop fronts in the Calle Correria, an archaeological museum, and museums of fine art and of playing cards.

▶ Zumaya (Zumaia)   85D1

In this pleasant Basque town, the house and studio of the Basque painter Ignacio Zuloaga (1870–1945) is joined to an ancient chapel in what was once a halting place for Santiago pilgrims taking the north coast route.

OLD CUSTOMS
Vitoria's Plaza del Machete gets its name from a genuine machete, a kind of straight-edged scythe for hacking at undergrowth. In former days, the ceremony of Basque rights, or *fueros*, was held every 1 January. The mayor of Vitoria would take up his stance here facing the town's representative in the national parliament. The latter had to swear to defend local rights under pain of beheading by the official machete. The ceremony ceased with the loss of Basque *fueros* (local rights) in 1841.

HAVE A CIGAR
All three of the main Basque cities (Bilbao, San Sebastián, and Vitoria) hold major fiestas in August, but one of them begins in a most unusual way. Vitoria's Fiestas de la Virgen Blanca starts on the evening of 4 August with the descent of the *celedón*, a dummy carrying an umbrella, which is lowered on a rope from the tower of the church of San Miguel to a house below in the Plaza de la Virgen Blanca. A man dressed in similar clothes to the dummy emerges from the house, the crowd applauds, and everyone lights a cigar.

THE *JOTA*

The *jota* of Navarra and Aragón is a hugely athletic dance, with much springing in the air and lusty kicking. The *jota* matches the landscape: hard and steep but always invigorating. Like flamenco, it is also danced in other parts of Spain, especially in Old Castile.

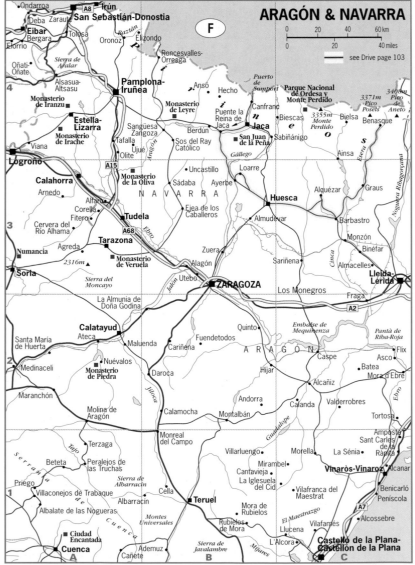

ARAGÓN & NAVARRA

0   20   40   60 km

0   20   40 miles

see Drive page 103

NOT AS WELL KNOWN as the adjoining Basque Country and Catalonia, Aragón and Navarra together occupy some of the most dramatically beautiful, if challenging, of Spanish landscapes.

THE LAND Both regions come tilting down from the high Pyrenees. To the west, in Navarra, the mountains are often moist and misty, subject to Atlantic weather. Aragón is higher and more "continental," meaning it is hotter and colder by turns and very much drier in summer. From the Pyrenean foothills, the land stretches out southwards, with vines and fruit and what might be called temperate farming. Next, the basin of the River Ebro runs through, west to east, agriculturally rich but often dreary in appearance. In Navarra, the Ebro area is known as La Ribera (the river-bank), and it marks the southern border of the region. Aragón stretches on far to the south of the Ebro, gaunt, sometimes tremendous, sometimes threatening, to reach such mountain ranges as the Montes Universales in the southwest and the formidable Maestrazgo in the southeast.

Physically, the visitor perceives Aragón and Navarra as one, linked in their northern reaches by the passage of the Pilgrims' Way to Santiago de Compostela. Historically, however, the two regions could scarcely be more different.

ARAGÓN'S PAST Aragón, larger and usually more prominent in Spanish affairs than Navarra, had its beginnings high in the Pyrenees in a pocket of resistance to the Moors. Little by little the infant kingdom advanced from Jaca, through Huesca and Tarazona and finally to Zaragoza, retaking the city in 1118. Zaragoza up to that time had been the major focus for Moorish civilization in northern Spain; Moorish subjects, now known as Moriscos, stayed on and constituted the majority of the population until they were expelled in 1609. The result is that while the northern part of the region has its fine Romanesque and, later, Gothic and Renaissance buildings, southern Aragón is Spain's grandest repository of the Mudéjar, the immensely evocative architectural forms created by Moriscos, working for Christian masters.

Almost from the start, Aragón looked east, forming a dynastic alliance with Catalonia (1137) and sharing in Catalonia's medieval empire. It produced Ferdinand of Aragón, husband of Castile's Isabella, then gradually over the centuries was forced into submission to a centralized Spain. Nowadays, though Zaragoza flourishes, the rural areas of Aragón are seriously depopulated. The people are reputed to be vigorous and friendly, loud-voiced, and direct speaking.

NAVARRA'S INDEPENDENT SPIRIT Where Aragón looked east to Catalonia, Navarra, by contrast, looked north and west, to France and the Basque Country. A proportion of its population is Basque, and there is a strong sense of Basque identity.

Always aloof from the Spanish mainstream, Navarra was in fact ruled by a French dynasty from 1234 until its

Aragón and Navarra

Roofs and towers of Calatayud. This largely Mudéjar town once guarded the Aragonese frontier

TOURIST INFORMATION

Benasque: Calle San Pedro (tel: 974 55 12 89).
Calatayud: Plaza el Fuerte (tel: 976 88 63 22).
Fuendetodos: Cortes de Aragón 7 (tel: 976 14 38 01).
Huesca: Plaza de la Catedral 1 (tel: 974 29 21 70).
Iruñea: Calle Eslava 1 (tel: 948 20 65 40).
Jaca: Calle Regimento de Galicia 2 (tel: 974 36 00 98).
Lizarra: Calle San Nicolás 1 (tel: 948 55 63 01).
Olite: Rua Mayor 1 (tel: 948 74 17 03).
Orreaga: Antiguo Molino de Roncesvalles (tel: 948 76 03 01).
Tarazona, Veruela: Calle Iglesia 5 (tel: 976 64 00 74).
Teruel, Valderrobres: Calle Tomás Nougués 1, Teruel (tel: 978 60 22 79).
Tudela: Plaza Vieja 1 (tel: 948 84 80 58).
Zaragoza: Plaza del Pilar s/n (tel: 976 39 35 37).

annexation to Spain by Ferdinand of Aragón in 1512. From then on, it struggled to hold on to its local rights (*fueros*) and freedoms, launching a series of bloody civil wars in the 19th century under the banner of Carlism, a reactionary, romantic creed.

The Carlists were still one of the strongest forces supporting General Franco in the 20th-century Spanish Civil War. Conservative, temperamentally rugged, and full of the relics of a battling past, Navarra has one visitor "spectacular": the running of the bulls during the fiesta of San Fermín at Pamplona, 6–14 July.

▶▶ Albarracín   98B1

This small town on the edge of the Montes Universales, an independent state from 1165 to 1333, is one of the most strikingly sited towns in all Spain and is remarkably unspoiled.

Arriving from Teruel, you see the whole facade of the town rising vertically before you in a concave crescent, brown ochre to strawberry in colour. The streets are narrow and the tall buildings have overhanging first storeys. The medieval walls are impressive; so is the high silhouette of the small cathedral, notable for its carved wooden *retablo* (altarpiece), which depicts the life of St. Peter, as well as the quirky treasures of its museum. There are numerous cave paintings in the sierra to the south.

▶ Alcañiz   98C2

A messy, rather disappointing town in parts, Alcañiz has an interesting old quarter running back from the River Guadalope to the impressive Plaza de España. Look out for the Renaissance town hall and the baroque facade of the town's huge collegiate church. The castle is now a parador, but was once one of the leading centres of the Knights of Calatrava.

▶ Alquézar 98C3

Alquézar is a little way north of Barbastro and is noted for the beauty of its setting and its collegiate church, on the site of a Moorish *alcázar* (fortress); hence its name.

▶ Alsasua (Altsasu) 98A4

This Navarrese town is an historic hub of commerce at a meeting place of mountains. The landscape of harsh, rocky cliffs above green pastures and ancient woods offers memorable approaches.

▶ Barbastro 98C3

Barbastro is undistinguished except for its cathedral. It is on the site where Petronila of Aragón married Ramón Berenguer IV of Catalonia in 1137, thus establishing Spain's grandest medieval alliance. It has a huge 16th-century *retablo* by Damián Forment.

▶▶ Baztán and the Regata del Bidasoa 98A4

The valley of the Bidasoa River, green with meadow and forest, runs down from the low peaks of the western Pyrenees, and becomes steeper and more dramatic as it nears the sea. The towns of Arantaz, Lesaca, Vera de Bidasoa, Yanci, and Echalar once formed the famous local alliance of the Cinco Villas. **Echalar** is the most impressive, with huge harmonious homesteads and mighty stones around their doors and windows. The town of **Elizondo** has fine old mansions along the river, heavy with the armorial bearings of emigrants returned from the Americas.

▶ Benasque 98C4

Benasque is a pretty, stone-built town, boasting such historic buildings as the Renaissance palace of the Counts of Ribazorga and the 13th-century church of San Marcial. It is popular with walkers, climbers, and skiers.

▶▶ Calatayud 98A2

A dilapidated but engaging Mudéjar town, lying below a ruined castle and the grey cliffs bounding the valley of the River Jalón. After centuries of neglect, the Mudéjar-towered brick-patterned churches of Santa María and San Andrés have been restored. The age-worn, part-arcaded Plaza de España is a delight. Elsewhere in the old town, in lanes no wider than an arm span, walls bulge ominously. Leave the main road here for the outstanding 12th-century **Monasterio de Piedra**, which is about 28km (17mi) to the south (see page 107).

▶ Daroca 98B2

Daroca was once a medieval craft centre, but has since shrunk back within the magnificent but ruinous walls and towers surrounding it. Glimpses from the main road above are a temptation to enter by the upper gate and pass downhill along a winding cobbled street; another fine gateway, carrying the imperial arms of Charles V, is at the Jiloca River exit far below. The collegiate church of Santa María and the church of San Miguel are the main monuments. **Maluenda** has a notable Mudéjar tower and church.

101

The watery setting of the popular Monasterio de Piedra

In almost all the cities, towns, and villages of Aragón, from Alcañiz to Huesca, from Teruel to Zaragoza and often, too, in nearby Catalonia and Navarra, it is worth tipping your head backwards now and then to admire the immense eaves protruding from the older buildings. Sometimes, as in the alleys of Daroca, they practically meet, forming a broad umbrella overhead. Aragonese eaves are generally wooden, and often elaborately carved, almost on the scale of a Chinese temple.

►► Estella (Lizarra) 98A4

As one of the many staging posts along the way to Santiago, this town was known to pilgrims as "Estella La Bella" (Estella the Beautiful); and so it remains.

The monumental sites include the Romanesque church of San Miguel with a magnificently sculpted north facade enclosed in a protective glass porch.

Across the river, the Plaza de San Martín is flanked by an early palace of the kings of Navarra (12th century) which houses a gallery of regional art. The fortified church of San Pedro, with fine carved cloisters, is at the top of a monumental stairway. (Guided tours are conducted by the tourist office.) A short way north, following signs to San Sebastián and turning left soon after Abárzuza, you will see the monastery of **Iranzu**, in a beautiful and calming valley (fine Cistercian church; great 13th-century kitchen).

► Fitero 98A3

The honey-coloured Cistercian monastery of Santa María in Fitero hides a Gothic church behind its Romanesque doorway, often closed. The key is kept in the Casa Parroquial opposite. The slightly tatty nearby spa, **Baños de Fitero**, on the edge of the sierra, is good for rheumatism. Waters issue forth at 11°C (52°F).

►► Fuendetodos 98B2

This solemn, stone-built village, birthplace in 1746 of the artist Goya, lies in country of forbidding vastness and aridity. The **Casa-Museo de Goya** (Calle Alfondiga, tel: 976 14 38 30; *Open* Tue–Sun 11–2, 4–7) is not as humble as its plaque maintains. The **Museo de Grabado** (Museum of Etching) shows the complete Goya *Caprichos* and *Disasters of War*.

►► Huesca 98B3

Modern Huesca is unremarkable, but old Huesca contains a rich ensemble of Aragonese art and architecture. The sculpted portals of the cathedral lead into a bare hall of stone, with nave and two side aisles and a fine Damián Forment *retablo* in alabaster. The handsome town hall has a famous painting of the Bell of Huesca.

Inside the restored Goya house, the main attraction in the artist's birthplace, Fuendetodos

High on its crag, the castle of the kings of Aragon at Loarre

Drive

Mountains and plain

See map on page 98.

This drive takes a minimum of two days, but could be used as the basis for a week or so of travelling.

Starting at Jaca (perhaps after a visit to the Ordesa National Park, see page 111), drive west on the main road (N240) to Pamplona.
After 10km (6mi), divert left to the monastery of **San Juan de la Peña** (see page 110).

Return to the main road and continue west. From Puente la Reina de Jaca, drop south on the N240. From Ayerbe, divert left to Loarre and follow signs to **Castillo de Loarre**.
Visit the splendid castle-eyrie of the kings of Aragón, one of Spain's great military buildings.

Continue to **Huesca** (see page 102).

You could possibly spend a night here, but certainly take an hour or two to visit the old town.

From here, take the N240 to Barbastro.
There is a potential side-trip to **Alquézar** (see page 101).

From Barbastro, the C138/9 leads to Graus.
The route is mainly through peach orchards, shortly picking up the lower reaches of the River Esera. **Graus** is faded but very pleasing, a town that time has forgotten. The once-grand Plaza de España has wide Aragonese eaves and traces of ornamental painting on the facades. The town is gathered under a rounded sandstone cliff and a large grey basilica.

Continue along the Esera Valley to **Benasque** (see page 101).
The valley opens and closes, at times forming a dramatic gorge. It leads eventually to a broader, grassy valley, with Benasque at its head. To the southeast of Benasque, the ski resort of Cerler is reached by a pine-flanked road with magnificent views. All the highest Pyrenean peaks—Aneto, Maladeta, Posets, and El Perdiguero—are close to Benasque.

Spain enjoys the largest area of uncultivated, wild land in all Europe. Rare creatures, including wolves, bears, and bearded vultures, survive here. As with all things Spanish, there is great regional variation.

NATIONAL PARKS
There are 12 national parks on Spanish soil, four of them in the Canary Islands, plus Archipélago de Cabrera in the Balearics. Mainland Spain's seven are: Picos de Europa; Ordesa y Monte Perdido and Aigüestortes i Estany de Sant Maurici in the Pyrenees; Tablas de Daimiel and Cabañeros in Castilla-La Mancha; Doñana in Andalucía; and the Sierra Nevada.

104

Tongue orchid (Serapias lingua). Many orchids grow in Spain's mountain regions

The north coast The northern provinces of Cantabria, Asturias, and Galicia are cool and green. Beyond the pockets of industrialization, the economy is based on fishing, small farming, timber, and hazelnuts. Much of the meadowland has degenerated into weed beds, but the late appearance of intensive farming methods has helped the preservation of wild flowers. Orchids, speedwell, saxifrages, and columbine are common. In the fastnesses of the Picos de Europa, there are over 40 recorded species of orchid. Rare butterflies also survive here. Some primary beech and oak woods still exist (particularly in the Sierra de Ancares), and newly planted chestnuts stand on hillsides clothed with broom, gorse, and heather. The planting of eucalyptus and pine as cash crops, which is heavily criticized on the grounds that the trees impoverish the soil and are of only short term benefit, has been reduced as a result of pressure by ICONA, the offical nature conservation body.

Northern Spain still has deer, wolves, and a few Iberian brown bears, now severely reduced in numbers (the majority of sightings has been in the Reserva Nacional de Somiedo, see panel page 94). Wild boar flourish here as in most wild places in Spain, though they are rarely seen. Easier to spot is the chamois, once endangered but now making a successful comeback. There are capercaillie in the woods, and in the sky you might see eagles (golden, Bonelli's, booted, and short-toed), as well as vultures (Egyptian and griffon). The rare eagle-owl shelters in caves and rock holes.

The rivers contain sea trout, brown trout, and salmon, with otters to hunt them. The wetlands area around the Bay of Santoña, between Bilbao and Santander, is an important stopping place for migratory birds such as spoonbills, avocets, plover, greenshank, and curlews. The Cíes islands, off the northwest coast, are a breeding ground for shags, guillemots, and gulls.

The Pyrenees The Spanish Pyrenees became accessible only in the 20th century and especially during the skiing boom of the past 25 years. The environmental pressures that other areas have had to resist for decades are comparatively new dangers for this region of mountains, lakes, waterfalls, trout streams, and flower-filled meadows.

The slopes of the Val d'Aran are prized for their profusion of orchids and rare butterflies. The Parque Nacional de Ordesa y Monte Perdido shelters gentians, edelweiss, anemones, alpine roses, and violets; there are roe deer, wild boar, eagles, vultures, foxes, and ermines. The Parc

Nacional d'Aigüestortes i Estany de Sant Maurici has chamois, otters, eagles, grouse, capercaillie, and the rare bearded vulture (see panel).

Central Spain The central area of the *meseta* is a landscape of open wheatfield, vineyards, and sheep tracks through barren plains, yet there is more diversity of flora and fauna than at first appears. The mountain ranges around the *meseta*, notably the sierras of Gredos, Guadarrama, Ayllón, Béjar, and Peña de Francia have wild boar, lynx (very rare), wolves, and roe deer, as well as imperial eagles, vultures, and kites. The Serranía de Cuenca to the east is rich in orchids. There is an abundance of smaller mammals such as rabbits and hares. Hunting (mostly of red and fallow deer) is a popular activity. The Tablas de Daimiel, an area of lagoons formed by the Río Guadiana, once supported a huge variety of bird-life, but is now endangered by water extraction (see page 195).

Mediterranean and Andalucía All the variations of topography, and flora, from near-desert to high mountain are represented in this area. The peaks of the Sierra Nevada are usually covered in snow, despite being within striking distance of the Mediterranean.

Mediterranean wetlands provide an important refuge for wildfowl and migrating birds, such as stone curlews and marsh harriers, spoonbills, and glossy ibis, as well as smaller warblers and shrikes. They find their way to Aiguamolls de L'Empordá in Catalonia, to the Ebro delta, to the Valencian Albufera, and to the Doñana National Park in the province of Huelva. All these areas are under threat from the pressures of intensive farming, industrial waste, and tourism.

Regional autonomies are responding by designating some key areas as *parques naturales*, thus providing an element of protection. Whether this will be enough is an open question. Meanwhile, some Spanish environmentalist groups put their faith in direct action, and the Doñana National Park has been the scene of pitched battles.

BIRDS OR SHEEP?
The great bustard, most notable of the steppes-type birds inhabiting Old Castile, is so large that when it is feeding with its head down in long grass, its back may be mistaken for that of a sheep. Other birds, smaller but equally fascinating, make heavy use of wetlands in the interior. Around the Laguna de la Nava, near Palencia, for example (an ancient wetland reflooded in the 1990s) during the winter months you may encounter geese in their thousands, plentiful marsh harriers, and Calandra larks (also in thousands). Up to 160 of Spain's 350 bird species have been spotted here.

105

THE BEARDED VULTURE
The lammergeyer, also known as the bearded vulture, is noted for dropping bones from a huge height in order to smash them so that it can eat the marrow. Already rare, this bird is, sadly, becoming rarer.

Nesting white stork, a common sight in central areas

Time out for a game of bowls in Jaca

THE BELL OF HUESCA
Legend claims that King Ramiro II of Aragón, thoroughly displeased with his nobles, summoned them one day to see the forging of a bell whose voice would ring across the kingdom. Welcoming them instead to a gloomy chamber in his palace, virtually a cellar, he promptly cut their heads off. His "bell" was the dreadful news of the event. The cellar is still to be seen within the late 17th-century Universidad Literaria, now housing the provincial museum in Huesca (see page 102). There is a dramatic painting of the scene (visits during office hours) on the first floor of the town hall.

▶▶ **Jaca**   *98B4*

Jaca, an attractive little Pyrenean town, was the city from which the tiny Kingdom of Aragón launched its comeback against the Moors. It soon became first point of call for Santiago pilgrims taking the eastern route from France. Today, it is the hub of an important skiing region in the Pyrenees.

The cathedral and its diocesan museum (entered via the cathedral) are musts for the culturally inclined. The cathedral portico contains a fine sculpted tympanum of the Wheel of the Trinity and archaic lions. The carved Romanesque capitals of the south porch (especially Abraham and Isaac, to the right of the door) are naively powerful. The **diocesan museum** (*Open* Tue–Sun 11–1.30, 4–6.30. *Admission charge*) has an excellent collection of Romanesque paintings and sculpture.

On the western edge of town is a huge citadel, open to the public, with deer grazing in its moat.

▶▶ **Leyre**   *98B4*

The monastery of San Salvador de Leyre (tel: 948 88 41 50; *Open* Mon–Sat 10.15–2, 3.30–7, Sun 10.15–2, 4–7. *Admission charge*), burial place of the kings of Navarra and the spiritual centre of the kingdom in the 11th century, lies beneath the cliffs of the Sierra de Leyre above the vast blue reservoir of Yesa. The 11th-century crypt and Romanesque church are surrounded by modern monastic buildings, including a hotel. Vespers with Gregorian chant are at 8PM and full service is at 10.15PM.

▶▶ **Maestrazgo**   *98C1*

The ancient domain of a knightly order (see pages 218–219), the Maestrazgo is a rugged territory of rock and gorge straggling the border of Teruel and Castellón provinces. It has many unspoiled, fortified medieval townships, notably Morella (the "capital" of the Maestrazgo, see page 217) and Cantavieja, on the Teruel side of the border, historically important because of its ridge-top vantage point. To the northwest of it is the enchanting, restored walled village of Mirambel. The most spectacular of all the Maestrazgo's towns, however, is Ares del Maestre, which is wrapped around the base of a 1,318m (4,323ft) rock. Another attractive spot is the shrine of La Balma (beyond Zorita, north of Forcall) where a church has been stuck precariously to a vertical wall of rock.

►► Monasterio de Piedra   98A2

Beyond the reservoir that threatens to engulf red-roofed Nuévalos, the Monasterio de Piedra (tel: 976 84 90 11; *Open* daily 9–6) is one of Aragón's most popular spots. Below the monastery, paths follow the Río Piedra; cool, arboreal, and full of waterfalls.

►► Olite   98A4

Olite sits on a plain—a surprising choice for the greatest castle of the kings of Navarra (tel: 948 74 00 35; *Open* daily 10–2, 4–6). Though heavily restored, it is a fine place to explore, with galleries, courtyards, and views of the town.

► La Oliva   98A3

The Cistercian monastery of La Oliva (tel: 948 72 50 06; *Open* 9–12, 4–6; ask to be shown around) was founded in the 12th century, in the lower valley of the Río Aragón, rich now in fruit trees and poplars. It was a major cultural centre for Navarra. The church has a Romanesque facade, Gothic cloister, and chapterhouse.

►►► Ordesa National Park   98C4

See page 111

►► Pamplona (Iruñea)   98A4

The city best known these days for its bull-running festival (Fiestas de San Fermín, see panel) was once the fortress capital of Navarra and an important stage in the Santiago pilgrimage. It was here (marked by a plaque) that the young Basque nobleman Ignatius Loyola fell wounded in 1521 during the defence of Pamplona against the French. He went on to found the Order of Jesuits, and to achieve sainthood. The walled old town contains a Gothic cathedral (*Open* Mon–Fri 10.30–1.30, 4–7; Sat 10–1.30. *Admission charge*). The neoclassical facade is disappointing but the cloisters, the Puerta de la Sala Preciosa, and the star vaulting in the Barbazan chapel more than compensate. Look out for the Museo de Navarra (tel: 948 42 64 92; *Open* Tue–Sat 10–2, 5–7; Sun 11–2. *Admission free*), the *ayuntamiento* (town hall), and the twin-towered church of San Saturnino as well.

►► Puente la Reina   98B4

Charming little Puente la Reina lies at the river crossing where pilgrims arriving via the Somport pass finally converged with those entering Spain via Roncesvalles (see page 110). The twin-aisled church of El Crucifijo contains a noted 14th-century German crucifix. The narrow main street, or Calle Mayor, with its handsome mansions and the baroque church of Santiago, leads to the 11th-century arched bridge of the pilgrims, for pedestrians only.

107

One of the waterfalls found along the Piedra River

For most of history, the Pyrenees have proved a substantial barrier between France and Spain, often regarded as one of the key reasons for the great differences in culture between the Iberian peninsula and the rest of Europe.

In the present century, with the immense pull now exerted by wild places, and the consequent development of Pyrenean tourism, the mountains have come to seem almost a unifying factor.

The highest peaks of the Pyrenees: Monte Perdido (known as the Lost Mountain; 3,355m/11,004ft), Pico Posets (3,371m/11,057ft), and Pico de Aneto (3,408m/11,178ft), rise in their year-round snow-cover in the Aragonese province of Huesca. Today, there are ski-resorts in the high valleys which provide for winter visitors. There are magnificent national parks to explore on foot in summer, one in Huesca (**Ordesa y Monte Perdido**, see page 111), one close by in the Catalan province of Lleida (**Aigüestortes i Estany de Sant Maurici**, see page 130). Tucked into the folds of this lofty terrain is an extraordinary and unexpected wealth of largely medieval art and architecture. At the same time, it must be acknowledged that the intrusions of skiing and ski facilities are considerable and very often discouraging.

Travellers' trials One major point about travel in the Pyrenees, Catalan, and Navarrese as well as in Aragón itself, is that the valleys on the Spanish side run down

THE SONG OF ROLAND
The *Chanson de Roland*, a medieval epic poem of chivalry, describes the retreat of Charlemagne's army into France through the Pyrenees. The poem tells how the rearguard is attacked by Moors but the leader, Roland, chivalrous to the end, refuses to sound his great horn, Oliphaunt, until it is too late. His army is cut down. In fact, the disaster was inflicted not by the Moors but by the Basques, wary then as now to the interference of outsiders.

Pyrenean church, Linas de Broto is typical of the many small Romanesque churches nestling among the green valleys and slopes of the Pyrenees

north to south. Roads up and down are good; but east–west roads between one valley and the next, where they exist at all, are usually slow, tortuous, and generally ignored by locals. The easiest way to understand the shape of the Pyrenees in Aragón is to consider the main valleys in order, starting in the west near Jaca, true capital of the locality, then moving eastwards to Benasque, fast emerging as a second focus.

To Ansó and Hecho Entering Aragón from Navarra, the first route northwards from the N240 doubles back into Navarra to ascend the **Roncal Valley**, famous for its cheeses. Next, north of depopulated but dramatic little Berdún, twin valleys ascend to **Ansó** and **Hecho**. They are linked towards the top by a good cross-wise road. Both little towns, Ansó and Hecho, are remarkably attractive, with solid stone houses, high wooden balconies, immense eaves, and the occasional conical chimney. Ansó in particular is now growing very rapidly. Cross-country skiing is the popular pastime here.

Puerto de Somport This pass above Jaca is a main point of access for France. Snow sometimes blocks the pass but an all-weather tunnel is being built. The border itself, beyond the pass and lower down, is open 24 hours a day. Starting from Jaca, the road winds up the valley of the River Aragón, offering extensive panoramas of peaks and, very often, swirling cloud. The pass itself is bleak and may be windy. The well-established ski resort of **Candanchú** is at a high altitude here, as is the newer resort of Astún. Canfranc, accessible by train, is lower down on the Spanish side.

Going north The River Gallego ascends next—from **Sabiñánigo**, which, although industrial, has an interesting art gallery. Moving north up the valley, there is soon a turn-off right to an intriguing scatter of Romanesque churches at Olivan, Oros Bajo, San Juan de Busa, Súsin, and Lárrede. Carrying on north up the main road past Biescas, where the C140 diverts right towards the Ordesa National Park, a much improved road carries you up and over into France (the valley from this point is known as Tena; the border closes in bad weather). It passes the attractive settlement of **Sallent de Gállego**, now a skiing resort. A side road to the right, climbing steeply up the formidable little gorge of Escalar, leads to the high-level spa of **Balneario de Panticosa**, known to the Romans for its medicinal waters. High rocky peaks rise round a small lake, with a dreary cluster of hotels. There is skiing here and at **El Formigal**.

From Barbastro A fair step southeast, **Barbastro** (see page 101) is the starting point for two more valleys. The Cinca valley leads up via Ainsa to Bielsa and beyond, with, finally, a high-level parador and entry to the Monte Perdido end of Ordesa National Park. The dramatically lovely valley of the Esera also leads up from Barbastro, past sleepy Graus (see **Drive**, page 103) and on towards the mountain cirque above Benasque, highest point of the whole Pyrenees.

The Puerto de Somport, historic pilgrims' crossing point from France

THE BEAR FACTS
The brown bear (*ursus arctos*) is one of the 10 most endangered species in Europe. In Spain, only a handful of individuals survive in remote enclaves of the mountains of the north, the population having been decimated during the 20th century by indiscriminate hunting and the destruction of the bears' forest habitat. In the central Pyrenees attempts are being made to boost the native population by reintroducing animals brought from Eastern Europe. These largely solitary omnivores hibernate for part of the year and survive the rest of the time on a diet of whatever they can find, such as nuts, berries, insects, fish, small mammals, and honey. Despite their size (up to 2.5m/8ft long) and fearsome reputation, bears have hardly ever been known to attack without provocation and they have more to fear from human beings than the other way round.

Part of the Ordesa National Park, an area of stunning beauty, covering a great expanse of mountains, valleys, and forests, rich in flora and fauna

BIRTHPLACE OF KING FERDINAND
The birthplace of Ferdinand of Aragón (1452), Sos del Rey Católico lies in wild sub-Pyrenean country. The town has steep stone streets, fine arched door-ways, and a tunnel under the church of San Esteban.

▶ **Roncesvalles (Orreaga)**   *98B4*

For centuries this was the main crossing point in the western Pyrenees. The village below the pass has a monastic 13th-century church containing the tomb of its founder, Sancho the Strong of Navarra, and a later building over the supposed site of Roland's tomb (see panel on page 108). Special masses are said in the church for pilgrims.

▶▶ **San Juan de la Peña**   *98B4*

This extraordinary monastery (tel: 974 35 51 19; *Open* Tue–Sun 11–2, 4–5.30. *Admission charge*), the burial place of Aragonese royalty and nobles, is under a huge overhang of rock. The monastery was originally built in Mozarabic style with horseshoe arches and painted frescoes. A Romanesque church was built on top, taking advantage of the rock for its roof, with a tiny open cloister and exquisitely carved capitals.

▶▶ **Sangüesa (Zangoza)**   *98B4*

Despite the pungent smell from its pulp mill, Sangüesa is a charming, rather serious little town. Here pilgrims who had followed the River Aragón from Jaca crossed it for the last time. The church of Santa María on the river bank has one of the most graceful carved facades in Spain (12th–13th centuries). Behind the wide-eaved town hall is the Castillo del Príncipe de Viana (palace of the Prince of Viana).

▶▶ **Tarazona**   *98A3*

Tarazona, historic Mudéjar town under the Sierra de Moncayo, has a fine brick-patterned cathedral tower and brilliant *celosía* plaster tracery in its cloister windows. The 12th- to 13th-century cathedral boasts an impressive Renaissance doorway, fine *retablos*, and Mudéjar cloisters. The 18th-century bullring is an octagon, its perimeter made up of ancient houses.

Walk

Ordesa National Park

This national park is one of the glories of the Pyrenees. Established in 1918 and extended in 1982, it embraces the mountain country round El Monte Perdido (3,355m/11,004ft) which rises on its northern flanks. Four valleys, Pineta in the east, Puertolas and Añisclo in the south, and Ordesa in the west, run up towards the inhospitable high ground. This is great walking country.

Enter the park from Torla (where there are hotels and places to camp).
    Maps and information are available from the shop by the parking area if the national parks office is shut. Walks of various levels of difficulty and duration start here.

For a long but easy walk, head straight up the valley to Cascada de Cola de Caballo (Horsetail Falls).
    There are astounding views of cliffs and many waterfalls.
    Return the same way (total distance 20km/12mi).

For a more rigorous outing (6–8 hours for moderate walkers) follow the signs for Senda de Cazadores.
    The hike starts with 1.5 to 2 hours' walking straight up a crag; steep but safe.
    Follow the cliffside Faja de Pelay path left at the top. Head slowly down towards Cascada de Cola de Caballo.

Return down the track as above.

❏ Less dramatic but greener and softer than the high Pyrenees in Aragón, the Pyrenees of Navarra are cut through by the valleys of Irati, Salazar, and Roncal as well as Roncesvalles and Baztán, closer to the sea. Salazar is most famous locally for its hard round cheeses which are good for picnics. ❏

Walk

Señorío de Bertiz

This is a compact but diverse botanical garden (tel: 948 59 24 21; *Open* daily 10–2, 4–6. *Admission charge*), at Oieregi, at the beginning of the Baztán valley on the N121 road. The garden was created at the turn of the 20th century by a wealthy Navarrese horticulturalist, who willed it to the government of Navarra.

You can simply walk or, for a longer, more rugged stroll, take the path behind the garden. This takes you into the 25sq km (10sq mi) of densely wooded natural park (*Open* at all times) immediately behind.

There are two unmarked walking trails, one over a hill and the other beside the river, both easy to follow beneath tall trees.

All minor paths lead to one or other of the trails.

The spectacular backdrop to Torla, gateway to the Ordesa National Park

Aragón and Navarra

THE LOVERS OF TERUEL
Teruel has its own Romeo and Juliet legend. Way back in the 13th century, Isabel de Segura fell in love with penniless Juan Diego Martínez de Marcilla, but was forced to marry another. Returning from the wars, Juan Diego met her secretly but died of a broken heart. She kissed his corpse at the funeral next day and promptly died herself. They were buried in the same grave, in the church of San Pedro. Today, their mummified corpses lie in a specially built mausoleum near the church.

BÉCQUER
While in Veruela, the Romantic writer Gustavo Adolfo Bécquer (1836–1870) wrote *Letters from my Cell* for the newspaper *El Contemporanéo*.

Plaza de los Fueros in the old episcopal town of Tudela

►► Teruel   98B1

Much fought over during the Civil War, Teruel has several astonishing Mudéjar towers, the best being San Martín and San Salvador, and a cathedral with a magnificent *artesonado* ceiling.

On the outskirts of the city is **Dinopolis** (off N234 towards Valcenia, tel: 902 44 80 00, *Open* Thu–Sun 11–9), a theme park about dinosaurs and other prehistoric creatures by way of interactive displays and a 3D cinema.

► Tudela   98A3

Tudela, Aragón's main settlement along the Ebro River, is a somnolent agricultural centre, trailing a Moorish past. Many tumbledown brick mansions bear Mudéjar patterning. The Gothic cathedral is splendid, and the doorway of the old mosque survives within the cloister.

►► Ujué   98A4

High on its crag, Ujué is tremendous with its church and ruined castle rising over what appears a ghost town from without, commanding huge, wild views. On the Sunday following St. Mark's Day, 25 April, thousands of barefoot, black-clad penitents descend from the surrounding towns to process round the church.

► Valderrobres   98C2

The remote and tiny village of Valderrobres retains a castle of the kings of Aragón and an impressive 12th-century church.

► Veruela   98A3

North of the Sierra de Moncayo, this 12th-century Cistercian monastery combines charm with solidity. A gateway through stout external walls leads to the facades of the church and abbots' palace. Within, the handsome two-storey cloister is Gothic below, Renaissance above.

► Viana   98A4

Cesare Borgia died in battle in this attractive Navarrese border city. The church of Santa María has one of Spain's best Renaissance portals.

►► Zaragoza

Lying on the west bank of the Ebro, Zaragoza (Saragossa in English) was a major Roman city and later spent 400 years as capital of Spain's most northerly Moorish kingdom. It still contains one splendid Moorish palace, the Aljafería. During the Reconquista, Zaragoza became the capital of advancing Aragón and a leading city in emergent Spain. Later, it gained fame from its resistance to Napoleon's forces during two great sieges in 1808–1809.

El Pilar The place to begin sightseeing is in the large open rectangle that forms the effective middle of the old city, separated from the river only by the awesome Basilica of El Pilar (*Open* daily 5.45AM–9.30PM). A huge brick building, 18th-century in its present form, El Pilar has high corner steeples and a central dome, flashy with ceramic tiles and heavy with statuary.

Within, it is huge and creamy coloured with vast fluted pilasters. An inner church or shrine shelters the immensely revered image of the Virgin on the very pillar (El Pilar) on which she is said to have appeared to St. James the Apostle in AD 40. There are ceiling paintings here by Goya and his brother-in-law Francisco Bayeu (not too easy to make out). In the main church, note also the expressive Forment *retablo*.

Other sights In the same square are the cathedral (closed since 1984, but now reopening in stages) and the Lonja (Exchange). The **Lonja** is built of tiny bricks, with bands of severe ornament under mighty eaves. The interior, open only for exhibitions but a must if open, displays magnificent reliefs and brilliant Gothic stone ornament. Excavations of the Roman forum in front of the cathedral are open to the public in a kind of "underground garage" display.

The **Aljafería** (tel: 976 28 95 28; *Closed* Feb–Mar and Nov–Dec, Thu–Fri. *Admission free*) is about 15 minutes' walk to the west, a castle much modified and restored over the ages but based around a Moorish courtyard and its original mosque. Ferdinand and Isabella contributed a grand stairway and fine *artesonado* ceiling on the first floor.

The huge El Pilar basilica, which stands on the banks of the River Ebro, has four slender towers and 11 cupolas covered in bright tiles

THE EXPLOITS OF EL CID
In the 11th century, Zaragoza was ruled by the super-civilized Beni-Hud dynasty, becoming a haven for scholars and poets. El Cid, who still enjoys something of a false reputation as a Christian hero, in fact served for five years, from 1085, as mercenary leader for the Beni-Huds, winning great victories against the Christians and capturing the Count of Barcelona not once, but twice. It seems quite likely he spoke Arabic as well as Castilian.

ROOTS OF ZARAGOZA
Once you know, it seems so obvious…Caesar Augusta…Zaragoza (by way of Moorish Sarakusta). The Roman Emperor gave his name to the city on the Ebro in AD 25.

Work began on Antoni Gaudí's Sagrada Família in 1882 but the church is still not finished

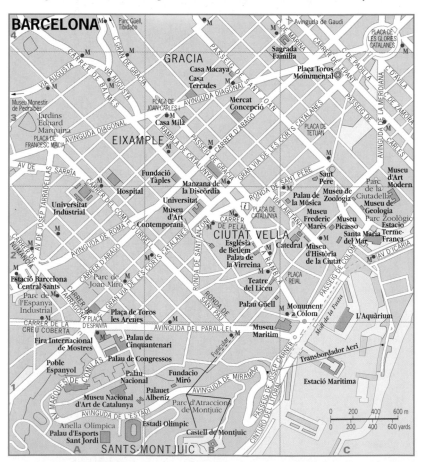

BARCELONA

GRACIA

EIXAMPLE

CIUTAT VELLA

SANTS-MONTJUÏC

Parc Güell, Tibidabo
Avinguda de Gaudi
PLAÇA DE LES GLORIES CATALANES
Sagrada Família
C. DE MARINA
C. DE PADILLA
C. D'AVILA
C. DE TETANI
AVINGUDA DE LA MERIDIANA
C. DE ZAMORA
Plaça Toros Monumental
Casa Macaya
Casa Terrades
VIA AUGUSTA
CARRER DE BALMES
Museu Monestir de Pedralbes
Mércat Concepció
PLAÇA DE JOAN CARLES I
AVINGUDA DIAGONAL
Casa Milà
Jardins Eduard Marquina
PLAÇA DE FRANCESC MACIÀ
RAMBLA DE CATALUNYA
PASSEIG DE GRÀCIA
CARRER D'ARAGÓ
PLAÇA DE TETUAN
AV DE SARRIÀ
GRAN VIA DE LES CORTS CATALANES
Sant Pere
Museu d'Art Modern
Fundació Tàples
Hospital
Manzana de la Discòrdia
Universitat
Ronda de Sant Pere
Palau de la Música
Museu de Zoologia
Parc de la Ciutadella
Museu de Geologia
Universitat Industrial
CARRER DEL COMTE D'URGELL
Museu d'Art Contemporani
CARRER DE PELAI
PLAÇA DE CATALUNYA
Museu Frederic Marès
Museu Picasso
Parc Zoològic
AVINGUDA DIAGONAL
CARRER DE ROMA
RONDA DE SANT ANTONI
CARRER
Santa Maria del Mar
Estació Terme-Franca
CARRER DE JOSEP TARRADELLAS
Estació Barcelona Central-Sants
CARRER D'ARAGÓ
Parc de Joan Miró
GRAN VIA DE LES CORTS CATALANES
Església de Betlem
Catedral
VIA LAIETANA
Museu d'Història de la Ciutat
AV D'ICARIA
PASSEIG DE COLOM
NUMANCIA
CARRER DE TARRAGONA
RONDA DE SANT PAU
Palau de la Virreina
PLAÇA REIAL
Parc de l'Espanya Industrial
PLAÇA D'ESPANYA
Plaça de Toros les Arenes
Teatre del Liceu
LA RAMBLA
Palau Güell
Monument a Colom
Moll de la Fusta
L'Aquàrium
CARRER DE LA CREU COBERTA
AVINGUDA DEL PARAL·LEL
Museu Marítim
Fira Internacional de Mostres
AV MARQUES DE COMILLAS
Palau de Cinquantenari
Funicular
Transbordador Aeri
Poble Espanyol
Palau de Congressos
Palau Nacional
Fundacio Miró
AVINGUDA DE MIRAMAR
PASSEIG DE JOSEP CARNER
Estació Marítima
Museu Nacional d'Art de Catalunya
Palauet Albéniz
Parc d'Atraccions de Montjuïc
AVINGUDA DE L'ESTADI
CINTURÓ DEL LITORAL
Anella Olímpica
Estadi Olímpic
Palau d'Esports Sant Jordi
Castell de Montjuïc

0 200 400 600 m
0 200 400 600 yards

CATALAN BARCELONA: SEABOARD CITY, capital of a nation within a nation of just over six million people, sophisticated, glamorous, and fast-moving is, for many people, Spain's top city, leaving Madrid in the shadows. The essence of Barcelona, as natives explain it, is that it is intensely Catalan (give or take a huge immigrant population from Andalucía and the rest of Spain) and simultaneously open to the whole world.

The history of the city is written eloquently into its various districts, starting with the earliest and probably most famous, the Barri Gòtic (Gothic quarter), behind the harbour. Up one side of it goes the wonderful strollers' avenue called Las Ramblas, full of flower stalls and cafés in the dappled shade. Within 100m (330ft) of the Ramblas, you find yourself in a stone-built warren of churches, palaces, the cathedral, and Roman remnants, the first Barcelona. Somehow it mostly survived two episodes of destruction by Spanish monarchs: first in 1652 and again in 1714. (The Franco period, 1939–1975, was another hard time for Barcelona, with repression of the language and Catalan identity itself.)

Inland from the Barri Gòtic lies the Eixample, the ample 19th-century extension laid out on a grid system. This was the building ground for the Catalan Modernista architects, the band whose works are cumulatively the most brilliant of Spain's 19th- and 20th-century artistic achievements. It is here that most Modernista buildings are found, including, of course, Gaudí's Sagrada Família.

On its southern side, the city is bounded by the great green hill of Montjuïc, site of some of the finest museums as well as a symbolic castle. It also holds the handsomely revamped Olympic Stadium and other buildings erected for the 1992 Olympics. The grand Port Vell development has opened up the port to the city, and it now boasts an attractive shoreline, marina, open-air cafés, restaurants, an aquarium, and large commercial base. The "Olympic Village" added considerably to the city's housing stock, while a brand new ring-road system and an agenda of *nou urbanisme* (new urbanism), open spaces filled with lively modern sculpture, create the impression of a city at ease with past, present, and future.

Barcelona

Decorative detail on a Modernista building. This type of art flourished in the 19th and 20th centuries

City visit

▶▶▶ Barri Gòtic

For descriptions of the main churches and museums in the Barri Gòtic, see within the listings on pages 117–123.

Nobody should visit this city without spending a few hours simply pottering in its medieval heart. Starting in Plaça Nova or the Plaça de la Seu (the cathedral square), dive down the Carrer del Bisbe Irurita through the Portal del Bisbe, whose towers date back to the Romans. Pass by the bishop's palace, with a right turn into picturesque Plaça Sant Felip Neri or a glimpse, left, into the cathedral cloister. The little lane then passes between the Casa dels Canonges and the elaborate Renaissance facade of the Palau de la Generalitat, home base for an autonomous Catalonia. Once into the Plaça Sant Jaume, you see that the Ajuntament (Casa de la Ciutat or Town Hall) is just opposite the Generalitat: thus the city government faces the would-be nation state and not always in friendship.

The Plaça del Rei, tucked in round the northern side of the cathedral, is even more impressive. As well as the Museu d'Història de la Ciutat, brought here stone by stone to complete the ensemble, it contains parts of the former royal palace and a noble Gothic hall, the Saló de Tinell, where Columbus allegedly reported to Ferdinand and Isabella the success of his first voyage. The Plaça Ramon Berenguer el Gran, with its equestrian statue of Berenguer III, Count of Barcelona, offers fine views of the Roman walls.

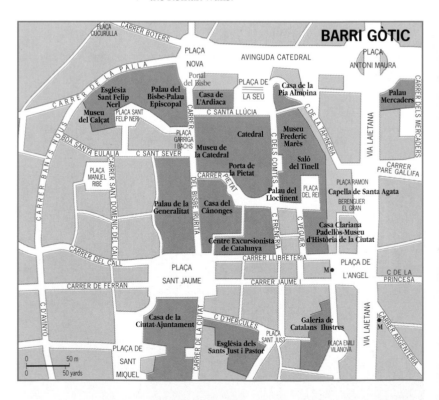

Casa Amatller/Casa Batlló/Casa Lleó Morera

see ►►► **Manzana de la Discòrdia** page 121

►►► Casa Milà or La Pedrera   114B3
(the Stone Quarry)

Passeig de Gràcia 92 (tel: 934 84 59 00)
Metro: Diagonal
Open: daily 10–7.30

Gaudí's triumphantly peculiar block of flats is a massive construction, combining the weight and dignity of stone with surging organic flow. Built between 1905 and 1911, its eight storeys weave sinuously around a corner block with hardly a straight line in evidence. The bristling ironwork of the balconies is by Gaudí's collaborator Josep Maria Jujol. You can visit the Gaudí exhibition (*Open* daily 10–8, guided tour at 6. *Admission charge*) and roof terrace for a closer look at the fantastical chimneys.

► Casa Terrades or Casa de les   114B3
Punxes (House of Spires)

Diagonal 416
Metro: Diagonal

This large, spiky apartment block by the Modernista architect Puig i Cadafalch mingles Rhineland castle turrets with a kind of Oxford college neo-Gothic.

►►► Catedral la Seu   114C2

Plaça de la Seu, Barri Gòtic (tel: 933 15 15 54)
Metro: Urquinaona, Licea. Bus: 17, 19, 45
Open: Mon–Fri 9–1, 4–7, Sat–Sun 9–1, 5–7. Admission free, but charge for sacristy, museum, and choir

This mainly 14th- and 15th-century Gothic building acquired its present facade and spire only in the late 19th century, although built to original designs. Yet the medieval ambience is impressive. The interior, with its multiplicity of chapels, one of them housing the remains of Ramon Berenguer I, Count of Barcelona (1018–1025), is also effective. Note the carved choir stalls (14th–15th century), choir screen (16th century), and cloister (15th century). Local martyr Santa Eulàlia is buried in the crypt.

The Gothic calm of Barcelona's cathedral

GETTING ABOUT
The Barri Gòtic is for walkers. For most other destinations, the metro is simplest and fastest. A range of tickets is available for multi-trips either on metro alone or combined with other forms; there are also passes ranging from one to five days. The Plaça de Catalunya is the focus for travelling; start the journey from here to Tibidabo by local train, finish by bus and funicular. For Montjuïc, take the metro to Plaça d'Espanya and climb or use the escalator; or take the funicular from Parallel metro station.

PIRATE OR HERO?
Roger de Flor is sometimes considered a pirate, more often a Catalan hero and patriot. At the head of a mercenary light infantry force called the Almogàvers, he adventured across the Mediterranean between 1302 and 1311, taking first Sicily, then Athens, and a chunk of the Greek mainland. The Catalans stayed in Greece for most of a century. They took Corsica and Sardinia later in the 14th century, then Naples in 1423. This remained a Spanish possession until 1714.

Walk

Las Ramblas

See map on page 119.

Las Ramblas is the city's beloved *paseo*. Formerly a dry river bed, it is really a series of five interconnecting avenues stretching from the corner of Plaça de Catalunya to the Columbus statue and the port (2km/1mi). It is a walkway crowded with open-air cafés, newspaper kiosks, shoppers, artists, and entertainers.

Begin at the Rambla Canaletas.
   If you want to ensure your return to Barcelona, they say, you must drink from the iron fountain here.

Pass the restored 17th-century baroque church of Església de Betlem on the corner of Carrer del Carme and the rococo **Palau de la Virreina**.
   This palace of the vicereine of Peru now houses an information office for cultural events in the city.

You have now reached the Rambla Sant Josep.
   Flower stalls fill the street. On your right is Barcelona's famous 19th-century covered **Mercat de la Boqueria**, a cornucopia of fruit and vegetables, meat, and fish. Look down at your feet, in the Plaça de la Boqueria, to find the mosaic pattern designed and signed by Joan Miró. Look up at the corner of Casa Bruno Quadras for the green Chinese dragon holding a lamp.

Continue to the Café de l'Opera on the same side.
   Opposite stands the **Gran Teatre del Liceu**, Spain's most prestigious opera house, destroyed by fire in 1994 but now rebuilt and reopened.

Walk on towards the port.
   The near end of Carrer Nou de la Rambla is distinguished by the **Palau Güell**, the Modernista mansion of Gaudí's foremost patron. This leads into the Barri Xines district (Chinese Quarter). There are few Chinese here but there is ample evidence of Barcelona low life. Avoid after dark.
   Off the northern side of the Rambla, to your left is the **Plaça Reial**, an elegant arcaded square, ringed with cafés, palm trees, and lampposts designed by Gaudí. Here, too, the atmosphere is more wholesome by day than by night. The wax museum, **Museu de Cera**, is on the left.

As the Rambla ends, the view ahead is of Columbus on his column, pointing confidently to Libya.

Time for refreshment at the end of the walk in Plaça Reial

►► Fundació Antoni Tàpies · 114B3

Carrer d'Aragó 255 (tel: 934 87 03 15)
Metro: Passeig de Gràcia
Open: Tue–Sun 10–8. Admission charge

The entire career of Catalan and international artist Antoni Tàpies (born 1923 in the Barri Gòtic), is shown here. The airy building is an early Modernista factory by Domènech i Montaner. The sculptural tangle of wire on top of the building, a typical Tàpies signature, aroused great antagonism when the Foundation was opened in 1990.

►►► Fundació Joan Miró · 114B1

Parc de Montjuïc s/n (tel: 934 43 94 70)
Metro: Espanya, then bus 61
Open: summer, Tue–Wed, Fri–Sat 10–8 (winter 10–7); Thu 10–9.30, Sun 10–2.30. Admission charge

The cool white building by Josep Luís Sert encloses a colourful riot of work (paintings, tapestry, *objets trouvés*) by Joan Miró (1893–1983), one of Barcelona's favourite sons. Miró's work leading up to the Civil War is distressed and distressing. Much of the rest seems playful, despite the artist's avowed pessimism. The Foundation actively promotes art and also holds outstanding exhibitions.

►► Hospital de la Santa Creu i de Sant Pau · 114A3

Avinguda de Gaudí (tel: 932 91 91 99)
Metro: Hospital de Sant Pau

Puig i Cadafalch's hospital proves that Modernista buildings can really work, though you may be surprised to see the fanciful elaboration of particular clinical departments around the pleasant open patio.

► Liceu, Gran Teatre del · 114B2

Ramblas (Sant Pau 1)

A famous Rambla landmark, in the opulent style of the 1840s, this is Spain's leading operatic venue, often featuring such Catalan talents as José Carreras and Montserrat Caballé.

Tapestry in the Fundació Joan Miró

LAS RAMBLAS

119

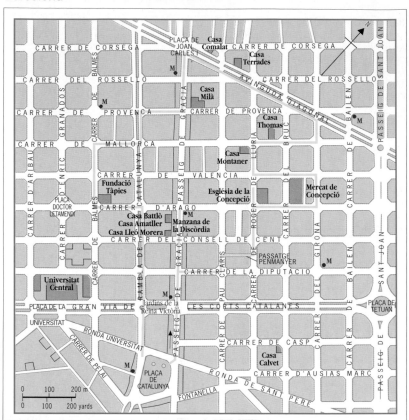

Walk

Eixample

Leave Plaça de Catalunya top right, by the broad Passeig de Gràcia.
Nos. 35, 41, and 43 make up the **Manzana de la Discòrdia**.

Retrace your steps for two blocks, then go left down Carrer de la Diputació, up Pau Claris, and cut through pretty Passatge Penmanyer (a private gated street). Continue left up Roger de Llúria.
There are pretty Modernista fronts at numbers 72, 74, and 80.

Go back a block and left down Carrer d'Aragó to Mercat de Concepció, up Girona and left down Valencia, right and up Roger de Llúria again.
Casa Montaner, designed by Domènech i Montaner, stands on the next corner.

Go right down Mallorca.
Modernista **Casa Thomas** is here.

Turn left up Girona and left into Avinguda Diagonal. You can get a glimpse of the Sagrada Família from here.

Turn left down Passeig de Gràcia.
Gaudí's **Casa Milà** is at No. 92.

Turn right here down elegant Provença, left down Rambla de Catalunya, with a diversion through Balmes and back down d'Aragó.
Fundació Tàpies is here at No. 225.

Finish the walk down Rambla de Catalunya.

►►► Manzana de la Discòrdia   114B2

35–43 Passeig de Gràcia
Metro: Passeig de Gràcia
This extraordinary block is distinguished by buildings from each of the three great Modernista architects, in styles that vary hugely. Domènech i Montaner's **Casa Lleó Morera** stands at No. 35; its interior is famous for its intricately carved woodwork and stained glass. Puig i Cadafalch's **Casa Amatller**, with stepped gables, ceramic decorations, and mock-medieval stairway is at No. 41. It houses a reception point for Modernista tours of the city. Gaudí's sparkling **Casa Batlló**, at No. 43, has an amazing sinuous roofline.

►► Museu d'Art Contemporani   114B2
de Barcelona

Plaça dels Angels 1 (tel: 934 12 08 10)
Metro: Plaça de Catalunya
Open: Mon, Wed–Fri 11–7.30, Sat 10–8, Sun 10–3.
Admission charge
The MACBA, designed by architect Richard Meier, opened in 1995 as a work of art in itself. Within are displays of Spanish and Catalan art post-1945.

►►► Museu Nacional d'Art de Catalunya 114A1

Palau Nacional, Parc de Montjuïc s/n (tel: 936 22 03 75)
Metro: Espanya
Open: Tue–Sat 10–7, Sun 10–2.30. Admission charge
This palatial relic of the 1929 Exhibition, the Palau Nacional, houses the city's pride and joy of an incomparable collection of Romanesque art. Mainly from Pyrenean churches in such remote areas as the Vall de Boí, these exceptional works were rescued from imminent threat of destruction and theft earlier in the century. There is also a collection of Gothic art.

► Museu d'Art Modern   114C2

Parc de la Ciutadella s/n (tel: 933 19 50 23)
Metro: Arc de Triomf
Open: Tue–Sat 10–7; Sun 10–2. Admission charge
"Modern" here means mainly late 19th- and early 20th-century Catalan, with painters such as Fortuny, Santiago Rusiñol, Ramon Casas, and Isidro Nonell reflecting local life and artistic aspiration.

► Museu Frederic Marès   114C2

Plaça de Sant Iú 5–6 (tel: 933 10 58 00)
Metro: Jaume I. Bus: 17, 19, 45
Open: Tue–Sat 10–5; Sun 10–2. Admission charge
Opened in 1946, this museum displays a private collection of religious paintings and sculpture and a vast array of everyday 19th-century objects, such as clocks and toys.

►► Museu d'Història de la Ciutat   114C2

Plaça del Rei s/n (tel: 933 15 11 11)
Metro: Jaume I. Bus: 16, 17, 19, 22, 45
Open: Tue–Sat 10–2, 4–8; Sun 10–2. Admission charge
This museum site shows the compacted layers of civilization of old Barcelona: Roman, Visigothic, Christian, Moorish, Carolingian.

Looking up at the unmistakable Torre de Calatrava, a communications tower built for the 1992 Olympic Games

MAJOR EVENTS
Barcelona has staged three major international events and has used each of them to make improvements to the city. For the 1888 Exhibition, notable Modernista buildings were erected. The 1929 Exhibition produced the much-praised Mies van der Rohe Pavelló and the huge Palau Nacional. The 1992 Olympics gave the city new sports venues, an Olympic village, a reopened shoreline, new ring roads, and sculpture in parks and public places; the so-called *nou urbanisme*.

A statue of Christopher Columbus overlooks traffic on Passeig de Colom, which runs along the waterfront of Port Vell

▶▶ Museu Marítim 114B1

Avinguda de les Drassanes 1 (tel: 933 42 99 20)
Metro: Drassanes. Bus: 14, 18, 36, 38, 57
Open: daily 10–7. Admission charge
This excellent museum has been assembled in the vaults of the Drassanes, the medieval shipbuilding sheds near the Columbus monument. The centrepiece is a gilded replica of *La Real*, flagship in the battle of Lepanto, 1571.

▶▶ Museu-Monestir de Pedralbés 114A3

Baixada Monestir 9 (tel: 932 03 92 82)
Metro: Reina Elisenda. Bus: 22 from Passeig de Gracia
Open: Tue–Sun 10–2. Admission charge
This Catalan-Gothic monastery, with its well-preserved church, cloisters, dormitories, and kitchens, was founded in 1326 by Elisenda de Montcada, wife of Jaume II. Highlights include the wall paintings of Ferrer Bassa from 1346, and the gallery of religious masterpieces.

▶▶▶ Museu Picasso 114C2

Carrer Montcada 15–19 (tel: 933 19 63 10)
Metro: Jaume I
Open: Tue–Sat 10–8; Sun 10–2.30. Admission charge
Housed in a Catalan-Gothic palace, this collection gives a view of Picasso's early years. From the first studies of doves and a bullfight through to portraits of his family, the childhood works are enthralling. The museum includes Picasso's early Parisian nightlife studies, and the best of his Blue Period with its sadly alienated figures. The *Harlequin* of 1917 is also here. Works from his maturity and old age include the series called *Las Meninas*, a deconstruction of Velázquez's greatest work.

▶▶ Palau Güell 114B2

Carrer Nou de la Rambla (tel: 933 17 39 74)
Metro: Liceu
Open: Mon–Fri 10–1, 4–6.30. Admission charge
Gaudí's chief patron, the industrialist Count Eusebi Güell, commissioned this mansion (1886–1888). It is built

HOMAGE TO CATALONIA
The British writer George Orwell went to Barcelona in December 1936 to join the Republicans in the Spanish Civil War. "It was the first time I had been in a city where the working class was in the saddle," he wrote in *Homage to Catalonia* (1938). He was struck by the fact that no formal modes of address were used, and hardly anyone was well dressed.

in neo-Gothic, early Gaudí style, and houses a theatrical museum, Museu de les Arts del Espectacle.

▶▶▶ Palau de la Música Catalana   114C2
San Francesc de Paula 2 (tel: 932 95 72 00)
Metro: Catalunya, Urquinaona
Open: Mon–Sun 10–3
This Modernista concert hall by Domènech showcases the work of master craftsmen in all the decorative arts. The auditorium is lit by a glorious stained-glass dome.

▶▶▶ Parc Güell   114A4
Carrer d'Olot 7 (tel: 932 13 04 88)
Metro: Lesseps
Open: daily 10–8; Nov–Feb, 10–6. Admission charge
The happier side of Gaudí's genius is evident in the curious buildings in this park on a flank of Tibidabo. Don't miss the cursive benches by Josep Maria Jujol.

▶ Poble Espanyol   114A1
Avinguda del Marqués de Comillas (tel: 933 25 78 66)
Metro: Espanya, then shuttle bus
Open: daily from 10; closes Mon–Sun midnight, Tue–Thu 2AM, Fri–Sat 4AM. Admission charge
Replicas of representative buildings from all over Spain were built here for the 1929 Universal Exhibition. It is now a lively evening entertainment spot.

▶ Port Vell, Barceloneta, and Port Olímpic 114C2
Hansonfront
Metro: Drassanes, Barceloneta
This redeveloped area boasts palm-lined walkways, new marinas, beaches, restaurants, shops, an IMAX cinema, aquarium, and a museum of Catalan history.

▶▶▶ Sagrada Família   114C4
Plaça Sagrada Família s/n (tel: 934 55 02 47)
Metro: Sagrada Família
Open: daily 9–7 (later in summer). Admission charge
Gaudí's unfinished Expiatory Temple of the Holy Family is unmissable. Gaudí took over the project in 1883 and worked on it obsessively until he died, struck by a tram, in 1926. The eastern end, with four honeycomb pinnacles and a cascade of organic sculpture representing the Nativity, went up under his direction.

▶▶ Santa María del Mar   114C2
Passeig del Born 1 (tel: 933 10 23 90)
Metro: Jaume I
Open: daily 9–1.30, 4.30–8 (Sun from 10AM); Mass at 1
Grandly solid, though definitely scruffy from outside, Santa María del Mar's high-rise interior establishes it as the most ambitious of Barcelona's Gothic churches.

▶▶ Tibidabo   114A4
Plaça Tibidabo 3–4 (tel: 932 11 79 42)
Metro: Avinguda Tibidabo, then tram via Blau
Open: summer, 12–10; winter, 12–6
This mountain-top (512m/1,680ft) behind Barcelona has a fun fair, basilica, and views of the city beneath.

A dragon covered with a mosaic of bright ceramic tiles stands guard over steps in Gaudí's Parc Güell

123

GAUDÍ'S FANTASY
Parc Güell was intended as open space for a building project which never happened due to lack of funds. A few houses were built, though, and Gaudí lived in one of them. It is rather dingy but open to the public.

TIBIDABO
"Tibidabo," the Latin for "Unto you will I give…" recalls Satan's promise to Jesus in the Wilderness.

Shopping

The city is readily divided into three main shopping areas: the Ciutat Vella or Old Town; the smart avenues of the Eixample, particularly the Passeig de Gràcia; and the Avinguda Diagonal and northwards to the Sant Gervasi district. Unusually, for Spain, large modern malls are an important shopping feature in Barcelona (see panel).

SHOPPING MALLS
Barcelona has several large shopping complexes. The newest is Diagonal-Mar on the waterfront, with cinemas, 220 shops, restaurants, and a play area for children. Barcelona Glories in Plaça de les Gloriès is similarly vast, while L'Illa de Diagonal (Pedralbes district) also has a hotel and conference facilities. In the heart of the city, on Plaça Catalunya, is El Triangle with chic shops such as Habitat (a household shop), Sephora (a perfume shop), and the legendary Café Zurich.

124

The harbourside area of city has a variety of shops and restaurants

DESIGN Barcelona prides itself on being at the cutting edge of style. Design is an obsession here. Start at **Vinçon**, Passeig de Gràcia 96, purveyor of the seriously designed household artefact, selling everything from lights and kitchen furniture to ashtrays. The store has another branch, **Tinçon**, Rosselló 246, dedicated solely to everything you need for a designer bedroom. For those interested in contemporary furniture, **B D Ediciones de Diseño** at Mallorca 291-3 is unbeatable, housed in a wonderful Modernista house. **La Manual Alpargatera** at Avinyó 7 is famous for its espadrilles while **Antonio Miró**, Consell de Cent 349 is the king of Catalan fashion design since the 1970s.

FOOD AND FUN GOODS The best food market is the revamped **La Boqueria** in the Ramblas. There are some excellent delicatessens, including **Múrria**, Roger de Llúria 85 with its mouth-watering window display. **La Seu**, Dagueria 16 has one of the finest collections of Spanish cheeses, while behind the handsome Modernista facade, **Escribà** at Rambla 83 is deservedly famous for its handmade chocolates. The flea market (Monday, Wednesday, and Saturday) is at Los Encantes at the Plaça de les Glòries. In the same area is **DOM**, Passeig de Gràcia 76; a fun shop full of kitsch, inventive solutions for household decorations. Light up your life with a candle from **Cereria Subirà**, Baixada Llibreteria 7, the oldest candle shop in town offering every shape and size of candle you could imagine.

Note: Large department stores like El Corte Inglés are often open during the long Spanish siesta.

Food and drink See also pages 282–283

One thing is sure, you are guaranteed to find a huge variety of food in Barcelona. Catalan cuisine is adventurous, with a ready use of herbs and spices and a mingling of sweet with savoury flavours.

TAPAS BARS La Bodegueta, Ramble Catalunya 98, is a haven of wine barrels and good ham. Try the anchovies washed down with cider at **Xampanayet**, Montcada 22; a good place to stop after a visit to the Picasso Museum. Try **Sol Soler**, Plaça del Sol 13 for alternative tapas like cous cous and chicken wings. **La Gran Bodega**, Valencia 193 is an old-style tapas bar renowned for its *patatas bravas*.

CIUTAT VELLA Can Culleretes, Quintana 5 serves excellent Catalan dishes. **Cal Pep**, Plaça Dies 8 is a wonderful place and it is worth the wait to sit at the bar. **Les Set Portes**, Passeig Isabel 14 is renowned for its rice dishes. **Cafè de l'Acadèmia** (Lledó 1), **Senyor Parellada** (Argentería 37), **Santa Maria** (Comerç 17), and **Estrella de Plata** (Pla de Palau), are all new generation Catalan restaurants providing creative twists to traditional fare.

EIXAMPLE Expect to pay out (and eat well) at the famed Galician fish restaurant, **Botafumeiro** (Gran de Gràcia 81), **La Dama** (Avinguda Diagonal 423), and **Drolma**, newly opened in Hotel Majestic (Passeig de Gràcia 68) under Catalan chef, Fermí Puig. For Catalan cooking fresh from the market, go to **Casa Amalia** (Passatge Mercat 4). **L'Hostal de Rita** (Arago 279) is excellent value and always crowded. **Flash Flash** (Granada del Penedes 25) has 1960s art decor and is good for tortillas.

BARCELONETA is famous for its fish and seafood restaurants. **Can Major**, Almirante Aixada 23 is smart but pricey. Enjoy harbourside views from **Merendero de la Mari**, Palau de Mar; a well-restored warehouse. At Port Olímpic check out **Agua**, Passeig Marítim 30, certainly the trendiest and one of the best places for paella. **Els Pescadors**, Plaça de Prim 1 serves excellent fish.

CHAMPAGNE BARS...
Barcelona is famed for Spanish cava (sparkling wine) and has a number of *xampanyeria*, or champagne bars. Try Xampanyeria at Provença 236. For cocktails as well as cava, Boadas, just off the Ramblas at Tallers 1, is long established.

125

...AND MILK BARS
Granjas are milk bars, the place to stop for a cake and a coffee.

The bright lights of Plaça d'Espanya, one of Barcelona's busy squares

BARCELONA FIESTAS
23 April is the day of Sant Jordi, Catalonia's patron saint, celebrated by the gift of a red rose from a man to a woman and a book from a woman to a man. 24 June, Sant Joan's day, is preceded by bonfires and fireworks the night before to mark midsummer.

MONTJUIC NIGHTLIFE
The Poble Espanyol, the Spanish Village on Montjuïc, built for the 1929 Exhibition fair is one of the livelier concentrations of night-time entertainments in the city, particularly at weekends. There are some good bars and restaurants and you can hear jazz as well as flamenco. Try the designer bar Torres de Avila, actually seven bars in one. There are good concerts held in the Village's Plaza Mayor during the Grec Summer Festival.

Nightlife

Barcelona's nightlife begins in the morning, at weekends, at about 2AM. However, those who prefer to be tucked up in bed by that time need not feel left out. A city as large and sophisticated as Barcelona offers a wide and varied choice of entertainments including plays, music, ballet, and modern dance, which begin and sometimes end long before the serious night revellers get going. It is useful to invest in a copy of the city's listings magazine, *Guía del Ocio*, to plan your entertainments.

LIVE MUSIC Flamenco is not a Catalan art form, but enthusiasts may enjoy an evening at **El Patio Andaluz**, Aribau 242; **El Tablao de Carmen**, Poble Espanyol, Montjuïc; or at **Los Tarantos** in Plaça Reial. Jazz fans should check out the **Harlem Jazz Club**, Comtessa de Sobradiel which has live music from 8PM and **La Cova del Drac**, Vallmajor 33. For blues, **La Boïte**, Diagonal 477 is a well-established club. If ballroom dancing is your passion, join the locals in the afternoon session, or enjoy the crooning orchestra in the evening at **La Paloma**, an amazing turn-of-the-20th century dance hall on Tigre.

UP AND DOWN Numancia 179 caters for old and young: parents upstairs and young people down. **Otto Zutz**, Lincoln 15, a designer nightspot on three floors, is open for members only, after 2AM, or so they say; but if your face and clothes fit, well, give it a try.

Open air clubbing is the answer for steamy nights; a trendy spot with cool music is **La Terrazza**, Poble Espanyol, Avinguda Marqués de Comillas 25, high up on Montjuïc.

BARS Margarita Blue, Josep Anslem Clavé is a Mexican bar/restaurant, open till 3AM and has a sister bar **Rita Blue** in Plaça Sant Agusti with a dance floor in the basement. **Boadas**, Tallers 1 is the ultimate 1930s cocktail bar. **Nick Havanna**, Rosselló 208 is one of Barcelona's famed designer bars from the 1980s, and still looks good.

Accommodation See also page 277

A spate of building and refurbishment in the 1990s left Barcelona with plenty of accommodation, much of it in the higher price ranges. The luxurious 44-storey **Arts Hotel**, in the Vila Olímpica, was part of the 1992 Olympic project. North of the Diagonal are excellent business hotels such as the **Hilton, Princess Sofía, Meliá Barcelona**, and **Tryp Presidente**.

Hotels in the Eixample, with exceptions such as the 5-star **Husa Avenida Palace**, are often smaller. Some, like the **Regente** and **Condes de Barcelona**, are former Modernista mansions. The **Hotel Claris**, a 1990s refurbishment of a 19th-century palace, with its own small museum of Egyptian antiquities, wins plaudits for luxury and style.

In the Old Town, there are 5-star luxury hotels like **Le Meridien**, favoured by international pop stars, the **Colón**, directly opposite the cathedral, or, less expensive but still elegant, art deco **Rivoli Ramblas** on Rambla del Estudis. The **Rialto** and **Suizo** are also recommended. *Aparthotels*, such as **Avenida Victoria**, on Pedralbes, are good for families and those who prefer to cook for themselves.

● **Stroll** *There are a number of objectives for a stroll on Montjuïc. Take the metro to the Plaça d'Espanya. First visit the La Caixa Foundation in former Modernista textile factory, Caixa Forum, Avinguda Marquès de Comillas, or the contrastingly impressive Mies van der Rohe pavilion opposite. Then return to steps and escalators up to the Palau Nacional (home of Museu Nacional d'Art de Catalunya), then another escalator to the Olympic Complex and the pretty Jardin d'Acclimatacio. You can then head for the cooling Fundacio Miró with its impressive collection of the Catalan artist's work. Alternatively, arrive by funicular from the Avinguda Parallel or cable car from the port, and enjoy walking in fresh air in the gardens overlooking the port, or visit the castle.*

ACCOMMODATION
The regulations of the Generalitat recognize two groups of establishments: Hotels (H) and Pensions (P), plus the Hotel Apartment (HA) subgroup.

THE FOUNTAINS OF MONTJUÏC
On Plaça de les Cascades, at the base of the hill, the fountains are illuminated at night in a rainbow of colours, accompanied by music from Thursday to Sunday evening in summer, and on special festivals.

You can stay in splendour in Barcelona as the city has a wide choice of hotels

It's easy to get around in populous, bustling Barcelona; Catalonia's capital city

see Drive page 132

3371m
Pico
Posets

Val d'Aran
Vielha-Viella

3408m
Pico de Aneto

3143m
Pic d'Estats

Benasque ■ Parc Nacional
d'Aigüestortes

■ Vall
de Boí

Esera

Graus

Noguera Pallaresa

Noguera Ribagorzana

Puigcerdà

La Seu d'Urgell-
Seo de Urgel
Sierra del Cadí

C A T A L U Ñ A

Sant Joan
de les
Abadesses

Sant Pau

Ripoll

Santa Pau

Castellfollit
de la Roca

Olot

Besalú

F

(AND)

Portbou
Sant Pere de Rodes
Cap de Creus
Perelada
Roses • Cadaqués
Figueres

A7

Golf de Roses
Empúries-Ampurias
L'Escala
L'Estartit
Peratallada
Platja de Pals
Begur

Berga

Solsona
Ponts
Cardona

Manlleu

Vic

Salt
Girona-
Gerona
Palafrugell

Aiguablava
Cap Roig
Palamós

Caldes de
Malavella

S'Agaró

Balaguer

Manresa

Parc Natural
del Montseny

Tossa de Mar

Sant
Feliu de Guíxols

Almacelles

Mollerussa

Cervera

Terrassa-
Tarrassa

Granollers

Argentona

A19

Lloret de Mar
Blanes

Calella

Costa Brava

Lleida-
Lérida

A2

Tàrrega

Montserrat

A18

Les Borges
Blanques

Igualada

Sant Cugat del Vallès

Sabadell

Mataró

C A T A L U N Y A

Montblanc

Santes
Creus

Vilafranca
del Penedès

Badalona

BARCELONA

Poblet

Valls

Castelldefels

L'Hospitalet
de Llobregat

*Pantà de
Riba-Roja*

Sitges

El Vendrell

Vilanova i la Geltrú

Flix
Asco

Port
Aventura

Reus

Tarragona

Batea

Mora
d'Ebre

Salou
Cambrils

Ebro

A7

*Golf de
Sant Jordi*

Tortosa

L'Ampolla

Cap de Tortosa

■ Pare Natural
del Delta de l'Ebre

La Sénia
Alcanar

Amposta
Sant Carles de la Ràpita

Vinaròs-
Vinaroz

A

*Costa Daurada-
Costa Dorada*

B

CATALONIA

0   20   40   60 km

0   20   40 miles

C

Catalonia

CATALONIA, THAT NORTHEASTERN TRIANGLE of the Iberian peninsula, within Spain but by no means entirely of it, has a strong sense of its own identity. Written "Cataluña" in Castilian Spanish but "Catalunya" in Catalan, the region has its own language and its own history, customs, culture, and achievements. The Catalans, solid in their self assurance, see themselves as hard-working, disciplined achievers. Catalonia is far from the stereotypical image of Spain and continually among the most exciting regions to visit. Its heart and symbol is the city of Barcelona (see pages 114–127).

The Catalan landscape is immensely varied. In the north are the Pyrenees, popular with skiers and walkers. The foothills give way southwards to orchard territory and then to bleak *meseta*. The Mediterranean east is defined by the rugged Costa Brava, heavily built up but still beautiful and wild in many places. After that the coast drops south through Barcelona to the tamer landscape and long sandy beaches of the Costa Daurada. The hinterland here yields the best white wines in the whole Iberian peninsula.

Catalonia was settled early by Greeks and Phoenicians. The Romans and Moors followed; then the area was conquered by the Carolingian kings of France, so setting it off on its distinctive course. Autonomous from 874, it was taken into the Kingdom of Aragón in 1137 but retained remarkable independence, continuously resisting the centralizing power of Madrid from the 17th century. Today Catalonia, with the Basque country, is the most solidly independent of the Spanish autonomous regions.

▶▶▶ REGION HIGHLIGHTS

Aigüestortes *page 130*
Barcelona *pages 114–127*
Costa Brava *pages 134–135*
Empúries *page 133*
Girona *page 137*
Montserrat *page 138*
Poblet *page 142*
Ripoll *page 142*
Tarragona *pages 146–147*
Val d'Aran *page 148*

The Catalan national sense of identity is focused on Barcelona

Catalonia

TOURIST INFORMATION
Aigüestortes, Vall de Boi:
Barruera
(tel: 973 69 40 00).
Banyoles: Passeig de la
Industria 25
(tel: 972 57 55 73).
Cervera: Carrer Major 115
(tel: 973 53 13 03).
Figueres: Plaça del Sol
(tel: 972 50 31 55).
Girona: Rambla de la
Llibertat 1
(tel: 972 22 65 75).
Montseny, Sant Cugat del
Vallès, Terrassa: Plaza de
Cataluña 17, Barcelona
(tel: 933 04 31 35).
Montserrat: Plaça Creu
(tel: 938 35 02 51).
Olot: Carrer Bisbe
Lorenzana 15
(tel: 972 26 01 41).
Ripoll: Plaça Abat Oliba
(tel: 972 70 23 51).
Sitges: Carrer Sínia
Morera 1
(tel: 938 94 42 51).
Tarragona: Carrer Major
39 (tel: 977 24 50 64).
Tortosa: Plaça Bimil-Lenari
(tel: 977 51 08 22).
Val d'Aran: Calle
Sarriulèra 10, Vielha
(tel: 973 64 01 10).
Vic: Ciutat 4
(tel: 938 86 20 91).
Vilafranca del Penedès:
Carrer Cort 14
(tel: 938 92 03 58).

In the gazetteer entries below, where both Castilian and Catalan names are given, the Castilian appears in brackets after the Catalan.

▶▶▶ Aigüestortes (Aigües Tortes)   128A3

The "Parc Nacional d'Aigüestortes i Estany de Sant Maurici," to give this enchanting tract of peaks and water its full name, is one of two national parks in the Pyrenees (see pages 108–109) and the only one in Catalonia. Aigüestortes means "twisting waters" and Estany means "lake." In the east, round Lake Sant Maurici, pines climb steeply from the lake shore to meadows that yield to scree and needle peaks, of which the Encantat peaks (2,747m/9,010ft) are the most memorable. From Sant Maurici, a trail leads westwards over the pass of Espot.

Getting there Apart from openings to east and west, the park is almost entirely enclosed by high mountain peaks. From the east, access is up the valley of the Noguera Pallaresa and through the village of Espot (train from Lleida to Pobla de Segur, then bus). From Espot, cars may drive as far into the park as the Sant Maurici lake. After that it is a matter of hiking or proceeding by jeep (for rent with driver or self-drive). From the west, follow the valley of Noguera Ribagorcana, then Vall de Boí, with its magnificent Romanesque churches, to the village of Boí. From Boí, approach the park entrance (6km/4mi) on foot, by bicycle or taxi. Fit hikers can walk between the two last car points in about four hours. Between December and April, the park is snowbound and open to cross-country and mountain skiers, though only those with good experience should try. Park offices (Espot, tel: 973 62 40 36; Boí, tel: 973 69 61 89) with maps and information are open at either end in summer. Contact the tourist information office at Barruera (tel: 973 69 40 00) for the latest, year-round information.

The charming white-washed houses of Cadaqués viewed from across the harbour

▶▶ Banyoles (Bañolas)   *128C3*

The lake here, 2.2km (1mi) of straight water between winding banks, has always been popular with watersports fans. After it was used for the 1992 Olympic rowing event, however, leisure activity both on and around the lake increased. The town has a pretty, arcaded square, lively in the early evening, and an archaeological museum, containing prehistoric remains. The Benedictine monastery of San Esteban, founded in 812, has a fine 16th-century high altar and 18th-century cloisters.

▶▶ Besalú   *128C3*

A delightful medieval town of creamy stone, Besalú stands beside the River Fluvia, spanned by a fortified Romanesque bridge. The town also has two especially lovely Romanesque churches, Sant Pere and Sant Vicenç. There is a profusely arched and arcaded main square, from which narrow streets lead through to the ancient Jewish quarter, and the remains of a ritual Jewish bath dating from 1264.

▶▶ Cadaqués   *128C3*

This former fishing village on Cape Creus, is lively but not noisy. Its small beach and artistic connections (Picasso, Magritte, Buñuel, and Lorca all came here) may have contributed to its slightly elevated tone. You can see surrealist Salvador Dalí's house (tel: 972 25 10 15 for an appointment; *Closed* 7 Jan–15 Mar), with giant eggs on the roof, at nearby Port Lligat.

▶ Cardona   *128B2*

A weird little Pyrenean foothill town, Cardona is dominated by a 13th-century castle (now a parador) and an austere Romanesque church.

▶ Cervera   *128A2*

Number 66 Carrer Major is where the marriage contract of Ferdinand and Isabella was signed in 1469. This town is also home to the university founded by Philip V when he closed Catalonia's other universities in the 18th century.

Besalú, with its Romanesque bridge, is a small medieval town of great charm

131

NATURAL WATER
Two major bottled waters, Vichy Catalan and Malavella, are produced in the quiet, pleasantly jumbled town of Caldes de Malavella. A grand old spa hotel and the remains of Roman baths testify to its health spa tradition.

A GREEK AND ROMAN HERITAGE
It was only natural for the ancient Greeks to push on from Massalia (Marseilles) to Empúries (see page 133) and other spots in Catalonia. They were traders, and business was good in this rich agricultural area. When the Romans first came in through Empúries in the Second Punic War, the intention was to defeat the Carthaginians. But victory gave the Roman Republic the mineral wealth of the peninsula, mainly from the Cartagena region in the southeast and from southwest Andalucía.

Drive

Behind the Costa Brava

See map on page 128.

This is essentially a drive inland from the Costa Brava, starting at Figueres and finishing at Girona. It encompasses much lovely scenery and takes in several of Catalonia's key shrines and a number of interesting natural phenomena. To complete it pleasurably in a day would require an early start; but there is a possible break-off point halfway, at Olot.

Starting from Figueres, take the N260 west for 26km (16mi) to Besalú.
 Olive groves in a semi-rural landscape give way to rolling plains of wheat fields and woods, with Pyrenean foothills rising ahead and to the right. Much in evidence in this peaceful landscape is the stout and ample Catalan *mas* (farmhouse). Many are now restaurants.

Continue for 14km (9mi) to **Castellfollit de la Roca**.
 This impressive pink-tiled village is built on the edge of a volcanic precipice, which falls 60m (197ft) into the Fluvià River.

From here the road to Ripoll ascends with fine views back over Olot and its

volcanic countryside of lushly forested hills rising from flattish valleys.

After climbing to the Col de Coubet pass, take the road angling obliquely right to **Sant Joan de les Abadesses** (see page 142).
 The road descends through glorious country to the town and the upper valley of the River Ter.

On leaving Sant Joan, follow the main road south through a steeply wooded valley to **Ripoll**.
 The magnificent monastery here has an even more spectacular place in Catalan history (see page 142).

From Ripoll, take the C150 directly back towards Olot.
 The road rises steeply and enticingly, but all this western end of the arrowhead is hard driving.

Rejoin the original road for a brief stretch down to Olot.
 The views are quite good enough to warrant a second look.

After a stop at **Olot**, home to a community of artists, take country back-roads for 33km (20mi), through Santa Pau and on to Banyoles lake.
 Before Santa Pau, a path leads to the 2km (1mi) wide crater of Santa Margarida, for an optional detour.

After a winding hill crossing, descend finally to the peaceful lake of Banyoles and drive 20km (12mi) to Girona.

The precipitous village of Castellfollit de la Roca

When the torch for the 1992 Barcelona Olympiad came ashore in Empúries (Ampurias), the symbolism was entirely fitting. For this was one of the foremost settlements in the westward drive of the ancient Greeks, ranking, for them, alongside their colonies at Nice and Marseille.

These days, though, **Empúries** is only a cluster of ruins beside the sea, much added to and partly built over by the Romans, with grey stone walls and remains of ancient streets running down to the intense green of pines and the glittering blue of the Mediterranean.

History The Phoenicians were here first, settling on an inshore island, now a knoll of mainland with a village a little way beyond the site. The Greeks arrived in about 600 BC. By the 5th century BC, their town was growing smartly, perhaps because of a lucrative trade in cereals, and in due course it became a proper Greek *"polis"* or city state. During the First Punic War Empúries was pro-Roman and anti-Carthaginian. At the start of the Second Punic War, in 218 BC, the Romans, led by Publius Cornelius Scipio, landed here before moving south against Sagunt. From then

onwards, Empúries was a powerful and important Greco-Roman city. The religious buildings and city market stood on the same sites right through Greek and Roman times. The Romans added villas and public buildings along the summit of the hill. When the Romans left, the town was slightly in decline, but became a Visigothic bishopric.

The site Visiting the site is fairly simple, with a route clearly indicated and explanatory signs along the way. The path leads from the parking area, and follows around the top of Cyclopean walls dating from the 2nd century BC. It takes in the main religious areas and temples, turns left through the *stoa* or market and then leads up to the small, helpful, site museum. The Roman villas lie beyond the museum (some excellent mosaics and a park-like atmosphere), with the Roman forum and other public buildings back along the ridge. The site ends in a Roman gate and walls with remains of an amphitheatre beyond.

Exploring the remains of the Greco-Roman coastal city of Empúries, where three settlements were founded between the 7th and the 3rd centuries BC

Catalonia

The system known as *pesca de la traiña*, or *traiña* fishing, involves a ring of boats with lamps at the stern laying a net around a central illuminated boat. The fishermen confidently expect fish, particularly their chief catch, the anchovy, to be attracted by the lights and to gather innocently together to be caught, and it seems to be foolproof. The sight of boats fishing at night with lights is one of the most romantic of the Mediterranean.

▶▶▶ **Costa Brava**   *128C2*

Spain's "wild coast" of rocky inlets, pine-covered hills falling sharply down to the sea, and sheltered coves alternating with wide golden beaches stretches from the border with France down to the town of Blanes in the south. The choice extends from lively high-decibel resorts to quietly secluded bays, and in general, the resorts to the north of Palamós are quietest. Yet just a short distance inland, tourist Spain is left far behind.

RESORTS AND SIGHTS

The beach at **Aiguablava** is reckoned to be top of the league on this coast of ravishing beaches. It is small, with a marina, a couple of beach restaurants, and a smart parador (with scenic views).

Begur (**Bagur**) is the point of access to several good beaches, including Aiguafreda, Fornells, and Aiguablava. This town, with its fine houses and lively market, is dominated by a 17th-century castle.

The most southerly resort of the Costa Brava is **Blanes**, an industrial town (of nylon manufacturing) with a large beach, marina, and fishing harbour. There are a few grand but decaying buildings in the old town. Spectacular coastal views can be had from the Marimurtra botanical gardens on the hill above the town.

A cheerful and busy tourist resort (mostly self-catering accommodation), **L'Estartit** is the main centre for diving on the Costa Brava. Enthusiasts come for the caves, tunnels, and coral reefs of the Illes Medés (Medés Islands) immediately off the coast, formerly the haunt of pirates. The area, with its coral, is now protected and visitors can see the coral beds and underwater life by glass-bottomed boat. The wide, gently sloping town beach is popular with families.

Lloret de Mar is a thrumming package tour destination with a good beach and esplanade. Bars, discos, and fast-food joints insulate the visitor from any experience that could be described as Spanish.

A floral corner in the old town of well-restored Pals

Popular Palamós, once a simple fishing village, has grown into a busy port and is now a resort with a mass of apartments and hotel blocks

The resort of **Palamós** is low on charm, busy with traffic, and hot in summer. There is a busy port near the middle of the old town at the top of an ear-shaped bay, with massed holiday apartment blocks. Less developed **Platja de la Fosca**, just to the north, has two attractive beaches inside a large bay. **La Platja d'Aro** has unfortunately grown up with no other function than as a holiday resort. Hotels and apartment blocks line its 3km (2mi) beach, which is its only recommendation.

Pals beach stretches from Estartit southwards to Begur in a wide sweep of sand. The town itself, neat, floral, historic, and beautifully restored, is some way inland and deservedly popular.

Roses (**Rosas**) has a fortunate position at the end of a wide bay backed by mountains and a good sandy beach, but this cannot compensate for the ugliness of its tourist development.

Much famed in the 1960s for its discreet development, **S'Agaró** has become increasingly popular and, like the nearby La Platja d'Aro, more densely built.

Formerly a spa and the centre of the 19th-century cork-producing industry, **Sant Feliu de Guíxols** is now a gentle commercial town and coastal resort. It has a charming promenade shaded with plane trees, a busy market, and the ruins of an 11th-century monastery.

Benedictine monks built the walled monastery of **Sant Pere de Rodes** in the 9th and 10th centuries. Though partly destroyed in the 18th century, it still stands imposingly on a high peak in the last foothills of the eastern Pyrenees sliced off by the sea, with extensive views along the coast. You can drive there, or walk (two hours) from the harbour town of El Port de la Selva.

The long-established, well-liked resort of **Tossa de Mar** has retained much of its character and charm, thanks to its position around a large semicircle of beach, backed by wooded hills, and to its Vila Vella (old town), with 12th-century walls, towers, and lighthouse. Boats from here call at various points along the Costa Brava.

SARDANAS

The *sardana* forms an integral part of Catalonian folklore. Thought to have its roots in Cerdanya, northern Catalonia, it is still danced today all over the province, usually at weekends and during festivals. Participants join hands and dance in a constantly moving circle, and anyone may join in or leave the dance at any time.

135

BOTANICAL GARDENS

In the Jardí Botànic de Cap Roig (Cape Roig Botanical Gardens. *Open* winter, daily 9–6; summer, daily 9–8), enjoy wonderful sweeping views of quiet bays and rocky cliffs from high terraces, as winding, leafy paths lead from one thrilling *mirador* (look-out point) to another among carefully tended flower beds.

Salou's beach, always crowded in summer

136

▶ Costa Daurada (Costa Dorada)   *128B1*

The Costa Daurada (Golden Coast) stretches from the Ebro delta in the south to Cunit in the north. Most of the shoreline is fairly ordinary: hot and flat, filled with resorts and rather uninspiring beaches. It does, however, have a state-of-the-art theme park at Port Aventura, near Salou (see opposite), the lovely Roman city of Tarragona (see page 146), and a magnificent hinterland. A short way inland is the world-famous monastery of Poblet (see page 142).

RESORTS AND SIGHTS
Adjoining the Costa to the south, the **delta of the River Ebro** protrudes into the Mediterranean like a flattened arrowhead. Though very hard pressed by towns and agriculture (rice fields, fruit, and vegetables), this is Spain's largest Mediterranean wetland, and an important aquatic habitat.

L'Ampolla, the most southerly Costa Daurada resort, is a place of low-rise apartments and small hotels, with yachts and fishing boats. Views south of the Ebro delta resemble a mangrove swamp with telephone poles.

The little seaside town of **Cambrils** has a good wide beach and a pleasantly old-fashioned esplanade. In the afternoons a crowd gathers on the harbourside to watch the fishing fleet unload the day's catch. The streets around the harbour are filled with excellent fish restaurants. The built-up area now connects Cambrils with **Salou**; popular with local Catalans and with Spaniards generally, it is doubly crowded on weekends. It benefits from a charming seaside promenade and some fine Modernista houses. Round the headland from Salou is the small but developing resort of **La Pineda**, which has a good water park.

▶▶▶ **Empúries** see page 133   *128C3*

▶▶ Figueres (Figueras)   *128C3*

Spaniards, and Catalans, have great respect for their own birthplace, a tradition followed by Salvador Dalí. He endowed his birthplace, the busy town of Figueres behind the Costa Brava, with an extraordinary surrealist museum (tel: 972 67 75 00; *Open* summer, daily 9–8; winter, Tue–Sun 10.30–5.15) of his own life and work. Full of visual jokes, this museum in an artfully converted theatre is a complex blend of exhibitionism and deep seriousness. Don't miss the living room designed as "The Face of Mae West," with the famous red sofa as her lips.

▶▶ Girona (Gerona)   *128C2*

Girona, meeting-place of rivers, possesses an old town packed deep with treasures and full of shadowy medieval arches, alleyways, and dark stairways. Old houses, now restored and painted in ochre, orange, and green, hang over the River Onyar, reflected artistically in its waters. The city has a long history, which goes back to the Celtiberians. It was called Gerunda under the Romans. Essential sights include the old Jewish quarter, an imposing cathedral with the widest single Gothic span in Christendom, the Museu d'Art (tel: 972 20 95 36; *Open* Tue–Sat 10–6, Sun 10–2. *Admission charge*) displaying a largish gallery of painting and ceramics, Arab baths, and the archaeological museum within a former Romanesque monastery.

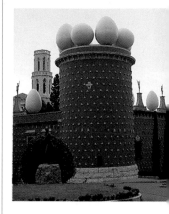

The visual humour at the Dalí museum in Figueres

PORT AVENTURA
This exciting theme park (tel: 977 38 46 56; *Open* end of Holy Week to Oct, daily 10–8. *Admission charge*) is based on the pleasures of five "continents," each with its own brand of entertainment. Rides range from giant teacups for kids to the largest roller-coaster in Europe. Reach it by train from Tarragona and Barcelona, or tour bus from the coastal resorts.

▶ Lleida (Lérida)   *128A2*

The Catalan provincial capital, Lleida looks uninviting from outside but will repay a visit. The skyline is dominated by La Zuda, a ruined Moorish fortress, and the Seu Vella (old cathedral), which has a fine south portal and soaring Gothic cloisters. Below it lies the old town, the new 18th-century cathedral (with a collection of tapestries) and, across from it, the magnificent Catalan Gothic Hospital de Santa María, which houses a modest archaeological museum.

Walk

Costa Brava patrol path

This is a coastal walk, following the old Cami de Ronda, or Civil Guard patrol path, between Cap Roig, Calella de Palafrugell, and Llafranch. It can be started or ended at any of these points and takes a short hour in each direction, allowing for stops.

Starting from the housing development just beneath Cap Roig Botanical Gardens, follow the sign "Al Cami de Ronda" on the Carrer del Cant del Ocells. Turn left at the sea, through a tunnel.

On approaching Calella beach, keep as close to the sea as possible, hitting the road again at Hotel Mediterrani and following it down along the arcaded front of Calella de Palafrugell.

Keep to the coast again round the cape to Llafranch.
   The views all the way are varied and often dramatic, a true Costa Brava blend of red rock, green pines, blue seas, and with new development and older towns.

Catalonia

LOCAL PRODUCTS

Catalan countrymen used to wear a kind of shortened stocking cap, bright red with a black band at the base. The best were made in Olot, where they are still produced, though mainly for "folklore" purposes (for dance teams and local costume). Olot also has sculpture workshops, turning out brightly painted religious statues. These go mainly to South America, the Spanish market being close to saturation.

138

CATALAN COSTUME

The red and black Catalan stocking cap is called a *barretina* and the red sash worn round the waist is a *faixa*.

The great monastery of Montserrat in its stupendous setting

▶ Montblanc   128A2

The 14th-century town of Montblanc, like its monastery neighbour Poblet, gains much from its proximity to the attractive sierra of Prades (1,201m/3,939ft). Tranquil today, its massive walls and turrets are a reminder of earlier, more perilous times. It is claimed that St. George slew the dragon in this very town. Consequently, the feast of Sant Jordi is a major springtime festival here. The town contains several important churches; the most impressive is Santa María, with baroque facade and Gothic interior. Note also the patio of the Hospital de Santa Magdalena.

▶ Montseny   128B2

High and wooded, the Montseny sierra rises not far north of Barcelona, making it good for hiking, cycling, or Sunday lunch among its restaurant-rich villages. There are lofty views of the mountains from the Girona road and from Vic to the north. The **Parc Natural del Montseny** has chestnuts, wild cherries, and great views. The towns of **Breda** and **Hostalric** are recommended stops.

▶▶▶ Montserrat   128B2

Montserrat, literally "the saw-toothed mountain," is chief of the spiritual homes of Catalonia. Its ancient Benedictine monastery, at 721m (2,365ft), was destroyed by Napoleonic invaders and rebuilt in forceful rather than attractive style beneath the rocks. The venerated 12th-century Virgin of Montserrat shelters in her great dark church (tel: 938 77 77 77; *Open* daily 8–8. *Admission free*). Her face is black, allegedly smoke-stained. The atmosphere is highly impressive, not least because the monks, even in the dark days of Franco, heroically took a stand for Catalanism. There are rich collections in the museums here, open to the public. A funicular takes you up the mountain for scenic views.

▶ Olot   128B3

This town at the centre of the Garrotxa volcanic area is famous for its late 19th-century school of landscape painting, which can be seen at the Museu Comarcal de la Garrotxa, Carrer de l'Hospici (tel: 972 27 91 30; *Open* Mon, Wed–Sat 11–2, 4–7, Sun 11–2). The same ticket allows you entry into the Museum of Volcanoes in the town's Botanical Gardens. Look out for a splendid Modernista mansion, the Casa Sola-Morales at No. 38 Paseo Blai. (See also **Drive** page 132.)

▶ Perelada   128C3

This ancient wine-growing settlement behind the coast produces a good sparkling wine. The local grandee family owns the castle (tel: 972 53 81 25; by appointment only) with library, wine museum, and crowd-pulling casino.

▶▶ Peratallada   128C2

Near to Pals, the lovely walled village of Peratallada is less restored, more rustic, and more medieval in atmosphere. Its Romanesque church stands in fields outside the walls. Inside, enjoy the palatial castle facade and the arches rising over narrow streets.

The exhilarating Catalan Pyrenees begin with the Costa Brava, and especially with rugged Cap de Creus, where the monastery of Sant Pere de Rodes has stood for many years like a last outpost overlooking the sea.

From here, with little intermission, the ground climbs ever higher, up through the grand, green hills and lesser mountains known as the Pre-Pyrenees and finally to the main ridge and glacial cirques of the highest mountains. These lie along the border with France, rising ever higher as they move east–west. The Pyrenees reach their highest point just across the Catalan border and into Aragón (see pages 108–109).

The northern mountains The Costa Brava end of the Pyrenees (Pirineus in Catalan), already quite high enough to offer numerous ski stations, is crossed diagonally by the historic route from Perpignan to Lleida. There is plenty of interest along the way; just north of the border town of Puigcerdà lies Llívia, a little Spanish enclave entirely surrounded by French territory. Just north of La Seu d'Urgell is Andorra, even more remarkable in its semi-autonomous survival.

All this is skiing territory and all along here to the south runs the splendid Cadí range, with magnificent rock-wall views and the handsome split peak of Pedraforca (2,497m/8,190ft). Pierced now by a north–south tunnel, affording access to Barcelona, the range is the key feature of the Cadí-Moixeró Natural Park.

Going south and west South again, the Pre-Pyrenees are a treasure store of Catalan Romanesque architecture, boasting such historic splendours as the monasteries of Sant Joan de les Abadesses and Ripoll (see page 142).

To the west, just before Aragón, come two quite lovely north–south valleys, the Noguera Pallaresa and the Noguera Ribagorcana, running up towards the highest ground and linked at the top by a narrow road over the high Bonaigua pass. This is the climax of the Catalan Pyrenees.

Between the two valleys lie the Parc Nacional d'Aigüestortes and the extraordinary Vall de Boí (see page 148), heartland of Catalonia's rural Romanesque architecture. Above again lies the equally extraordinary Val d'Aran, decanting downwards into France, rather than Spain, with a language of its own. For beauty, walking, and winter sports, this area is beyond compare. The inhabitants here are hardy people, sometimes more reserved than in other parts of Catalonia.

139

The wild spaces of the Pyrenees near the French border

Spain is a country where every small town celebrates its saint's day as well as the highlights of the Christian calendar. In an increasingly secular society, these festivals are more than Christian feasts, indeed, many of them date from pre-Christian times. They also mark the bonds of locality, community, and tradition.

140

Semana Santa The Holy Week before Easter is the chief religious festival, celebrated with dour and dreadful sombreness in Old Castilian towns like Burgos and Valladolid. In Cuenca, Holy Week forms the occasion for a sacred music festival; for Sevillanos, it is a theatrical showcase of religious fervour.

In every case, the week begins with the blessing of palms on Palm Sunday, progressing to a climax of grief through Thursday night and emerging to triumphant joy on Sunday. Throughout the week, activity is focused on church services and street processions. Huge floats, or *pasos*, decorated with flowers and lit by candles, bear polychrome, life-sized statues in mute reenactment of the events of Holy Week. Timetables of processions and services are usually printed in the local press.

The participants The bearers are members of various town brotherhoods, who have often paid for the privilege of carrying the floats on their shoulders. The penitents, many dressed in pointed hoods and robes, may walk barefoot beneath the weight of crosses or self-inflicted blows.

Often a *paso* will wait while muffled drums echo from another street. Suddenly the ululating cry of a *saeta* (literally an arrow), directed at Heaven from an onlooker moved by grief, pierces the air. Sometimes an oppressive and dreadful silence hangs in the incense-filled air, interrupted by a sharp rattle as the bearers resume their load and continue their dolorous progress.

Yet the general atmosphere is not one of lamentation. Locals will expound at length on the techniques of carrying the *pasos* and the subtleties of footwork involved. Youngsters emerge from town discos to see a procession go by and exchange a joke with a friend in the *paso* before ducking back into the party.

Corpus Christi This festival, like Semana Santa, is a moveable feast, generally falling at the end of May. It celebrates the triumph of good over evil and culminates in the procession of the Host through the streets, which in some towns have been carpeted with flowers and scented herbs. Even young children stay up through the night to make these carpets, knowing their perfection will last only until the first step of the procession.

Christmas and Carnival Christmas Day itself is a family rather than public celebration. The main feast is on 6 January. This is the Feast of the Three Kings, Los Tres Reyes Magos, and the occasion for the exchange of gifts. Carnival takes place in February before the austerities of Lent and is celebrated with variable fervour throughout the country. For many, it is the occasion for a great deal of dressing up and processions and general merrymaking.

Romerías, or pilgrimages, often involve all the inhabitants of a small town or village. They set out to some remote and venerated place, usually a shrine to the Virgin or saint, in a day trip that may have all the appearances of a village picnic. Sometimes they dress in traditional costume and sing as they go along. The *romería* in Ujué, though, is a notable exception. Pilgrims walk silently through the night in chains, flagellating themselves at the Stations of the Cross.

ROMERÍA TO EL ROCÍO
The most famous *romería*, to the shrine of Nuestra Señora del Rocío (Our Lady of the Dew) in the province of Huelva, takes place at Whitsun and is undoubtedly of pre-Christian origin. It has a strong southern and even gypsy character as the vast cavalcade of people on horseback or decorated carts travels to the shrine on the edge of Doñana National Park. The journey involves camping out and is the occasion for as much music, dancing, drinking, and horsemanship as piety.

141

Religion comes out onto the streets for numerous festivals which take place throughout Spain. They tend to evoke deep feelings among the locals and sometimes the whole town joins the procession

Opposite: It is a great honour to carry the holy image

142

WILFRED THE HAIRY
Wilfred the Hairy, stout ally of the Frankish Emperor Charles the Bald, was the key figure in the evolution of Catalonia, gathering several territories into an independent County of Barcelona in 878. Soon after, he founded the Abbey of Ripoll (where his remains reside in a casket of waxen smoothness, cantilevered from the wall of the north transept), and Sant Joan de les Abadesses in 885. He died in 897, founder of a dynasty which was to rule till the 15th century, when Catalonia was taken over by the Kingdom of Aragón.

ANCIENT CULTURES
Even before the Ancient Greeks, the Phoenicians, and the Romans, the Costa Brava was surprisingly well populated. The megalithic peoples of 4,000 and more years ago left standing stones and a good supply of dolmens (at Fitor in the Gavarres hills and La Cova d'En Daina, inland from Palamós). At Santa Cristina d'Aro, near Sant Feliu, is an 80-ton granite block precariously balanced upon another.

▶▶▶ Poblet　　　　　　128A2
Poblet monastery (tel: 977 87 00 89; *Open* daily 10–12.30, 3–5.30. Guided tours. *Admission charge*) ranks with Ripoll in importance but is much more attractive, its stone and architecture a golden testament to Catalan history and religious aspiration. Founded by Ramón Berenguer IV in 1150, the triple-walled monastery was largely destroyed by mob violence in the 19th century but has now been restored and reoccupied by monks. Tours reveal cloisters and *locutorio*, kitchen, refectory, and library. The huge church contains mock-Gothic, reproduction tombs of the kings of Aragón-Catalonia and a Damián Forment *retablo*, many of its lower figures decapitated in revolutionary periods. There is an 87m (285ft) long dormitory, and an informative museum illustrating the reconstruction of the monastery.

▶ Puigcerdà　　　　　　128B3
A frontier ski resort town, Puigcerdà is also popular with people from Barcelona who build rather lavish holiday chalets here. The self-proclaimed "capital of snow," the town has an octagonal belltower and is well worth a visit. The tiny Spanish enclave of Llívia lies 5km (3mi) onwards, in France. The mountain views are splendid.

▶▶ Ripoll and Sant Joan de les　　128B3
Abadesses (San Juan de las Abadesas)
These two great Benedictine monastic foundations, both established in the 9th century by Wilfred the Hairy, are often called the cradle of the Catalan nation. The splendour of **Ripoll** (Monestir de Santa María. *Open* daily 10–1, 3–7, closing 6PM Sep–May. *Admission free.* Cloisters *Open* as church. *Admission charge*) is best illustrated by its now glassed-in portico, with its large, detailed, and lively sculptured facade. Though worn by pollution, it remains one of Spain's great set pieces of early Christian art. Ripoll was a major place of learning and transmitted much of Arab culture, especially mathematics, into northern Europe. **Sant Joan de les Abadesses** (Monastir de Sant Joan de les Abadesses, tel: 972 72 23 53; *Open* daily, summer 10–7; winter 10–2, 4–6. *Admission charge*), 10km (6mi) up the valley, is another gem. Wilfred's daughter Emma was first abbess of this foundation for high-born ladies. Don't miss the Romanesque church, Gothic cloister, and the major works of sculpture inside the abbey. The town has an attractive Plaça Major.

▶ Sant Cugat del Vallès　　　128B2
Behind Tibidabo mountain lies the little monastery town of Sant Cugat. The church of the one-time Benedictine monastery (tel: 935 90 29 74; *Open* Tue–Sat 9.30–12.30, 3.30–5.30; Sun 9.30–12.30) is extremely handsome, with rose windows over the main portal, and triple apse.

▶▶ Santes Creus　　　　128A2
Santes Creus monastery (tel: 977 63 83 29; *Open* Tue–Sun 10–1.30, 3–7; last admission 20 minutess from closing. *Admission charge*), is one of the many burial places of the kings and queens of Aragón. Their remains were moved here from an earlier site by Ramón Berenguer IV in 1158. The monastery's gateways, with ornamental plasterwork

and complete with sundial, give way to a handsome, quiet square. The monastery is battlemented; on the church facade a Gothic window surmounts a Romanesque door. The traceried cloister is a delight.

▶ La Seu d'Urgell (Seo d'Urgel)   128B3
Today La Seu d'Urgell, seat of the archbishop (who happens to be joint titular ruler of Andorra) is essentially a point of passage on the way to Andorra. The 12th-century cathedral is a fraction militaristic, but elegant with a pretty gallery high on the exterior of the apse. Don't miss the 13th-century cloister and diocesan museum (tel: 973 35 32 42; *Open* Jun–Sep, Mon–Sat 10–1, 4–7, Sun 10–1; Oct–May, Mon–Fri 12–1, Sat–Sun 11–1. *Admission charge*).

▶▶ Sitges   128B2
Sitges is a seaside town built around an older nucleus on a knoll beside the sea. It is a resort where gay life and family holidays exist comfortably side by side. The original old town, with baroque parish church, a diminutive square, fine mansions, and a section of rampart, divides two very satisfactory beaches from one another. The small northern beach of San Sebastián is backed by palms and cafés and 1920s apartments. The large beach to the south, the Playa de Oro, is divided into segments by breakwaters and backed by a fuller display of palms. Most of the restaurants are around the Carrer de Parelladas. Among several museums the best is the Museu Cau Ferrat (tel: 938 94 03 64; *Open* Tue–Fri 10–1.30, 3–6.30, Sat 10–7, Sun 10–3. *Admission charge*), up on the knoll. Once the home of the Catalan painter-playwright Santiago Rusiñol (1861–1931), it is stuffed with ceramics, ironwork, glass, and paintings galore, including five Picassos and two El Grecos.

▶▶ Solsona   128B2
This rather tatty little town of medieval alleys lies in a wide bowl in the pine-clad Pyrenees. One corner of it is formed by the combination of the bishop's palace with the Romanesque and baroque cathedral. The slender and much venerated Romanesque Virgin of the Cloister is displayed in the cathedral, well worth a coin in the light box. The diocesan museum (tel: 973 48 21 01; *Open* Tue–Sat 10–1, 4–6. *Admission charge*) has prehistoric galleries, polychrome Romanesque statuary in the cloister, and a fine assemblage of Romanesque murals from local churches, as well as some Catalan Gothic religious art.

The resort of Sitges has 11 beaches to choose from, as well as good restaurants and nightclubs, and several highly distinctive museums

143

CORK-OAK FORESTS
The extensive cork-oak forests of the Costa Brava hinterland have always produced much of Spain's cork exports. Now, with plastic replacing cork, and in the face of Portuguese competition, Catalan factories confine themselves mostly to cleaning, steaming, and pressing high-quality cork from Portugal. Local cultivation has declined, but the trees can still be seen.

Would-be artists should move to Catalonia. There seems to be something in the air that inspires great achievements. Catalonia in the 20th century gave us such artistic giants as Miró, Tàpies, Dalí, and Picasso.

THE SAGRADA FAMÍLIA

The Expiatory Temple of the Holy Family was the brain-child of Josep Bocabella, a rich publisher, who commissioned it to atone for the excesses of left-wing Catalans. In 1883, Antoni Gaudí i Cornet, a 31-year-old architect, took over the project, and continued to work on the Sagrada Família until his death in 1926. The church was Gaudí's obsession, and he became an ascetic, dressed in rags, and working and sleeping on site.

144

The restored monastery of Poblet, founded in the 12th century

The Romanesque The story starts, however, with Wilfred the Hairy, first count of independent Barcelona, and his 9th-century Monasterio de Santa María at Ripoll. By the end of the Romanesque period the monastery had not only acquired its great carved portals, it stood at the heart of international learning and Catalan self-aware-ness. Another great foundation, the later Cistercian monastery at Poblet in mid-Catalonia, was to be equally important. Meanwhile, in the Pyrenean valleys, Romanesque churches with tall-stacked towers were acquiring some of the most outstanding frescoes in Spain. Catalan Romanesque mixes a local earthiness with Byzantine gravity and an Italianate sense of charac-ter (there was strong influence from Lombardy).

A flowering culture Architecture thrived mightily during the Gothic period, when Catalan architects specialized in vast single-span hall-churches. The cathedral in Girona has the widest Gothic vault in Christendom. This style spread beyond the Pyrenees into France. Meanwhile, Catalan intel-lectuals like the 13th-century mystic, polymath, and poet Ramón Llull were continuing to influence the pattern of culture throughout Europe.

Cultural rebirth Spain's centralist centuries, especially under the Bourbons, were not good for Catalonia. How-ever, the 1840s saw the start of a great linguistic and literary revival known as the *Renaixença* (Renaissance). It was a period of literary creation, choral singing, and lively folklore, all in Catalan. It led, in a clear succession, to the curious glories of Modernista architecture (see opposite).

Suppression and revival Catalan art also emerged, with artists like Santiago Rusiñol (1861–1931), the influential impressionist Ramón Casas (1866–1932), the legendary Pablo Picasso (born in Andalucía, but who spent a forma-tive period in Barcelona), and the eccentric Salvador Dalí. In music, Pablo Casals (1876–1973) came to be regarded by many as the greatest cellist who has ever lived. In the aftermath of the Civil War the Franco dictator-ship tried to ban the Catalan language and suppress Catalan culture in an attempt to impose a cultural homo-geneity on Spain. Far from disappearing, however, Catalan creativity went underground, ready to break out again on Franco's death with the joyful exuberance that characterizes the region today. This can be seen in the striking design sense of contemporary Barcelona and in the performances of such greats as tenor José Maria Carreras and soprano Montserrat Caballé.

Gaudí—Catalan architect, fantasist, and creator of the astonishing spiky and organic-looking church of the Sagrada Família, Barcelona's foremost picture-postcard image—has become the most famous of a remarkable generation.

But we should not forget the 50 or so other Catalan architects, most notable among them Lluís Domènech i Montaner and Josep Puig i Cadafalch, and an army of hundreds of master craftsmen who supported these brilliant designers in every domestic manufacture from stained glass to ceramics, from furniture to door locks.

The Modernista movement The depth and richness of the movement transformed Barcelona itself, made a real impact on other Catalan towns from Olot in the north to Reus in the south, and reached out into Valencia and many other provinces.

The style was a close cousin to German Jugendstil and British, Belgian, and Austrian art nouveau, based on a flowing organic line and a richly romantic use of colours and materials. Yet the motivating force behind the movement was Catalan cultural nationalism.

Domènech, Gaudí, and Puig
Domènech made his mark first. As a 28-year-old architecture professor he called, in 1879, for a "national"

approach. He went on to define it in a long series of buildings, ranging from houses and hospitals to the Palau de la Música Catalana in Barcelona (see page 123). Preferring to build in brick with bright ceramic ornament, he leaned quite heavily on Gothic antecedents. Stained glass was a favourite Domènech medium.

Antoni Gaudí, born in 1852, was conservative and rigid in his philosophy where Domènech was open and eclectic. Gaudí would certainly have repudiated the label "Modernista." But his technical daring matched a soaring imagination and he gathered around him a tight network of disciples, all achieving unprecedented effects, even though in the service of a restrictive ideology. Concrete and wrought iron were his forte; the list of craftsmen who worked with him is immense.

Puig, the last of the trio, was both younger and fractionally less inventive, more inclined to rely on historical precedent. But his range is also surprisingly great; and he went on to become head of the regional government which Catalonia briefly achieved at the start of the 20th century.

145

Inside Antoni Gaudí's Casa Batlló, which has a phantasmagorical facade and a scaly roof

Tarragona's cathedral
is a fine example of
Romanesque-Gothic
transition architecture

146

NATURAL SPRINGS
Names beginning with
"Caldas de" are extremely
common and imply both a
profusion of local mineral
waters and many spas.

▶ ▶ ▶ **Tarragona**   *128A1*

Leaving Barcelona out of the equation, Tarragona is by far
the most agreeable of the larger towns along the coast of
Catalonia. Open, airy, pleasantly modern in parts, it also
possesses some of the best Roman remains in Spain (and a
strong sense of antiquity) confined, but by no means
entirely, within attractive, high city walls and a tangled
old town.

The city is a provincial capital. Despite some dreary
apartment blocks on its southern approach, the middle of
town has a remarkable atmosphere, full of light and a
sense of civilization. This is best sampled on the Rambla
Nova, a modern street which leads to a fine *mirador* (look-
out point), the well-named Balcó del Mediterrani.

Here, from beside the statue of the town's medieval
hero Roger de Lauria, the slope falls away steeply
beneath to the railway station, beach (the renovated
Platja del Miracle), the harbour, and the remains of the
Roman amphitheatre.

Publius Scipio, driving south from Empúries against the
Carthaginians in 218 BC (in the Second Punic War),
adopted Tarragona as a Roman city. Later the Emperor
Augustus lived here, and Pontius Pilate was born here. It
was the main Roman city in Spain.

Chief ancient sites Pretori Romà (Roman Praesidium)
is physically linked to the vaults of the Roman
Circus (these two form the Museu de la Romanitat, see
opposite). The **Archaeological Museum** (tel: 977 23 62 09;
Open summer, Tue–Sat 10–8, Sun 10–2; winter, Tue–Sat
10.30–1.30, 4–7, Sun 10–2) is in a modern building linked
to Pretori. It has fine sculpture and mosaics, including the
famous Medusa head, which has become almost a stock
image of Tarragona.

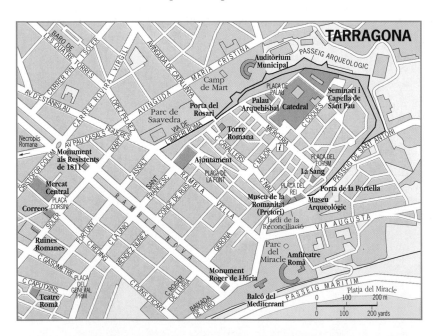

TARRAGONA

Roman aqueduct of les Ferreres, near Tarragona. Also known as the Puento del Diablo (Devil's Bridge), this impressive aqueduct, which extends for some 198m (650ft), once carried water from the Gayá River over a valley of the Francolí River

147

Passeig Arqueológic (tel: 977 24 57 96; *Open* summer, Tue–Sat 9–9, and illuminated Sun 9–3. *Admission free with museum pass*), Tarragona's massive town walls are thought to have been built onto bases constructed by an ancient Iberian tribe called the Cerretani. This walkway takes you round the outside of the inner wall, pre-Roman, Roman, medieval, and 18th century.

The **Amfiteatre Romà** (tel: 977 24 25 79; closed for refurbishment; call in advance) is a short walk down towards the sea. Modern seating follows the old shape of the theatre, with the ruins of the Christian basilica of Santa María del Miracle superimposed. Divided by a modern street, the site of the **Forum**, beyond the Rambla Nova, is extremely fetching, with elegant golden brown columns, cypresses, and geraniums. Also interesting are the **Pretoric i Circ Romans**, the Roman circus (tel: 977 24 19 52; *Open* Tue–Sat 9–9, Sun 9–3. *Admission charge*).

Christian Tarragona Until the 11th century, this was the seat of the Primate of Christian Iberia. The cathedral (*Closed* Sun, except for Mass) is built on the site of the Roman temple of Jupiter and succeeds a mosque. Broad stone stairs ascend to a time-worn square and the sculpted portals of the cathedral. Within, a magnificent *retablo* soars up in Gothic pinnacles. The ancient Romano-Christian necropolis, on Passeig de la Indepèndancia 15, has a rich assortment of tombs and sarcophagi.

Around Tarragona On the road east towards Barcelona, look for the funerary tower named after the Scipio brothers, which has a pair of half-obliterated statues on its upper portions (at 16km/10mi, to the left). At 20km (12mi), now on a floral roundabout, is the **Arco de Bará**, an impressive 2nd-century arch, which once straddled the highway. About 4km (2.5mi) along the road north to Lleida, there is a two-storey Roman aqueduct, one of Spain's best. It can be seen from a stopping-point on the A1 to Barcelona.

HUMAN PYRAMIDS
For reasons which remain unknown, Catalans love building human pyramids. Strong men, often assisted by a tight-packed crowd, put their arms on each other's shoulders to form a tight circle. Working to a well-rehearsed plan, men and women, boys and girls climb on to their shoulders and form up to nine human tiers. A very young boy or girl is the last to go up and quickly raise a hand to show that the pyramid is complete. Dismantling the pyramid safely is an integral part of the operation. Many of the teams of *castellers*, or pyramid-builders, come from Tarragona, El Vendrell, Valls, and Vilafranca de Penedès, but they travel all over Catalonia to give feast-day displays.

Catalonia is one of the regions leading Spain's "green tourism" revolution. Over the last 10 years a large number of rural bed and breakfasts have sprung up, offering a relaxing change from lying on the beach or slogging round a city. In Catalonia these family-run guest houses are called *casas de pages* and they usually offer an inexpensive, welcoming way to explore the countryside. Ask for details in any tourist office.

BATTLE OF THE EBRO
The last and most heroic Republican offensive of the Civil War was begun at the end of July, 1938, when 100,000 men crossed east to west over the Ebro River at different points, and successfully gained the high ground on the other side. The Nationalists soon countered with devastating air and artillery attacks. It is estimated that up to 200 planes flew daily over Republican-held posts to drop an average of 10,000 bombs. With virtually no air cover of their own, the Republicans were beleaguered but continued to fight a hopeless war of attrition. The battle began in scorching summer heat, but, by mid-November, when snows began to cover the peaks of the sierra, it was over. It had cost the lives of 70,000 Republicans and half that number of Nationalists. Ernest Hemingway, in his role as war reporter, was among the last to cross the Ebro with the retreating Republicans.

▶ **Terrassa (Tarrassa)** *128B2*

Close to Montserrat but very much in the busy hinterland of Barcelona, this important textile town is little visited by tourists. It has a handful of monuments of great interest and charm: notably the churches of Santa María, San Pedro, and San Miguel, which contain ancient elements, including Visigothic horseshoe arches and Gothic paintings. There is also a varied and interesting textile museum, at Calle Salmerón 25 (*Open* Tue, Wed, Fri 9–6, Thu 9–9, Sat–Sun 10–2. *Admission charge*).

▶ **Tortosa** *128A1*

Close to the mouth of the Ebro, Tortosa has a long history both as a meeting place and point of division between the Moorish and Christian cultures. Taken by the Moors in the 8th century, it was conquered for the Christians by Ramon Berenguer IV in 1148. The Moorish *zuda* (hill fortress), today containing a parador, has lovely views of the town and its setting, and of the multi-buttressed, largely Gothic cathedral below. The 16th-century Collegi de Sant Lluís, now the town museum (*Open* Mon–Fri 9–2, 3.30–6; *Closed* Thu afternoons), was built by Charles V for the sons of Moorish converts. In the river is a spiky steel memorial to those who died in the Battle of the Ebro.

▶▶ **Val d'Aran** *128A3*

The Val d'Aran is the high valley of the Garonne (Garona), with popular walking trails and some of the best skiing in Spain. It was cut off from the rest of Spain each winter until the construction of the road tunnel from the south after the Civil War. The language is a mixture of old Gascon and Catalan, although many people can speak Catalan, Castilian, and French, and the local spirit is one of sturdy independence. The valley's capital is Viella (Vielha); prettier Artiés, 6km (4mi) to the east, is best for food and accommodation.

▶▶ **Vall de Boí** *128A3*

This beautiful high Pyrenean valley has become well known for its winter skiing and summer trekking. Its earlier and greater fame resided in its extraordinary collection of Romanesque churches.

▶ **Valls** *128A2*

Valls is famous for human pyramids (see page 147), which seem to be echoed by the lofty open stonework belfry of San Juan, the principal church. The place features the remnants of an old castle, ancient ramparts, a few faded Modernista houses in the Carrer de la Cort, and handsome 19th-century street lighting.

▶▶ **Vic (Vich)** *128B2*

A pleasant broad valley, northwest of the Montseny range, is home to the old Catalan city of Vic, which remains a busy place. The best part is the quieter old town, especially the Plaça Major and the cathedral square, the Plaça del Bispe Oliva. In the latter, the 18th-century neoclassical cathedral with elaborate Romanesque tower is made extraordinary by the vast grisaille-to-sepia frescoes, depicting scenes from the lives of Jesus' disciples, by the 20th-century Catalan painter Josep Maria Sert. They are not to all tastes, but some find them strangely stirring. Opposite is Catalonia's leading episcopal museum (tel: 938 86 22 14, closed for refurbishment), one of the most important in Spain. Its Romanesque collection of painted wooden panels and altar fronts and frescoes, drawn from the surrounding region, is spectacular. Don't miss the *Last Supper* from La Seu d'Urgell. There is also notable Gothic work (by 15th-century artists Lluís Borrassa and Jaime Huguet, in particular).

Once a Roman settlement, the town also possesses the ruins of a 2nd-century Roman temple.

► **Vilafranca del Penedès**   *128B2*
(Villafranca) and Olèrdola

Capital of the Penedès wine region, where wagon-loads of grapes can be seen bowling through the town at harvest time, **Vilafranca del Penedès** is certainly worth a stop. A pleasant main road *rambla* opens into a square confusingly known as the Rambla Sant Francesc. Behind here is the old town. The town hall is half monumental-medieval, half florid-19th century; the parish church is quite baronial, and across from its main portal, in Plaça Jaume, is the local museum, its various archaeological displays housed in a fine building with Aragonese royal connections. Conoisseurs will also enjoy the Museu del Vi (Wine Museum, tel: 938 90 05 32; *Open* winter, Tue–Sat 10–2, 4–7, Sun 10–2; summer, Tue–Sat 9–9, Sun 10–2. *Admission charge*), which shows a history of wine from Egyptian and Roman times to the 19th century. The Torres winery, one of Spain's most reliable, is 3km (2mi) away. Plaça Jaume is also home to other mansions, and a monument dedicated "Als Castellers" or "to the human pyramid-builders."

Olèrdola, above the Sitges road, has an ancient site with a Romanesque church, which has Mozarabic elements and a castle. Wineries in Vilafranca and nearby Sant Sadurni d'Anoia, many of which can be visited, produce cava, Spain's answer to champagne.

ROMANESQUE CHURCHES
The Romanesque churches in the high Pyrenean Vall de Boí, including San Clemente de Taüll, are among Catalonia's most remarkable riches. Free-standing towers rise up to six storeys, with little arched windows in ones, twos, and threes, against the mountains. Rounded apses are decorated with the rings of blind arches known as Lombard banding. Inside were the famous frescoes, rescued in the nick of time from theft and the elements for the Museo d'Art de Catalunya in Barcelona.

ARCHITECTURAL STYLES
Forget the nasty blocks put up for skiers in the 1960s. Traditional Val d'Aran architecture is one of the most distinctive styles in Spain. The villages are built in dark stone, with fly-away eaves and dark slates reaching up to encircle the Romanesque church tower which rises in each.

149

Cathedral and bridge in Vic, an old Catalan city, now a busy industrial centre

THE CHRISTIAN RECONQUEST of Spain threw up first the kingdom of León, and then that of Castilla, which surpassed its parent in power, creating in the process a landscape bristling with castles (the *castillos*, from which it takes its name). These fortresses, strongest along the River Duero, stretched right down towards Madrid. The provincial capitals of Castilla-León (León itself, Zamora, Palencia, Burgos, Valladolid, Soria, Salamanca, Ávila, and Segovia) all have their roots in this expansion, and together form a roll-call of Spanish history. Two-thirds of the land is plain, the rest mountain; it comprises the largest single region in the European Union and one of the most sparsely populated. Its agriculture is suffering from the competition of other European countries.

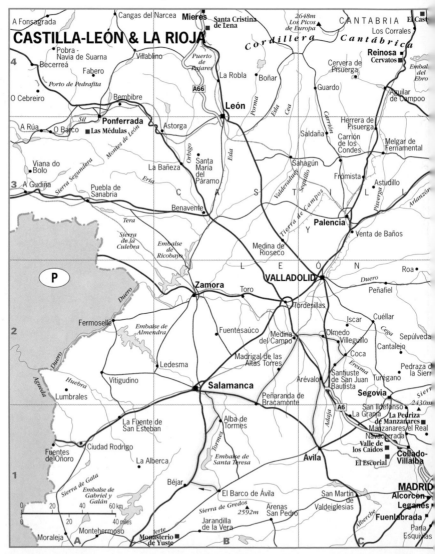

La Rioja, bordering Castilla-León to the east and closer to the coast, is a different proposition. It too has its wide plains, its gorges, and mountains, but it seems to have drawn a greater cordiality from the richer lands along the Ebro. Some people find it a more easy-going place. One of Europe's smallest regions, it is noted for producing some of the best red wines of Spain. La Rioja is also famous for its excellent peppers. Fresh vegetables, in fact, characterize the cuisine of the area. This is another feature of contrast with adjoining Castilla-León, where meat, such as spicy sausage, roast kid, lamb, and suckling pig, is the basis of regional cooking.

One unifying aspect, however, is the Pilgrims' Way to Compostela, which passes through, linking the regions in history, architecture, and spirituality.

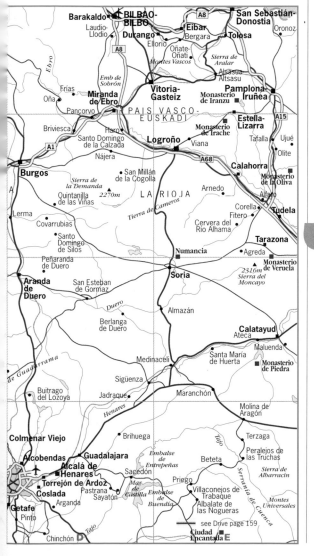

152

▶ Agreda   151E3

Agreda marked the early frontier between Castile and
Aragón, as witnessed by its castle and the fortified tower
of the church of San Miguel. Later it was home to Sor
María de Agreda, nun and confidante of King Philip IV.

▶ Aguilar de Campoo   150C4

Aguilar, dominated by a castle, a communications mast,
and a biscuit factory, is a satisfying town, with plenty of
ancient mansions. The long arcaded main square leads up
to the large collegiate church of San Miguel (Gothic interior), with kneeling funerary couples. The heavily restored
monastery of Santa María La Real (tel: 979 12 50 00; *Open*
summer, Tue–Fri 10.30–2, 4.30–7.30, Sat–Sun 10.30–2, 5–8;
winter, Tue–Fri 4–7, Sat–Sun 10.30–2, 4.30–7.30. *Admission
charge*) contains a permanent exhibition of Romanesque
church architecture.

▶▶ Alba de Tormes   150B1

The town gave its name to the Dukes of Alba, and later
St. Teresa died here. Though pleasantly set on the River
Tormes, it is now rather dismal. All that is left of the
dukes is a huge tower, closed for reconstruction.
St. Teresa fares better. Visitors enter the convent church of
La Anunciación (tel: 923 30 02 11; *Open* daily 8–1.30, 4–8)
under a fine Plateresque rendering of the Annunciation.
Opposite, behind a grille, is a reconstruction of the cell
where St. Teresa died, showing her on her deathbed.
Farther along the left-hand wall is her original burial
place. She is now in a casket high above the altar, her arm
behind a door to the left, her heart behind a door to the
right. The index finger of St. John of the Cross is kept in
the museum of the Teresian opposite.

▶▶ La Alberca   150A1

This beautiful half-timbered village in the Sierra de
Francia, southwest of Salamanca, has become very
touristy. The district, once spectacularly poor and
neglected, retains ancient architecture and customs.
Rustic La Alberca has a little stream, a cobbled opening
for a square, and a pretty stone cross, while old trades are
actively pursued. On the peak of La Peña de Francia
above, reached by a road that winds round the mountain,
is a monastic retreat. The views are awesome.

▶ Almazán   151E2

This is a pleasing walled town with three gates, on the
River Duero. One of the gates leads straight into the main
square, with flower beds, a statue of 16th-century local
worthy Diego de Laynez, and the classical 16th- to 17th-
century palace of the Counts of Altamira. In one corner of
the square is San Miguel, a Romanesque church whose
octagonal tower is topped with patterned brickwork
showing a clear Mudéjar influence.

▶ Aranda de Duero   151D2

This river crossing on the Duero was a busy place until
the main road bypassed it. It is still good for Castilian
roast dinners, and its church of Santa María has one of
Spain's finest facades. Isabelline elaboration is tamed by

harmony of composition; scenes from the Passion and Resurrection mingle with the richest dynastic heraldry.

▶ **Arévalo**   *150C2*

Reputedly the home of Spain's best suckling pig, Arévalo stands on the confluence of the Adaja and Arevalillo rivers, and was once protected by the huge 14th-century castle, childhood home of Queen Isabella. The modern town sprawls, but the old town around the Plaza de la Villa has noble mansions and fine churches, such as Romanesque Santa María and San Martín.

▶ **Arnedo**   *151F3*

The capital of Rioja Baja (Lower Rioja), Arnedo has a ruined Moorish castle and two fine Gothic churches, Santo Tomás and Santa Eulalia. Under a line of cliff and hill with man-made caves, its setting is dramatic.

▶▶ **Astorga**   *150B3*

Now only a medium-sized town, Astorga was one of Spain's earliest bishoprics and, later, an important stopping point on the Pilgrims' Way. The Romans called it "Asturica Augusta." It has a fine Gothic/baroque **cathedral**, with a Renaissance *retablo* by Gaspar Becerrá, pupil of Michelangelo (*Open* daily, summer 9–12, 5–6.30; winter 9.30–12, 4.30–6. *Admission charge*). Note especially the marvellous central porch, with carvings. The adjoining Diocesan Museum (tel: 987 61 58 20; *Open* daily, summer 10–2, 4–8; winter 11–2, 3.30–6.30. *Admission charge*) is also worth a visit.

The **bishop's palace**, begun by Gaudí and finished by Ricardo Guereta, has a Gothic-baronial exterior, but with a Gothic-Mudéjar interior. Never actually used by a bishop, it now houses the motley collection of the **Museo de los Caminos** (Museum of the Pilgrims' Way; tel: 987 61 68 82; *Open* summer, Tue–Sat 10–2, 4–8, Sun 10–2; winter, Tue–Sat 11–2, 4–8, Sun 11–2. *Admission charge*) and provides a fairly rare chance to see the inside of a building decorated by Gaudí.

153

Scene from the life of Christ in Astorga's cathedral

▶▶▶ Ávila   150C1

Ávila provides a key to understanding Spain. The stern remains of military might, in the form of Europe's greatest medieval walls, and the reminders of religious intensity in the many convents and churches, combine to offer an awesome vision of Old Castile.

THE PAST PRESERVED Inhabited earlier by Celts, whose carved stone bulls and boars are found everywhere in the area, Ávila became a much contested buffer zone between Moors and Christians until King Alfonso VI, on retaking the city, ordered his son-in-law Ramón de Borgoña (Count Raymond of Burgundy) to build a definitive set of **walls**. Between 1088 and 1091, the count constructed a circuit of 2.4km (1.5mi), with 88 round towers and nine gates. The whole complex is still standing. Following the old Roman line, the walls form a rectangle, running downhill to a river in the west. The apse of the city's rugged cathedral, an essential part of the defensive scheme, forms a protrusion in the wall on the higher, eastern side where it was most open to attack. The two most impressive city gates, with low arches for entry and high walkways above to join the towers, are also here. The future St. Teresa (see panel) was born here in 1515 and lived much of her life within sight of the medieval walls. Few notable contributions to the city have been made since. It has survived because it was so thoroughly bypassed by subsequent history. Spain's highest provincial capital, Ávila is very bleak in winter, which is arguably the most fitting time to see this atmospheric city.

WITHIN THE WALLS The main feature is the early Gothic cathedral (tel: 920 21 16 41; *Open* Mon–Fri 10–5, Sat 10–6.30, Sun 12–6. *Admission charge*), rather dour outside with an unfortunate late 18th-century main facade. The interior is relieved by sculptural scenes on the Plateresque retrochoir, notably the *Massacre of the Infants*; by the strangely mottled red and white stone of apse and transepts; and, in the ambulatory, by the alabaster tomb

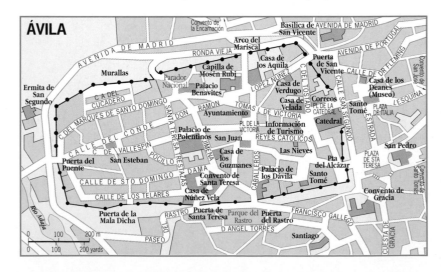

ÁVILA

Carvings above a doorway of Ávila cathedral

of El Tostado (the Toasted or Swarthy One), otherwise known as Bishop Alfonso de Madrigal. The cathedral **museum** includes the sacristy, where the leaders of the 16th-century Comuneros rebellion met, and there is a fine *Ecce Homo* by Luis de Morales.

Of the **palaces** within the walls, the best, including those of the Nuñez Vela, Guzman Oñate, and Dávila families, cluster to the south. In the middle is the impressively vast Polentinos palace, with a further, less remarkable cluster, on the north side.

OUTSIDE THE WALLS All the best religious architecture, and some of the more agreeable parts of town, are here. Beyond the northeast corner of the fortifications is the very fine Romanesque church of **San Vicente** (*Open* daily 10–1.30, 4–6.30. *Admission charge*). It was built as a shrine on the site of a triple martyrdom (Vicente and his sisters Cristeta and Sabina), with colonnaded side gallery and a remarkably sculpted west entrance. At the heart of this part of town is the Renaissance **Casa de los Deanes**, housing a good provincial museum (tel: 920 21 10 03; *Open* Tue–Sat 10–2, 4.30–7.30; Sun 10–2. *Admission charge*), and the Romanesque church of **San Pedro** (*Open* daily 10–12 and for services. *Admission free*). Behind San Pedro is **St. Teresa's birthplace** (*Open* daily 9.30–1.30, 3.30–7. *Admission free*), which is now encased within a baroque church, and **San José**, the first convent founded by Teresa (*Open* daily 10–1.30, 3.30–6. *Admission charge*), which has a small museum about the saint's life, next door.

It is worth taking a car to the magnificent church and monastery of **Santo Tomás** (tel: 920 22 04 00; *Open* daily 10–1, 4–8. *Admission charge*), on the south side of town, once used by Ferdinand and Isabella as their Ávila residence. The poignant alabaster effigy of their only son, Prince Juan, dead at 19 years of age, looks up at a *retablo* painted by Pedro Berruguete. There is a series of three magnificent cloisters, one of which contains a museum with oriental art.

On the northern side of town is the **Convento de la Encarnación** (tel: 920 21 12 12; *Open* daily 9.30–1.30, 3.30–6. *Admission charge*). Young ladies conducting visitors about the convent point out the very spots where St. Teresa saw visions. The small museum is highly evocative of both her life and of that of her confessor, that other great Spanish mystic, San Juan de la Cruz (St. John of the Cross).

...AND DEATH
St. Teresa's body, though treated with quicklime after death, gave off a smell of roses, provoking an investigation during which her left hand was removed. This eventually came into the possession of General Franco, who clutched it on his own deathbed. The saint's heart was removed to gauge the effect of a vision in which she felt her heart and bowels had been pierced by a burning spear. Her left arm was also removed and small parts progressively trimmed for reliquaries. The practice was stopped by Pope Clement IX.

St. Teresa in stained glass in the Convento de la Encarnación

The castle of Berlanga de Duero was built in the 15th century and features two rings of walls and a keep

EL COLACHO
An unusual event takes place in Castrillo de Murcia, due west of Burgos, at Corpus Christi (which falls in either May or June). Babies born during the previous 12 months are laid on a mattress in the street and a sinister character dressed in a bright red and yellow costume, called El Colacho, jumps over them. It is said that by jumping over the babies, El Colacho frees them from illnesses associated with the devil, especially hernias.

▶ **Astudillo**   *150C3*

Astudillo (40km/25mi north of Palencia), with its 13th-century walls and the Mudéjar church of Santa Clara, is another reminder of the richness of Palencia, once residence of the Kings of Castile (see also Frómista, page 160).

▶ **Béjar**   *150B1*

A messy but interesting walled town under its own sierra (good views of the town from N630 to the northeast), Béjar occupies a promontory that juts into an enclosed valley. Continue to its end for the Plaza Mayor and the palace of the dukes of Osuna, now a school.

▶ **Benavente**   *150B3*

Benavente, set at an important crossroads and familiar to many travellers in northwest Spain, is unremarkable except for its hill-top parador, which incorporates the one remaining tower of the ruined and rebuilt castle of Ferdinand II of León.

▶ **Berlanga de Duero**   *151D2*

Berlanga is one of a chain of Christian fortresses, built along the Duero valley stretching from Soria to Valladolid, marking the first stage of the Reconquista. (Others are at Gormaz, Peñaranda, and Peñafiel.) Its looming curtain walls and turrets, seen from the south, rival those of Ávila. The town is dour, with arcades and a large collegiate church.

▶ **Briviesca**   *151D3*

The heir to the Spanish throne receives the title of Principe de Asturias (Prince of Asturias), a practice established by the Castilian Cortes, which met in this little Burgos town in 1388. Briviesca is otherwise known for its convent church of Santa Clara and the shrine of Santa Casilda, which is just outside the village.

▶▶▶ **Burgos**   *151D3*

The best approach to Burgos is along the Madrid road. Arriving this way, you get an early view of the open stonework of the cathedral towers, rising in knobbly, thrilling eccentricity from under the castle hill.

Early prominence Fernán González, count of Castile, pronounced himself independent of León in the mid-10th century, thus becoming, in the Castilian-based view of Spain, a national hero. His descendant Fernando (Ferdinand) I became first king of Castile, then of León as well. Alfonso VI was the last king to rule from Burgos, shifting the court to Toledo in 1085 soon after the capture of that city. Rodrigo Díaz de Vivar, better known as El Cid, and rather notionally a vassal of Alfonso, was born a short way north at Vivar del Cid. He is as much a presence in the city as Fernán González.

In 1221 Fernando III, El Santo, laid the first stone of a Gothic cathedral which was to be among the finest in Spain. Successive kings and queens used the nearby Monastery of Las Huelgas as a residence when in Burgos. Isabella I commissioned family tombs in the Cartuja de Miraflores, Burgos's other great monastery.

Up to the present The city was headquarters of the Mesta (see panel page 176), and gathered wool from all Castile for dispatch down to the coast then to Flanders. This trade collapsed during the 16th century. Despite declining wealth, Burgos remained a military and religious capital. Franco used it as his Civil War headquarters from 1937 and, later, its military courts played a large part in his suppression of the Basques, notably in the Burgos trials of 1970, when international protest prevented the execution of Basque dissidents.

Visiting Burgos The old town rises on the north side of the little River Arlanzón. Only the municipal museum, which is fairly central, and the two great monasteries, Las Huelgas (1km/0.6mi) and the Cartuja de Miraflores (4km/2.5mi), are on the south side, which is best visited by car. For the rest, Burgos is very much a walker's city. Approaching the old town across the Santa María bridge, with the attractive riverside *alameda* called the Paseo del Espolón, the city's favourite strolling place, to the right, pass under the Arco de Santa María, a splendid 11th-century gateway with two semicircular towers and four turrets. Originally part of the old 11th-century city walls, it was remodelled in the 15th century. This route will bring you directly to the cathedral.

The cathedral The exterior of the cathedral (tel: 947 20 47 12; *Open* Mon–Sat 9.30–1, 4–7, Sun 9.30–11.45, 4–7. *Admission charge*) is a festival of spires, towers, and pinnacles. Right in the middle of the interior, and next to a choir carved by Felipe Vigarni (circa 1500), El Cid and his wife Jimena lie under a simple slab. A replica of their marriage settlement and a trunk belonging to El Cid are displayed in the cloister museum. The first chapel to the right on entry (Capilla del Santo Cristo) has an early image of Christ, made of leather and supposedly with human hair. Both hair and nails are said to grow.

GREAT ARCHITECTS
Gil de Siloé was one of the immensely talented group of architects and sculptors on whose services the Catholic Monarchs, Ferdinand and Isabella, were able to call. He was responsible not only for the exquisite royal tombs in the Cartuja de Miraflores at Burgos, but also for the *retablo* and triptych of the Capilla del Constable in Burgos cathedral.

157

Enjoying the view from the remains of Burgos's 11th-century city walls

The Gothic cathedral of Burgos was adapted to its site on a slope, with staircases both inside and out

An architectural high point is the magnificent double stairway descending to the north transept from a high outer door, the so-called Escalera Dorada (Golden Staircase) of 1519–1523 by Diego de Siloé. At the east end of the cathedral is the late 15th-century Capilla del Condestable (Chapel of the Constable), by Simón de Colonia, magnificent in Isabelline Gothic, and with the fine tomb of the constable of Castile and his wife.

CASTLE, CHURCHES, AND CASA DEL CORDON

The **castillo**, where both El Cid and Edward I of England were married, was blown up during the 18th century and finally demolished by the French in 1813. At the base of the castle hill there are several Romanesque and Gothic churches, including **Santa Agueda** (open for services only) where El Cid supposedly forced Alfonso VI to swear a great oath that he had not killed his brother at Zamora. Lower in the city, close to the main shopping street of Calle Santander, stands the handsome mansion where Columbus reported to Ferdinand and Isabella after his second voyage. Its door is surrounded by a stout stone cord, hence its name, the **Casa del Cordón**.

Monasterio de las Huelgas Las Huelgas (tel: 947 20 16 30; *Open* Tue–Sat 11–1.15, 4–5.15; Sun 10.30–2.15) was founded by Alfonso VIII in 1187, at the request of his queen, Eleanor of England, after victory against the Moors at Navas de Tolosa. Its Sala Capitular still holds the tent-flap of the Moorish leaders, as well as the banner from the battle of Lepanto. The church served as mausoleum to the early kings of Castile. There is a museum of textiles containing important grave-goods. The monastery's Mudéjar remnants include the chapel of Santiago. Here, the moveable arm of St. James' image was used by Ferdinand III to dub himself a knight.

Cartuja de Miraflores The church (*Open* Mon–Sat 10.15–3, 4–6; Sun 11.20–12.30, 1–3, 4–6) contains a *retablo* by Gil de Siloé said to have been gilded with the first consignment of gold brought from the New World, and two of Spain's finest funerary monuments, both commissioned by Isabella la Catolica and carved by de Siloé. These are the tombs of her parents and her brother.

MONASTERIES FOR RETIREMENT

From an early date, the royal families of Spain's tiny Christian kingdoms were almost obsessed by the desire to live, at least during their later years, in pious monastic settings. They founded numerous monasteries and stayed in them during the peripatetic course of medieval rule. This tradition was carried on by the Habsburgs, Charles V at Yuste, Philip II at El Escorial, and even, to a lesser degree, by the Bourbons. Las Huelgas, a royal foundation at Burgos, is an earlier example.

▶▶ Carrión de los Condes   150C3

Lovely Carrión, in rolling wheat country between Burgos and León, has retained two pilgrims' churches with Romanesque carving: Santa María del Camino and the more elaborate Santiago, which has a fine frieze topping its west facade. The former monastery of San Zoilo to the west has admirable Renaissance cloisters.

▶ Cervera de Pisuerga   150C4

Though set on the bubbling Río Pisuerga, this is a disappointing village, except for the fortified church of Santa María del Castillo (with cloisters), which stands on a great rock in the village. The nearby parador has fine views into the mountains of the Reserva Nacional de Fuentes Carrión.

▶▶ Ciudad Rodrigo   150A1

A place above all for strolling and relaxing, Ciudad Rodrigo rises over the Río Agueda not far from Portugal. Walls dating from the 12th century still enclose the old town, and their whole circumference can be walked, offering fine country views and glimpses into streets still somewhat scarred from the Napoleonic Wars. The French held the town; the Duke of Wellington besieged and finally took it in 1812. He became Duke of Ciudad Rodrigo, a title still held by his descendants. The castle, once belonging to Enrique de Trastámara, is now an ivy-covered parador. As well as cannon-ball dents, the cathedral has fine choir stalls and an interesting rebuilt nave. Of the two palaces in the Plaza Mayor, the one from the 16th century is now a town hall. This square also sees the climax of wild bull-running festivities at Carnival time. A popular local bar is called El Sanatorio.

FAMILY HONOUR
The Infantes of Carrión married the daughters of El Cid and then behaved in a surprising manner. They beat them up and stripped them naked and left them in an oakwood—all this according to the epic poem of El Cid's deeds. The Cid caught up with the Infantes and unsurprisingly killed them. Their tombs are in the San Zoilo Monastery.

ANCIENT MONASTERIES
The kings of Navarra, León, and Castile supported the great Benedictine monastery at Cluny, in France, with tribute money paid in by the Moorish *taifa* kingdoms. They positively welcomed the French order, who soon established the Santiago pilgrimage on an international scale and built Romanesque monasteries along the route. The biggest, at Sahagún, is a ruin. The Cistercians who followed in the 12th century were even more prolific builders, their monasteries now Gothic in style.

159

Drive

Historic Castile
(see map on pages 150–151)
This varied drive is seen as a continuation of, or prelude to, the Extremadura drive on page 186.

Picking up the route at El Barco de Ávila, strike north. Divert 5km (3mi) left to scruffy, well-positioned **Béjar** (see page 156).

Return up N630 towards Salamanca.
Turn right for **Alba de Tormes**, with St. Teresa connections (see page 152).

Continue to Salamanca and then out towards Ávila on N501.

At Peñaranda de Bracamonte, you go north across the flat plain to visit **Madrigal de las Altas Torres** and **Medina del Campo** (see page 165).

Leave Medina on the Olmedo road. Head very briefly right on N403, following signs to Llano de Olmedo, Villeguillo, and then to **Coca** (see page 160).
Return via Santiuste for **Arévalo** and finally south for Ávila on the fast minor road.

Relaxing Ciudad Rodrigo

EL CID

The romanticized legend of El Cid (ca 1043–1099) as Christian hero of the Reconquest has reached posterity through a wonderful 12th-century epic poem. In reality, the Cid (Arabic for leader) was a minor aristocrat named Rodrigo Díaz de Vivar, who became an over-powerful military chieftain. Banished by his king, Alfonso VI, he took service with the Muslim ruler of Zaragoza, winning him great victories. He finally carved out a private territory for himself in Valencia.

The turrets and towers of Coca Castle are an extraordinary sight

►► Coca Castle   150C2

A castle of extraordinary elaboration, white and pink and set in pine woods roughly midway between Segovia and Valladolid, Coca (tel: 921 58 60 62; *Open* Mon–Fri 10.30–1.30, 4–5.30; Sat–Sun 11–1, 4–6; *Closed* 1st Tue every month) is a true phenomenon. It was constructed for an archbishop of the ecclesiastically powerful Fonseca family in the late 15th century and swarms with turrets like swallow nests, so numerous they seem at least partly ornamental. The castle has a deep, dry moat.

► Covarrubias   151D3

This well-preserved, not to say prettified, little township in the green Arlanza valley, is these days no stranger to tourism. With the tomb of Fernán González (see Burgos, page 156) in its Gothic collegiate church, it feels very close to the heart of Old Castile. The church has a rich museum and the tower of Fernán González still stands.

► Frías   151D4

With its castle tower alarmingly perched on a crag and houses hanging by their fingertips like those in Cuenca, Frías rises above the Ebro just west of the Sobrón *embalse* (reservoir). The village's 13th-century bridge springs from Roman foundations.

►► Frómista   150C3

Here, in a tiny town on the Pilgrims' Way to Santiago, one of the finest Romanesque buildings in all Spain was erected around 1066: the beautiful church of San Martín. Roof levels stack up from a triple apse (reflecting triple aisles) through transepts to the nave, their heavy tiles creating an almost Byzantine effect. Capitals are profusely carved; there are no fewer than 315 carved corbels and a mass of tightly controlled decoration. This was a popular stopping place for numerous pilgrims, who had the choice of four hospices in which to stay.

►► Gredos, Sierra de 150B1

The Gredos Mountains, some of Spain's loveliest, begin to rise at the western edge of the Comunidad de Madrid. Their lofty central section falls mostly into the province of Ávila and they run on westwards, becoming more and more remote, some would say more beautiful, right into Extremadura.

The range itself centres on the Pico de Almanzor (2,592m/8,503ft), the highest point of a north-facing cirque, or corrie, rising over a high lagoon. The peaks may all be seen from the upper terrace of the first-ever parador, personally sited by Alfonso XIII in 1928, a little way northeast of the cirque. This side of the range, though good for serious walking, is a little bleak and cold except in high summer. The Río Alberche flows laterally along it, then swings down round the Madrid end of the range.

The southern side, with the valley of the River Tiétar (see page 186) following it east to west, is far warmer, with crops such as tobacco and red peppers; the mountains rise above, sometimes to straight, sometimes to jagged crests. Summer settlements at the head of the Tiétar Valley dwindle away with distance from Madrid. Towns like **Arenas de San Pedro** (with the castle of Alvaro de Luna) and the village of **Guisando** above it have an interesting vernacular architecture of jutting upper storeys and wooden balconies. This reaches a climax farther down the valley in **Villanueva de la Vera** and especially **Valverde** (see page 186). As you cross the main pass above Arenas, the old Roman road is clearly visible and may be walked above Cuevas del Valle. There is an attractive 14th-century castle at Mombeltrán.

WALKING IN THE GREDOS MOUNTAINS
The high mountains are magnificent walking terrain, but difficult tracks require experience. Maps are in short supply and guides, like the useful *Andar por la Sierra de Gredos*, by Jorge Lobo, No. 30 in the Penthalon *Aire Libre* series, tend to be in Spanish only. Mountain refuges are fairly plentiful. Many fine walks can be made upwards from the Tiétar valley, from spots close into the sierra like Casillas in the east and from Guijo de Santa Barbara above Jarandilla in the west.

161

Walk

Walk in increasingly lovely country, with pine, oak, and chestnut trees, and mountains rising above.

A taste of the Gredos Mountains

This is an undemanding stroll (though with some gradients), which can be combined with a trip to San Martín de Valdeiglesias and the Toros de Guisando (see page 202).

To reach the start, take the road north from San Martín for Ávila and at the point of entry to El Tiemblo, turn left up an unpromising-looking asphalt road, which later turns into a good dirt road. Ascend some 10km (6mi) and park where the road doubles back over the bridge, or go a little higher straight up.

In Arenas de San Pedro

The south facade of León's Gothic cathedral, pierced by one of the three great rose windows of stained glass

162

MINING IN ROMAN TIMES
When the Romans came to Spain, the peninsula was still rich in gold, silver, and other valuable minerals. The Romans mined prodigiously, nowhere more so than at Las Médulas, in the wild Bierzo mountains of León. They used a combination of slave labour and water to wash away whole mountain sides, creating an enormous, empty amphitheatre riddled with red rock spires left unaccountably standing. Galleries the size of cathedral naves disappear into the hills; tunnel mouths gape darkly in the middle of cliff faces.

Opposite: the impressive 13th-century Hostal de San Marcos in León

▶▶▶ **León**   *150B4*

Capital of a province of plain and mountain, and with a full-ranking university, León has a strongly individual character. The city's huge importance in early Spanish history has left it with three of Spain's most remarkable monuments: the Romanesque royal pantheon of San Isidoro, a great Gothic cathedral, and the pilgrimage hospital of San Marcos, now a parador.

History León was founded by the Romans; its name derives from "Septima Legion." Occupied by the Visigoths and then rather briefly by the Moors, it became chief city of the Christian advance across the Cantabrian mountains into the wide frontier zone of the northern *meseta*. In 998, Almanzor, on a raid from Córdoba, destroyed the city utterly, pulling down the Roman walls. But the Christians

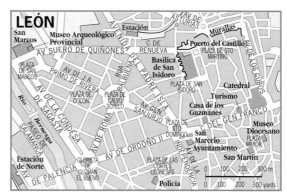

soon rebuilt it, and in the following century Ferdinand I of emergent Castile combined the two young kingdoms by marrying Sancha of León. With the influx of Santiago pilgrims, French influence was now not only pouring in but was also welcome. The cathedral of León was built almost entirely in French style during the 13th century. Meanwhile, the vast and monumental hostel of San Marcos was assembled by the Knights of Santiago. Later, when the tide of history brought Castile to the fore, León disappeared from prominence to reemerge in the present generation.

City exploration The city is small enough to explore on foot. Its main contemporary focus is the Plaza de Santo Domingo and adjacent Plaza San Marcelo, with the patioed Renaissance Casa de los Guzmanes, now the Diputación, on the site where Guzman el Bueno was born. Opposite is the Savings Bank headquarters, built by Gaudí in something close to Scottish baronial style (see also **Astorga**, page 153). From here the pilgrim route led along La Rua, now a shopping street. Following it, then bearing left, leads you to the pleasing if dilapidated Plaza Mayor with the old town hall, the bar-district or Barrio Húmedo, and substantial 14th-century city walls.

The cathedral The cathedral of Santa María de la Regla (tel: 987 87 57 70; *Open* Mon–Sat 8.30–1.30, 4–7. *Admission free*) is a magnificent example of early Gothic architecture.

Begun in 1205, its two unmatched but evocative spires rise above a great rose window. The richly carved triple doorway beneath, though widely praised for its scenes from the lives of Christ and the Virgin and for its Final Judgment, is not as well preserved as some elsewhere (see **Huesca**, for example, page 102), while the statue of the Virgen Blanca (White Virgin) at the heart is a substitute for the real thing, now sheltered in a chapel behind the altar. The transcendent glory of the cathedral, however, is its glass; light floods through in gorgeous blues, reds, purple, and a seemingly omnipresent golden yellow. Different colours dominate at different times of day and the light inside the cathedral when the cloud gives way outdoors to sunlight is magnificient.

The walls themselves were kept minimal so as to provide maximum window space, 1,800sq m (19,375sq ft)

JUAN DE JUNI

The French sculptor Juan de Juni, influential on his Castilian successors, first made an appearance in about 1533 in León, where his *retablo* of the Virgin and St. John in the church of Santa Marina was much admired. By 1541 he had made his way to Valladolid, which then embarked on the great tradition of sculpture so well displayed in its Museo Nacional de Escultura. He is buried in the convent of Santa Catalina.

The glowing interior of León cathedral is notable for the beautiful light produced by its unique collection of stained-glass windows—there are over 700 panes in all

THE WOOL TRADE
Wool was the life blood of Castile and sheep fairs or markets were central to the organization of stock rearing. The greatest fair of all was held at Medina del Campo (see opposite). Mass was conducted from a balcony in the flank of the collegiate church of San Antolín in the Plaza Mayor, and only then could dealing begin. The burning of much of Medina by the troops of Charles V greatly embittered the Comuneros, or Commons, who were as interested as the next man in maintaining income from wool. It was during Charles V's reign (1516–1556) that the wool trade began its slide to ruin.

of glass in 125 window openings, mainly dating from the 12th to 16th centuries. There is a two-tiered choir with retrochoir by Juan de Badajoz. The cathedral museum (tel: 987 87 57 70; *Open* Mon–Sat 9.30–1.30, 4–7; Sat mornings only in winter. *Admission charge*) is in the 14th-century cloister.

Panteón (royal mausoleum) and San Isidoro Virtually part of the city walls, León's Basílica de San Isidoro (tel: 987 87 61 61; *Open* Mon–Sat 10–1.30, 4–6.30; Sun 10–1.30; extended hours Jul–Aug. *Admission charge*) was reconstructed late in the 11th century to house the relics of St. Isidore, the great early Christian polymath of Seville, whose bones had been negotiated away from the Moors. The building which it replaced had as its porch (now at lower level and reached by a separate entrance) a crypt-like space, which still survives. Until disturbed by the French in the Napoleonic Wars, it was the resting place of 23 kings and queens and 12 royal children. Its vaults are supported by columns with massive capitals carved with mainly Visigothic motifs. Some smaller capitals, one showing the raising of Lazarus, are among Spain's earliest Romanesque sculpture. Even more extraordinary are the frescoes which cover the vaults, painted about a century later. Massively imposing, they spread over all surfaces, their designs adapted to ceiling shape, and show the Last Supper, scenes from the Passion, and many from the Bible and Apocrypha. The depiction of country pursuits, in the Annunciation and in a country calendar made up of round medallions, is especially touching. The guided tour includes the treasury upstairs.

San Marcos Inevitably one is struck first by the facade of the Monasterio de San Marcos: a majestic 100m (328ft) stretch, in a double-decker arrangement, composed of windows, columns, niches, and medallions. Above the main door rides a fantastical Santiago Matamoros (St. James the Moorslayer), while above him a decorative gable protrudes high above the skyline with imperial arms and a statue of Fame. Behind the main entrance a grand stone stairway, now part of the parador, ascends, with many hotel rooms in the old part of the building. There is a fine Renaissance cloister, which gives access to the **provincial museum** (tel: 987 24 50 61; *Open* Tue–Sat 10–2, 4.30–8; Sun 10–2. *Admission charge*). This houses a miniature masterpiece, the Carrizo ivory, a small and affecting 11th-century Crucifixion. The church on the right, heavily decorated with pilgrim shells, is unfinished but contains a finely carved, raised choir (ask at the hotel if it is closed). The whole building, one of Spain's finest, has survived many vicissitudes and, at one point, proposed demolition.

▶ Lerma   *151D3*

The Duke of Lerma (1550–1625), favourite of King Philip III, built himself a monstrously ungainly palace here at the top of the town from which he took his title, and a modest accumulation of churches, convents, and cobbled streets. The town is entered through a fortified gateway and remnants of the old town walls can still be seen.

▶ Logroño   *151E3*

Modern Logroño, capital of La Rioja, is set around the Espolón, a one-block city park distinguished only by a statue of General Espartero, a local hero and 19th-century military dictator. Pilgrims to Santiago, crossing the Ebro here, filed along La Rua, now one block in behind the river. The large church of Santiago is also along here, with St. James' horse prominent on the southern facade. If you take the pleasantly arcaded Calle Portales past the cathedral, instead, you will soon pass General Espartero's stout stone mansion, now the **provincial museum** (tel: 941 29 12 59; *Open* Tue–Sat 10–2, 4–9; Sun 11.30–2. *Admission free*).

▶▶ Medinaceli   *151E2*

From its height, Medinaceli controlled the crossing of the southern route out of Soria and the east–west route between Zaragoza and the old cities round modern Madrid. The Romans built a fine triumphal arch, still standing though with worn inscriptions. Almanzor, Moorish scourge of Christians, died here in 1002. It is a lovely place, all stone, with walls and castle remnants, ivy and huge trees in monumental settings. The mansion of the Dukes of Medinaceli stands on the Plaza Mayor.

▶ Medina del Campo   *150B2*

Medina's Plaza Mayor was the site of the medieval wool trade fairs which were the centre of the Castilian economy. Queen Isabella died in the fine house over the arch in the corner of the same side (beside the gabled *ayuntamiento*). The pink **Castillo de la Mota** (*Open* Mon–Sat 11–2, 4–6 (7 in summer), Sun 11–2. *Admission charge*), across the main road, is one of Spain's grandest castles.

WINE CELLARS
Haro, capital of the Rioja Alta, is preeminent as a wine town, with the bodegas of houses as famous as CUNE (also written CVNE, the Compañía Vinícola del Norte de España), Federico Paternina, and the Bodegas Bilbaínas. Several are open for visits.

If wine seems like a serious business in Haro you'd get the opposite impression on 29 June, when the town holds its annual Batalla del Vino (Wine Battle). For two hours thousands of people pour, squirt, spray, and throw red wine at each other. The commonest weapon is a leather drinking bottle, but almost anything goes, and serious combatants use tree-spraying equipment to deliver their liquid ammunition. It is traditional to wear white clothes for the battle and these are quickly and permanently stained a light purple.

Passing the time of day in Medina del Campo. In medieval times, the Plaza Mayor was the scene of regular wool trade fairs; today it is a busy agricultural centre

At an altitude of 1,379m (4,524ft), the pass between León and Asturias is one of the most scenic routes in the region

▶ **Medina de Rioseco**   *150B3*

The stately churches of this rather decrepit town, north of Valladolid, testify to former wool wealth. Gothic Santa María stands under a baroque tower; the church of Santiago has a fine Churriguera *retablo*.

▶▶ **Nájera**   *151D3*

Nájera is on the Pilgrims' Way in La Rioja. In the monastery church of Santa María la Real (tel: 941 36 36 50; *Open* summer, Tue–Sat 9.30–1.30, 4–7, Sun 4–6.30; winter, Tue–Sat 10–1, 4–5.30, Sun 10–12.30, 4–5.30. *Admission charge*), are the tombs of kings and queens of Castile, León, and Navarra.

▶ **Olmedo**   *150C2*

This former strong-point on the plain retains an impressive quantity of its town walls and gates. The Casa Consistorial and adjoining church of San Julián have been restored to make a pleasing complex.

▶ **Oña**   *151D4*

Oña, on a bend in the gorge of the Río Oca, is the burial place of the descendants of Fernán González. It has an abbey, a lovely Plaza Mayor, and Roman bridge.

▶ **Pajares, Puerto de**   *150B4*

This pass from León into Asturias is one of the steepest points of interchange between the high *meseta* and the north coast's verdant strip. Valgrande has a ski station.

▶▶ **Palencia**   *150C3*

Palencia, on the Río Carrión is set around its beautiful late Gothic **cathedral** (tel: 979 70 13 47; *Open* Mon–Sat 10.30–1.30, 4.30–6.30, Sun 11.15–1.30. *Admission charge*). In the handsome *retablo* of the Capilla Mayor, the Renaissance statuary of Felipe de Vigarny combines with painted panels by Juan de Flandes and Juan de Valmaseda. Beneath is a crypt with Visigothic columns and arches. The cathedral museum has Flemish tapestries and a much-prized *San Sebastián* by El Greco. **San Miguel** church is said locally to have been the marriage place of El Cid and Jimena.

▶ **Pancorvo, Desfiladero de**   *151D3*

Just east of the village of Pancorvo, the N1 highway and the railway make their way through an impressive ravine, staked out with a Moorish castle.

▶ **Pedraza de la Sierra**   *150C2*

This pretty walled town lies north of the Sierra de Guadarrama. It is arranged around what could be a model Spanish town square, which is formed by the town hall (marked by its clock), church, noble mansions, and porticoes providing shade for stalls and shops. Many of its houses have been restored, a service originally performed for the castle by the Basque painter Ignacio Zuloaga. Pedraza's two hotels are popular haunts for weekenders escaping Madrid. The town is also an archetypal Sunday lunch spot, full of restaurants boasting an *horno de asar*: a Castilian wood-fired oven for roasting meat.

▶▶ **Peñafiel**   *150C2*

On the banks of the Río Duratón, this small town has one of the most astonishing castles (*Open* Tue–Fri 11.30–2.30, 4.30–7.30; Sat–Sun 11.30–2.30, 4.30–8.30. *Admission charge*) in the whole Duero region (14th to 15th centuries). From below, it appears like a battleship riding the crest above the town. From inside, the keep feels like the ship's bridge and the walls are genuinely ship-shaped.

▶ **Peñaranda de Duero**   *151D2*

Hardly a mouse stirs in Peñaranda, a little Duero town suffering serious agricultural decline. But a castle and city walls survive in parts and the collegiate church stares across the Plaza Mayor at the palace of the dukes of Avellaneda.

▶ **Ponferrada**   *150A4*

Ponferrada, industrial town with important monuments including a 12th-century Templar castle and elaborate 17th-century *ayuntamiento*, lies at the end of a rewarding stretch of the Pilgrims' Way, running south from Astorga through beautiful country. On approaching Ponferrada from the west, take the side turn for the 10th-century Mozarabic **Santo Tomás de las Ollas** (*Open* Tue–Sat 10–2, 5–8, Sun 10–2), which has nine horseshoe arches in its apse and good views en route of Ponferrada on its mountain-ringed plain, complete with coal tip. In the town itself, the crenellated Templar castle guards the crossing of the River Sil.

▶ **Puebla de Sanabria**   *150A3*

Modest but beautiful medieval houses in this little hilltop town lead upwards to a Romanesque church and 15th-century castle. The town is the main point of access to a large lake/reservoir; extremely popular in summer.

▶ **Quintanilla de las Viñas**   *151D3*

The main attraction of Quintanilla is the remarkable Visigothic church (*Open* summer, Wed–Sun 9.30–2, 5–7; winter, 10–5; *Closed* last weekend of every month. *Admission charge*) close to the village, with its strange and unexplained carvings.

CENTRE FOR SCULPTURE
The great art of Castile is sculpture. Santo Domingo de Silos is the epicentre of Romanesque; Burgos has tremendous work from the time of the Catholic Monarchs. Valladolid came into its own in the 16th century with Juan de Juni and, above all, the emotional work of Alonso Berruguete, his subjects always in passionate movement. After Berruguete comes the great if sometimes excessive Gregorio Fernández. The work of both men can be seen in churches and cathedrals and in the Museo Nacional de Escultura in Valladolid.

167

The castle at Pedraza de la Sierra, perched on a hilltop, retains a medieval feel. This is much-loved by Spanish families as a spot for Sunday lunch al fresco

The face of Europe changed in the 9th century when the Catholic Church let it be known that the tomb of St. James the Apostle had been discovered in Santiago de Compostela, in far Galicia, in the northwest corner of Spain.

THE ANCIENT PILGRIMS

The pilgrims wore wide hats to keep off the sun and rain, and carried a leather pouch or scrip and a stout stave. When they arrived at Santiago they would buy a scallop and stick the shell in their hats as proof that they had made the journey. The scallop shell has become the symbol of the pilgrimage.

The story told how the saint had come to Spain on a long ministry after the death of Christ. Returning to Jerusalem, he was beheaded by Herod. When burial was refused, angels conveyed his body by boat to Padrón in Galicia and took it onto the place we now call Santiago de Compostela. The hermit who found St. James (Santiago) was guided by a star, to a "field of stars," in Latin *campus stellae*, whence the name Compostela. Or possibly the name might come from *compostum*, a Roman burial place, for there was in fact a tomb and it seems to have been Roman.

Theodemir, the local bishop, authenticated the remains as those of St. James and the claim was accepted by the King of Asturias. The presence of the holy corpse began to exercise a mesmeric fascination in Europe.

Journeying for salvation Pilgrimages had been important in the ancient world. Among Christians, the greatest was originally to Jerusalem. Now Santiago became another sacred goal, possibly along the route of a far more ancient and magical pilgrimage to the "world's end" at Fisterra on the Galician coast west of Santiago. When the Holy Sepulchre in Jerusalem fell to Islam in 1078, making travel there impossible, Santiago became the European Pilgrims' Way *par excellence*.

Most of the earliest pilgrims were French and the main route was often called the Camino Francés, the French Way. Later pilgrims came from all over Europe. The enterprise was difficult and dangerous and the pilgrims travelled in large groups.

Upon arrival at Santiago, they spent at least a night in prayer and song and gained remission of their sins according to a complicated sliding scale. All social classes were represented; some were criminals or murderers, seeking redemption; some were making the pilgrimage in proxy for wealthy folk at home. They flowed in an incessant stream from the 9th to the 16th centuries and now, once again, in modern times.

How they came The main routes out of France, spelled out in the world's first guidebook (*Liber Sancti Jacobi*), written by the French monk Aimeric Picaud in the 12th century, led across the Pyrenees, either by the Somport pass and down to Jaca, or across the more westerly pass at Roncesvalles and so down to Pamplona. The routes met at Puente la Reina and flowed across northern Spain in a broad stripe, finally crossing the Bierzo Mountains into Galicia and so on to Santiago. There was a north coast route as well; and Christian pilgrims from Muslim

Spain used the old Vía de la Plata, the Roman route through Mérida, Salamanca, and Zamora.

Hopes of a Christian reconquest of the Iberian peninsula were matched by a new story: that St. James in person had helped the Christians to victory in the (apparently mythical) battle of Clavijo in 844. By the 11th century, when reconquest first began to seem a real possibility, St. James the Pilgrim had become St. James the Moorslayer (Santiago Matamoros), riding triumphantly over his victims on a thousand church facades in Christian Spain.

Pilgrims' Way architecture From the early days, the pilgrimage brought its own architecture. The monks of Cluny in France were heavily involved, subsidized by the Spanish kingdoms. Churches of much greater size were now built (as were some very pretty small ones), using the normal Romanesque round arch. The large ones had galleries along the nave and transepts, to handle the great numbers of pilgrims. Best of all was the sculpture, simultaneously assured and innocent. Indeed the architectural delights of the Camino de Santiago are one of the main reasons for a modern pilgrimage.

MODERN DAY PILGRIMS
Following in the footsteps of earlier pilgrims who were treading these paths in the 11th and 12th centuries, are modern-day international pilgrims who continue to be drawn into taking the road to Santiago. Those completing the journey on foot, or by other allowable means, including cycling or on horseback, may be entitled to receive a certificate known as "La Compostela," provided certain basic requirements are fulfilled (such as having the *carnet del peregrino* regularly stamped at churches or pilgrim refuges as evidence of genuine itinerary).

The rich baroque west facade of Santiago de Compostela cathedral, traditional entrance for pilgrims arriving in the city

The town hall presides over Salamanca's Plaza Mayor, one of the largest and most harmoniously arranged public squares in Spain

►►► Salamanca   150B2

Up from the Roman bridge across the Río Tormes, down from the Plaza Mayor to the twin cathedrals and the university, a magnificent display in golden stone, Salamanca is one of Europe's greatest and most agreeable cities. If almost a third of it had not been blown apart during the Napoleonic Wars (thus producing a district long called Los Caídos or the Fallen Ones), the accumulation of splendour might have been overwhelming.

Though lively with young people, the atmosphere is rather different from that of Spain's other major university cities. For here there is not just a meeting between youth and a respectably inclined provincial city society. Salamanca is also unmistakably part of a province that is still strongly agricultural. The local economy is based on cattle breeding, with large landholdings, traditional if rather battered villages, and the complement of gypsies that is usually associated with stock-rearing in Spain.

History Salamanca is also a very ancient place. Captured by Hannibal in 217 BC, it retained its importance under Rome and the Visigoths. The Moors took it in the 8th century, and during the early centuries of the Reconquista, it fell into the vast no man's land south of the Duero and was twice sacked by Almanzor.

Like Ávila, it was walled and repopulated by Count Raymond of Burgundy late in the 11th century, and in 1218, Alfonso IX of Castile founded the university. It was from here that Arabic science and learning was shared with Europe. Establishing the international reputation of Salamanca, the university competed with those of

Oxford, Paris, and Bologna until the 17th century. It was supported to wonderful architectural effect by the Catholic Monarchs, Ferdinand and Isabella. They also provided funds for a great Gothic cathedral that was simply pinned on to the side of the existing Romanesque structure. By now the city had also acquired a huge array of churches, convents, palaces, and towers.

During the Napoleonic Wars, Salamanca was occupied by the French. Wellington defeated them nearby at Arapiles (the Battle of Salamanca in English), but promptly retreated, leaving the city to be sacked. General Franco used it as his headquarters during the early part of the Civil War, removing to Burgos after an assassination attempt. Today the city is busy and active, with its university forever longing to regain the leading place which it lost over the centuries to Madrid and Barcelona.

Finding your way It is possible to walk all of central Salamanca. Starting at the Plaza Mayor, down the old main street or Rua Mayor, go off right to the university, passing several notable Gothic and Renaissance buildings on the way. Alternatively, carrying straight on down the Rua Mayor, you will soon reach the city's twin cathedrals and then, by walking a little eastwards, rather uphill and down, a series of outstanding churches and convents. Each of these routes is discussed below, beginning with the Plaza Mayor.

Plaza Mayor Salamanca's beautiful main square (built in the second quarter of the 18th century) is the hub of the city, spiritually, practically, and for recreation, the place where everybody meets for a drink and a chat, where cattlemen still make deals, and where civil and religious celebrations are focused. Three members of the Churriguera family were involved, proving that not all their works involved the wild excess associated with their name. Andrés García de Quiñones designed the *ayuntamiento* (town hall). These names can go down in a special hall of fame, since this is undoubtedly Spain's most admired Plaza Mayor. Three residential storeys rise serenely, with small wrought-iron balconies, shutters, and the most regular of windows, above an arcaded ground floor with shops and cafés; the grander and more florid *ayuntamiento* is on the north side, topped by clock

THE SILVER ROUTE
The Roman road that led from Sevilla to Mérida and all the way north to Gijón is traditionally known as the Vía de la Plata, and is vigorously promoted by tourist offices along the route for its association with silver. Alas, the reason for the name is quite unclear, though it could be something perfectly simple like the way the old road shone in moonlight.

MARÍA LA BRAVA
During the 15th century, Salamanca was the scene of bitter family feuding, heightened by the tragic event of 1465, when two brothers of the Enrique family were killed by the Manzano brothers during an argument at a game of *pelota*. The wronged mother, afterwards known as María la Brava, took swift vengeance by tracking down the assassins in Portugal, killing them, and throwing their heads onto her sons' tombs, in the church of Santo Tomé. The city became divided into two enemy groups, taking on the name of the parishes of either Santo Tomé or San Benito.

171

Children in Salamanca in traditional dress. Local folk costumes can be seen in the city's annual fiesta in June

"V" FOR VICTOR
When you earned your doctorate in Salamanca you were allowed to daub your initials, entwined with a "V" for "Victor," in red paint on almost any suitable wall. The courtyard of the Palacio de Anaya is full of them. During the Civil War, Franco appropriated the symbol for the Nationalist cause.

and belfry. Medallions of heroes and would-be heroes are carved in the structure, including General Franco.

Off the main street Start down the Rua Mayor, then turn right at the **Casa de las Conchas** (House of the Shells. *Open* Mon–Fri 9–9; Sat 9–2, 4–7; Sun 10–2, 4–7. *Admission free*). This mansion of the late 15th and early 16th centuries was entirely encrusted with the stone scallop shells symbolic of the pilgrimage to Santiago by its owner, a knight of Santiago. It has very fine Gothic wrought iron, the shield of the Catholic Monarchs at the top of the facade, and a notable Plateresque stairway. The next building of note is the twin-spired, baroque **Clerecía**, a church built for the Jesuits starting in 1617. From here it is a short step south to the university.

The University To visit the university (tel: 923 29 44 00; *Open* Mon–Sat 9.30–1, 4–7; Sun 10–1. *Admission charge, free Mon mornings*), start in the Patio de Escuelas, which contains a statue of Fray Luis de León, mystic and university teacher, standing before the main university **facade**, a Plateresque (see page 35) front to the slightly earlier cloister of the old university (or Escuelas Mayores) within. This facade, with a medallion of the Catholic Monarchs, a portrait of the pope, statues of Hercules and Venus, and any quantity of heraldry and elaborate shallow carving, is arguably the finest in Spain.

Scholarly argument suggests it is intended as a humanistic dialogue on the nature of Sacred and Profane love, the former winning out, of course, along with Learning and the Monarchy. It also includes a skull with a frog on top of it, a symbolic coupling of death and sexual sin ominous for the young scholar. Important rooms give off the cloister within, including chapel and *paraninfo*, the main formal hall of the old university.

It was here, at the start of the Civil War, that university rector and philosopher Miguel de Unamuno became involved in a confrontation with Franco's General Millán Astray, who finally shouted "Death to intellectuals. Long live death!" Unamuno retired to his home, notionally disgraced, to die there shortly afterwards. Next door is the lecture room used by Luis de León and with its original furniture. From here he was taken to imprisonment by the Inquisition, returning five years later with the phrase "As we were saying yesterday…."

These words were invoked again by Unamuno in the 1920s after a period of internal exile under the dictator Primo de Rivera. A beautifully carved staircase leads to the first floor, still containing the university's once world-famous library.

On the far side of the Patio de Escuelas is the cloister of the **Escuelas Menores**, with thrilling mixtilinear arches. Another doorway leads into a room which now contains the **Salamanca Sky**, a considerable portion of the original library ceiling that was moved here for safe keeping when the original ceiling began to crumble.

This strange painting, depicting the serpent Hydra and astrological signs, shows that the university, visited by Columbus, placed as much faith in astrology as it did in astronomy.

Salamanca's twin cathedrals The **Catedral Nueva** (New Cathedral) on the cathedral square (*Open* daily 10–1, 4–6. *Admission free*) is a festive concourse of pinnacles and domes. Juan Gil de Hontañon worked here as well as at Segovia. Within, there is late Gothic vaulting and the regulation chapels, but fewer artworks than expected. The best moments are external: the whole north side and skyline and the west facade, grandly Plateresque, with relief carvings of scenes from the life of Christ. Crossing the interior of the New Cathedral, you step through a common wall into the **Catedral Vieja**, the massive Old (12th-century) Cathedral (*Open* daily 10–12.30, 4–5.30; closed Nov–Feb on Sun. *Admission charge*), with cloisters, frescoes, and a magnificent *retablo* from the 15th century. Again the finest feature is external: the strangely fish-scaled, elongated pyramid of the Torre de Gallo, which recalls the domed roofs of Toro, Zamora, and Plasencia.

On from the cathedral The imposing **Palacio de Anaya**, opposite on the right as you leave the New Cathedral, belongs to the university.

It is worth descending eastwards to the **Convento de las Dueñas**, or Dominicans (tel: 923 21 54 42; *Open* summer, daily 10.30–1, 4.30–6; winter 4.30–5.30, Sun 10.30–1. *Admission charge*). The convent has a strange cloister, architecturally harmonious but incorporating in its capitals and other ornamentation a ghastly accumulation of portraits of death, dismemberment, and agony, human, animal, and fantastical. The nuns also sell sweetmeats.

Shortly after comes the Dominican church of **San Esteban** (16th century, with cloister and a magnificent 17th-century western facade showing the stoning of San Esteban). Like the facades of the University and New Cathedral, this is best seen in evening light. The cloister contains prophets' heads in medallions, together with a staircase by Rodrigo Gil de Hontañon. This leads to the choir gallery, which features a richly gilded altarpiece by José Churriguera.

Past San Esteban to the left, you will come to the small but pleasing Romanesque church of **Santo Tomás Cantuarensis**, the first in Europe to be dedicated to the martyr of Canterbury in England.

BULL-BREEDING COUNTRY
Salamanca province is bull-breeding country *par excellence*. You will see many of the wild black cattle grazing under the holm-oaks and cork oaks in the occasionally park-like countryside. The ranches, called *fincas*, are often very large. Their entrances are marked by stone pillars which sometimes bear the brand-mark of the *finca*. The homesteads frequently have both a chapel and a small bullring where the activity of the animals, especially the females, is studied as an aid to breeding. This is where young *toreros* first learn their skills.

173

The dramatic outlines of Salamanca's twin cathedrals, across the Río Tormes, rise together in harmony. The pair combine the solid lines of the Spanish Romanesque style of the Catedral Vieja (Old Cathedral) with the Catedral Nueva (New Cathedral); Gothic with Plateresque and baroque elements

The monastery of Santo Domingo de Silos

174

BIRTH OF CASTILIAN
The first syntactically complete Castilian sentences known to scholars are in the margin of a Latin manuscript from San Millán. They are like a photograph of the language at the moment of its birth. The first known Castilian poet, Gonzalo de Berceo, was a monk at San Millán. Fragments of Basque are recorded here in association with early Castilian, showing the debt of the new language to the older.

THE LEGEND OF THE COCKEREL
A maid at the inn in Santo Domingo de la Calzada fell in love with a German pilgrim. When he rejected her, she planted the hotel silver in his knapsack and told the authorities. He was arrested and hanged. On their return from Santiago, his parents found him still alive on the gibbet and interrupted the judge's dinner with the news. "If it's true," he scoffed, "this cockerel on my dish will crow." It did, and the young man was rescued. A cock and hen have been kept in the cathedral ever since.

►► San Millán de la Cogolla　　151D3

The hermitage of San Millán (6th-century Riojan ascetic) is reached through halcyon country with mountain views, above the little town. The church is split into two naves by a row of Romanesque and Mozarabic arches. In one of two burial caves hollowed in the rock lies a green jade statue of the saint. The church is called San Millán de Suso (San Millán of Up Above. *Closed for restoration*). Later the community moved down into the valley, founding a larger monastery, San Millán de Yuso (tel: 941 37 30 49; *Open* Tue–Sun 10.30–1, 4–6).

► Santa María de Huerta　　151E2

This dominating monastery, just over the Castile-Aragón border, has a vaulted 13th-century refectory, 15th- to 16th-century cloister, and florid 18th-century church.

►► Santo Domingo de la Calzada　　151D3

It was the lifelong work of St. Dominic (Santo Domingo) to build a pilgrims' *calzada* (causeway) here. An engineering saint, he also built bridges and a pilgrim hospital, now a luxurious parador. The 12th- to 13th-century cathedral of this agricultural town is celebrated for its cock and hen (see panel). It also houses the saint's shrine-tomb and a fine Damián Forment *retablo*.

►► Santo Domingo de Silos　　151D3

Not to be confused with Santo Domingo de la Calzada (see above) or the local Santo Domingo (St. Dominic de Guzman) who founded the Dominican Order, the 11th-century saint of Silos rebuilt a monastery sacked by Almanzor. The monastery (*Open* Tue–Sat 10–1, 4.30–6, Mon–Sun 4.30–6. *Admission charge*) lies in mountain country south of Burgos. The cloister is delightful; the carved capitals (possibly incorporating Moorish workmanship) constitute one of Europe's finest assemblages of Romanesque sculpture. The corner reliefs give a moving account of Christ's life and resurrection. The monastery, though dissolved in the 19th century, is once again a religious community; visitors are welcome at services, made internationally famous through the monks' recording of Gregorian plainsong.

SEGOVIA

Iglesia de
la Vera Cruz
Capilla de
San Blas
Monasterio
de El Parral
PASEO DE LA ALAMEDA
Eresma
Río
Antigua Casa
de la Moneda
Convento de
Santa Cruz
PASEO DE SANTO DOMINGO DE GUZMÁN
CARDENAL ZÚÑIGA
SAN MARCOS
CERRO DE LAS NIEVES
VELASCO PASEO
VALLEJO
Alcázar
VELARDE
DAOÍZ
PLAZA DEL ALCÁZAR
PASEO DE JUAN II
San
Esteban
SAN NICOLÁS
Iglesia de
S Nicolás
PLAZA
SAN NICOLÁS
DEL OBISPO
Casa del
Marqués
del Arco
PLAZA SAN
ESTEBAN
La
Trinidad
S QUIRCE
DR LAGUNA
SAN AGUSTÍN
San Juan de
los Caballeros
(Museo Zuloaga)
MARQUÉS DEL ARCO
PLAZA DE
LA MERCED
Ayuntamiento
PLAZA
MAYOR
LECEA SERAFÍN
COLÓN
Museo
Provincial de
Bellas Artes
PLAZA
DEL CONDE
DE CHESTE
Arroyo
SOCORRO
SAN GEROTEO
i
Catedral
Corpus
Christi
San
Martín
San Sebastián
Torreón de
los Lozoya
VÍA DE ROMA
Clamores
CUESTA DE LOS HOYOS
SAN VALENTÍN
Casa de
Juan Bravo
JUAN BRAVO
PASEO DEL SALÓN
PLAZA
DEL
AZOGUEJO
Acueducto
Romano
El Pinarillo
Casa de
los Picos
San Millán

0   100   200 m
0   100   200 yards

▶▶▶ Segovia   150C2

Gracefully ornamental in appearance, even a little frilly,
Segovia is considered fun where nearby Ávila is
thought to be stern. The look of its architecture seems to
carry over into its engaging present-day ambience.
Segovia's best-known monuments are its lofty and
intriguing Roman aqueduct, one of Spain's main icons,
the almost equally famous ship-shaped medieval *alcázar*,
which was remodelled in 19th-century Gothic fantasy,
and the pinnacled 16th-century cathedral which towers,
more lovingly than threateningly, above the town.
Segovia also offers a fistful of good Romanesque
churches, a smaller number of palatial mansions, one of
Spain's best "military" churches (Vera Cruz, which
legend says was founded by the Knights Templar), and
the bad-taste resting place of St. John of the Cross nearby.
There are many good restaurants; most visitors being day
trippers. Segovia nevertheless makes an excellent base for
touring in Castile and the Guadarrama mountains.

History Roman, Visigothic, Moorish in its time, the town
was refortified—like Ávila—by a triumphant Alfonso VI
in the late 11th century. Most of the walls and three of the
five gates survive. It was a well-liked stopping place for
the Trastámara kings of Castile and it was here that
Isabella was proclaimed Queen in 1474. Its greatest
wealth came with the Mesta (see panel page 176) and the
wool boom of the 15th and early 16th centuries. After this,
like the rest of Castile, Segovia entered a steep decline.
Nowadays, a sense of liveliness has returned.

The Roman aqueduct brought water from 15km (9mi)
south, reaching a height of 28m (92ft) on a double tier of
granite arches, which were built with amazing exactitude
(and pincer-holes for the lifting of each block). The last
stretch is now well within the city confines, in the Plaza de
Azoguejo. Not far away from it, down a broad shopping
street, is the large and attractive Romanesque church of
San Millán, built in the early 12th century, with external
galleries and carved capitals.

THE PALACE OF
LA GRANJA

The summer palace of the
Bourbon dynasty at La
Granja de San Ildefonso
lies 11km (7mi) south of
Segovia. The interior, now
housing one of Spain's
leading tapestry
collections, was restored
after a fire in 1918. The
gardens combine the
formality of Versailles with
a mountain setting and
magnificently monumental
fountains, which are
turned on at 6PM in spring
and summer "when there
is water." In the attractive
little town, the 18th-
century Royal Glass
Works, which once
produced the great mirrors
and windows of the
Spanish royal palaces,
has been reopened as
Spain's National Museum
of Glass.

175

Segovia's spectacularly positioned Alcázar was rebuilt in the 19th century after a fire

THE MESTA
The Honourable Council of the Mesta, established by Alfonso X in 1273, was the immensely powerful association of sheep-owners who held sway in much of medieval Castile and other parts of Spain. It controlled the drovers' roads or *cañadas* along which the enormous merino flocks were moved with each change of season. The Mesta helped keep Spain a ranching country which preferred stock-rearing to cultivation. There was a law that any land where once the flocks had grazed remained Mesta territory.

The Alcázar With slated turrets that might have been an inspiration to Gaudí, this old Castilian fortress (*Open* May–Sep, daily 10–7; Oct–Apr, 10–6. *Admission charge*) stands on the farthest westward point of the hilltop site. Inside, there is a surfeit of suits of armour, splendid 15th-century Mudéjar ceilings (Rooms 3 and 5), and great views out through modern plate-glass windows; a thoughtful safety precaution since at least one royal prince has fallen to his death here.

The cathedral Right on top of the hill stands the huge sandy-golden cathedral (*Open* Jun–Sep, daily 9–6.30; Oct–May, 9.30–5; *Closed* Sun mornings. *Admission charge*), last of Spain's Gothic constructions, and one of its finest, at least from outside, with pinnacled apse and added Renaissance domes. It is mostly the work of father and son architects, Juan Gil and Rodrigo Gil de Hontañon, fresh from their triumph in Salamanca. A museum off the cloister displays church treasures, pictures, and tapestries.

Further exploration From the adjoining Plaza Mayor, starting in Calle Isabel la Catolica, the evening *paseo* drifts down to the aqueduct, passing the Romanesque church of San Martín; a statue of the Comunero leader Juan Bravo, who was executed here; the tower of the **Lozoya palace**; and finally, after a good viewing point, the **Casa de los Picos** (tel: 921 46 26 74; *Open* Mon–Fri 12–2, 7–9; *Closed* August. *Admission free*), covered all over with ornaments like cross-cut mace heads. Romanesque **San Esteban** with its tall tower stands closer to the cathedral.

There is also an outer circuit, or *ruta monumental*, with specially fine views of the *alcázar*. This takes in the **Convento de Carmelitas Descalzas** (tel: 921 43 13 49; *Open* daily 10–1.30, 4–7; *Closed* Mon mornings. *Donation accepted*), founded by San Juan de la Cruz and, with a brief diversion, the supposedly Templar church of **Vera Cruz**. Its nave runs in a circle round a kind of two-storey central column containing a chapel on the first floor where entrants to knighthood may have watched over their armour throughout the night.

▶ **Sepúlveda**   *150C2*

The Río Duratón, on its way down from the Sierra Guadarrama to the Duero, loops between steep banks, with this grey stone town on its northern side. The Romanesque church of San Salvador has good views.

▶▶ **Soria**   *151E2*

Soria marked the limit of the Christian advance against the Moors. This, and its place in the poetry of Antonio Machado, gives it a special resonance for Spaniards. The town displays fine Romanesque monuments, particularly San Juan de la Rabanera and Santo Domingo. Note also the grandiloquent Renaissance Palacio de la Gómara. The **Museo Numantino** (tel: 975 22 13 97; *Open* summer, Tue–Sat 10–2, 5–8, Sun 10–2; winter, Tue–Sat 10–2, 4–7; *Admission charge*) on Paseo de Espolón has excellent displays from the Iberian-Roman archaeological sites at nearby Numantia and Tiermes.

▶▶ **Tordesillas**   *150B2*

It was in this decayed Castilian town on the River Duero that the Treaty of Demarcation was signed in 1494, under the authority of the Borgia Pope Alexander VI. Spain was given all of Latin America except Brazil, which went to Portugal. Here, too, Queen Juana II of Castile (Juana La Loca) was confined during 40 years of madness. At her death in 1555, she was buried in the **Monasterio de Santa Clara** (tel: 983 77 00 71; *Open* summer, Tue–Sat 10–1, 3.30–6.30; winter, 10.30–1, 4–5.30, Sun 10.30–1.30, 3.30–5.30. *Admission charge*), a former royal palace. With its decorated plasterwork and artesonado ceilings, it is one of the finest Mudéjar buildings in Spain. The deconsecrated church of San Antolín (tel: 983 77 09 80; *Open* Tue–Sun 10.30–1.30, 4.30–6.30. *Admission charge*) holds a collection of religious sculpture.

ANTONIO MACHADO
Antonio Machado (1875–1939) was a French teacher from Sevilla. He made his emotional home in Castile, especially in Soria, where he lived from 1907 to 1913 and which he celebrated in lean, lyrical poetry. Later, after the death of his much-loved wife, he lived in Ubeda, where he is also much remembered. He died in 1939, in Collioure in the south of France, a refugee from Franco. Many consider him a finer poet than the more dramatic Lorca.

177

Walk

Laguna Negra

Laguna Negra, the Black Lagoon, is a natural lake, backed by sheer cliffs.

To get there from Soria, 16km (10mi) along the Burgos road take a right turn after Cidones, then follow signs. Alternatively, dropping south from Logroño on the N111, pass through extremely remote country. Shortly after Villanueva de Cameros, take the road to Villoslada de Cameros, and then south through Montenegro.

There is a five-minute walk up to the Laguna from the road's end (angle left in the first clearing).

For the fit and active there follows an enthralling walk-cum-rock scramble right round the lake.

ROMAN RUINS
Numantia (modern Numancia), 5km (3mi) from Soria on the Logroño road, was an Iberian settlement which resisted Roman conquest. The Romans devoted 20 years to an economic blockade. When defeat became inevitable in 133 BC, after a year's tight siege by Scipio Aemilianus, the inhabitants killed themselves. The site was later built over by the Romans and has now been carefully excavated.

AN OLD SAYING
"Rome was not built in a day," most Europeans say, when speaking of the need to continue steadily with a chosen course. Spaniards, recalling the wars and sieges of northwest Castile, more often use the phrase: "Zamora was not taken in one day."

▶ **Toro**   *150B2*

Toro is becoming well known outside Spain for its sturdy red wines. Like Tordesillas, this is an ancient town built on the high northern bank of the Duero. There are old mansions (many outside the early walls), a ruined castle, and above all the 12th-century collegiate church of **Santa María la Mayor** (*Open* summer, daily 10–1, 5–8; winter, Fri–Sat 10–2, 4.30–6.30, Sun 10–2), one of Spain's most admired Romanesque buildings, with a finely carved west door and three naves. It is given a curiously Byzantine aspect by its polygonal dome.

▶ **Turégano**   *150C2*

Easily visited from Madrid, Turégano has good shops and restaurants. The castle, founded by Fernán González, enfolds the Romanesque church of San Miguel.

▶▶ **Valladolid** see opposite

▶▶ **Zamora**   *150B2*

Zamora, fortified by strong if stubby walls, lies on a hill above the Duero, within 50km (30mi) or so of modern Portugal. Here, to the mortification of El Cid, who served him, King Sancho II of Castile was murdered, thus opening the way for his brother, Alfonso VI. The old town is rather sporadically preserved, but its monuments have a romantically medieval feeling.

The castle to the west is now a school for the applied arts. Just next to it is the remarkable **cathedral**, with a 12-sided Byzantine dome similar to that at Toro. It also has a fine and solid Romanesque tower and a less appropriate 18th-century facade. There is a severely dignified cloister and a museum that contains some gorgeous 15th-century Flemish tapestries. Outside the city walls and beneath the castle is the tiny Romanesque church of **Santiago de los Caballeros** (closed to the public; ask at tourist office), where El Cid is said to have been knighted. Other sights include the church of **La Magdalena** (*Open* summer, Tue–Sun 10–1, 5–8; winter, Fri–Sat 10–2, 4.30–6.30, Sun 10–2) with fine doorway; the Renaissance palace of the Counts of Alba and Aliste, now a parador; a Holy Week museum (*Open* Mon–Sat 10–2, 5–8, Sun 10–2. *Admission charge*) with work by 19th-century local sculptor Ramón Alvarez, and the pretty church of Santa María de la Horta.

Zamora, seen across the Río Duero, is the seat of a bishop. It was once the scene of many fierce battles between Christians and Moors

►► Valladolid   150C2

Valladolid was for centuries the chief city of emergent Spain, main centre of the court, and birthplace of kings and queens. Columbus died here and Cervantes also spent time here. Today it remains a large and active city, richly studded with monuments.

In the Plaza de San Pablo, north of the cathedral, are two of Spain's greatest facades. That of **San Pablo** itself falls into two elaborate sections, the lower part Isabelline-Gothic, the upper Plateresque. Round the corner to the right is the majestic portal and facade of the **Colegio de San Gregorio**, its many motifs dominated by the shield of Isabella and Ferdinand. Inside, round the cloisters, is the **Museo Nacional de Escultura** (Spain's National Sculpture Museum; tel: 983 25 03 75; for opening times, see page 267). Concentrating heavily on polychrome wood statuary, something Spain is famed for, it has an unrivalled display. The main exhibit is the remarkable *retablo* from the Valladolid monastery of San Benito, the greatest masterpiece of Alonso Berruguete. Nearby is the house where Philip II was born.

The **cathedral** (tel: 983 30 43 62; *Open* Mon–Fri 10–1.30, 4.30–7, Sat–Sun 10–2), a gaunt work by Herrera, Philip II's architect for the Escorial, was finished off in Churrigueresque baroque. Its museum, in a Gothic-Mudéjar setting, houses works by major sculptors. Close by are the elegantly Gothic church of Santa María la Antigua, the university square and, just down Calle Librería, the **Colegio de Santa Cruz**, part of the university, with a particularly fine patio.

The Plaza Mayor, with arcades and statue, is at the heart of town. The surprisingly grand house occupied by Cervantes (1603–1606), now a museum dedicated to Spain's best known writer, is nearby. The town is also famed for the solemnity of its Holy Week celebrations.

Plaza de Zorrilla, Valladolid. Known as an important university city and episcopal see, this modern industrial town has ancient monasteries and varied architecture

DEATH OF THE DISCOVERER
His name may have gone down in history but Christopher Columbus died in Valladolid on 20 May, 1506, aged 55, a poor, bedridden, and disillusioned man. His fortunes were never to recover after his first moment of triumph in 1492. After having been arrested and shipped back to Spain in chains for his mismanagement of the colony he founded, he set sail again only to be shipwrecked in Jamaica on his fourth and final voyage. He spent his later years trying in vain to persuade the king and queen of Spain to grant him the titles he said he had been promised. And he was never able to appreciate the scale of his discovery, maintaining until his last breath, not that he had discovered a continent, but that he had found a new route to the Far East.

Extremadura

EXTREMADURA ACQUIRED ITS NAME as the land "beyond the Duero." Since *duro* means "hard," the name also evokes the toughness of frontier country. As the frontier against the Moors was pushed farther and farther down into the peninsula, so the name at last became attached to a tract of country a good distance from the Duero and far enough south to share a border with Andalucía. Today's Extremadura is a cultural midway point between the lively good humour of Mediterranean Spain and the severity of Old Castile. Its people remain rural, often traditional, though also aspiring to modernize. Their greatest hope is to break the historic cycle of deprivation. The countryside they live in is intensely beautiful, with wild and sweeping landscapes, though a few districts are bare to a fault. Except in the mountains, Extremadura is burning hot in summer.

THE LAND Portugal lies to the west. The region's northern rim is formed by the Sierra de Gata and the last outposts of the Peña de Francia, both ranges pungent with cistus in late spring. The Sierra de Gredos creeps in from the east, diminishing but still magnificent. From this mountainous

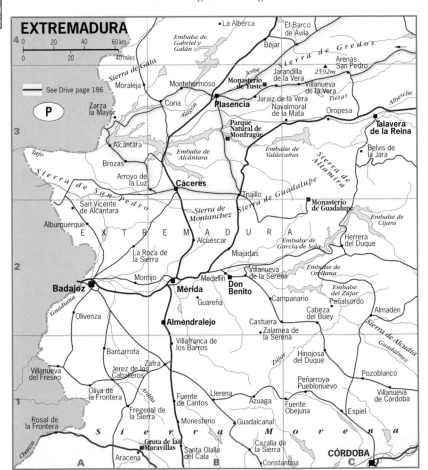

beginning, open terrain runs away south. Mostly this is archetypal Spanish cattle country, with holm-oak and sometimes cork-oak growing well spaced apart, throwing pools of shade on grassland that is tawny by summertime. Black cattle stand beneath the trees. Black pigs roam free in autumn, growing fat on acorns. Red kites and other hawks are common; griffon vultures nest in the mountains and the Tagus gorge. Cotton, tobacco, and other warm-country crops grow where valley land has been irrigated, usually as part of the post-Civil War "Badajoz plan." There are also grapes and olives.

THE BACKGROUND The towns, such as Plasencia, Cáceres, and Villanueva de la Vera, are often exceptionally lovely, well-matched by castles and monasteries. Two of the great orders of military knights, those of Alcántara and Santiago, were founded here, the latter in Cáceres. From here, too, came that fierce breed named the *conquistadores*. An extraordinary proportion of their leaders (see pages 188–189) were Extremadurans, taking with them to the New World a militant Catholicism and an untameable hunger for wealth. Survivors brought their riches home, building palaces that are still on show today, such as the Pizarro residences in Trujillo. At the latest count, three Extremaduran towns, Cáceres, Guadalupe, and Mérida, have been declared World Heritage Sites.

The beautiful Monasterio de Guadalupe rises above the rugged sierra

Extremadura

TOURIST INFORMATION

Badajoz: Plaza de
la Libertad 3
(tel: 924 22 27 63).
Cáceres: Plaza Mayor s/n
(tel: 927 62 50 47).
Guadalupe: Plaza Mayor
(tel: 927 15 41 28).
Mérida: Paseo José
Álvarez de Buruaga
(tel: 924 31 53 53).
Plasencia: Calle El Rey 8
(tel: 927 42 21 59).

VELAZQUEZ'S JESTER

The El Bobo de Coria
restaurant in Coria
(at Calle Pizarro 6, tel:
927 50 07 95) recalls
Juan Calabazas, the sad-
eyed court jester twice
painted by Velázquez. He
was born in Las Hurdes
and taken into service by
the Duke of Alba (who
also held the title of
Marquis of Coria). From
Alba's retinue, Juan
Calabazas passed to
Philip IV and so to the
canvas of Velázquez. The
restaurant serves excel-
lent potato and spinach
soup, and the wine is
Pitarra.

RETIREMENT IN YUSTE

Charles V abdicated in
1556, retiring to Yuste
with his family portraits,
100 servants, and a
friendly clockmaker. He
found it difficult, however,
to refrain from seeking
news, and Yuste became
a place of pilgrimage for
important folk and impe-
rial servants. Ravaged by
gout, Charles built a
rampart for riding straight
up to his first floor apartments in his litter. His
winter bedroom gave onto
the altar of the monastery
church. He heard Mass
four times a day and
fished in a pool beneath
his living room; a source
of the malaria which
finally killed him.

*The granite Roman
bridge across the Tagus
at Alcántara dates back
to AD 105*

► Alcántara   180A3

The extraordinary six-arched bridge across the Tagus
gorge, rising almost 70m (230ft) from the water and
surmounted by a triumphal arch, looks as if it was built
yesterday, not in AD 105. It was restored in 1860. Although
they do not diminish the phenomenon of *el kantara*
(Arabic for bridge), the huge dam wall and hydroelectric
installations above do rather spoil the atmosphere. The
little town above the gorge was once the headquarters of
the Knights of Alcántara (see also page 219). It has a
slightly crumbling air from outside but is well kept and
tidy within.

► Badajoz   180A2

Badajoz, an architecturally dull frontier town, does have
some good points, including the narrow streets in attractive flat-fronted 19th-century style. The 13th-century
cathedral with 17th-century facade and **Museo de Bellas
Artes** (tel: 924 21 24 69; *Open* winter, Tue–Fri 10–2, 4–6,
Sat–Sun 10–2; summer, Tue–Fri 10–2, 6–8, Sat–Sun 10–2.
Admission free) have paintings by the Badajoz-born 16th-
century painter, Luis de Morales.

►►► Cáceres see opposite   180B3

► Coria   180B3

This little sleepy town, with almost a Portuguese air, rises
above the Río Alagón. The bank is commanded by a 16th-
century cathedral with massive baroque tower and
Plateresque filigree carving to either side of its main door.
On the north side, some of the stout Roman walls survive.

►►► Guadalupe see page 184

►► Jarandilla and Yuste   180B3

Emperor Charles V chose the monastery at Yuste, set
above the Tiétar Valley (see page 161 and panel) as his
place of retirement. The Emperor built his palace/villa
(tel: 927 17 21 30; *Open* Mon–Sat 9.30–12.30, 3–6; Sun
9.30–11.30, 3.30–6.30. Guided tours available as groups
form) up against the side of the existing monastery. While
his palace was under construction, Charles lived nearby
at Jarandilla in the castle of the Counts of Oropesa, now
the **Parador of Charles V**. There are hotels in Jarandilla,
and it is a natural base for exploring the area.
   The old town below the road, with two churches and a
castle, is not spectacular, but there is a pretty stroll below
to the "Roman bridge" and strenuous mountain walks
from Guijo de Santa Barbara above.

Nowhere in Spain is there so dense a concentration of monuments as in ancient Cáceres. Confined within Moorish walls built up on Roman foundations, this is a hilltop town solid with Spanish grandeur and with a mass of storks in springtime. The buildings, mostly Renaissance, are in a rough brown stone with heraldic crests and severe, if sometimes elaborate frontages. It is even more astonishing at night, with the details picked out by floodlighting.

The main square of Cáceres is built on a slope, with arcades and cafés, just below the ancient town. You can enter the old town from here under the wide **Arco de la Estrella** (Arch of the Star). Turning immediately right inside the city wall you will encounter the **Generala** house, the **Palacio de los Golfines de Arriba**, and several towers on the city wall. Left at the end, left again, and up the narrow Calle Ancha past the parador in the 14th-century Ulloa palace, you come to an open square in front of the church of **San Mateo**, which was constructed during the 14th to 16th centuries.

Immediately to the right is the magnificent **Casa de las Cigüeñas** (House of Storks). In 1477, the towers of the town were torn down on the orders of Queen Isabella (many of them were rebuilt afterwards), but here the original was allowed to stand. Diagonally to the right behind the viewer is the **Casa de las Veletas** (House of the Weather-vanes). This contains the Cáceres Museum (tel: 927 24 72 34; *Open* Tue–Sat 9–2; Sun 10.15–2.30. *Admission free*) and a fine Arab cistern.

183

Down past San Mateo, tucked in under the large white church of San Francisco Javier, are **Santa María**, used as the cathedral, the **bishop's palace**, **Palacio de los Golfines de Abajo**, and **Palacio de Carvajal**. The church of **Santiago**, where the Order of Santiago was founded, lies straight below outside the walls with an energetic *retablo* of the saint by Alonso Berruguete (1558).

Cáceres' walls enclose one of Spain's finest architectural ensembles

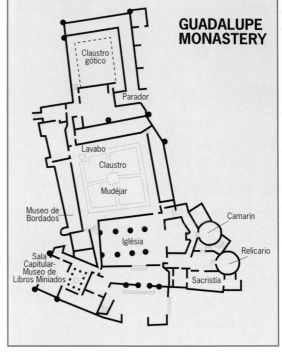

The massive walls of Guadalupe monastery dominate this small Extremaduran town, the strongest religious link between Spain and Latin America

GUADALUPE MONASTERY

Claustro gótico

Parador

Lavabo

Claustro

Mudéjar

Museo de Bordados

Camarín

Iglésia

Relicario

Sala Capitular-Museo de Libros Miniados

Sacristía

THE STORKS OF EXTREMADURA

Right through Extremadura and western Spain, the storks arrive in February to take up nests left vacant over the winter months. In villages, these are usually on the highest available spot on the church. Cathedrals sometimes attract clusters of nests, and often they are to be found incongruously perched on disused factory chimneys. Nobody bothers the storks, who chatter with an odd rattling sound and wheel about the sky, long necks extended. When the nests are floodlit, as happens, for example, in old Cáceres, the disturbed birds peer down with a look of perpetual surprise.

▶▶▶ **Guadalupe**   *180C2*

The beautiful monastery of Guadalupe (tel: 927 36 70 00; *Open* summer, daily 9.30–12.45, 3.30–6.45; winter, 3.30–6.30. Guided tours only. *Admission charge*) rises from rugged sierra over a tiny town full of cobbled streets and jutting, wood-beamed balconies.

It is said that a shepherd discovered the dark-faced image of the Virgin in the 13th century. The hermitage he built became a Hieronymite monastery, receiving rich gifts from Alfonso XI. It was both a stopping place for royalty and foremost of Spanish holy places to be linked with the discovery of America. Columbus named an island after Guadalupe; and Guadalupe gave its name to the Virgin of Mexico. Today the monastery stands as the heart of "Hispanidad," the supposed common bond between Spain and its former American colonies.

Uncompromising towers give the building a military look. Close up, the facade is an array of swirling Gothic-Mudéjar tracery. The tour of the monastery (now Franciscan) includes arguably the finest Mudéjar cloister in Spain. The **Museo de Bordados** (Embroidery Museum) is a display of ecclesiastical wealth and elaboration in its vestments and altar frontals. Scenes by the great Extremaduran painter Zurbarán hang in the sacristy, the only such series in Spain still in its original setting. Behind the altar, visitors are shown the Virgin of Guadalupe herself and may touch or kiss her robes.

The monastery runs its own hotel around another Gothic cloister. There is also a patioed parador, founded as a monastery hostel in 1402.

▶▶ Jerez de los Caballeros   180A1

Jerez, a compact little town in the middle of the empty sierra, is full of churches, convents, and mansions built by *conquistador* gold. The churches of San Bartolomé, San Miguel, Santa Catalina, and Santa María, make up an astonishingly rich quartet. Núñez de Balboa ("discoverer" of the Pacific) was born here, as was Hernando de Soto, who explored the Mississippi. The 13th-century castle recalls Jerez's history as a frontier stronghold of the Templars and the Knights of Santiago.

▶ Medellín   180B2

The birthplace of Hernán Cortés (see panel, page 188) is a village dominated by a castle, beside the River Guadiana. In the main square is a statue of Cortés and a stone said to mark the exact spot of his birth.

▶▶▶ Mérida   180B2

Mérida was once the capital of Roman Lusitania. There are many fine Roman monuments to be found here. Just by the impressive 60-arched **Roman bridge** is the huge *alcazaba* (Arab fortress), built on Roman foundations and with Roman blocks. There is a Roman **theatre** (retaining a splendid backdrop of marble columns) and an **amphitheatre** (with a seating capacity of 15,000). The excavated **Casa del Anfiteatro** has engaging mosaics of wine-pressing. The adjoining **Museo Nacional de Arte Romano** (*Open* summer, Tue–Sat 10–2, 5–7, Sun 10–2; winter, Tue–Sat 10–2, 4–6, Sun 10–2. *Admission charge; free Sun*) should not be missed. The Temple of Mars, farther on and down the hill, has a shrine to the child saint Eulalia. **The Casa de Mitra** (House of Mithras), across town by the bullring, has some more fine mosaics.

▶ Olivenza   180A2

Olivenza passed to Spain from Portugal only in 1801 and some of its buildings are Portuguese in style. The castle holds the local museum, and there are 18th-century barracks and an interesting bullring.

The modern bullring in Roman Mérida is decorated in Moorish style

THE QUEEN'S CHOICE
The lazy good looks of Manuel Godoy, caught in a portrait by Goya (Real Academia de Bellas Artes de San Fernando, Madrid), transformed Spain's fortunes for the worse. The young guards officer became the lover of Queen María Luisa and, at the same time, a friend and confidant to her husband Charles IV. Prime minister by the age of 25, he devised the treaty which gave Spain Olivenza. He and Charles IV finally signed away Spanish independence to Napoleon.

ROMAN ART AT MÉRIDA
Opened in 1986, the Museo Nacional de Arte Romano, incorporating a stretch of well-paved Roman road, is an essential stop on any Roman pilgrimage through Spain. Along with sculpture, glass, pottery, coins, and mosaics, it shows you many other aspects of life in Emerita Augusta, or Mérida.

Drive

Along the Tiétar Valley

The valley of the River Tiétar, lying warm and protected from north winds by the Sierra de Gredos, is one of the loveliest in Spain.

Drive east to west into the district

Drive

Scenic Extremadura

See map on page 180.

This roughly circular drive will require at least two days and could easily be extended by a trip to the great monastery shrine of Guadalupe.

Combined with the Castile drive (see page 159), picked up in El Barco de Ávila, it would make a possible week's tour from Madrid.

Leave Madrid and pass to the south of the Sierra de Gredos by highway C501 and enter Extremadura along the Tiétar Valley.

called La Vera. The road runs a little above the valley floor on the northern side, with villages below the road that are easy to miss.

Villanueva de la Vera has an ancient town centre and main square, with jutting wooden balconies and protruding first storeys. **Valverde de la Vera** is still more spectacular with hugely projecting first floors. Beautiful **Cuacos** has a galleried main square and many seigneurial houses. All these villages are worth a leisurely stroll round.

Make sure you have enough time to enjoy **La Vera** and **Plasencia**.

Now drive west through open country to **Coria**. Take the road south, and then strike farther west for Alcántara. **Garrovillas**, on the way, has an interesting plaza.

Head southeast to **Cáceres** via Brozas, following road signs. Take the N521 to **Trujillo**.
  The reward in taking the main road lies in the impressive profile of that *conquistador* town.

Drive north now across wild cattle country from Trujillo to Plasencia again.
  You pass the Monfragüe nature reserve where griffon vultures nest on crags above the Tagus.

Leave Extremadura on the N110. The beautiful **Jerte Valley** is best in cherry-blossom season.

Jarandilla, in the Tiétar Valley, temporary lodging for Emperor Charles V

▶▶ Plasencia 180B3

The old town at the crossing of the Río Jerte is full of noble mansions, ancient walls and towers, and hidden churches. Life focuses around the cafés of the **Plaza Mayor**. The chief monument is the cathedral, or rather the two (both unfinished) **cathedrals** (tel: 927 41 48 52; *Open* daily 10–12.30, 4–5.30; closes Fri 7PM. *Admission charge*). The one in use is newer, Gothic within, with a fine Plateresque door. The old cathedral, backing onto it, is now a museum. It has a lovely Romanesque/Gothic transitional cloister, where you can see the joins in the composite building. The ethnographic museum (tel: 927 42 18 43; *Open* Wed–Sat 11–2, 5–8, Sun 11–2) is outstanding.

▶▶ Trujillo 180B3

Trujillo produced the *conquistador* Francisco Pizarro (see pages 188–189) and still lives in his shadow. The main square, with steps and road leading up and down to different levels, is dominated by a large statue of Pizarro, astride a helmeted horse. The mansions in the square express the wealth of the *conquistadores*. The palace of Francisco Pizarro's brother Hernando, Palacio del Marqués de la Conquista, is diagonally across from the statue, grandly solemn, but with a Plateresque window and balcony let into the corner and a swashbuckling shield above, literally wrapped round the edge of the building. On the lower side of the square, with gracious balconies, is the palace of the Marqués de Piedras Albas. Behind the Pizarro statue rises the large, lichen-encrusted church of San Martín and just below this, with more fine balconies, is the Palacio de los Duques de San Carlos, now a convent (Trujillo tourist office, tel: 927 32 26 77; *Guided tours only Mon–Sat 9.30–1, 4.30–6.30, Sun 10.30–12.30. Admission charge*). It is also worth climbing up to the old Moorish castle that stands on a prominent ledge overlooking the town; it features great solid towers.

▶▶ Zafra 180B1

With delightful arcaded squares and narrow white streets, Zafra is dominated by the nine-towered castle where Hernán Cortés of Medellín stayed as a guest before departing for Mexico. It is now a parador, with a marbled Renaissance patio by Juan de Herrera at its heart.

TASTY HAMS
Air-cured mountain ham, cut thin and raw, is one of Spain's great delicacies. *Jamón serrano* is the generic name for it and often refers to the ham of the unglamorous white pig. The black pig, or black-foot, *pata negra*, is an Iberian native, traditionally reared on acorns, roaming free in Extremadura and western Andalucía. The best *pata negra* hams are known by place names; *jamón dc Montánchez* in Extremadura, for instance. The best known from Andalucía are *Jabugo* (Huelva) and *Trevélez* (Granada). Ask the price first when ordering in bars.

187

Ten years after Columbus' discovery of America, the only Spanish settlements in the New World were in Cuba and Hispaniola (modern Haiti and the Dominican Republic). Yet by 1540, the brutal heyday of the conquistadores *was over, replaced by a generation of settlers.*

HERNAN CORTÉS

Although Cortés defeated the Aztec Empire and established his own from the Caribbean Sea to the Pacific Ocean, the difficulties of administration and the political intrigues against him were too much. He returned to Spain where, in his own words, "old, poor, and in debt," he died in 1547.

SMALLPOX

The hardiness and the bravery, as well as the brutality, of the *conquistadores* are beyond dispute. But the Spaniards were also aided by the catastrophe of smallpox, which they had introduced unwittingly during the latter stages of the three-year campaign in Mexico. It killed up to half of the native population in central Mexico, among them Cuitlahuac, who had taken over the leadership on the death of his brother Montezuma and appeared likely to be a far more formidable opponent. The Europeans, having greater resistance to the disease, were less affected by it, and so more able to continue fighting.

A significant number of those who set out for the New World in search of gold came from Extremadura. In the same way that today's poor and dispossessed are often drawn to large cities in search of a new life, so the lands across the Atlantic beckoned irresistibly to those trapped in the poverty and hopelessness of rural life in this deeply deprived region of Spain.

Conquest of Mexico Vasco Núñez de Balboa made the first settlement in Panama in 1508 and within five years had pushed through to the Pacific Ocean. Yucatán and its Mayan civilization were "discovered" by Hernández de Córdoba. Inspired by this, Hernán Cortés sailed from Cuba for the mainland with 11 ships and 600 men. Cortés came from a poor but respectable family in Medellín in Extremadura, had arrived in Hispaniola at the age of 19, and quickly established a power base there. Now on the mainland, with the help of an Indian mistress, he defeated what opposition he met, set up a capital at Veracruz, and marched into Mexico.

The Spanish party were open-mouthed at the wealth they saw. Initially they were welcomed and housed in a palace in the Aztec capital. When one of their party was killed, they seized the occasion to demand that Montezuma, the Aztec king, should pay allegiance and tribute to Charles V. Montezuma was held hostage and later killed.

Pizarro and the Inca Empire The next stage was the defeat of the Inca civilization and the conquest of Peru. The chief protagonist in this venture was Francisco Pizarro of Trujillo. Born illegitimate in around 1475, he spent his early life as a swineherd. It is likely he had a spell fighting in Italy before he left for Hispaniola. In 1524, already wealthy and well into middle age, he formed a partnership with Diego de Almagro and Hernando de Luque to explore the west coast of South America.

Early difficulties led to a request for reinforcements from Panama, but Pizarro was ordered to return. His response, so the story goes, was to draw a line on the ground with his sword and invite those who wished to continue with him to step over the line. Of the 13 who crossed the line, some were to reap an eventual reward of untold wealth and honour, though many, like Pizarro, eventually died a violent death.

They knew already that an Inca empire existed and it was equally clear that the resources of the original syndicate were inadequate. Pizarro returned to Spain to get

funds from Charles V. In the process he was made governor and captain-general of all he conquered. He returned, joined by his four brothers, and in 1531 Pizarro, Almagro, and 168 Spaniards set out to defeat a mighty empire of millions. Like Cortés with Montezuma, Pizarro knew his easiest tactic lay in capturing the emperor/sun god Atahualpa. Pizarro succeeded in this, and held Atahualpa hostage; the condition for Atahualpa's release was that the room in which he was imprisoned should be filled with gold and silver. But after fulfilling the condition, Atahualpa was accused of the murder of his brother, baptized, and then garotted.

Predictably, rivalries and dissensions arose between Almagro and Pizarro, which ended with Almagro's death, at the hands of one of Pizarro's brother, followed by Pizarro's, stabbed in his palace by Almagro's son.

One of the results of the colonization was the decimation of the native Indian population; due more to the ravages of disease than to war. At the end of the era of conquest, some 15,000 Spaniards had taken part, leaving the mother country to cross the Atlantic in their tiny ships. Many were never to come home again, casualties of hardship and disease.

RELIGION
Most of the indigenous population was soon converted to Christianity. Latin America remains exceptionally devout, although Catholic dominance is now being challenged, increasingly, by Protestant missionaries. The task of conversion fell mainly on the Jesuits, whose surviving mission churches from Paraguay to Mexico remain a major part of the architectural legacy.

189

A bronze statue of Pizarro in Trujillo

Castilla-La Mancha and the Madrid Region

South, east, and west of Madrid is the autonomous region of Castilla-La Mancha, once known as New Castile; Old Castile is the heartland north of Madrid. With the Community of Madrid, it makes a shield-shaped territory right in the heart of Spain. The Community of Madrid is well populated, but with mountains and plenty of appealing and historic spots. Castilla-La Mancha, though spoiled in parts by industry, an over-enthusiasm for reservoirs, and some ugly roads, remains one of the most exciting parts of the whole peninsula. It ranges from the pine-forested Serranía de Cuenca in the east, with the weird rock formations of La Ciudad Encantada, through the

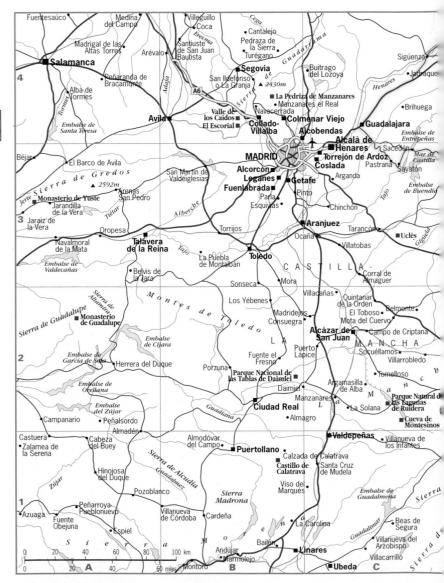

flatness of La Mancha, to the empty Montes de Toledo in the west. The Madrid region is bordered by the Guadarrama Mountains to the north; Castilla-La Mancha is set apart from Andalucía by the Sierra Morena. Leaving aside Toledo, which often seems close cousin to such stern spots as Ávila, Castilla-La Mancha is an affable, relaxed part of Spain. However, over 500 castles, Moorish and Christian, bear witness to its warring past. The military orders, Knights of Calatrava and Santiago, ruled huge tracts of the territory. There are also monasteries and aristocratic palaces, surviving alongside a vernacular architecture.

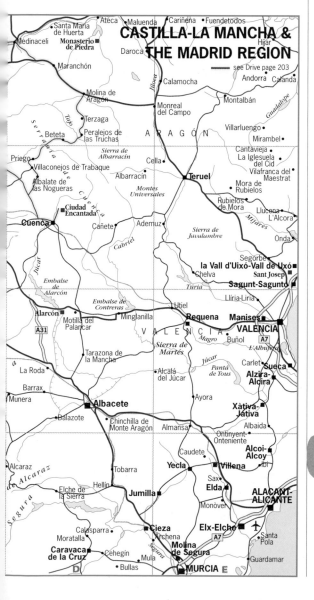

CASTILLA-LA MANCHA &
THE MADRID REGION

see Drive page 203

The palace in Alcalá de Henares. An important university town in the 16th and 17th centuries, Alcalá was the birthplace of Miguel Cervantes, creator of Don Quixote

TOURIST INFORMATION
Albacete: Calle del Tinte 2 (tel: 967 58 05 22).
Alcalá de Henares: Callejón Santa María (tel: 918 89 26 94).
Cuenca: Plaza Mayor 1 (tel: 969 23 21 19).
Ciudad Real: Avenida Alarcos 21 (tel: 926 20 00 37).
Guadalajara: Plaza de los Caídos 6 (tel: 949 21 16 26).
Parque Nacional de las Tablas de Daimiel: (tel: 926 69 31 18).
Toledo: Puerta de Bisagra (tel: 925 22 08 43).
Valdepeñas: Plaza de España (tel: 926 31 25 52).

CARDINAL CISNEROS
Francisco Jiménez de Cisneros, cardinal and archbishop of Toledo, was one of Spain's mixed blessings. He founded a great university at Alcalá and commissioned the Polyglot Bible. In Toledo, he made it possible for the Mozarabic form of service to be preserved in perpetuity. But it was his severity that provoked the Moors of Granada into a hopeless rebellion; and after the death of Queen Isabella I, Cisneros squandered resources on crusades against North Africa.

► Alarcón   191D2
A fierce twist in the gorge of the Río Júcar offered the Moorish kingdom of Toledo the site for an impregnable castle—impregnable, that is, until 1184, when Hernán Martínez de Cevellos used two daggers to scale the walls. The site and the castle (now containing a parador) still combine to make a stirring impression. A village with three churches is contained within the walls.

► Albacete   191D2
Always a nerve centre in Spanish communications, Albacete, on the La Mancha plain, is famous for the manufacture of knives, but has little of historic interest. There are a number of Modernista houses (one by the cathedral in green tiles) and a provincial museum (*Open* Tue–Sat 10–2, 4.30–7, Sun 9–2. *Admission charge*), which has good archaeological exhibits.

►► Alcalá de Henares   190C3
Just 31km (19mi) east of Madrid, industrial Alcalá has at its venerable core the fine Renaissance facade of the university founded here in 1508 by Cardinal Cisneros (*Guided tours* every 45 minutes Mon–Fri 11.30–5.30, Sat–Sun 11–2, 4–7, from the entrance facing Plaza de San Diego). Cervantes was born here (a 1950s version of his house in Calle Mayor contains editions of his works) and here Queen Isabella gave birth to Catherine of Aragón, who married England's Henry VIII. The university facade, by Rodrigo Gil de Hontañón, is a 1540s replacement of the brick original. The swans in evidence are a pun on Cisneros' name (*cisne* means "swan"). Don't miss the Gothic-Mudéjar Capilla de San Ildefonso where Cervantes was christened, or the university's Patio Trilingüe, named after the trilingual or Polyglot Bible produced here at Cisneros' orders.

► Alcalá del Júcar   191E2
This tiny township in the Júcar gorge, with castle perched on top of a great cake of cliff, extracts effortless drama from its troglodyte houses and cliff-side site. Although damaged during the Civil War, the town has been well restored and retains a number of medieval buildings.

► Alcaraz 190C1

Alcaraz is marked by earlier grandeur, with castle ruins and a handsome Calle Mayor running along the sloping hillside. The largely Renaissance Plaza Mayor reflects the style and spirit of local architect Andrés de Vandelvira, born here in 1509. There is a fine Plateresque doorway at the Plaza Mayor end of the Calle Mayor.

►► Almagro 190B2

The historic home of the Knights of Calatrava lies white and peaceful in the plains of New Castile. Its extraordinary main square has long sides formed by what seems an infinite extension of glassed-in balconies, two storeys high, riding over stone arcades. The Corral de las Comedias is a uniquely surviving theatre of the Golden Age; churches and noble houses abound; the Fugger banking family retained a large warehouse now known as the Palacio Fucar. The convent of the Calatrava Order, with Gothic church and calm Renaissance cloister, is another notable survivor. Lace-making and aubergine pickling are modern classics.

► Almansa 191E2

The small town of Almansa lies gathered round a rock with a crenellated fairy-tale castle, which was built by the Infante Don Juan Manuel. Below lies the fine church of the Asunción and the Renaissance Casa Grande next door.

►► Aranjuez 190C3

Aranjuez, with its shady groves of trees beside the Tagus, is an easy day trip from Toledo or Madrid and site of a major Bourbon palace (tel: 918 91 03 05; *Open* Apr–Sep, Tue–Sun 10–6.15; Oct–Mar, Tue–Sun 10–5.15. *Admission charge; free Wed for EU citizens.* Guided tours only). The palace exterior mainly reflects the taste of Charles III. So do parts of the interior, especially the porcelain room, which is decorated with the work of the Royal Porcelain Factory in Madrid. Both Charles IV and Queen Isabella II have left their mark here as well. Note the 203 Chinese drawings presented to Isabella, some showing scenes of torture. The palace has fine chandeliers and mirrors.

The delightful formal Jardín de la Isla, just behind the palace, was originally planted by Habsburg Philip II. The Jardín del Principe, a little west along the river and set in acres of forest-parkland, contains the royal boathouse, now rebuilt as a museum to show the royal barges, and a "cottage" palace, known as the Casa del Labrador (call 918 91 03 05 to reserve a guided tour).

PRINCE KARL OF AUSTRIA
Prince Karl of Austria was toe-to-toe with Philip of Anjou in the War of the Spanish Succession. Hostilities had opened all across Europe in 1702. In 1705, Karl's British and German forces landed in Barcelona and Valencia. They twice succeeded in taking Madrid but in 1707 were decisively beaten at Almansa by French troops under the Duke of Berwick. It was the beginning of the end for Karl in this particular contest, though he went on to be Holy Roman Emperor. Philip of Anjou was confirmed as Philip V of Spain and reigned, with a brief interruption, right up to 1746.

193

The palace at Aranjuez, one of the rural refuges of the royal family in former times

Belmonte castle and its crenellated walls. Built in the mid-15th century, the castle features cylindrical towers, bastions, and battlements, with a sweeping view of the landscapes of La Mancha

ROYAL JELLY
The raw material of royal jelly is "pollen" or *pan de abeja*, meaning bread of bees. Used by Alcarria locals (see page 202) to stir into milk or water, it is reputedly very good for prostate problems, stress control, and as an aphrodisiac. It doesn't taste very good, though.

▶ **Belmonte**   *190C2*

Belmonte is guarded by an impressive 15th-century castle on a hill overlooking the plains of La Mancha (*Open* daily 10–1, 3.30–6. *Admission charge*). From the castle, which retains fine Mudéjar ceilings, walls run down the hillside; there are several gates still remaining. The whole town has been declared a monument of interest to the visitor, and lies on the Don Quixote tourist route (see pages 198–199).

▶ **Caídos, Valle de los**   *190B4*

As much as the Alcázar of Toledo (see page 206), the Valley of the Fallen (*Open* Tue–Sun 10–6. *Admission charge*), is a monument to those who died in the Spanish Civil War, at least on the Nationalist side. It is only a short distance northeast of the Escorial (see page 200).

Following his victory in 1939, Franco set his political prisoners to work hollowing a monstrous cavern from the rock at the foot of a pine-clad valley of the Sierra de Guadarrama. The result was a tunnel-like church almost as grandiose as the Escorial. Franco himself is now buried on one side of the High Altar; José Antonio, theorist of Spain's Falange party, or national socialists (see page 45), on the other. On a rock above the cave-shrine rears a cross 125m (410ft) high; a tiny funicular ascends to its base, from where there are stunning views.

A visit here, combined with the Escorial (there is a useful bus link between the two), will greatly enhance an understanding of Spanish history between 1939 and Franco's death in 1975.

▶ **Calatrava**   *190B1*

This ruined and romantic castle (*Open* Apr–Sep, Tue–Sun 10–2, 5–8; Oct–Mar, Tue–Sun 10–2, 6–7. *Admission charge*) of the Knights of Calatrava looms immense over a southerly pass out of La Mancha. Within encircling walls, the castle itself rises in a final crag, with a convent church tucked in behind.

Walk

Parque Nacional de las Tablas de Daimiel

A visit to this national park (*Open* 8AM–8.30PM in spring; 9PM in summer; 6.30PM in winter) is a chance to see the last of the once extensive wetlands of La Mancha, episodic home to a huge population of migratory water birds.

This final outpost, formed by the confluence of the Guadiana and Cigüela rivers, is, alas, under threat. Excessive water-pumping for the fields and vineyards of La Mancha, and the failure of an emergency scheme to divert more water in the direction of the Tablas, has dried up the area. Where once it was rich in bird-life all the year, now there is a guarantee of water only from January to June, naturally the popular months to visit. It is best in spring, but avoid Holy Week and weekends.

About 10km (6mi) along a winding road north of the village of Daimiel, park at an information point.

A terrain of rushes and small elevated islands among water courses now reveals itself. Paths and large railed bridges made of railway sleepers link islands and mainland, with observation points, a hide overlooking the one small permanent lagoon, and another peeping into an enclosed aviary.

A well-marked walk circuit to Isla del Pan takes 2 hours; to Permanent Lagoon 30–40 minutes; and to Prado Ancho 1.5 hours.

195

Walk

Ciudad Encantada

At 36km (22mi) northeast of Cuenca, well signposted via Villalba de la Sierra, La Ciudad Encantada (Enchanted City. *Open* daily 9.30–sunset. *Admission charge*) is an extraordinary rockscape set at 1,400m (4,593ft) among pine woods.

A 3km (2mi) circuit of gravel path is laid out among the rocks (white arrows out, red arrows home); allow perhaps 1.5 hours for a leisurely circuit including diversions.

Huge individual clumps or long parallel ridges of rock have been eroded near their bases leaving forms that rise up like inverted clubs. The owners of this private patch of land (20sq km/8sq mi) have posted up fanciful names such as "The Theatre" and "The Tortoise" alongside each of the main phenomena.

The flat, watery expanses of Las Tablas de Daimiel

Unspoiled Chinchón is famed for its extremely picturesque Plaza Mayor. Following old customs, it still stages the occasional bullfight, with spectators watching from the balconies of the houses which surround the square

PARTRIDGE-SHOOTING
La Mancha and the rough land thereabouts have always been partridge-shooting territory. Nowadays, this has become something of a mania, both for Madrileños and well-to-do foreign tourists. Don't be surprised to meet men with guns lumbering towards you out of the winter mists.

196

► Chinchilla de Monte Aragón   *191D2*

Some 12km (7mi) south of Albacete, on a rocky outcrop above the plains of La Mancha, stand the ruins of a 15th-century castle, once a stronghold of the Marquis of Villena, Grand Master of the Knights of Santiago. The little town which grew up around the castle is now somewhat decayed but still attractive with a pleasing main square, La Plaza de La Mancha, a town hall, and the 15th-century church of San Salvador. The castle (good views) is reached by a very narrow road, passing ruined houses and some cave dwellings.

►► Chinchón   *190C3*

Chinchón, within easy striking distance of Madrid, is justly famous for its Plaza Mayor, the genuine, archetypal, arcaded Spanish square, nestled in a valley, with town rising above. Above the ground-floor arches rise two or three storeys of wooden balconies. These are used for viewing bullfights, but many have been turned into restaurants, with tables set along the balconies. On Sundays, delicious smells waft upwards to the grand stone church of La Asunción, which contains a Goya *Virgin*. The pleasant stone-and-brick, 17th-century Augustinian convent is now a parador. Chinchón is well known for *anís*, a fiery aniseed liquor. Popular with Spaniards, it may seem strong to others.

► Ciudad Real   *190B2*

Ciudad Real, the Royal City, received its title in 1420, but was founded about 200 years earlier by Alfonso X, the Learned, as a check on the power of the Knights, with territory nearby at Almagro and beyond. Interesting sights include the large and bare cathedral, with Renaissance *retablo*; the adjoining house of the *conquistador* Hernán Perez de Pulgar (1451–1531), now used for exhibitions; the **Museo Provincial** (tel: 926 22 68 96; *Open* Tue–Sat 10–2, 5–8), demonstrating the rich archaeology of the region; and the **Museo El Quijote** (tel: 926 20 04 57; *Open* 10–2, 4–6. *Admission charge*) with displays on Don Quixote and his creator, Miguel de Cervantes. The church of Santiago has an elegant, Gothic interior, San Pedro a swirling rose window, and best of all is the horseshoe Mudéjar arch of the Puerta de Toledo.

Crossing the gorge to old Cuenca along the foot-bridge provides a worth-while view of the town's famous Casas Colgadas *(Hanging Houses)*

OSIER BARK
Osiers grow dense and reddish coloured in valley bottoms north of Cuenca. Harvested in February/ March, the osier bark is stripped by steaming and then dyed in primitive-look-ing pits. This picturesque trade is diminished, although still very evident.

197

▶▶▶ **Cuenca**   *191D3*

Cuenca, capital of its province, is the supreme picture postcard town. This medieval gem clings to the summit of two deep gorges formed by the Huécar and Júcar rivers passing far below. Some houses are built into the vertical side of a gorge, thereby earning them the description *Las Casas Colgadas* ("the Hanging Houses") of Cuenca. For best views of the Hanging Houses, you should cross the gorge by the footbridge (Puente de San Pablo) to the left of the gallery and look back at the town. The bridge was originally constructed for the benefit of the Dominican monks of the monastery of San Pablo on the other side, now converted into a parador. The pleasant modern town beneath is almost a separate entity.

Architecturally, Cuenca is a modest town, but note the **mansions** on the Calle de la Correduría and Calle Alfonso VIII, built by *conquistadores* returning from the Americas, and the cathedral that dominates the Plaza Mayor. Built between the 12th and 13th centuries, it is an imposing structure with a pale Renaissance facade. The interior is largely Gothic and richly decorated.

A few steps to the south is the cluster of buildings offi-cially designated as **Las Casas Colgadas**. This strange and lovely architectural ensemble, heavily restored, houses the outstanding **Museo de Arte Abstracto Español** (tel: 969 21 29 83; *Open* Tue–Fri 11–2, 4–6, Sat 11–2, 4–8, Sun 11–2), a collection of Spanish abstract paintings and sculpture owned by the Juan March Foundation. Artists exhibited include Millares, Rueda, Saura, Tàpies, and the sculptors Chillida and Serrano. A restaurant next to the gallery serves local delicacies. The **Diocesan Museum** (tel: 969 22 42 10; *Open* Tue–Fri 11–2, 4–6, Sat 11–2, 4–8, Sun 11–2) near the cathedral is worth visiting for its paintings, the cathedral treasury, and a display of early carpets, their production formerly a local industry. The **Science Museum** is another interesting place (tel: 969 24 03 20; *Open* Tue–Sat 10–2, 4–7, Sun 10–2).

ROMAN "CONCA"
The Romans knew Cuenca as Conca. It was part of a marriage settlement to King Alfonso VI by the Moorish ruler and was at one time headquarters of the Knights of Santiago. In subsequent centuries it was fought over by the French and the Carlists, and during the 20th-century Civil War.

In Don Quixote de La Mancha and Sancho Panza, his earthy squire, Miguel de Cervantes immortalized not only two extraordinary characters but also the landscape of La Mancha, from which Quixote took his name. And it was on this strange, flat plain, not so very far south of Madrid, that many of the pair's adventures came to pass. By far the best known is Quixote's tilting at the windmills, which lifted him up, complete with his horse Rocinante, and dumped him down again.

Windmills of La Mancha, Don Quixote's "giants," are still a prominent feature of the landscape

198

LOCAL CERAMICS
The region has a long tradition of pottery, basketwork, and popular crafts in general. A variety of glazed utensils in various forms is produced in Consuegra and Cuerva, southwest of Toledo, which is also known for its attractively decorated jugs known as *ollas majas*. Some interesting pottery is produced in Mota del Cuervo, where "turntable moulding" is carried out exclusively by women. It is also known for its small, slim, polished jugs with flat handles, called *tinajas*.

But there is more to the Knight than windmills and more landscape to the story than just the plain, extraordinary as it is. Much of the tale in fact takes place in the surrounding mountains and, in the final chapters, ranges as far as Aragón and Barcelona.

The Quixote route The "official" (and signposted) Quixote route can be done in a single day. It sticks to the northern part of La Mancha and concentrates quite heavily on windmills.

The route starts at **Consuegra**, just to the west of the NIV, the main traffic artery between Madrid and the south. From here, it drops a little south to Puerto Lápice, then continues, eastwards, along the line of the N420.

At Consuegra, restored windmills stand along a crest above the town, gaunt against the sky, stone-built and white-painted, with four great latticed sails.

Unlike Consuegra, **Puerto Lápice** gets a mention in the book. It has a lovely old *corral*, a farm building with courtyard, done up as the inn on the Sevilla road which features so heavily in the Don Quixote story, and a bar with *tinajas*, the enormous storage jars that are typical of this wine-growing area.

Next stop, **Alcázar de San Juan**, has 15th- and 16th-century monuments, but is essentially a railway town.

Campo de Criptana has an impressive cluster of windmills above the town, though some are modern constructions. With a stretch of the imagination one might almost visualize the windmills as great giants against whom the chivalrous Don Quixote battled so valiantly.

Up to the northeast is **El Toboso**, home of the lady, imaginary or otherwise, to whom Don Quixote plighted his troth. Visitors are shown "Dulcinea's house," a handsome old dwelling furnished in the style of the period. There is a "Cervantine Centre" with a collection of editions of *Don Quixote*. The route continues on through **Mota del Cuervo** (ruined windmills stand in fields of litter above the town) and finishes in **Belmonte**, rather dubiously attached to the Quixote legend but with a fine castle on a hill (see page 194).

Off the beaten track Those with time will be well repaid by extending the route deeper into the country. From Mota del Cuervo, for instance, you could drop south to Tomelloso and nearby **Argamasilla** where, according to another doubtful legend, Cervantes was held in prison and began his masterpiece. The countryside around, however, is pure La Mancha.

South to the hills South again, but still within the territory of the story, are the lagoons of **Ruidera**, set in rough, wild country (see page 202) and the strange and prominently featured **cave of Montesinos** (reached from Ossa de Montiel or 3km/2mi from the southernmost lagoon). By now, you are among the Campos de Montiel (fields of Montiel), the first place actually mentioned by name in *Don Quixote*. Beyond here, almost at once, come the thoroughly Quixotic mountains of the Sierra Morena.

199

Almost every town on the Quixote route has its statue of the melancholy knight, who was immortalized by the pen of Miguel de Cervantes. The exploits of Don Quixote and his faithful servant Sancho Panza are world famous

San Lorenzo del Escorial is the most extreme of all the monastery-palaces and pantheons built by Spanish royalty. Vast in hard-edged granite, it rises from the southern slopes of the Sierra Guadarrama on a site chosen by Philip II, who had promised his father Charles V a mausoleum and had vowed to dedicate a monastery to St. Lawrence. In its ostentatious, penitential gloom (relieved by a collection of artworks and religious relics, and a magnificent library), it symbolizes Habsburg Spain.

200

At the heart of the Escorial (tel: 918 90 59 02; *Open* Tue–Sun 10–6. *Admission charge, free Wed for EU citizens*) are the private chambers of Philip II. A recess off his austere bedchamber, where he died in 1598, gave on to the high altar of the basilica.

Beneath the pompous basilica, with kneeling sculptural groups of Charles V, Philip II, and their families, the gaudy Royal Pantheon contains the remains of virtually all the Spanish kings and queens from Charles V on. In the adjoining Palacio Real (Royal Palace), the Salas Capitulares or Chapter Rooms have paintings by

Flemish, Italian, and Spanish masters. There is also a museum of architecture.

The Bourbon rooms are decorated with tapestries, some Goya-based. The rooms of Philip II and his daughter Isabella have terracotta floors, tiled dados, and creakingly ancient furniture. There is the sedan chair in which Philip was brought here to his deathbed.

The library, under ceilings by Tibaldi and Carducho, contains a sumptuous display of manuscripts.

The monastery and town can be visited on a day trip from Madrid, by train or tour bus.

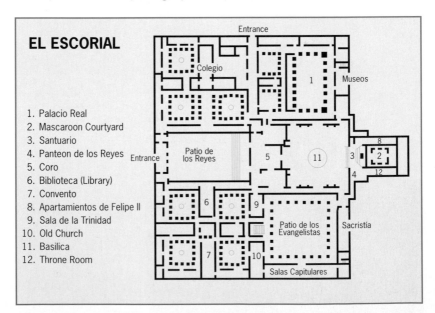

EL ESCORIAL

1. Palacio Real
2. Mascaroon Courtyard
3. Santuario
4. Panteon de los Reyes
5. Coro
6. Biblioteca (Library)
7. Convento
8. Apartamientos de Felipe II
9. Sala de la Trinidad
10. Old Church
11. Basilica
12. Throne Room

Entrance

Colegio

Museos

Entrance

Patio de los Reyes

Patio de los Evangelistas

Sacristía

Salas Capitulares

▶ **Guadalajara** *190C4*

The capital of Guadalajara province is remarkable for one monument: the **Palacio del Infantado** (tel: 949 21 33 01; *Open* winter, Tue–Sat 10–2, 4–7, Sun 10–2; summer, Tue–Sun 9.30–2.30. *Admission charge*). It was the ducal palace of the Infantados, part of the important Mendoza family. Here Juan Guas' Plateresque facade is decorated with stone protrusions, heraldry, and "wild men." Inside are cloisters and Guadalajara's provincial museum.

▶▶ **Guadarrama, Sierra de** *190B4*

The Sierra de Guadarrama is only about an hour's drive from Madrid. Rocky and pine-forested, it angles up in a northeasterly direction from the Escorial, featuring the ski station of Navacerrada and attractive spots to visit. **Manzanares El Real**, on the southern approaches, boasts the region's most exuberant and decorative castle (15th century, restored). Nearby is the regional park of **La Cuenca Alta del Río Manzanares**, with the famous tumbled rockscapes of La Pedriza. Over the pass at Navacerrada is the sumptuously beautiful monastery of **El Paular**, founded in 1390 by Juan I of Castile. Farther east, on the main road to Burgos, **Buitrago del Lozoya** retains an old walled precinct with medieval houses and a Picasso museum endowed by Picasso's own hairdresser, a loyal son of the village.

▶ **Mar de Castilla** *190C3*

This inland "sea" of artificial lakes was created by the damming of the River Tagus. Beside the three largest reservoirs of Entrepeñas, Buendía, and Bolarque there is growing tourist development catering for fishing and watersports enthusiasts.

▶ **Molina de Aragón** *191D4*

Stern walls and a keep, four stalwart towers aloft— Molina's much fought-over border status between the kingdoms of Aragón and Castile is still evident. The town, both new and old, lies below. There are mansions and churches with ancient facades, some crumbling, others shored up with rather functional restoration. A murky river passes through, spanned by a Roman bridge of huge red sandstone blocks.

▶ **Montes de Toledo** *190B2*

Venison and wild boar feature on menus in this region, with little sense of surprise or special luxury. The sparsely populated Pico Corocho de Rocigalpo rises to 1,447m (4,747ft); genuine huntsman's territory.

RESERVOIRS
General Franco probably opened more reservoirs in history, sometimes with devastating consequences for Spain's landscape. It was an essential part of his agricultural policy, and compulsory land purchase was rather easy for dictators. The story goes that on his deathbed his hand fell into his chamber pot. "I bless this reservoir…" he mumbled, which were supposedly his last words.

201

Walking in the Sierra de Guadarrama is a healthy pastime. With its scenery of green forests and slopes rising to snow-capped peaks, the area is an oasis amid the dry Castilian plains

Lake San Juan, San Martín de Valdeiglesias. Nestling in the foothills of the Gredos mountains, this is a popular weekend destination for Madrileños, who flock here to practise water sports

THE WILD PRINCESS
The tempestuous one-eyed Princess of Eboli from Guadalajara married the Duke of Pastrana, many years older than herself, and had 13 children by him. She was also the lover of the Spanish King Philip II, among others. In the course of time and devil-ish intrigues, she fell out of favour. Escaping death, she was nevertheless kept under house arrest in the Palacio de los Duques de Pastrana. She was allowed to sit on a balcony overlook-ing the square for one hour each day; a routine remembered in the square's name, Plaza de la Hora.

▶▶ Pastrana   190C3

A charming town of quiet, twisting streets and grey mottled roofs, Pastrana lies in the Alcarria hills above the Río Tagus. It was once held by the Knights of Calatrava, then given by Charles V to Ruiz Gómez da Silva, who later became the Duke of Pastrana and built a silk factory here. The grand ducal palace occupies an entire side of the lovely town square. The nearby late Gothic collegiate church has a treasury with fine 15th-century Brussels tapestries commemorating the war fought against the Moors in North Africa by King Alfonso V of Portugal. There is also a Franciscan monastery just out of town.

▶ Priego   191D3

Perched on the lip of a valley on the edge of the Serranía de Cuenca, the town of Priego looks rather run down in contrast with its wonderful position. There is no evidence of any wealth gained from its famous wickerwork and ceramic handicrafts.

▶ Ruidera   190C2

Las Lagunas de Ruidera (the Ruidera lagoons) are a succession of narrow natural lakes in marshy land along the Pinilla River (dammed farther downstream). All are popular in summer. Nearby is the Cueva de Montesinos, where Don Quixote had extraordinary visions.

▶ San Martín de Valdeiglesias   190B3

Barely an hour's drive from Madrid, this agreeable little town marks the eastern beginnings of the Sierra de Gredos. From here, take the Ávila road, and follow sign-posts for **Toros de Guisando** to see these four stone bulls, believed to be Celtiberian, in an enclosure by the road. Nearby is San Juan Lake in an attractive setting amid pines which reach the water's edge.

Drive

Sigüenza circular route
(see map page 191)

This route describes a two-day drive, either a circle based on Sigüenza or a scenic two-day extra to the direct route between Zaragoza and Madrid. Stop overnight in Cuenca.

From Sigüenza, follow the road east to **Medinaceli** (a corner of the adjoining province of Soria, see page 165). Leave Medinaceli by the old Madrid road, turning left for Maranchón, and cross the railway tracks.
　The route now goes through barren rolling countryside and depopulated villages.

From Maranchón, head south to **Molina de Aragón** (see page 201). Leave the town by the C202 signposted to Peralejos and follow the Alto Tajo tourist route.
　This part of the route is through agricultural villages and the wild ravines of the Serranía de Cuenca. The landscape becomes more wooded and mountainous near **Peralejos de las**

Truchas, a fishing and hunting settlement. Pass through the Tajo (Tagus) gorge and onto **Beteta** (castle on top and old town below). Continue down the course of the Beteta gorge, Hoz de Beteta, to **Priego** then southwards to **Villaconejos** (literally, Rabbit Town), with its troglodyte dwellings.

Follow the road southwards towards Albalate de las Nogueras and join the N320 towards Cuenca.
　Cuenca has both its famous Hanging Houses and a parador, in a former monastery. Make a detour to the extraordinary rock formations of **La Ciudad Encantada**.

Leave Cuenca as you entered, by the Madrid road, then continue northwards on the N320 around the reservoirs of the Mar de Castilla.
　At Sacedón, there is a sign to Buendía, one of the holiday resorts on the lake and somewhere to relax or indulge in watersports.

Continue on the N320 out of Sacedón across the Entrepeñas reservoir, turn left to Sayatón, then right to **Pastrana**.
　It is worth spending some time in this delightful medieval town.

From here follow the N320 to Guadalajara. Head back to Sigüenza or westwards to Madrid.

203

Quiet Sigüenza comes to life at fiesta time in the Plaza Mayor

ANCIENT TRANSLATIONS

Among Toledo's large and cultured Jewish community there were many scholars. They and colleagues from all over Europe were employed by Alfonso X, the Learned (1252–1284), in his Translators' School in Toledo. The idea was to translate works from Arabic for the general benefit of Christian Europe. The Arabs, and with them the Moors, were not only skilled philosophers, mathematicians, and navigators, but it was they, with their capture centuries earlier of much of the Byzantine Empire, who had become the guardians of the texts of Ancient Greece. Translations were also undertaken earlier at the monastery of Ripoll in Catalonia.

►►► Toledo 190B3

Toledo may be a tourist trap, but it is still unmissable: compact, awesome, often described as mystical. Certainly El Greco made it seem so, painting it in livid hues under a livid sky; and Cervantes referred to Toledo's "rocky gravity."

Toledo's past The history of the peninsula is encapsulated here: Romans, Visigoths (they made Toledo their capital), Moors (for whom it was a frontier city of great learning and cultivation), and Jews (who in early days lived here in some numbers, at peace with Moors and Christians). Alfonso VI of Castile conquered it in 1085. For a while, the tradition of scholarship persisted under the Christians, and Alfonso X (the Learned) maintained a school of translators here, salvaging Greek, Latin, and Arabic texts for emerging Europe. Toledo's Jews, who were central to this process, were eventually to be persecuted at the instigation of Vicente Ferrer (who was later sanctified), and finally expelled from Toledo and Spain in 1492.

As well as scholars, Toledo produced silks and fine-tooled, damascene daggers and swords. "The Greek," El Greco, was its finest painter. It was, and remains, chief city of the Spanish Church, seat of the Primate, and so far as Spain had a capital, Toledo was it, until Philip II moved the court to Madrid in 1561. Between then and the coming of the tourists, the only power Toledo retained was spiritual. Its most bitter battle was the siege of the Alcázar, held by the Nationalists, in the Civil War.

Economic decay from the 16th century on ironically helped to preserve the historic buildings and Moorish atmosphere of Toledo, which nowadays attracts huge numbers of visitors.

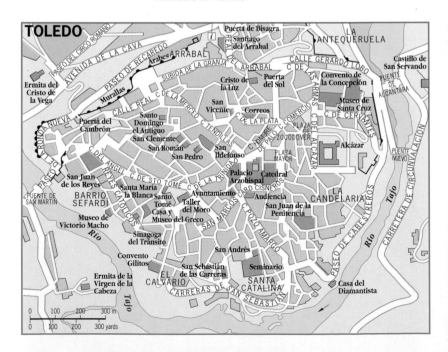

Toledo's "New" Bisagra Gate (Puerta Nueva de Bisagra), with its twin towers and imperial symbol, was enlarged and rebuilt by Covarrubias in 1550. Entry to the town was formerly through the early 10th-century Bisagra Gate, which lies a short distance away

Sightseeing Toledo lies draped over high ground in a tight loop of the Tagus gorge. The city is without doubt one of Spain's brightest jewels, with its spectacular setting, splendid mansions, and great wealth of art treasures. For drivers, there is a road around the outside, the Carretera de Circunvalación, or Ronda, which has fine views. El Greco painted the city from close to the site of the parador, reached from this road. It is best to park outside the city and walk up by the 14th-century Mudéjar Puerta del Sol on the north side. From Madrid, there are many buses, trains, and day-trip buses. The point of departure inside the city is the roughly triangular Plaza de Zocodover (the "Zoco" or souk), site of ancient horse fairs and now of a Tuesday market. The most visited sights can be walked by making a rough semicircle, starting from Zocodover down the Calle Comercio.

The cathedral Toledo's cathedral (*Open* Mon–Sat 10.30–12, 4–6, Sun 2–6. *Admission charge*) was founded by Fernando III, El Santo, in 1227. Entry is normally to the left of the main facade (under a single tower and with the *ayuntamiento* opposite, designed by El Greco's son). The interior, centre of Spanish Catholicism, is lit darkly by stained glass and is dense with works of art. There is a shrine to the Visigothic San Ildefonso, featuring the rock on which the Virgin set foot when she presented him with a chasuble. The magnificent choir contains scenes of the capture of Granada, by Rodrigo Alemán. The vast *retablo* opposite includes a representation of the shepherd who guided the Catholic troops to their great victory at Navas de Tolosa (halfway up on the left, on the pillar). Behind the sanctuary is the *Transparente*, a super-baroque work of wings and plunging figures, lit by the sun's rays through a round window. At the southeast corner of the cathedral is the Mudéjar chapel, where the ancient Mozarabic order of service is still in use. The cathedral sacristy contains an impressive collection of Italian and Spanish masterworks, focused on El Greco's *Expolio, Christ Stripped of his Robes*. In the tiny church of Santo

THE BURIAL OF THE COUNT OF ORGAZ El Greco's *The Burial of the Count of Orgaz* shows the miraculous appearance of Saints Augustine and Stephen, who lower the count, a benefactor of the Church of Santo Tomé, into his grave, still wearing his damascene armour. A line of Castilian gentlemen looks calmly on. The upper portion of the painting stands for Heaven, with the Virgin waiting to welcome the soul of the dead man. This is portrayed as a baby ascending through a shape like a birth canal. Non-Spaniards have come to see this work, with its gravely bearded, aristocratic faces, and swooning sense of divinity, as somehow epitomizing an aspect of Spanishness, even though the artist (who is pictured in the painting) was born in Crete.

205

EL GRECO

El Greco came to Toledo in 1576 or 1577. He quickly found work with the church, and the success (despite occasional rows over commissions) that always eluded him with Philip II. He never moved again. It is tempting to suggest that he identified personally both with the dramatic landscape of the city and with the rarefied spirituality which he portrayed. If this seems particularly Castilian, so be it; Domenicos Theotocopoulos, the Greek, had come a long way from his native Crete.

THE SIEGE OF THE ALCÁZAR

The Nationalist defence of the Toledo Alcázar was one of the great epics of the early months of the Civil War. The story has it that the son of the Nationalist officer in command, Colonel José Moscardó, was captured by the Republicans, who threatened to kill him. Moscardó spoke to his son on the telephone, exhorting him: "If it be true, commend your soul to God, cry Viva España and die like a hero," an uncanny echo of Guzmán el Bueno (see panel, page 237). Moscardó's battered operations room, even his telephone, can still be seen in the Alcázar.

Tomé (*Open* daily 10–5.45, 6.45 in summer. *Admission charge*) not far away from the cathedral, is El Greco's enormous painting, *El Entierro del Conde de Orgaz* (*The Burial of the Count of Orgaz*).

Casa y Museo del Greco (El Greco's House and Museum)

This 16th-century building (tel: 925 22 40 46; *closed for refurbishment*) is set out as if it really were El Greco's. It contains paintings by the artist, and in the well-stocked museum there is the famous *View and Plan of Toledo*, which was a major source of information on the city in the artist's own day.

Santa María la Blanca In the Judería, or Jewish Quarter, is the stunning little church (originally a synagogue) called Santa María la Blanca (tel: 925 22 72 57; *Open* Apr–Sep, daily 10–2, 3.30–7; Oct–Mar, 10–2, 3.30–6. *Admission charge*), built in Almohad style in the 12th century. Snowy white within, it rises on graceful horseshoe arches to raised geometrical patterning.

Sinagoga del Tránsito This 14th-century synagogue is elegant in Mudéjar style. It was built by Samuel Leví, treasurer to Pedro I (who finally had him executed). It now contains a small Jewish museum (tel: 925 22 36 55; *closed for refurbishment*).

San Juan de los Reyes (St. John of the Kings)

The monastery church (tel: 925 22 38 02; *Open* Apr–Sep, daily 10–1.45, 3.30–6.45; Oct–Mar, 10–1.45, 3.30–5.45. *Admission charge*) built by Isabella and Ferdinand is a grand display of Isabelline Gothic, encrusted with royal monograms and with their yoke-and-arrow symbol (borrowed by Franco for Spanish Fascism). Outsize stone shields tilt at rakish angles on the walls. The cloister is delightful; the church's outer facade is hung with chains removed from Christian captives of the Moors.

Other central sights The **Alcázar** (*Open* Tue–Sat 9.30–2.30. *Admission charge*), rebuilt in 16th-century form after the Civil War, is a fascinating museum of the 68-day siege of the fortress, and a monument to the Nationalist cause (see panel). Try not to miss it, whatever your views.

The **Museo/Hospital de Santa Cruz**, an airy hospital of the late 15th and early 16th centuries, with Plateresque facade and patio, is just under the Alcázar. It has an impressive collection of paintings by El Greco and others and it is a stunning architectural space (see page 267 for opening times).

North of Plaza del Zocodover As you cross over to the Old (Moorish) and New (16th-century) Bisagra gates on the north side of town, you pass by the ancient mosque now named **Cristo de la Luz**. This building, with its echoes of the Great Mosque of Córdoba, may be the oldest in Toledo. Beyond the gates, the **Hospital de Tavera** (tel: 925 22 04 51; *Open* daily 10.30–1.30, 3.30–6. *Admission charge*) has sundry works of art and curiosities including Ribera's *Bearded Woman*, often, alas, away on loan for exhibition.

Wine-tasting in a Valdepeñas cellar. Known for its wines, which are mainly white and characterized by a fruity taste, the town has numerous bodegas, or wine cellars, which can be visited

EL DONCEL
In the chapel of San Juan y Santa Catalina in Sigüenza's cathedral, the delicate 15th-century effigy of Martín Vázquez de Arce shows him as an armed knight at ease, one leg folded over the other, reading a book, no doubt religious. Known as El Doncel, normally meaning a page-boy or even virgin but here perhaps "young person of delicate beauty," this is one of Spain's most famous funerary statues.

▶▶ Sigüenza   190C4

From the *alameda* at the bottom of town to the castle at the top, little Sigüenza is a delightful, old-fashioned provincial town. The **cathedral** (tel: 619 36 27 15 and ask for Diego; *Open* Mon–Sat 9.30–2, 4.30–7. Guided tours Tue–Sun 11, 12, 12.45, 4.30, 5.30. *Admission charge*) is the chief monument, a composite of Romanesque, Gothic, Plateresque, and even 20th-century styles. Despite a sombre outward appearance, it has a rich interior. The cathedral museum has one good painting each by El Greco and Zurbarán; the sacristy ceiling bears over 300 intricately carved heads by Covarrubias.

▶ Talavera de la Reina   190A3

Wellington's forces defeated the French here in 1809; otherwise this busy town means only ceramics. These rely on floral patterning and naturalistic designs such as lolloping large-eared rabbits. There are many commercial showrooms as well as a local ceramics museum.

▶ Uclés   190C3

The remarkable **monastery** (tel: 969 13 60 14; *Open* daily 10–2, 4–7. *Admission charge*) here, 16th- to 18th-century in its present form but founded in 1174, was a key site for the Knights of Santiago (see page 219). The refectory retains busts of the Masters.

▶ Valdepeñas   190C1

Workaday Valdepeñas handles the wines produced in this part of La Mancha. There are numerous bodegas, and *tinajas*, enormous wine storage jars, stand by the road.

▶ Villanueva de los Infantes   190C1

In the Campos de Montiel, this little town, with its extra-ordinary collection of monuments, is a good example of how history once touched New Castile, then passed it by. The Plaza Mayor has a huge parochial church, arcades, and wooden balconies. There is a lovely little patio and enough shields and escutcheons to fill a book of drawings, literally, as one has been published locally.

TALAVERA POTTERY
Ever since Renaissance times, the liveliest pottery in Castile has come from Talavera de la Reina and nearby Puente del Arzobispo. Using light greens, browns, yellows, and often red for flowers, the potters decorate their wares with cheerful scenes of rural pursuits and nature generally. Floral designs, often rimmed in blue, are also traditional. There are masses of pottery shops in Talavera itself, and Talavera ware, along with a great deal of junk pottery, is commonly sold elsewhere in shops and markets. Some of the dishes are huge and intended for walls; others are small and inexpensive enough for domestic use.

BETWEEN CATALONIA IN THE NORTH and Andalucía in the south, there lies a tract of coastal Spain composed of the autonomous regions of Valencia and Murcia and popularly known as the Levante, the land of the rising sun. The two "autonomies" are very different, for the Valencia region is historically intertwined with Catalonia and speaks its own language, Valenciano, which has similarities to Catalan. Murcia is more Spanish.

SPAIN'S FOOD BOWL The whole of the area, with once-poor Murcia now beginning to come into its own, is Spain's chief market garden. Valencia's fertile *huerta* (market garden) has been one of history's choicest prizes.

208

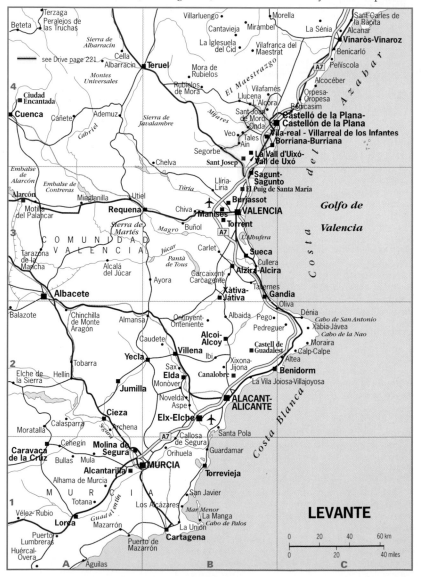

LEVANTE

Women of Morella in the Maestrazgo having a good gossip about the events of the day

El Cid captured the city in the 11th century and founded a private kingdom here, but both the city and its famous *huerta* soon reverted to the Moors, who held on for two more centuries.

The present-day system of irrigation still owes much to the Moors. The basic crops, now as then, are oranges, vegetables, and rice (paella is a dish from Valencia). But the *huerta* is also a very messy area, full of light industry and litter. One pleasing relief is the Albufera lake, south of Valencia, though itself badly threatened by pesticides and encroaching building.

TOURIST ATTRACTIONS There are three important *costas*. The Costa del Azahar or Orange Blossom Coast, undramatic but much used by families, lies mainly north of Valencia. Running south from around the Cabo de la Nao headland lies the packed mass-tourism Costa Blanca, focused on Benidorm, a very well-run resort. The Murcian coast (or Costa Cálida) has a semi-inland sea, the Mar Menor, with new resorts emerging around it.

Valencia, Spain's third city, has some fine old buildings and a very pleasant atmosphere. Architecturally, Murcia is one of Spain's most baroque cities. Behind, round, and between the two big cities are plenty of interesting places, ranging from Sagunt, the tragic site of one of the great sieges of the Punic War, to Xàtiva and Gandia, home of the Borgia family. And behind all of them rises the magnificent sierra, gaunt above the sea.

Local produce in Castelló de la Plana

TOURIST INFORMATION

Albufera Lake: Raco de L'Olla (tel: 961 62 01 72).
Alcoi: San Lorenzo 2 (tel: 965 53 71 55).
Caravaca de la Cruz: Calle de las Monjas 17 (tel: 968 70 24 24).
Cartagena: Plaza Basterreche s/n (tel: 968 50 64 83).
Castelló de la Plana, Costa del Azahar: Plaza María Agustina 5, Castelló de la Plana (tel: 964 35 86 88).
Costa Blanca: Rambla de Mendez Nuñez 23, Alacant (tel: 965 20 00 00).
Costa Cálida: Plaza Julián Romea 4, Murcia (tel: 902 10 10 70).
Elx: Parque Municipal s/n (tcl: 965 45 27 47).
Murcia: Calle Plano de San Francisco 5 (tel: 968 35 87 20).
Puig, Segorbe, Vilafamés, Villena: Calle de la Paz 48, Valencia (tel: 963 98 64 22).
Sagunt: Plaza Cronista Chabret (tel: 962 66 22 13).
Valencia: Plaza del Ayuntamiento 1 (tel: 963 5104 17).
Xàtiva: Calle Alameda de Jaime 1 50 (tel: 962 27 33 46).

THE CROSS OF CARAVACA

Caravaca is the site of one of Spain's most exciting miracles. It seems that the local Moorish ruler was curious to hear the Christian Mass. A priest whom he was holding captive prepared to perform the ceremony, but suddenly remembered he had no cross. Quick as a flash, two angels arrived to remedy the deficiency. This celebrated cross disappeared during the Civil War, but the Pope made good the loss with the gift of a fragment of the True Cross. This is now embedded in the cross currently on display in Caravaca.

In the gazetteer entries below, where both Valenciano and Castilian place-names are given, the Castilian appears in brackets after the Valenciano.

▶ Alcoi (Alcoy) 208B2

North of Alacant (see page 214), in pleasant sierra dotted with pine and almond trees, Alcoi is a textile town with an industrial history. During the first Republic of 1874–1875, it declared itself independent and so it remained for several months. The town hosts Spain's best "Moors and Christians" festival (see the costumes exhibited in the Museo de Fiestas del Casal de Sant Jordi), and is home to the sugared almond or *peladilla*.

▶ Caravaca de la Cruz 208A1

This hill town in inland Murcia is dominated by the pink Real Alcázar, Santuario de la Vera Cruz, a restored 15th-century Templar castle with a 17th-century church within it. The church was built to house a cross delivered by angels (see panel). The town has some rumbustious "Moors versus Christians" parades in early May.

▶ Cartagena 208B1

Cartagena, on the south Murcian coast, has been an important mining and naval town since the Carthaginians first exploited its deep-water harbour and dug out minerals from the surrounding area. A densely jumbled town with a lively bustling air, it is now home to the Spanish Mediterranean fleet. Little remains of its tumultuous past except the old fort and ruins of a Romanesque church, the arsenal established by Charles III, and a submarine designed in 1888 by a naval officer, Isaac Peral.

▶ Castelló de la Plana (Castellón de la Plana) 208C4

Castelló de la Plana is a small provincial capital, set between the mountains and its busy port, El Grao. Castelló itself was largely destroyed during the Civil War, but despite being rebuilt during an undistinguished period of architecture, it has a pleasant, open feel. The cathedral, the 16th-century bell tower, the Convento de Capuchinas (containing paintings attributed to Francisco Zurbarán), and the Museo de Bellas Artes are the chief attractions.

South of Valencia lies the Albufera, a large
freshwater lake divided from the Mediterranean only by a sandbank. Though shrunk to
a tenth of its original size, it remains rich in
ducks, herons, fish, and eels. Parts are dense
with reed-banks; parts are fringed by rice
fields. This lake is at its best on misty mornings and at its most scenic at sunset.

Boat trip Boats ply for hire from **El Palmar** and **El Saler**.
The trip from El Saler lasts about 30 to 40 minutes, at an
all-in price for the boat. This is a traditional wooden craft,
long and lowish, once punted, now motorized. The trip is
highly recommended for views of the lake and its bird-life
and also, alas, for a vivid glimpse of the fragility of the
ecosystem. Though now subject to restriction, devastating out-of-scale building has occurred to the north and on
the protective sand-spit, La Dehesa; the waters, once
clear, are green.

The rice harvest used to come home by boat; now
nobody would dream of using anything except a truck
or tractor. The best months for spotting wildlife, as also
for duck-hunters, so keep your head down, are from
September to March.

Old and new Around the lake, particularly on the southern
side, there still survives a sprinkling of the original lake-
landers' *barracas*: long, thin, thatched houses with long,
narrow gardens. However, coastal apartment blocks all
too often tower above them.

A little south again, behind the dunes that back the
beach, there is the very pleasant **Parador de El Saler**, a
haunt of golfers who come for the course which backs
right onto the hotel.

*The Albufera lake,
rewarding for wildlife
enthusiasts and for
duck-hunters*

Walk

Gardens of Valencia

This is a walk of about 3.5 hours, combining two of Valencia's most pleasant and interesting open spaces, the **Jardines del Real** (also called Los Viveros) and the **Jardín Botánico** (Botanical Gardens). They are linked by a stroll along the bed of the diverted River Turia.
(See also page 222.)

Start at the Tourist Information Office, Calle de la Paz 48. Turn right to skirt round Plaza Alfonso el Magnánimo, then left up Calle General Tovar and through Plaza de Tetuán.

Now cross the fine old 16th-century bridge, Puente del Real, over the Turia.

Diagonally to the right now is the city's most expensive housing, diagonally left the entrance to **Jardines del Real**, graceful and southern in style. A 20-minute stroll takes you to the far end of the park.

Return to the same entrance, cross the road, and descend to the bed of the old Turia. Turn right.

Some parts of the river bed have been newly planted, others are older; some areas are football pitches. You will pass the handsome medieval city gates, the **Serrano Towers**.

Emerge from the river bed opposite the Nuevo Centro shopping centre and then walk away from the river at right angles along Calle Beato Gaspar Bono.

The entrance to the **Botanical Gardens** (tel: 963 15 68 00; *Open* summer, Tue–Sun 10–9; winter, 10–6; *Closed* in bad weather) is at the end of this long defile. Quiet and mature, founded in 1802, the gardens embody much of the Enlightenment quest for a scientific understanding of the flora of Spain and her dominions.

Return to the city centre down Carrer Quart, which becomes Caballeros. Turn right at the Plaza de la Virgen into an alley beside the cathedral leading to Plaza de la Reina at the end of Calle de la Paz.

Valencia, Spain's third city, is rich in parks and gardens

► **Costa del Azahar and Costa de Valencia** *208C4*
The Costa del Azahar (Orange Blossom Coast) runs south from just below the mouth of the Ebro towards the major city of Valencia, then on again to meet the Costa Blanca. It consists of a fringe of often flattish shoreline, backed in many parts by orange groves.

The mountains behind, unimpressive in the north, become increasingly dramatic as they near Valencia. Though this is one of the less stylish Spanish costas, some of its beaches are excellent and the generally calm atmosphere makes it suitable for families. Camping is popular in the area.

Alcossebre (Alcocéber) Midway down the Costa, Alcocéber has five beaches. The town beach is good; La Romana and La Tropicana, farther south, are both outstanding, though not smart.

Benicarló This fair-sized town towards the Costa's northern end has a small but busy beach, a fishing port, a parador, and a lively restaurant scene in summer. Wide streets and old buildings give it charm; note in particular the fine 18th-century church.

Benicasim Pleasant and well placed among palms, Benicasim is a northerly seaside suburb of Castelló de la Plana (see page 210). It is an agreeable but busy spot for family holidays.

Cullera South of Valencia, Cullera is definitely mass-tourism, and receives plenty of French visitors. It lies under a rocky hill and 13th-century castle, with a wide beach and many apartment blocks.

Gandía This southernmost resort on the Costa is backed by a forest of apartment blocks, and noisome with heavy through-traffic. It does boast long stretches of fine sandy beaches, however. It is also the birthplace of San Francisco Borja (St. Francis Borgia), who became the second head of the Jesuits. The ducal palace in which the saint was born is now a school run by Jesuits but can be visited on a guided tour (tel: 962 87 14 65; *Open* Tue–Sat 10.30–12.30, 5–7, Sun 10.30–12.30). Grouped around the handsome Gothic courtyard are several richly decorated chambers. Notable among them are the 17th-century Golden Gallery (in baroque style), the dukes' private chapel, and a room whose floor is covered in ceramics depicting the four elements of creation: earth, air, water, and fire. For more on the Borjas see Xàtiva, page 221. See also Peñíscola (page 220), Castelló de la Plana (page 210), and Sagunt (pages 220–221).

Grutas de San Josep (St. Joseph's Caves) Follow the road signs to "Grutas" from Vall de Uxó (just north of Sagunt). The grotto (tel: 964 69 05 76; *Open* Apr–Sep, Tue–Sun 11–1.15, 3.30–6.30; Oct–Mar, 11–1.15, 3.30–5.30. *Admission charge*) experience involves a boat trip along an underground river (you will see caves and rock formations artfully lit), followed by a short walk along a gallery, and a boat trip back again (45 minutes).

THE *HUERTA*
The true Valencia orange is as much a symbol of the Levante as the rice that goes into *paella*. Orange groves punctuate the rich market-garden land or *huerta* behind the coast, and lorries full of the chilled fruit go pounding off to northern Europe. As well as being skilled hi-tech horticulturalists, Valencianos are well known as some of Spain's shrewdest and most internationally minded traders.

213

The fishing harbour in Benicarló is a focal point in the afternoon when the boats come in and the fish auction is held; always a lively event

Levante

THE TASTE OF *TURRÓN*
In Spanish *turrón*, in Valencian *terró*, in English "nougat": Spaniards love this Arabic sweetmeat, made of almonds, honey, sugar, and the white of egg. It comes in two forms in Spanish sweet shops: *blando* (soft), and the hard kind more familiar to northern Europeans, known as *duro* or *imperial*. The little town of Jijona, above Alacant in a region of almond orchards, is the nougat capital. Factories cluster thickly here, and there is a delicious smell. You can visit the El Lobo factory, just before the bridge on the northern exit from Jijona.

214

Oropesa del Mar With a scrap of old town around a ruined castle inland, this resort north of Castellón de la Plana has a long beach to the north and a cove beach to the south.

►► **Peñíscola** see page 220

Vinaròs (Vinaroz) The most northerly port and resort on the Costa del Azahar, Vinaroz is scruffy but cheerful. The fishing fleet brings in giant prawns and scampi.

►► **Costa Blanca**   *208C2*
The Costa Blanca (White Coast) of Alacant province is a phenomenon. In the north its offerings range from huge headlands and inaccessible coves, through the pleasant villa territory of retired foreigners to the mass pleasure domes of Benidorm. At its southern extreme, it has some of the most dense and dismal villa/apartment developments in all Spain.

Alacant (Alicante) Elegant Alacant, with its tree-lined squares and boulevards, bustling modern town, magnificently baroque *ayuntamiento*, wide clean beaches, and bright waterfront Esplanada de España, is the undisputed capital of the Costa Blanca. For sightseers there is the Carthaginian **Castillo de Santa Barbara** (*Open* daily Apr–Sep, 9.30–7.30; Oct–Mar, 9.30–6.30. *Admission free*), with views; the 17th-century church of San Nicolás; and a small but interesting collection of 20th-century art in the **Museo Asegurada** (*Open* summer, Tue–Sat 10–2, 5–9, Sun 10.30–2.30; winter, Tue–Sat 10–2, 4–8, Sun 10.30–2.30. *Admission free*).

Altea Though centred still on its pretty, old town on a hill, Altea has now become a major tourist venue.

Benidorm Arguably Spain's capital of mass tourism, Benidorm is now almost a city behind its two long, crowded and excellent beaches. Having opted early for

Benidorm, high-rise holiday mecca for the volumes of tourists who flock here each year. One of Spain's most popular resorts, this international fun city is crammed with hotels, apartment blocks, and restaurants, with an excessive nightlife provided by bars and discos

Quiet beach near Xàbia (Jávea). Its attractive setting between two rock masses, international ambience, and lively yacht harbour make it one of the Costa Blanca's most desirable resorts

high-rise building, it pursues this course with great professionalism. Once very British in atmosphere, it is now international. It has the best water park on the Costa.

Calp (Calpe) The mighty upthrust rock here, the Penyal d'Ifac (Peñón de Ifach), is a surreal landmark of the Costa Blanca. Rising from the sea, it towers over the resort of Calp and is now a natural park. The ascent on foot takes one hour. An isthmus of high-rise blocks links it to the mainland, with beaches to the north and south, and fishing harbour under the rock.

Dénia A self-catering holiday place, Dénia has the excellent Las Marinas beach to the north. To the south, pretty Les Rotes leads to Cabo de San Antonio and the resort of **Xàbia (Jávea)**. Here, the hoop of sandy beach is overlooked by a parador with Roman ruins in its garden.

Terra Mitica (*Open* 16 June–16 Sep 10AM–midnight; 15 Mar–15 Jun, 17 Sep–4 Nov 10–8PM; 6 Jan–11 Mar, 10 Nov–30 Dec 10–6PM. *Admission charge*) This theme park is just outside Benidorm and designed around the civilizations of the Mediterranean with several water rides, a ghost train based on the Minotaur's labyrinth, and a large wooden big dipper.

Torrevieja As well as a white Andalucian-style kitsch development, Torrevieja has salt pans, a semi-natural park with passing flamingos, and a beach.

▶▶ Costa Cálida   *208B1*

Costa Cálida (the Warm Coast) is the coastline of Murcia, hitherto the playground of locals, now known for the Mar Menor (Lesser Sea), with its pulsating resort of **La Manga**. Golf is a major pastime.

Águilas Sailing and windsurfing are the attractions of this resort. The best beaches are southwest of town.

Mar Menor A large expanse of shallow water, the Mar Menor has a resort, La Manga, which is one of the concrete playgrounds of the Med. Strong winds make this an energetic paradise for windsurfers.

THE CANELOBRE CAVES
The Canelobre caves (*Open* Oct–Jun daily 11–5.30; Easter and summer daily 10.30–7.30) are a great destination for outings from Benidorm, reached via the village of Busot. At 700m (2,296ft), they are claimed as the richest stalactite caves in southeastern Spain. Lights illuminate the rock formations and concerts are sometimes held here. Don't expect to find yourself alone.

BUSINESS AND THE BIRDS
Commerce and wildlife coexist in the salt pans outside Torrevieja. These shallow lagoons produce a large proportion of Spain's salt and provide a vital habitat for wildfowl at the same time. Species which can be seen with binoculars from the shore (depending on the time of year) include pochard, kentish plover, squacco heron, shelduck, avocet, and, most spectacular of all, the greater flamingo. The salt works, meanwhile, can be visited by asking at the offices at the end of the square beside Torrevieja harbour.

Elx is a busy, commercial town, densely packed with small squares, fountains, and old buildings. It is famous for its exotic groves of date palms and for shoe manufacture. The date palms, of which there are around 200,000, radiate out from the middle of town. Though much reduced since they were planted by the Romans, they remain the largest palm plantation in Europe. They're best seen in the Parque Municipal (Municipal Park).

Another palm park is the **Huerto del Cura** (*Open* summer, daily 9–8.30; winter, daily 9–6. *Admission charge*), on the east side of town. Here, many of the trees in a well-maintained garden are named after celebrity visitors. The US palm, presumably for the ambassador, stands next to the late Señora Franco. At 150 years old, a famous seven-branched palm tree, known as the Palmera Imperial, leans perilously, much buttressed by iron hoops.

> ❏ The unusual sight of palm trees with their branches trussed in black polythene, shooting into the sky like tall spears, is a common one in Elx. Their fronds, protected from sunlight by the plastic, are being bleached for the Palm Sunday processions. Palm fronds are thought to divert lightning and are left to decorate balconies long after the religious celebrations are over. ❏

Mystery of Elx The 17th-century baroque Basilica de Santa María, beautiful in golden stone, surmounted by a tower and two domes of brightest blue, was built for the performance of the famous Elx medieval mystery play about the death, or dormition, of the Virgin (played by a small boy) and her coronation as Queen of Heaven and Earth. The action unfolds over two days, 14 and 15 August, but the full dress rehearsal of the whole play takes place the day before.

Next to the basilica are the sloping walls of the Moorish **fortress** and, within a short walking distance, the **Palacio de Altamira**, now an archaeological museum. Just out of town is **La Alcudia,** another archaeological museum (*Open* Oct–Mar, Tue–Sat 10–5; Apr–Sep, Tue–Sat 10–2, 4–8, Sun 10–2. *Admission charge*), where the beautiful 5th-century BC Iberian head of La Dama de Elx (now in Madrid) was discovered.

Elx palm fronds: prized throughout Spain

The remains of a Moorish castle occupy a lofty mountain crag at Guadalest. Much of the village was destroyed by an earthquake, but the steep climb up to the fortress is worth it for the splendid views of the area

▶▶ **Elx** see page 216   *208B2*

▶▶ **Guadalest**   *208B2*

In spite of being one of the Costa Blanca's star attractions, the pretty little town of Guadalest, 12km (8mi) inland from Benidorm, within the walls of a one-time Moorish fortress, remains relatively unspoiled thanks to its inaccessibility to cars. The entrance to the village is through a short sloping pedestrian tunnel cut in the rock over 1,000 years ago. It is famous for its lace and now most of its well-kept houses are craft and souvenir shops. From the old castle there is a wonderful view of the whole valley with its terraced fields of almond trees, and the belfry, perched precariously on a rock outcrop. For many, an excursion to Guadalest is a first intimation of the beauty and historical riches of the coastal sierra.

▶ **Lorca**   *208A1*

Lorca is famous for the manufacture of ceramics and textiles. The old town on a hill is dominated by a castle, with views of the modern town spreading out into the *huerta* below. Much of the old town was rebuilt in grand baroque style after it was partially razed by an earthquake in the 17th century. The Plaza de España has an arcaded town hall and the collegiate church of San Patricio; just above, on the Plazita del Cano, are the law courts together with archive buildings.

▶▶ **Maestrazgo** see pages 218–219   *208B4*

▶▶ **Morella**   *208B4*

A rugged but delightful mountain village in the upper Maestrazgo region, Morella has steep streets topped by a castle (tel: 964 17 30 32; castle grounds: *Open* May–Aug, daily 10.30–7.30; Sep–Apr, 10.30–6.30. *Admission charge*) on an immense rocky hill with great views. Skirted by its medieval walls and gates, it is the epitome of the fortified hill-top town. Look out for the Gothic Basilica de Santa María la Mayor, which has finely carved portals; pass through the old Franciscan monastery and museum to the castle.

THE MIRACLE OF MORELLA
In the Calle de la Virgen (behind the main street of Morella), there is a tiled plaque on the wall that tells a bizarre story. It marks the house where, in the early 15th-century, St. Vincent Ferrer performed a strange miracle. A distraught woman, worried because she had no meat to offer to the saint, who was coming for supper, cut up her son, and put him in the paella pan. Just before dinner, St. Vincent discovered what had happened and he reconstituted the boy's body, except for one little finger, which his mother had eaten to see if her dish was well salted.

The Maestrazgo (Maestrat) is a fiercely beautiful area of mountain and medieval townships in southern Aragón and the northern Levante. Its name means "the Dominion of the Grand Masters." The Knights Templar, Knights of St. John, and Knights of Calatrava were all active in this bitterly disputed frontier area between the Moors and Christians. Nothing in Spain more eloquently sums up the later stages of the Reconquest than the story of these Knights of the Church Militant.

218

EL MAESTRAZGO

Gradually the Templars began to acquire large estates, which were granted by the rulers of Aragón in return for their active role in the Reconquest. In addition, the Order became further enriched through gifts and donations received in various forms. These could be straightforward donations of money, or presents of horses and weapons to be used for battle. Many of these acquisitions were received as bequests from *confrates*, or fraternities, which started to form around the mid-12th century, increasing gradually over the following century.

The trend began in 1064, when Pope Alexander II granted indulgences to all French knights willing to fight the Muslims in Aragón. So off they went, dreaming of their "castles in Spain." Soon after the First Crusade in 1097, the Knights Templar and the Hospitallers were established in the Holy Land. Both quickly became active in Spain. The Templars received their first land grant in the peninsula, in Catalonia, in 1149. Even before that, Alfonso the Battler, King of Aragón, dying without an heir in 1131, had willed his whole kingdom jointly to the Templars, the Hospitallers, and the Holy Sepulchre in Jerusalem.

The astonished nobles of Aragón rejected the will and in Alfonso's place elected his brother Ramiro the Monk, obliging him to renounce Holy Orders to father a son and heir.

The Templar network Accompanied by strange symbols and rituals and octagonal church shrines modelled on the Holy Sepulchre in Jerusalem, the network spread rapidly through Spain. One of the best Templar churches is **Vera Cruz**, outside the walls of Segovia. The lovely little church of **Eunate**, an octagon set in meadows beside the Pilgrims' Way in Navarra, borrows the Templar style, though probably it was a burial place for pilgrims erected by the Knights of St. John of Jerusalem. Many Spanish castles, since refortified and reconstructed, have Templar origins. The most spectacular is that at **Ponferrada** in León. The Templars were interested in arcane knowledge; they were also strong supporters of the Jewish community and of the Moorish communities living in Christian territory.

Other orders Meanwhile, several other, entirely Hispanic orders, came into being. When the Templars conceded they could no longer hold their fortress at **Calatrava**, south of Ciudad Real, the abbot of Fitero in Navarra, a former soldier, stepped in to mount a heroic defence. As a consequence, a new order, that of Calatrava, was founded in 1158. The new Knights, who followed strict Benedictine rules, eventually lost the castle to the Moors, recovered it in the next century and massively rebuilt it into a sacred convent-castle. To stand on its battlements as sunset strikes the sierra is an awesome experience. The Knights of Alcántara were formed in 1165 and the Order of Santiago was established in Cáceres in 1170. The Knights of St. John meanwhile occupied a sturdy castle at Consuegra in La Mancha. Almost all held land in the Maestrazgo.

Threat and suppression The Templars became drastically overpowerful. Accused of everything from sodomy to Satanism, they were suppressed throughout Europe in a papal plot early in the 14th century. In Spain, those who would not disown the order were tried for heresy in the Old Cathedral in Salamanca. These events were the signal for the Hispanic Orders, including the new Knights of Montesa in Valencia, to expand into the vacuum. They continued to battle for Christendom along the borders but they, too, grew overpowerful. Their dominions were huge; they dominated the nomadic routes of the sheep flocks, and their military forces were uncomfortably strong.

Their comeuppance came with the Catholic Monarchs. In 1476, the death of the Marquis of Villena, Grand Master of the Order of Santiago, created a vacancy at the top. As the chapter went into conclave to choose a successor, at their monastery-headquarters at Uclés in Castilla-La Mancha, rebuilt in the Renaissance, the young Queen Isabella arrived, hastening from Valladolid, and persuaded them, after a little arm-twisting, to elect her husband Ferdinand.

He initially delegated the office, then took over in 1499. Meanwhile, he had been elected head of the Knights of Calatrava and of Alcántara. The Catholic Monarchs had scored another victory for the centre; from the reign of Charles V, the orders became purely ceremonial.

EL CID CAMPEADOR
Scattered about this wild and rugged region is an abundance of small fortified towns with medieval echoes and reminders of the exploits of the legendary Rodrigo Díaz de Vivar, more commonly known as El Cid Campeador. Some towns still carry the name of El Cid and numerous coats of arms can be seen, bearing witness to the valiant battles that took place here in the 11th century.

219

Salamanca's Old Cathedral, scene of Templar trials for heresy in the 14th century

EASTER *PASOS*

Francisco Salzillo's figures (*pasos*) are remarkable for their sweet-visaged portrayal of wild emotion. You can see the enormously long, multi-scene Nativity model which helped to make his name, in the Museo Salzillo in Murcia, where nativities (or cribs) are still made today, many for export.

MURCIAN VEGETABLES

Flat and fertile, Murcia prides itself on its Moorish tradition of intensive agriculture. Consequently, fruit and vegetables feature strongly on every menu. This is unusual for Spain, where the quality of a meal is judged more by the content of protein than vitamin C. Murcia is a province of artichokes, broad beans, mangoes, and custard apples.

VALENCIAN RICE DISHES

Paella is the most famous: a huge open pan of Valencian short-grained, saffron-flavoured and tinted rice, rich chicken and rabbit or seafood. Paella, however, is just one of many rice dishes in Catalonia and the Levante. Others include *arroz abanda*, with rice cooked in fish stock and the fish served separately, and, from Alacant, "crusty rice" (*arroz amb costra*), which contains chick peas, sausage, and pork with an eggy crust.

►► Murcia   208B1

Murcia, in the deep southeast, is a city apart. Despite its grimy outskirts and the erosion of its fertile *huerta* by ill-considered building, the city has much to recommend it.

The **cathedral** (*Open* daily 10–1, 5–7. *Admission charge*) displays an impressive mixture of rival styles. There is a grand baroque facade and fine carved Renaissance choir stalls. Though much of the interior is Gothic, Renaissance decoration runs riot in certain of the chapels. The tower (good views from the top) is Renaissance-Plateresque below, Gothic above. The nearby **casino** on Calle de la Trapería (tel: 968 21 53 99; *Open* 9–9. *Admission charge*) is a gentlemen's club. Its fake Mudéjar and neoclassical rooms provide a fine civic amenity. Away from the main town, the **Museo Salzillo** (*Open* autumn and winter, Tue–Sat 9.30–1, 3–6, Sun 11–1; spring, Tue–Sat 9.30–1, 4–7, Sun 11–1; Jul–Aug, Mon–Fri 9.30–1, 4–7. *Admission charge*) holds life-size polychrome figures for Easter processions created by the local 18th-century master, Francisco Salzillo. Further strolls in the city will reveal many more baroque facades, pleasant river embankments, and Spain's first-ever Jesuit college.

► Onda   208B4

Overlooked by its high castle, formerly ringed by three walls, and known locally as "the castle of 300 towers," Onda is a ceramics town. At the end of the Civil War, its citizens took refuge from Nationalist forces in the complex of tunnels (now mostly fallen in) under the castle.

► Orihuela   208B1

A splendid but decaying town, Orihuela was once the capital of Murcia, as seen by the 14th-century cathedral and fine manorial buildings (mostly in a state of collapse). Also notable is its extensive palm grove, **El Palmeral**.

►► Peñíscola   208C4

Now a tourist spot, Peñíscola is a rocky promontory jutting into the sea. Girdled with high walls, it is crowned by a castle. It was given its present form in the 15th century by the Spanish anti-pope, Pedro de Luna, alias Benedict XIII. The white, Andalucian old town lies below the castle. The new town is a mass of hotels and apartments behind a long beach.

► Puig   208B3

Just north of Valencia, the huge 13th-century monastery of Santa María in Puig is a major centre for pilgrimage and devotion, based on the 6th-century Byzantine stone relief of the Virgin and Child housed here.

► Requena   208B3

A pretty, old wine-making town in a wide plain, Requena has a couple of charming 15th-century churches and a Moorish castle, which now houses a wine museum.

►► Sagunt (Sagunto)   208B3

The ancient town of Sagunt, much fought over by Romans and Carthaginians and enclosed by high walls, sits high and tremendous on the crest of a long hill overlooking the

Drive

To the heart of the Levante
(see map page 208)

This is a drive into the Levante hinterland with its hard-edged ceramic manufacturing towns and spectacular mountain scenery.

From Sagunt take the N340 north. There is a possible diversion off this road to **Grutas de San Josep** (St. Joseph's Caves, see page 213).

On the approach to Castelló de la Plana, turn left towards Llucena del Cid. After 13km (8mi), turn right, passing local industry, through Sant Joan de Moró to the lovely town of **Vilafamés**.

Retrace your route and turn right, towards L'Alcora. Note the town hall in **L'Alcora**, with its baroque ceramic decoration.

Turn southwards through **Onda**, then inland towards Tales, past the tiny villages of Veo and Alcudia de Veo and then right for **Segorbe** shortly before Aín. The drive now becomes spectacular: high, narrow, and tremendous.

From Segorbe, take the N234 back to Sagunt.

Levante *huerta*. The modern town and busy port lie below. Sights include the **castle** and a **Roman theatre** (tel: 962 66 55 81; *Open* summer, 10–8; winter, 10–6. *Admission free*), controversially restored for modern use.

▶ Segorbe 208B4
Tranquil Segorbe stands high above the Palancia River. Its cathedral, over-restored and neoclassical, houses an art collection, with 15th-century religious panels.

▶▶ Valencia see pages 222–223

▶ Vilafamés 208B4
Vilafamés lies on the edge of a dense ceramic manufacturing area and wild sierra. It has an ancient high castle, pink-coloured stone houses, a Renaissance town hall, a baroque church, and a 15th-century former palace, which now houses a museum of contemporary art.

▶ Villena 208B2
A four-square castle, built in the 15th century for the Infante Don Manuel, presides over a modern town and fertile valley. Nearby castles are south at **Sax** and **Petrer**, guarding the way down to Alacant and the coast.

▶▶ Xàtiva (Játiva) 208B3
This is the site of one of Spain's great Moorish fortresses, the **Castillo Major** (tel: 962 27 33 46; *Open* Tue–Sun, summer, 10.30–7; winter, 10.30–6. *Admission free*), with centuries of accumulated castle-building rising along a high ridge where *huerta* meets sierra.

The old town has many fine facades and doorways, and can also claim that two Borgia popes were born here; their statues stand outside the grand Renaissance Colegiata (collegiate church), which is itself a step away from the fine municipal hospital. Halfway up the mountain, the whitewashed chapel of St. Felix contains fine Flemish primitive paintings.

THE BORJAS
Borja in Aragón produced the Borja family, dukes of Gandía, in Valencia, known as the Borgias in Italy. Cesare Borja was imprisoned at Xàtiva and Medina del Campo and died in Aragón in 1507. His nephew, Francisco Borja became second General of the Jesuit Order and is better known as San Francisco de Borja.

221

In the backstreets of the wine-making town of Requena

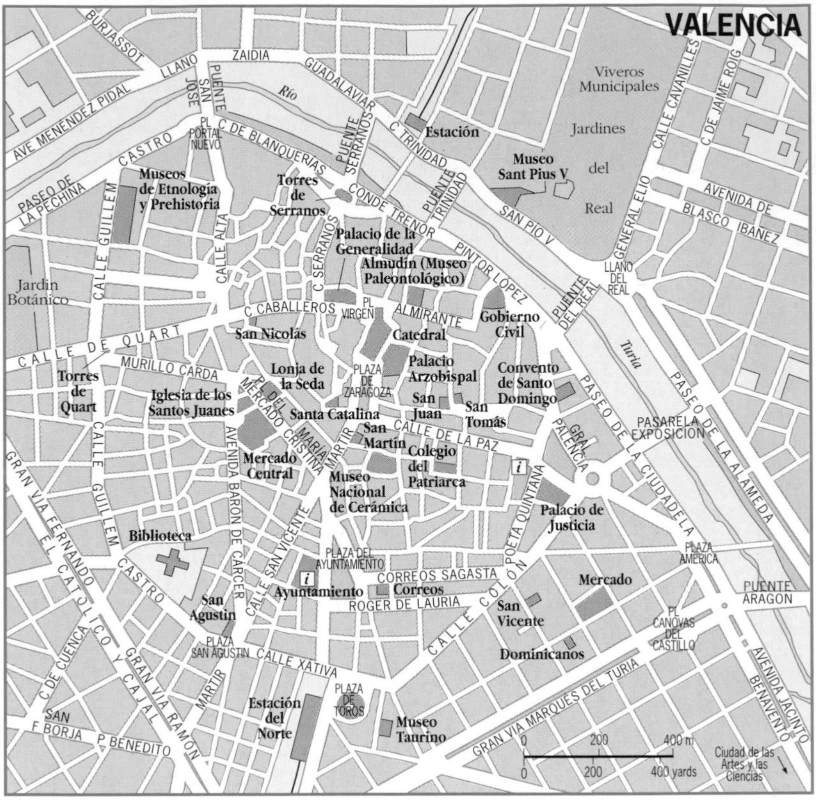

VALENCIA

(map of Valencia with labels including:)

ZAIDIA

Río

Viveros Municipales

Jardines

Estación

Museo Sant Pius V

del

Real

AVENIDA DE BLASCO IBAÑEZ

Museos de Etnología y Prehistoria

Torres de Serranos

Palacio de la Generalidad

Almudín (Museo Paleontológico)

Jardín Botánico

San Nicolás

Catedral

Gobierno Civil

Torres de Quart

Lonja de la Seda

Palacio Arzobispal

Convento de Santo Domingo

Iglesia de los Santos Juanes

Santa Catalina

San Juan

San Tomás

San Martín

Mercado Central

Colegio del Patriarca

Museo Nacional de Cerámica

Palacio de Justicia

Biblioteca

San Agustín

Ayuntamiento

Correos

Mercado

San Vicente

Dominicanos

Estación del Norte

Museo Taurino

Ciudad de las Artes y las Ciencias

0   200   400 m
0   200   400 yards

STROLLING IN VALENCIA
A short walk in Valencia's 19th-century districts reveals the charm of a hundred years ago: agreeable old houses, open octagons at street intersections, and much liveliness. There are many restaurants, especially round Calle Císcar, and good shops in Calle Salamanca.

▶▶ Valencia   *208B3*

Valencia is Spain's third city and capital of the Comunidad Valenciana region. It was founded by the Romans in 138 BC, later becoming one of the chief cities of the Moors. After Valencia fell to the Christians in 1238, the Moors lived on as agricultural workers and craftsmen until finally expelled in 1609. Valencia was the seat of the retreating Republican government of Spain in 1936–1937; but it was also here, during the abortive coup attempt in 1981, that a rebellious general rolled his tanks out on to the street. The city's old town, which takes about 20 minutes to cross on foot, is confined by a bend of the now-diverted Río Turia. This empty watercourse is crossed by ancient bridges and mostly planted as a park. To the east of the old town lies the 19th-century extension of the city. Modern Valencia is ranged round this nucleus.

Cathedral Valencia's cathedral is famous for its claim to possession of the Holy Grail, kept in the soaring Gothic chapterhouse (to the right on entry). The so-called Grail is an agate chalice. The museum (tel: 963 91 81 27; *Open* Tue–Fri 10.30–1, 4.30–6, Sat–Mon 10.30–1. *Admission charge*) beyond has splendid paintings, including Goya's brilliant rendering of St. Francis Borja exorcizing spirits. The cathedral *retablo* is by Juan de Juanes, one of Valencia's Renaissance heroes. The facade is baroque with Gothic and Romanesque portals north and south respectively; and the octagonal 14th- to 15th-century tower, the Miguelete, offers lovely views.

Behind the cathedral is the 17th-century shrine of Nuestra Señora de los Desemparados. In front, recessed from the square, is the brilliantly decorative baroque tower of the church of Santa Catalina.

For parks and gardens, see **Walk** on page 212.

Lonja de la Seda (Silk Exchange) Magnificently vaulted, this is one of Spain's finest buildings (tel: 963 52 54 78; *Open* Tue–Sat 9.15–2, 5–9; Sun 9.15–2. *Admission free*). Note the sinuous Gothic doorways.

Palacio de la Generalidad Valencia's ancient parliament building (tel: 963 86 34 61; visits by appointment only) is the nerve centre for the Valencia region. It has two glorious *artesonado* ceilings.

Key museums
Museo Sant Pius V (formerly Bellas Artes, tel: 963 60 57 93; *Open* Tue–Sun 10–8. *Admission free*) With works by Valencia's notable Renaissance painters and many Spanish masters, this is one of the best galleries outside Madrid.

Ciudad de las Artes y las Ciencias (tel: 902 10 00 31; *Open* Mon–Thu 10–8, Fri–Sun 10–9. *Admission charge*). The ambitious City of Arts and Sciences is taking shape in the bed of the Río Turia, a bus ride from the city. The IMAX cinema and Science Museum have already proved successful.

Colegio del Patriarca Another fine art collection (*Open* daily 11–1.30. *Admission charge*) is housed in beautiful buildings, with a lovely patio.

IVAM (tel: 963 86 30 00; *Open* Tue–Sun 10–7. *Admission free*) is a renowned gallery displaying modern art.

The **Museo Nacional de Cerámica** (*Open* Tue–Sat 10–2, 4–8, Sun 10–2), housed in an old mansion, is undergoing restoration, but part of its collection of ceramics from Valencia and the rest of Spain is still on display.

THE WATER TRIBUNAL
Valencia's Water Tribunal was founded by the Moors to allocate water supplies in the irrigated *huerta* round the city, and to punish those who took too much. It met at the door of the main mosque each Thursday morning. Though the mosque has been replaced with a Christian cathedral and the Moors with Christians, the Water Tribunal still meets on the very same spot on the same day of the week.

LOCAL FIESTAS
There are plenty of fiestas throughout the Valencia region. Las Fallas is the most spectacular. In the city of Valencia, in the week culminating on 19 March, St. Joseph's Day, vast papier-mâché satirical figures are set alight amid a continuing explosion of fireworks. In towns and villages which have a particular Moorish connection, like Alcoi (see page 210), a good-humoured mock battle between Moors and Christians takes place in the streets. Some fiestas are new creations, such as Cartagena's battle between Romans and Carthaginians.

223

Valencia's museum of ceramics is housed behind this extravagant entrance to the Palacio del Marqués de Dos Aguas

Andalucía

TOURIST INFORMATION
Antequera: Plaza San
Sebastián 7
(tel: 952 70 25 05).
Cádiz: Plaza San Juan de
Dios 11
(tel: 956 24 10 01).
Casares, Costa del Sol:
Pasaje Chinitas 4, Málaga
(tel: 952 21 34 45).
Córdoba: Palacio de
Congresos, Calle Torrijos
10 (tel: 957 47 12 35).
Costa de la Luz: Avda.
Ramón de Carranza s/n,
Cádiz (tel: 956 25 86 46).
Granada: Calle Mariana
Pineda, Corral del Carbon
(tel: 958 22 59 90).
Jaén: Calle Maestra 13
(tel: 953 24 26 24).
Parque Nacional de
Doñana: El Acebuche
(tel: 959 44 87 11).
Sevilla: Avenida de la
Constitución 21
(tel: 954 22 14 04).

SO POTENT AND EXCITING is the image of Andalucía; the dark, slender horseman, the sultry señorita side-saddle behind, the wild sounds and movements of flamenco, the heat, the wine, that many people see it, quite mistakenly, as a shorthand for the whole of Spain.

Visit Sevilla, Granada, Jerez, Córdoba and you will see that some part of this vibrant and tantalizing world really does exist. But Andalucía is many things besides.

First, there is the age-old poverty of Andalucía, born of a system of huge estates which left workers as badly off as Russian serfs. It is hardly surprising that left-wing parties have made their mark here.

Then there are the southern costas, from the popular, populous, boisterous Costa del Sol, to the wilder, far less exploited Costa de la Luz, out west on the Atlantic.

Mountains are another key factor: Andalucía has some of the most magnificent of Spanish landscapes, including the mighty Sierra Nevada. The Moors gave the region much of its cultural base, most apparent in the major cities of Córdoba, Granada, and Sevilla. But lesser-known places, such as Úbeda and Baeza, are treasure-houses of Christian Renaissance architecture, while among the mountains are jewel-like White Towns blending to perfection Christian and Moorish heritage.

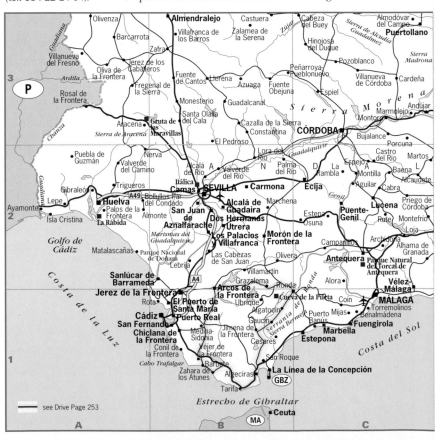

Antequera, topped by its Moorish castle

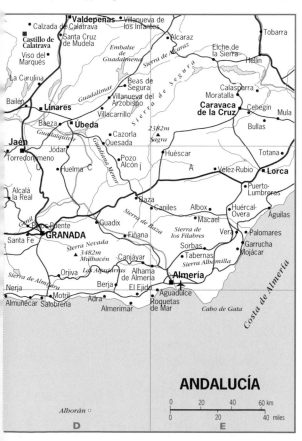

ANDALUCÍA

| | 0 | 20 | 40 | 60 km |
| 0 | | 20 | | 40 miles |

Alborán ○

D   E

Andalucía

Gibraltar as seen from Algeciras. On a clear day "the Rock" is visible from far along the coast

▶ Algeciras *224B1*

Algeciras stands opposite the Rock of Gibraltar. A pedestrian central area and a pleasant park are its main features.

▶ Alhama de Granada *224C2*

This town, high on the rolling terrain of Granada, was a key point in the Christian Reconquest against the Moors. The Catholic Monarchs themselves founded the parish church. Moorish baths remain as testimony to its long history as a spa town.

▶▶ Almería *225E2*

Almería is a sun-baked city in an arid landscape, its summit dominated by a Moorish fortress. It reached the height of its fame in the 11th century under the Arab ruler, Motacín. Then, it is said, the city was all palaces and gardens and was the centre of learned discourse. The remains of walls and towers show that defence was an equal preoccupation. The old city falls steeply down from the *alcazaba* to busy, narrow streets of ochre houses leading to the 16th-century fortified cathedral. The modern city has a confident air, but suffers from heavy traffic.

▶▶▶ Las Alpujarras *225D2*

The villages of these steep-sided valleys below the peaks of the Sierra Nevada National Park have a unique architecture with clear influences by the Moors who took refuge here after the fall of Granada. The whitewashed houses merge into each other, with tall chimneys protruding from flat roofs. The streets vary erratically in width, dwindling into passageways or steps, and often passing beneath bridges where two houses have been connected. Outside the villages, paths meander up and down the slopes beside hedgerows and meadows. Most visitors get as far as Bubión and Capileira in the Poqueira valley but to get to know the Alpujarras properly it is best to carry farther on and explore (see **Drive** on page 252).

▶ Andújar *224C3*

The old centre of Andújar has dignified mansions; the Gothic church of Santa María features an El Greco and a handsome Renaissance facade. Olive and sunflower oil are processed in the town today. Nearby, along the main road east of Córdoba, are historic Bailén and Linares.

▶▶ Antequera   224C2

Antequera's castle, built on the site of a Roman fort, has splendid views of the town and countryside. Below its maze-like garden sheltered with cypresses stands the handsome 16th-century church of Santa María. From here, the town flows down the hill, a mass of white, studded with brown churches. In the corner of the square, the 18th-century Palacio de Najera houses an excellent municipal museum with an eclectic collection of sculpture, paintings, and processional vestments. Outside the town, on the Granada road, is the huge, tumulus-covered dolmen of Menga. The stone slabs that comprise Spain's earliest piece of architecture (it dates from around 2500 BC) are massive, one weighing 180 tonnes. There is a smaller dolmen adjacent, and another 4km (2.5 mi) down the road.

▶ Aracena   224A3

Among the olive groves and almond orchards of the Sierra Morena, the small White Town of Aracena is built on the slopes of a hill with a ruined Moorish castle above. Beneath the hill, the Cuevas de las Maravillas have rock formations remarkable for their bizarre shapes and unusual hues, illuminated and reflected in the waters of subterranean pools. The mining museum in the nearby village of Río Tinto is worth a visit.

▶▶ Arcos de la Frontera   224B2

Arcos de la Frontera, a half-hour drive inland from Jerez, is one of the most spectacular of the White Towns, and has fine vistas (and splendid photographic angles) as you approach. Climbing steeply up one side of a hill, it meets a dramatic precipice at the hill's summit. The main square is perched right on the edge, backed by the church of Santa María de la Asunción (with Plateresque west portal) and a handsome castle, now converted into a parador. Another landmark is the 16th-century Gothic church of San Pedro, which features a large baroque bell tower.

The White Town of Arcos de la Frontera perches atop a high rock overlooking the Guadalete River

227

DEPARTURE OF COLUMBUS

Christopher Columbus (Cristóbal Colón in Spanish) waited at the monastery of La Rabida in the province of Huelva while Ferdinand and Isabella pondered his plan to seek a new route to the Orient. Their decision to support him was finally announced in the small town of Santa Fe, near Granada. Columbus set sail from the old port of Palos de la Frontera, near Huelva, in August 1492. His subsequent American expeditions left from Cádiz.

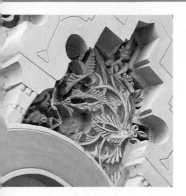

Baeza and nearby Úbeda, though slightly scruffy round the edges, are architectural delights. In the upper valley of the Guadalquivir, Baeza became the Christian capital of the area after its reconquest by Ferdinand III of Castile in 1227. Its greatest glories came just at the end of the Gothic and the start of the Renaissance periods with the Isabelline style; a truer Renaissance style evolved under Charles V. Little has happened in uncorrupted Baeza since.

Plaza de España to Plaza del Pópulo
Start at the Plaza de España. Walking downhill through the Plaza de la Constitución, you pass the three-storey, arcaded front of the Corn Exchange (1554) to the left and, diagonally across, the two-storey Lower Town Hall. On the left, enter the Plaza del Pópulo, a miniature marvel. The fountain contains badly damaged but ancient Iberian lions. Over to the left is the gloriously escutcheoned Butchers' Hall and in front the equally fine 16th-century facade of the Casa del Pópulo, now containing the tourist office. Farther to the right are two arches: the Jaén arch, built to celebrate Charles V's journey to his wedding in Sevilla, and the Villalar, built as atonement to Charles V for the town's rebellion during the Comuneros movement.

The Jaén arch, one of two gates built for Charles V

From Plaza Santa María The Plaza Santa María is just below the cathedral (*Open* summer, Mon–Sun 10–1, 5–7; winter, Mon–Sun 10.30–1, 4–6); the important seminary of San Felipe Neri (1660) is behind you. Central in the square is a 16th-century three-arched fountain. To the left is the Gothic facade of the Upper Town Hall, bearing the arms of Juana la Loca (Joanna the Mad) and Philip the Fair. The much-rebuilt cathedral is now essentially Renaissance. Within, note the beaten-metal, polychrome pulpit, and arches of the old mosque in the cloister.

As you descend past the seminary, on the left is the magnificently fanciful Isabelline Gothic facade of the Jabalquinto Palace (late 15th century; *Open* Tue–Sun 10–1, 4–6). It confronts the stylish Romanesque church of Santa Cruz (*Open* Mon–Sat 11–1, 4–6, Sun 12–2). Turn left here and on the right is the Old University (operative from 1544 to the 19th century).

Not just bird-watchers, but anyone who feels the slightest stirrings of interest in nature will wish to make the excursion to this greatest of surviving southern European wetlands. Here herons, egrets, and spoonbills share the marshy spaces with flamingos, ducks, and avocets. The area is made unique by its position on bird migration routes, and the availability of water in a variety of marginally differing habitats. Almost 130 species breed in the Doñana and many more pass through during migration.

On the drier ground around the fringes, red deer are plentiful and lynx continue to hold their own. Sea-birds throng the beaches on the far side of the ever-moving sand-dunes that divide the marshes from the Atlantic. Kites wheel overhead while, above them all, vultures sweep the sky. You might even see a very rare imperial eagle, which is recognizable by its white shoulders.

Getting there The official name of the area is the Parque Nacional de Doñana. In order to protect the extremely delicate environment, visits are by conducted tour only in large, high jeeps, at 8.30AM and 3PM from Tuesday to Sunday. Pre-booking is absolutely essential; tel: 959 43 04 32 as far in advance as possible. The park is reached from Sevilla by taking the main road for Huelva and turning south at Bollullos par del Condado. Park entry is after El Rocío.

Alternatively, you can take the bus to the resort of Matalascañas a little farther on and backtrack from there. (You will need to stay the night, as bus and park schedules combine badly.)

A unique wetland The Doñana park is on an effective bridge between Europe and Africa. It is bounded to the east by the River Guadalquivir, which flows out here into the Atlantic. The shifting dunes to the west restrain the water, creating permanent lagoons, some parallel to the coast and others farther inland, and an area of *marismas*, or seasonal marshes. Around them are pine and scrub.

A question of survival Excessive water extraction is a major problem, however, with high demands from tourism and agriculture. Growing pollution from industries higher up the Guadalquivir, from mining inland, and from pesticides used locally, have made the difficulties more acute; in 1986, 30,000 birds died of pesticide poisoning. A massive chemical overspill from a defective dam owned by a mining company threatened to destroy the wetlands in 1998. Amid national panic and international concern, a major catastrophe was averted, but only just.

SALT MARSHES
The area is divided into a humid and a dry Doñana. The humid Doñana consists of flat salt marshes and lagoons, which are dry in the summer and full of water the rest of the year, with scenery changing constantly according to the season. The depressions filled with water are known as *caños*, while the salt marsh lagoons, in general roughly circular in shape and fairly shallow, are called *lucios*. In the dry area are cork trees. Known as the Doñana Avaries, they give shelter to many bird colonies. An interesting feature is the movement of the dunes, which are swept inland by the wind. These pile up around the pine trees, forming so-called *corrales*, which can eventually choke the trees and bury them.

229

Cadiz's baroque and neo-classical cathedral, which stands by the seafront, contains the tomb of the great Spanish composer, Manuel de Falla

DEFEAT OF THE ARMADA
In 1588 Philip II of Spain was an unhappy man. The dark forces of Protestant heresy were gathering strength in the Low Countries and in England; and the English pirate Francis Drake had just destroyed the Spanish fleet at Cádiz. Philip began to assemble another fleet, an "invincible Armada" of 130 ships. It set sail from A Coruña on 22 July, 1588, but the planned invasion of England was thwarted by the successful guerrilla tactics of the English navy combined with the foul weather, and nearly half the ships were lost. The Armada was the death knell of Spanish maritime power.

▶▶ **Cádiz**   *224B1*

Despite its modern blocks and the growth of hotels beside its beaches, this is no ephemeral town: Cádiz is the doughty repository of all ages of Spanish history. Legend goes that it was founded by Hercules; historians verify that it has been settled for 3,000 years. Phoenician, Roman, and Moorish by turns, it later enjoyed huge wealth as the transit port for Latin American commerce. In 1812, it was the birthplace of an early republican constitution, which failed. At least the attempt reflected an open, liberal attitude among the town's citizens, which continues to this day.

The old town Sitting on a rocky peninsula, its jaw jutting into the Atlantic, old Cádiz is mildly dilapidated but charming, rough, and breezy on its Atlantic side and has a pleasant esplanade along its inner, eastern edge. The **Museo de Cádiz** (*Open* Wed–Sat 9–8, Sun 9–2, Tue 2.30–8. *Admission charge*) on the Plaza de Miña houses some excellent paintings by Zurburán and has a rich archaeological section documenting the city's past. The **Museo Histórico Municipal** (tel: 956 21 22 81; *Open* Wed–Sat 9–8, Tue 2.30–8, Sun 9.30–2.30. *Admission free for EU citizens*) boasts an 18th-century mahogany and ivory scale model of the town as well as reminders of the Cortés' bid for a democratic constitution in 1812, during the war against Napoleon. The nearby church of San Felipe Neri was where this constitution was first proclaimed and where the deputies gathered for debate. The public watched from the galleries and the press took notes in a side chapel. At the altar, there is a sweet-faced Murillo painting of the Virgin (the Immaculate Conception).

The cathedral On the outskirts of the old town, behind the southern beach, lies the neoclassical Catedral Nueva (New Cathedral) whose origins lie in much earlier times; the tower looks uncommonly like a surviving minaret. Immediately adjacent are the ruins of a large Roman theatre (*Open* Tue–Fri 10–1, 4.30–7.30, Sat–Sun 10–1. *Admission charge*). There is also a so-called "old cathedral," which is the Renaissance church of the Sagrario.

►► Carmona   224B2

Carmona, 30km (19mi) northeast of Sevilla, rises high on a bluff. Like its great lowland neighbour, Carmona went through Roman, Visigothic, and Moorish periods; both fell to Ferdinand III (el Santo), and both had Mudéjar palaces built by Pedro the Cruel. Carmona's palace, a ruin high on the clifftop, now has a parador within the ancient walls. The old town runs gently downhill beneath. The church of San Pedro has a tower built in imitation of Sevilla's Giralda. Another church, Santa María, occupies the site of the former mosque, retaining its patio. The town hall has an intact Roman mosaic courtyard. There are fine, fortified gateways and on the Sevilla road, an underground Roman necropolis (2nd century BC to 4th century AD, (tel: 954 14 08 11; *Open* Tue–Fri 8.30–2, Sat 10–2), full of rock-cut shafts and chambers, domes, niches, and carved reliefs. It held 900 families.

► Casares   224B1

This pretty White Town sits beneath its Moorish castle just inland from the coast in the Sierra Bermeja, cattle country with cork-oak and pines.

► Cazorla   225D3

A remote, high town, Cazorla is the base of hunters and visitors to the Coto Nacional de Cazorla (nature reserve). The town is set in a magnificent landscape of rugged mountains and pine forests with fine views of the Guadalquivir Valley. It has an excellent parador.

POTATO CHIPS AND CHURROS
Potato chips are still made on the premises in a shop or two in most Andalucian cities. The comparison with factory-made ones are a revelation. Usually potato chips are made along side *churros*: deep-fried pipes and rings of batter, traditionally consumed along with a cup of chocolate, though coffee will also do. Many Spaniards start the day with *churros*.

231

Walk

El Torcal de Antequera

To reach the starting point of this popular, geologically fascinating park, go south out of Antequera on the minor C3310 for Málaga (12km/8mi), then 4km (2.5mi), right, up a mountain road.

Here the visitor encounters one of Spain's most extraordinary rockscapes. Whole mountainsides ascend, constructed out of thin layers of rock laid sideways. Countless individual rock formations stand among the larger hills, some like piles of folded shirts, others like stacked plates or human vertebrae.

The road ends at an information office. Here you can learn about the formation of the bewildering rock shapes. A small display illustrates the pattern of waymarked paths in the area, with buttons to light up photographs of major formations en route. The length of waymarked routes varies from 30 minutes to 2 hours.

The going is on earth and rock, quite easy but up and down. The area is good for wild flowers but often very crowded (less so on longer paths).

PERSONALITIES OF CÓRDOBA

Perhaps it is no wonder a city as large as Córdoba produced so many figures remembered by posterity; among them, during Roman times, the two Senecas, father and son, and Lucan, author of the *Pharsalia*. Greatest of all were two Córdoban contemporaries, Averroës (1126–1198), an Arab philosopher who wrested the philosophy of Plato back from the neo-Platonists, and the Jewish polymath Maimonides (1135–1204), who codified Jewish law and is commemorated with a statue in Córdoba's old Jewish quarter.

►►► Córdoba   224C3

If the name of Córdoba has a romantic ring, so it should. Along with Sevilla and Granada, this is one of the great trio of Moorish cities of southern Spain, and indeed the greatest of them all in its own day. Today, however, it is by far the quietest, and to many tastes the prettiest and most sympathetic. In the old quarter, narrow white-washed streets, seldom higher than two storeys, burst with geraniums that seem to push their way through iron window grilles and positively tumble over balconies. Delectable floral patios can be glimpsed within. All is the purest essence of southern Spain. Add to this the magnificent presence of the Mezquita, the huge mosque that was the spiritual home of the Moorish caliphate, and the brew is rich indeed.

Historical background The conquering Moors, arriving in AD 711, made Córdoba their capital. In 929, Abd al-Rahman III declared Al-Andalus an independent caliphate, separate from Baghdad. Córdoba now rose to be the largest and most cultured city of Europe, before

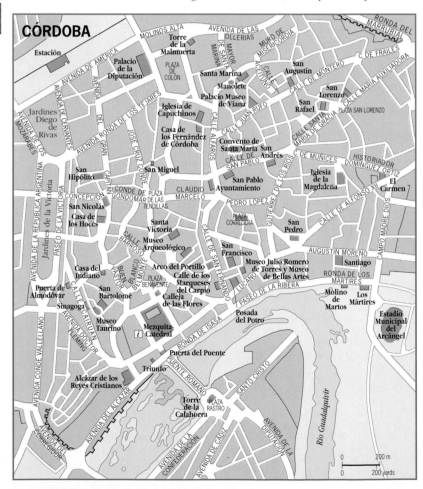

collapsing progressively from the early 11th century. It was retaken by the Christians in 1236 (see pages 30–31).

Mezquita This is one of Spain's great buildings, unique within Islamic architecture, and with the added peculiarity of having a Christian cathedral inserted in its midst. Apart from the cathedral, the huge interior of the Mezquita (tel: 957 47 05 12; *Open* Mon–Sat 10–6, Sun 2–6, winter till 5.30. *Admission charge; free* during Mass 9–10AM), not high but covering an ample area, is a forest of two-tiered red-and-white striped horseshoe arches on gleaming columns. The effect, in the semi-darkness, is at first breathtaking, after a while meditational. Some believe the pattern is derived from Roman aqueducts, others that it was simply an engineering device to gain height; at all events, it was and remains quite revolutionary. The mosque, whose holiest sanctum is against the rear wall to the right, was built in three main phases as described on page 234. Part was then scooped out in the 16th century, and the Christian cathedral installed in its place, with devastating effect on the cool, columnar vistas of the mosque and bursting up through the roof like a surfacing whale. The Emperor Charles V was horrified when he saw it, despite having built a palace for himself inside the Alhambra. He is said to have uttered with dismay words to the effect, "You have destroyed something unique, to build something commonplace."

Inside the mosque You enter by the Puerta del Perdón (Gate of Absolution) with 14th-century Mudéjar-style bronze doors. A former minaret converted into a belfry stands just beside the gate on the perimeter wall on the north, or city side farther from the river. Entry to the

Córdoba is full of charming corners and tiny squares. With white-washed houses and flower-filled balconies, it has a Moorish look

FLOWER-FILLED PATIOS
No Spanish city has lovelier inner patios than Córdoba, glimpsed through doorways heady and heavy with blossom. The tradition is maintained by a competition for best patio, run in May each year.

THE LIGHT FROM CÓRDOBA

"La luz que desde la catedral de Córdoba nos alumbra no es mortecina ni temblorosa. Es intensa. Penetrante, ilumina el camino. Propone el abrazo de las comunidades del mundo."

"The light which shines on us from Córdoba cathedral is neither wasting nor wavering. It points the way forward penetratingly. It proposes the mutual fellowship of the communities of the world."
King Juan Carlos, plaque on the Mezquita wall.

The gardens of the Alcázar. The Moors loved the sight and sound of water, which produced a cooling effect. In true Arab style the gardens are terraced with pools and fountains and lined with cypresses. On warm summer evenings they are enhanced by illuminations

mosque itself is diagonally to the left across the old ablutions courtyard, the Patio de los Naranjos (Court of Orange Trees).

The door immediately opposite the Puerta del Perdón leads directly into the oldest part of the mosque, built by Abd al-Rahman I in a single year, 786, mainly with columns retrieved earlier from Roman and Visigothic sites. Uneven in height, these are supported on bases of varying heights.

Walking straight forwards towards the rear wall of the mosque from Abd al-Rahman I's original construction, the visitor enters a section built by Abd al-Rahman II in 848 but interfered with by the later cathedral. This section contained a *mihrab* (prayer niche), the symbolic sacred centre of this period, within an area of gloriously complex architectural display. Following Islamic custom these are always built to face Mecca in the East, but in this case, supposedly due to some miscalculation, the wall runs more to the south than towards the east. Beyond this again is the most magnificent section of all, contributed by the last of the great caliphs, Al-Hakam II, in 964. Here arches become interlocked and multi-lobed, heavy with decoration. Ceilings of enormous intricacy, vaulted and with jewel-like ribbed domes, act as a prelude to the sacred *mihrab* of Al-Hakam's period, sadly roped off from visitors, but decorated on the outside with mosaics made up of tesserae that were a gift from the emperor of Byzantium. The colours and patterning and the use of elegant Arabic script create an effect which is piercingly beautiful.

Away to the left, on the east side (the zone of first entry for the visitor), the military dictator Almanzor created a large extension from 987, seven aisles deep and running the depth of the whole construction. The cathedral, jutting out into this as well, blends both Gothic and Renaissance work. The pulpits and choir stalls however, are highly praised but the cathedral's placing makes it quite unattractive.

Alcázar The old Umayyad castle (tel: 957 42 01 51; *Open* Tue–Sat 10–2, 4.30–6.30, Sun 9.30–2.30. *Admission charge; free* Fri), adapted by Alfonso XI and used by the Catholic Monarchs during the wars against Granada, has terraced water-gardens, outstanding Roman mosaics, and a 3rd-century Roman sarcophagus. From its Torre de los Leones (Tower of the Lions), there are golden views of the old city, the much-mended Roman Bridge, and the defensive Torre de la Calahorra on the far side of the Guadalquivir, which now houses the Museo de las Tres Culturas.

Barrio de la Judería The old Jewish quarter of Córdoba clusters close to the key buildings of the Arab city: the mosque and caliph's palace (now Christianized as the cathedral and site of the archbishop's palace, which contains a diocesan museum). This is Córdoba's inner sanctum of narrow streets and patios bright with geraniums. The former synagogue (tel: 957 20 29 28; *Open* Tue–Sat 10–1.30, 3.30–5.30, Sun 10–1.30. *Admission charge, free to EU citizens*) is here, in Calle Judíos, and is a simple building, in Mudéjar style, with Hebrew script instead of Arabic. There are restaurants, bars, and tourist shops in the Judería. In the Zoco, arts and crafts are sold by day; flamenco is performed on summer evenings.

Key museums
Museo Arqueológico (Plaza Don Jerónimo Páez; tel: 957 47 40 11; *Open* Tue 3–8, Wed–Sat 9–8; Sun 9–3. *Admission charge, free to EU citizens*). An important and attractive collection of Iberian and especially Roman remains, set in the Renaissance Páez Palace, itself worth visiting.
Museo de Bellas Artes (Plazuela del Potro; tel: 957 47 33 45; *Open* Tue 3–8, Wed–Sat 9–8; Sun 9–3. *Admission charge, free to EU citizens*). Less impressive than those in Sevilla or Cádiz, the Fine Arts Museum nevertheless has works by such masters as Luis Morales and Alonso Cano, as well as good Goyas.
Museo Julio Romero de Torres (Plazuela del Potro; tel: 957 49 10 09; *Open* Tue–Sat 10–2, 4.30–6.30; Sun 9.30–3. *Admission charge, free to EU citizens*). The museum dedicated to local painter Romero, who painted the women of Córdoba in the early years of the 20th century, is a curiosity loaded with heavy symbolism.
Palacio Museo de Viana This 17th-century mansion (tel: 957 49 67 41; *Open* Mon–Fri 10–1, 4–6, Sat 10–1. Guided tour of house. *Admission charge; for access to patios, separate tickets for each*), once belonging to the Viana family, has rambling rooms full of fine furniture and luxurious domestic accessories. It is most famous for its 13 patios.

Excursion: Medina Azahara
The later caliphs built themselves a spectacular palace 8km (5mi) east of Córdoba: the Medina Azahara (tel: 957 31 91 30; *Open* Tue–Sat 10–6.30, Sun 10–2. *Admission charge, free for EU citizens*). Destroyed at the fall of the caliphate, the site has been excavated and partially restored. Visitors descend towards the central terrace with caliphal apartments physically reminiscent of the Mezquita. Note the uniquely early cursive stone and vegetal wall-cladding.

CÓRDOBA ON FOOT
Córdoba is a walking city. It generally feels safe, though normal precautions are always in order. Road and rail connections to Madrid and other parts of Andalucía are very good.

BULL'S TAIL
Oxtail often features on Andalucian menus, not literally as *rabo de buey* but as the more glamorous *rabo de toro*, or bull's tail. Sometimes it's true. The carcases of bulls killed in the *corrida* are indeed sold off afterwards and not just the tail, either.

235

HISTORY MUSEUM
Housed in the Torre de la Calahorra, on the other side of the river, is the Museo de las Tres Culturas, where multiscreen presentations and audio-visual guides offer an insight into Córdoba's past.

SILVER AND LEATHER
Córdoba is renowned for intricate filigree work, where silver threads are used to make exquisite, lightweight designs. Typical Córdoban leather, which has Moorish origins, is decorative, involving very complex procedures such as embossing and chiselling.

Undeveloped beach near Mojácar. With its cluster of whitewashed houses climbing up the hillside, the town still has a Moorish look

THE LOST NUCLEAR BOMB
Palomares, where the Americans lost a nuclear bomb after a mid-air crash and could not find it for a month, is just to the north of Garrucha.

▶ **Costa de Almería** 225E2

This Costa is a very strange affair, with a North African feel to the northern part of it, especially round Garrucha and Mojácar, followed by the almost oppressive wildness of the Cabo de Gata.

The south is ushered in by plastic greenhouses galore, horrible to look at, though richly filled with vegetables for the markets of northern Europe. West from the capital city, Almería (see page 226), plastic greenhouses become enlaced with large, mass-tourism resorts. The Costa ends with a grim and grey corniche.

RESORTS
Aguadulce is a fair-sized resort 9km (6mi) west of Almería, with large-scale development behind the beach and below the main road. The grey-sand beach is quite wide and the whole front is made more pleasant by palm and pine.

West of Almería, an apron of flat land, filled largely with plastic greenhouses, spills out towards the sea. To the west of this is the rather swaggering development of **Almerimar**. With its water-sprinklers, golf courses, and young palms, this is an attempt at gracious holiday living. Once a dismal fishing village, **Garrucha** has prospered and blossomed into a substantial seaside town.

Hilltop **Mojácar**, once very Moorish in appearance, is now a mass of low development. Building now comes right down to the shoreline, enhanced by a parador. South lies the much wilder country of **Cabo de Gata**, with good beaches, though difficult to reach. One of them, Isleta del Moro, is very popular. Cabo de Gata itself has a lighthouse, salt pans, and a sadly romantic old fort.

On the apron of land west of Almería, **Roquetas** is an important resort, low-rise and with a large accumulation of "villas." Its atmosphere is better than its looks. The resort offers long beaches, water sports, and many activities including tennis, riding, and golf.

►► Costa de la Luz 224A1
RESORTS

Just across the River Guadiana from Portugal, **Ayamonte** is a busy port and a low-key resort. A road bridge connects Spain with Portugal, replacing the river ferry boat.

Isla Cristina, a little tuna-fishing town close to the Portuguese border, is friendly if rather decrepit. A long sandy beach runs east, backed by pine and dune.

Matalascañas is a characterless concrete resort, with a lovely beach but immediately abutting the Doñana National Park (see page 229).

El Puerto de Santa María is famous for fresh fish and sherry. It is also known for its sherry bodegas and there are tours available to visit them. Buy your seafood at a *cocedero*, or take-away, and eat it in a nearby bar. Mansions, castle, bullring, casino, or a ferry to Cádiz are noteworthy alternative diversions.

On the northern end of the Bay of Cádiz, **Rota** has a long sandy beach backed by mostly low-rise tourist development. It is home to an air and naval base.

Sanlúcar de Barrameda was the starting point for major voyages of discovery in the 15th and 16th centuries (Columbus and Magellan). The 16th-century church of Santa María de la O stands next to the Renaissance palace of the Medina Sidonia family.

A beautiful old town with a slightly hippy feel to it, **Tarifa** has a grandstand view of Africa. Famous as the landing place of the invading Moors in 711, it has extensive walls, a gate with a horseshoe arch, and the seafront castle of Guzmán El Bueno. A huge beach continues westwards for a long way. Its final stretch is reckoned to be Europe's top spot for windsurfing, but beware of high winds and strong currents. Tarifa's high winds have also given rise to giant windfarms above the town.

Protected from development by a military zone, **Zahara de los Atunes** lies north of Tarifa. Its wild and windy beach is typical of this stretch of the Costa de la Luz.

FOOD AND DRINK
Sanlúcar de Barrameda is renowned for its *manzanilla* sherry, matured here in *soleras*, supposedly gaining flavour from the salt sea breeze. As an accompaniment, try local (but expensive) langostinos, or king prawns.

GUZMÁN EL BUENO
Alonso Pérez de Guzmán received the title El Bueno, the Good, as a result of his behaviour at Tarifa in 1292. His own son was page to the Infante Don Juan, turncoat brother of the king, who had joined the Moors in their assault. When Don Juan threatened to kill the son unless Guzmán surrendered, the father threw down his own dagger in a gesture of defiance. The decision to sacrifice his son before his honour has traditionally excited intense admiration in Spain, though maybe times are now changing.

237

Tarifa, the Moors' gateway to Spain, is the most southerly point of Europe, with the coast of Africa only 14km (8mi) away. The town has narrow cobbled streets, whitewashed houses, and medieval ramparts

►► Costa del Sol   224C1

The Costa del Sol, the southern coast of Spain, used to be the pack leader in mass tourism. In the late 1980s, the tide of package holiday-makers ebbed, leaving the Costa in gloom and disarray. Since then, considerable efforts have gone into improvements all along the coast; beaches, promenades, and hotels have all been refurbished, and marinas and many golf courses built.

238

RESORTS
An outsize resort, **Almuñécar** has a large grey castle and little White Town behind. There are fine views eastwards of Salobreña and its castle.

Lower **Benalmádena** is really a westwards continuation of Torremolinos with a new marina (lots of nightlife here). The older part of the town, a little inland, is white and well kept, with plenty of foreign residents.

Out to the west of the real mass building of the Costa del Sol, **Estepona** is rather quieter and once again very foreign. There are plenty of apartment blocks but also a pleasant old town and a harbour.

Quite a city today, **Fuengirola** has massed apartment blocks and a promenade. There are some pleasant spots in town, and the western beach, Los Boliches, is popular.

The pleasures of **Málaga** lie in its essential Spanishness on a coast populated with foreigners. It is a modern town and working port with a long and settled history. It has a Roman amphitheatre, a 9th-century Moorish fortress, an 11th-century former Moorish palace (now partly restored as a museum), and the Gibralfaro castle and gardens on the summit of the hill. (Beware of muggings if walking alone up to the castle.) The 16th-century cathedral is sumptuous; the Sagrario, abutting it, was formerly a mosque and much of its Arabic decoration remains on the exterior wall. East of the harbour front there is a cemetery, which dates back to 1830 and was the first Protestant cemetery to appear in Spain. Pablo Picasso was born in Málaga (the refurbished Casa Natal de Picasso; Plaza de la Merced 15). As a break from the built-up coast, the hinterland includes the picturesque hills of the Montes de Malaga (take the C345 towards Colmenar) with good views on the way.

The Moorish castle overlooking Málaga sits amid attractive gardens on top of the Gibralfaro Hill. Nearby are the remains of a Roman amphitheatre

The marina at Marbella
has expanded over the
years into a busy
harbour against a back-
drop of modern, high-rise
apartment blocks. All
year round, luxurious
yachts are moored here
next to small boats, and
there are numerous
sporting events

Marbella's charms are fairly evident: well-kept apartment blocks, good restaurants, designer boutiques, an attractive marina (and a rather less impressive beach). The old town behind, rising above the Plaza de los Naranjos with its ceramic benches, has castle walls and stately buildings as well as narrow white streets. The focal point of the old town is the Plaza de los Naranjos. To the east, at Banana Beach, an oasis-like development of tented bars is intended as a focus for the town's nightlife. The coast on either side of Marbella has a reputation as the playground of Spain's smart set.

High above Benalmádena and Fuengirola, beautifully tended **Mijas**, with its small white streets and startling views, is a very commercialized but attractive hill village. Visitors come for carriage rides and souvenirs. Plenty of visitors stay forever.

Nerja, east of Málaga, is for many the most attractive town on the Costa del Sol. White, well kept, low-rise, with plenty of green in its gardens, it has good tourist amenities without the over-insistence of places like Torremolinos. The main attraction is the Balcón de Europa, a central viewpoint giving a wonderful eastwards panorama. At **Burriana** to the east, there is an excellent beach and coves. Behind is the rest of the agriculturally rich Axarquía region. The **Cuevas de Nerja** (Nerja Caves; tel: 952 52 95 20; *Open* daily 10–2, 4–6.30. *Admission charge*) are worth a visit.

Even smarter than nearby Marbella, **Puerto Banús** is a purpose-built development, with a marina, a clever pastiche of an old town, and expensive shops and restaurants. Anyone can come to look at Puerto Banús; only the wealthy stay.

Torremolinos has always been a popular resort. Almost a suburb of Málaga these days, it has an increasingly Spanish flavour, especially at weekends. As the name suggests, there is an old tower here, up on a point. There is also a scrap of old town heaving with tourist shops, Chinese restaurants, and discos. Hotels and apartment blocks abound and the beaches have been developed. At La Carihuela, for example, to the west, fresh sand has been shipped in and a multitude of fish restaurants can be found immediately behind.

239

GOLFING
Golf is the great sporting passion of the Costa del Sol. Some of its older courses enjoy great fame, Las Brisas, Sotogrande, Río Real, Torrequebrada, but green fees are high. The many new courses that have been built should bring prices down, improve public access, and generally help players. Meanwhile, the Dama de Noche at Puerto Banús is one of the first floodlit courses.

Spanish newspapers cover bullfighting in their arts reviews rather than their sports pages. This is a clear indication of its status as an art form for its aficionados.

THE BULLFIGHT
Most Spaniards regard the bullfight as a test of a man's intelligence and will against the formidable strength of the bull. In some respects, the contest is an atavistic Mediterranean ritual about virility and sacrifice, the "death in the afternoon"; almost a transfer of potency from vanquished to victor.

Although increasing numbers of Spaniards oppose bullfighting on the grounds of cruelty, it comes second only to soccer as the most popular national sport. In the Middle Ages, the contest was between a man on horseback and a bull. By the 18th century, it had become a folk pastime. The rules of combat were introduced about this time. Rather like soccer, modern bullfighting is occasionally tainted with charges of corruption involving breeders, veterinary surgeons, horn-shaving, matadors, and their teams.

Where to see it The biggest names in the bullfighting world can be seen at the Plaza de Toros (bullring) in Madrid or Barcelona (if tickets appear to be sold out, try a tour operator). The bullring at Sevilla, though much smaller, is still very prestigious, while a bullfight in Ronda, where the rules and rituals were first propounded, has a special resonance. These are the very special venues; many small towns, particularly in the south, celebrate their fiestas, and their Sunday afternoons, with a humbler bullfight.

It may be popular, but it is not cheap. The most expensive seats are in the shade or "Sombra." Those in the sun, "Sol," are least expensive and in between there are the "Sol y Sombra." The seats nearest the ring are called *barrera* (best avoided if this is your first bullfight), the *contra-barrera* are the next row, then come the *tendidos*, and right at the back, the *gradas*.

The Real Maestranza bullring in Sevilla awaiting the crowds

The black fighting bulls of Spain are raised mainly on ranges by the Guadalquivir in Andalucía and farther up on the dry Castilian plains which stretch between Salamanca and Ciudad Rodrigo

The introduction The whole ritual begins with a brass fanfare as each matador in his traditional costume, the *traje de luces* (suit of lights; each matador performs a ritual when donning his suit), accompanied by his team of *banderilleros* and *picadores*, heavy men on horseback, processes round the ring. Three matadors fight two bulls each in the course of the afternoon and each fight is divided into three distinct parts, their division heralded by bugle blasts.

The first stage lies in testing the bull's reaction to the cape and gauging his strength and temperament. This is done initially by the bullfighter's team. The matador first watches, then tests the bull himself with especially flamboyant passes. If, at this stage, the animal appears to have some weakness, it is replaced by another.

The fight When the bugles sound for the second stage, the *picadores* enter and wait on the edge of the ring. As the bull charges they extend their pikes to penetrate the bull's shoulder muscles, to test, damage, and tire him. Next, it is the turn of the *banderilleros* to attract the bull's attention. Balancing practically motionless over the horns momentarily, they thrust ribboned darts into his shoulders as he charges. Finally the matador, the star of the show, makes a dramatic re-entry. His aim is to demonstrate his skill, courage, grace, and poise through a series of clever feints and daring passes by deft work with the *muleta*, and to establish his supremacy over the bull. As the animal lowers his head, almost mesmerized into submission, the matador advances for the final stage, the *estocada;* he positions the animal square on his legs and thrusts his sword between the bull's shoulder blades, straight through his heart.

In reality the end rarely happens this cleanly. More often than not, the matador makes several efforts to deliver the fatal blow, all the time sweating under the disapproving boos of the crowd. If, on the other hand, he has done well after executing a particularly good *faena de muleta* and killed cleanly, he may be rewarded by the president of the day with an ear of the bull, even perhaps both ears. If the performance has been spectacular, he may win the bull's tail. Then he will be chaired out of the ring on the shoulders of supporters.

THE SEASON
The bullfighting season extends from April to October. Fights, or *corridas*, begin at 5PM sharp between April and June and sometimes at 6 or 7PM between June and October.

241

SPECIAL RITUALS
Bullfighters and their teams feel real fear before the start of the fight. You have only to watch them waiting in the tunnel before their first entry to understand how bad it is. Not surprisingly, they have developed all kinds of good luck rituals and beliefs. Here is an example. The *torero*, head of his team, always takes a room in a local hotel and uses it to be hauled and squeezed into his suit of lights, the brilliant garb he will wear at the *corrida*. Most *toreros* believe that they are sure to be gored if anyone goes into that room before they come back to collect their everyday clothes.

LORCA AND DE FALLA
The poet Federico García Lorca and the composer Manuel de Falla lived and worked, and occasionally collaborated, in Granada. De Falla's house, at Calle Antequeruela Alta 11, is now a museum (*closed for refurbishment*). Lorca's family home, the Huerta de San Vicente, at Calle Arabial, is also a museum (*Open* summer, Tue–Sun 10–12.30, 4–6.30. *Admission charge*), run by the poet's niece, Laura. Also well worth a visit is Lorca's birthplace at Calle Poeta García Lorca, Fuentevaqueros (*Open* Tue–Sun 10–1, 4–6. Guided tours on the hour. *Admission charge*).

►►► **Granada** *225D2*

In most people's minds, the name of Granada is inseparable from that of the Alhambra. This magical fortress-palace, the name in Arabic means literally "The Red One," quite properly stands as shorthand for all that was most graceful and intricate, most extravagant, and most accomplished in the long-lost Moorish civilization of Spain. Modern Granada is by no means an empty cipher, but it is the Alhambra and the Generalife gardens that visitors come to see, discovering the rest of the town almost by accident.

While most of Moorish Spain succumbed to the Christian Reconquest, Granada somehow held out, remaining in Arab hands two centuries longer than anywhere else. Militarily formidable, though often paying tribute to the Christians, this mountain kingdom excelled in all the arts of peace: in silk and ceramics, in tile-making, and above all in architecture and the decorative arts. Ferdinand and Isabella finally conquered it in January 1492, after a 10-year war, and they chose the city as their own burial place.

The Alhambra stands high on a spur of mountain under the Sierra Nevada. A second hill, to the north, is occupied by the Albaicín, an ancient and intriguing residential quarter. The "modern" city (post-1492) lies at the foot of the two hills. Today Granada is a commercial centre and university city, as well as being a popular venue for conferences.

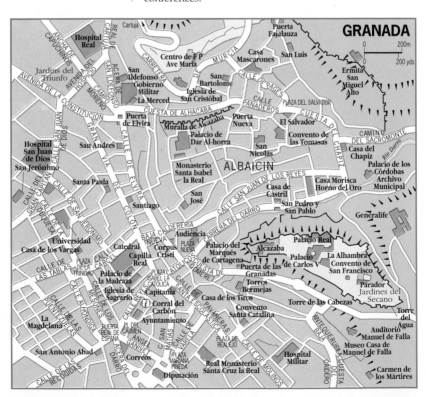

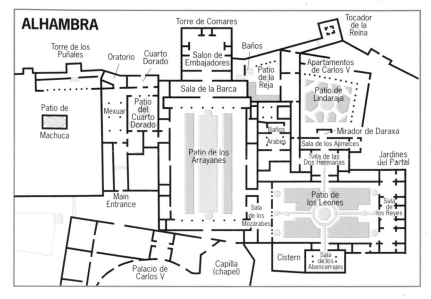

ALHAMBRA

Torre de Comares · Tocador de la Reina · Torre de los Puñales · Oratorio · Cuarto Dorado · Salon de Embajadores · Baños · Apartamentos de Carlos V · Patio de la Reja · Sala de la Barca · Patio de Lindaraja · Patio de Machuca · Mexuar · Patio del Cuarto Dorado · Mirador de Daraxa · Baños Arabes · Sala de los Ajimeces · Patio de los Arrayanes · Sala de los Dos Hermanas · Jardines del Partal · Main Entrance · Sala de los Mozárabes · Patio de los Leones · Sala de los Reyes · Palacio de Carlos V · Capilla (chapel) · Cistern · Sala de los Abencerrajes

243

The Alhambra

The Alhambra (*Open* daily 8.30–6. Night visits: Fri–Sat 8–9.30 (palaces only); tel: 902 22 44 60 in Spain, from abroad 34 913 46 59 36; www.alhambratickets.com; booking recommended. *Admission charge*) came into being as a massive castle, built by the founder of the Nasrid dynasty in the 13th century. Later kings created palace buildings and the summer gardens of the Generalife above. It was an American, Washington Irving, who invented the ultra-romantic image in his 1832 *Tales from the Alhambra*.

Alcazaba (Fortress) The Alcazaba, oldest part of the Alhambra, stands on the tip of the spur above the River Darro. Entry was from beneath, through huge gates, still surviving. Modern visitors enter from above. There is a courtyard with several impressive towers.

The palaces Various rulers built palaces on the site at different times. The tour route, made at the visitor's own pace, necessarily ignores chronology. The Mexuar (14th century), which was the audience room, is the first room entered. It gives an anticipatory glimpse of the brilliant mixture of tilework and plasterwork, rich in Arabic script, that characterizes the whole. Its oratory balconies, with a view over the Darro and Albaicín, have graceful paired windows (*ajimeces*), of which there are many in the palace complex. After the Patio del Mexuar and its Cuarto Dorado (Golden Room), the ensuing Patio de los Arrayanes (Myrtle Court) is serious and harmonious. Wooden galleries adorn one end. The other, over the river, is blocked off by the large Torre de Comares, a tower containing the huge and ornate 13th-century throne room of Yusuf I. There is a long pool and a vista clear through the throne room and out to the Albaicín. Next is the impressive Patio de los Leones (Court of the Lions from the 14th century), ranking with the Myrtle

The Alcazaba, the oldest of the Alhambra buildings

Sunset over the Alhambra in Granada and the 3,000m (9,840ft) snow-capped peaks of the Sierra Nevada, 20km (12mi) southeast of the city

GARCÍA LORCA
The brief and brilliant life of Federico García Lorca, born in Granada in 1898, ended with the bullets of Nationalist killers near the same city in July 1936, at the start of the Spanish Civil War. His lyrical and highly evocative poetry showed his sympathy with the gypsies of Andalucía, while such powerful and disturbing plays as *Blood Wedding* and *The House of Bernarda Alba* are still widely performed. A friend of leading musicians and painters, Lorca was a natural target for the Nationalists because of his homosexuality and Bohemian lifestyle.

Court as focal point of the Alhambra. The rooms around its elegant little pavilions with their groups of slender columns are all spectacular. The Sala de los Reyes (Royal Chamber) at the far end has beautiful Islamic ceiling paintings, a great rarity. The Sala de las Dos Hermanas (the Hall of the Two Sisters, or rather two marble slabs in the floor), on the riverside, has one of the greatest ceilings of all time, an amazing honeycomb dome.

Palacio de Carlos V (Palace of Charles V) The Emperor Charles V placed a palace of his own among the buildings of the Alhambra. Though out of place, it has great merit as an example of High Renaissance architecture. Within, there is a fine circular courtyard and an interesting collection of paintings in the Museo de Bellas Artes on the first floor. Downstairs is the important Museo de La Alhambra, which contains one of the seven famous "vases of La Alhambra" of glazed ceramic, along with exhibits from on-site excavations (tel: 958 22 48 43; *Open* Tue 2.30–6, Wed–Sat 9–6, Sun 9–2.30. *Admission charge, free for EU citizens*).

Palacio del Generalife Walk up the gardens to the Palacio del Generalife just above, built in the 14th century by the Moorish rulers as a summer retreat. The gardens here are even lovelier than those of the Alhambra. Pavilions lean out over the Darro valley offering magnificent views of the town and countryside. Marigolds and custard-apple trees delight the eye. The whole is cooled by water in cleverly designed pools and fountains.

OTHER SIGHTS
Albaicín
The labyrinthine suburbs of steep and narrow streets and steps on this ancient hill across from the Alhambra is also full of Moorish remnants, including Moorish houses. The typical Albaicín homestead or *carmen* is an ancient house, set behind high walls in steeply ascending lanes, its garden full of jasmine, cypresses, and orange trees. There is a magnificent view of the Alhambra from the church of San Nicolás, and a lovely walk down, but not at night, through the Plaza de San Miguel Bajo (turn right at the bottom of the square).

Capilla Real (Royal Chapel) and Catedral (Cathedral)
Isabella and Ferdinand ordered for their final resting place a splendid chapel (*Open* Mon–Sat 10.30–1, 3.30–6.30, Sun 11–1. *Admission charge*) in the style now known as Isabelline Gothic, profusely decorated, soaring in sinuous lines of masonry and vaulting.

Behind a magnificent screen, the sculpted effigies of the Catholic Monarchs (on the right) lie close to those of their unfortunate daughter and son-in-law, Joanna the Mad (Juana la Loca) and Philip the Fair. The coffins themselves are in a crypt below. The youthful kneeling figures of Isabella and Ferdinand on either side of the Plateresque *retablo* are attributed to Diego de Siloé.

Isabella's personal picture collection, with its strong allegiance to the Low Countries, is displayed in the sacristy to the side. She clearly liked small paintings; even her prized Botticelli is tiny. Across the road, with baroque exterior, is La Madraza, a building of Moorish origin, sometimes open for exhibitions. The patio is absolutely delightful.

Diego de Siloé worked on the large and airy cathedral building from 1528. The great artistic polymath Alonso Cano (you can also see his work in the Prado) contributed the main facade in the 17th century.

Cartuja
This stout 16th-century Carthusian monastery (tel: 958 16 19 32; *Open* summer, daily 10–1, 4–8; 3.30–6 in winter; Sun 10–noon. *Admission charge*) on the northern outskirts of town has a cloister, an impressive church, and a sacristy in the most florid baroque imaginable. In the refectory there are many large paintings by the fine monk-artist Sanchez Cotán.

Corral del Carbón
This balconied Moorish *caravanserai* (inn), set round a courtyard in the heart of town, later did duty as a coal store, whence its name (coal-yard). It now has an arts centre and a tourist information office.

GETTING THERE
To get to the Alhambra, take bus No. 30 from Plaza Isabel la Católica or a taxi. For the Albaicín take bus No. 31 from Plaza Nueva or a taxi to the top and then stroll down. Many buses start on the Carrera del Genil or just behind in the Plaza de Bibataubín. Number 11 takes a useful circular route, 8 goes to the Cartuja. As in Sevilla, the major risks are bag-snatching and car-window-smashing. Avoid walking in the Albaicín and Sacromonte areas at night.

245

HIGH PEAKS
Granada and the Alhambra lie under the Sierra Nevada (Snowy Mountains), the highest range of mainland Spain. Skiing in the area has developed enormously in recent years, giving Granada an extra tourist season. There is a good road to the Pico de Veleta, Spain's second highest summit; a fine and cooling summer excursion.

LOCAL FLAMENCO
Sacromonte is an area of caves behind the Albaicín, where you can hear local gypsy families perform the indigenous, flamenco song and dance routine called Zambra. The shows are heavily commercialized, the dancing often poor, the ambience faked. If you feel you really have to experience it, go with a group or you will get hassled.

Andalucía

CAVE HOMES
Cave dwellings have enjoyed a revival in this part of Spain. The advantages of constant temperatures and flexible accommodation (you can just dig a spare room) have sent sophisticated apartment-dwellers back to old cave-dwelling ways. It has become fashionable to own a cave as a second home.

SHERRY PRODUCTION
Sherry is made on the *solera* principle. The *solera* is a system of wooden butts or, increasingly these days, stainless-steel containers, all linked to one another and fed from the top with young wine year by year. The finished sherry is drawn from the bottom butt. Each *solera* always contains elements of the wine put into the system when it was originally laid down, often many years previously.

► **Guadix**   *225D2*
This town has a cathedral (*Open* Mon–Sat 11–1, 5–7; 4–6 in winter. *Admission free*), begun by Diego de Siloé, and a substantial Moorish *alcazaba* (castle). Visitors are often more interested in the cave dwellings of Guadix, complete with windows, TV sets, and, occasionally, even a garage extension. The Cave Museum in the Plaza de la Ermita Nuerva (*Open* Mon–Sat 10–2, 5–7 or 4–6 in winter, Sun 10–2. *Admission charge*) is worth a visit.

► **Huelva**   *224A2*
Although Huelva is one of Spain's most important commercial ports, there are important sites in the area, including **La Rábida**, delightful **Moguer**, and **Niebla**, still surrounded by Moorish walls and gateways.

► **Itálica**   *224B2*
The ruins of the once-great Roman city of Itálica can be visited near Santiponce, just outside Sevilla. Itálica was founded in 206 BC and the emperors Trajan and Hadrian were both born here in the first century AD. The town enjoyed a heyday in the 2nd century AD but subsequently fell into decline and was plundered. The most impressive building on the site is the amphitheatre.

► **Jaén**   *225D2*
Jaén is the tame capital of one of Andalucía's largest and wildest provinces. The old town, with its cluster of steep, narrow streets, is dominated by the Renaissance cathedral. High above is the hilltop castle of Santa Catalina.

►► **Jerez de la Frontera**   *224B1*
The word "sherry," an English corruption of Jerez, the business of this town is evident. Long before you enter it, vineyards and sherry bodegas, or wineries signal its most important produce. The sherry-producing region is a triangle formed by Jerez de la Frontera, El Puerto de Santa María, and Sanlúcar de Barrameda. Most bodegas have guided tours and tastings on weekday mornings followed by invitations to buy a bottle or two. They may be closed in August, however, in preparation for the September harvest and festival. Jerez itself is substantial, with palm- and orange-lined avenues, fine mansions, churches, including a Gothic-Renaissance cathedral, an 11th-century *alcázar*, and remains of Moorish walls now planted with gardens. Each Thursday visitors flock to the **Real Escuela Andaluza de Arte Ecuestre** (Royal Andalucian School of Equestrian Art) for a vivid and musical display of horsemanship (tel: 956 31 80 08; *Open* Mar–Jul, Mon, Wed, Fri 10–1; Jul–Oct, Mon, Wed 10–1. Shows: Mar–Oct, Tue, Thu; Nov–Dec, Thu show only. *Admission charge*).

►► **Osuna**   *224C2*
A small southern White Town, Osuna has a plain outward appearance that belies the splendour of its fine buildings: 16th-century mansions from the days of the Reconquest when the dukes of Osuna ruled over much of Andalucía. The Renaissance church, Colegiata de Santa María de la Asunción (*Open* Tue–Sun 10–1.30, 3.30–6.30. Guided tours only) has four paintings by Ribera.

▶▶ Ronda   224B1

Ronda is the best known of the Andalucian White Towns and much visited by coastal tourists. Surrounded by wild and rugged mountains that once sheltered smugglers and bandits, the town sits on two sides of a dramatic 100m (330ft) gorge with the River Guadalevín far below. The gorge is spanned by the Puente Nuevo, the "new" 18th-century bridge. There are awe-inspiring views from here down into the gorge. Unfortunately, the bridge claimed the life of the architect, who fell to his death from here while inspecting the works.

The old half of the town, the Ciudad, is a delightful quarter of narrow streets and quiet squares. The Collegiate Church of Santa María la Mayor (*Open* summer, daily 10–8; winter, 10–6. *Admission charge*) stands in one such square (Plaza de la Ciudad), its belfry formerly a minaret, with an arcaded facade. Part of the Moorish *mihrab* is visible in the entrance lobby. The grand houses are almost all Christian superimpositions on original Arab buildings following the Reconquest. The Renaissance Casa Mondragón, occupied for a short time by Ferdinand and Isabella, is rich in patios and horseshoe arches.

The 16th-century Palacio Salvatierra (not open to public visits) has a fine facade, and is decorated with a carved "wild" couple, signifying Inca "primitives." The old Moorish baths stand at the foot of the steep hill by the Puente Viejo, the old (17th-century) bridge.

The newer extension of Ronda, which is laid out on the other side of the bridge, is called the Mercadillo, the market-place. Construction began in 1485 by the Catholic Monarchs, who had recovered Ronda from the Moors. Its chief sights include the late 18th-century Plaza de Toros (museum, tel: 952 87 15 39; *Open* Jun–Sep, daily 10–8; Oct–May, 10–6. *Admission charge*), one of the oldest bullrings in Spain. The park behind the bullring, with its *alameda*, fountains and flower beds, has dramatic views over the gorge and the distant hills.

THE CRADLE OF BULLFIGHTING

"Dicen que hubo un torero
Que cuando hacía el paseíllo
El sol perdía su brillo
Se llamó Pedro Romero."

"They say there was a *torero*/his entry to the ring so fine/it did the very sun outshine/his name—Pedro Romero."

Lines written on the wall of the Pedro Romero restaurant opposite the bullring in Ronda. The restaurant was named after the famous bullfighter, whose grandfather, Francisco Romero, codified the rules of bullfighting early in the 18th century.

247

Ronda, spectacularly set on two sides of a gorge, is a popular spot for visitors and has long attracted artists

IN AND AROUND SEVILLA
Just under an hour's flying time from Madrid, 2.5 hours by high-speed rail and connected by road, Sevilla is readily accessible. Once in the heart of town, most places can be reached on foot. Buses are a little complicated, giving a clear edge to taxis (metered, not prohibitive). Agree the price of horse-drawn carriages beforehand.

▶▶▶ Sevilla (Seville)   224B2

Celebrated in operas, in poetry, and prose, Sevilla deserves its reputation. Its lovely setting on the River Guadalquivir, the old town, and, above all, the astonishing atmosphere of the place, ranging from the grief and lamentation of the Holy Week processions to the exuberant Feria (Fair) immediately afterwards, all combine to make this one of the most enchanting places to visit in Europe. A full 115km (71mi) up-river from the sea, Sevilla has been a major port for most of its history. It had an important Roman period, then came the Visigoths; and the Moors arrived in 712 to stay more than 500 years. Moorish Sevilla was at its height under the Almohads, new invaders from Africa who constructed stunning

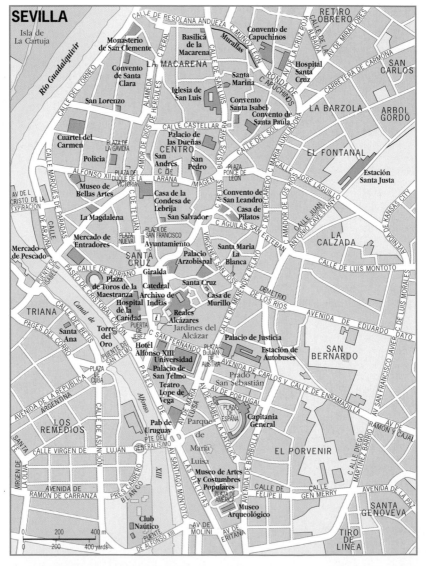

buildings, many of which still survive. The Christians, winning the city back in 1248, made it their southern capital. From 1503 to 1717, Sevilla enjoyed a trade monopoly with the Americas, becoming the wealthiest place in Spain. Decline and decadence soon followed, though, with the restoration of Spanish democracy and devolution of powers to regions, the Andalucian capital has enjoyed a revival in its fortunes over the last two decades.

Sevilla's massive Gothic cathedral, with its rich interior, is considered one of the most impressive in Spain. The Giralda adjoining is seen as a symbol of Sevilla

The Sights

Alcázar (Reales Alcázares) This mainly 14th-century palace (tel: 954 50 23 23; *open* Tue–Sat 9.30–5, Sun 9.30–1.30. *Admission charge*) in Mudéjar style, all ornamental patios, glorious tilework, and sumptuously decorated chambers, is one of the most thrilling building complexes in Spain. The grandest room is the Salón de Ambajadores (Hall of the Ambassadors), with brilliant plasterwork and Mudéjar honeycombed dome. The once-private Patio de las Doncellas (maidens) and the Patio de las Muñecas (dolls) are a triumph of delicacy. The garden, still beautiful today, incorporates a fine Mudéjar pavilion. Known as Carlos V's pavilion, it is surrounded by a maze and English gardens.

Archivo de Indias Latin America was ruled from here. The paperwork of an unrivalled archive is kept in the Casa de Contratación or House of Contracting *(closed for refurbishment)*, otherwise Casa Lonja (Exchange), built by Juan de Herrero, sombre architect of El Escorial.

Barrio de Santa Cruz Close to the cathedral and *alcázar*, this former Jewish ghetto is an ancient area of narrow whitewashed alleys and deep-set houses with graceful patios. Popular with visitors, its bars are high-priced. At its heart is the delightful Plaza de Santa Cruz.

HOLY WEEK PROCESSIONS
Sevilla has the most awesome Holy Week processions in Spain. The two images which are most intensely revered are La Macarena, a Virgin whose face is streaked with crystal tears, and Jesús del Gran Poder, Jesus of the Great Power. Both take their names from parish churches where they reside during the rest of the year.

TAPAS BARS
Sevilla is good for tapas bars and eating out. The liveliest tapas hour is from 1PM to 2PM, with the evenings less frenetic. Start the tapas trail behind the cathedral in the traditional bar, La Giralda, Calle Mateos Gago.

ORANGE MARMALADE
The traditional bitter marmalade of England and Scotland, often referred to as Seville marmalade, really does have a connection with the city. The municipally owned orange trees that grow in Sevilla's streets and squares are almost all of the bitter-fruiting variety which carries the city's name. When the oranges are picked, by municipal workers, they are shipped to Britain and there converted into marmalade.

BE PRUDENT
As in other southern cities, security requires some thought. Leave cars empty; don't wear extravagant jewellery; don't carry passports or too much money.

Casa de Pilatos A blend of Mudéjar and Renaissance, with arcaded patio, and magnificent tile- and plasterwork, this mansion (tel: 954 22 52 98; *Open* daily 9–7. *Admission charge; separate tickets for ground and first floor*) is supposedly modelled on Pontius Pilate's home in Jerusalem.

Catedral and La Giralda Built in a spirit of pure triumphalism by Sevilla's 15th-century Christian rulers, the cathedral (tel: 954 21 49 71; *Open* Mon–Sat 11–5, Sun 2.30–6. *Admission charge*) is the world's largest Gothic structure and third largest cathedral. Inside, note especially the Capilla Mayor or Great Chapel, with its Gothic *retablo* and fine grille of 1533; the huge tomb in which Columbus may (or may not) lie, and the rich treasury, chapterhouse, and sacristy, the latter with many notable paintings. The old ablutions courtyard of the former mosque (now the cathedral cloister or Patio de los Naranjos) is divided from the street outside by a magnificent Almohad bronze door. The **Giralda**, world-famous landmark and symbol of Sevilla, is the minaret of the former mosque, built to be the "most beautiful tower on earth." It now has a Christian belfry and outsize weathervane on top. Climb the long ramp for spectacular views.

Hospital de la Caridad Legend mistakenly asserts that the spectacular sinner-turned-penitent who headed this charity in the 17th century was the original for Don Juan. The hospital-church (tel: 954 22 32 32; *Open* Mon–Sat 9–1, 3.30–6.30. *Admission charge*) has Murillo paintings and ghastly scenes of death by Valdés Leal.

Isla de la Cartuja The Expo site of 1992, now a science and leisure park with some of the pavilions still in use, lies on an island to the west of town, accessible by road bridges, a footpath, and cable car. The Pabellón de la Navegación, a seafaring museum with particular emphasis on Sevilla's maritime contribution, a giant-screen cinema, and the Isla Mágica theme park, are all efforts to bring the site into contemporary use. One original building on the site was the fine old Carthusian monastery or Charterhouse, La Cartuja, where Columbus stayed and left his personal archive. Kilns survive from an old ceramics factory here.

La Maestranza (Plaza de Toros) Sevilla's whitewashed bullring (tel: 954 22 45 77; *Open* daily 9.30–2, 3–7) on the river is one of Spain's most picturesque.

Parque de María Luisa Tall trees from Latin America grace this fine park. Its dappled shade makes it a great spot for carriage-riding.

Plaza de España The brick-built Plaza, decorated with bright ceramics and evoking all Spain's provinces, was erected for the 1929 Ibero-American exhibition.

Torre del Oro The octagonal tower (tel: 954 22 24 19; *Open* Tue–Fri 10–2; Sat and Sun 11–2; *Closed* Aug. *Admission charge*) on the river, built by the Almohads and still casting a golden reflection in the water, is one of the trademarks of Sevilla.

Triana Across the river from the old town, Triana was once a gypsy quarter, haunt of flamenco singers. Some of that tradition still persists.

Universidad The former Fábrica de Tabacos (Tobacco Factory) on Calle San Fernando, the focus of Bizet's *Carmen*, is now the main building of the university.

Key museums
Centro Andaluz de Arte Contemporáneo (tel: 955 03 70 70; *Open* Tue–Fri 10–8, Sat 11–8, Sun 10–3. *Admission charge*). Set in the Monasterio de la Cartuja, it has a collection of major modern artists, such as Miró, Tàpies, and Chillida.
Museo Arqueológico (Plaza de América, tel: 954 23 24 01; *Open* Wed–Sat 9–8, Sun 9–2, Tue 3–8. *Admission charge, free for EU citizens*). The most interesting material here is Roman, due to the closeness of Roman Itálica, birthplace of the Emperor Hadrian. The magnificent Carambolo Treasure, discovered in the late 1950s, is outstanding.
Museo de Artes y Costumbres Populares (Plaza de América, tel: 954 23 25 76; *Open* Wed–Sat 9–8, Tue 3–8, Sun 9–2. *Admission charge, free for EU citizens*). This is in one of the buildings in the María Luisa Park constructed for the 1929 Ibero-American exhibition. Find out exactly how to wear your mantilla.
Museo de Bellas Artes (Plaza del Museo, tel: 954 22 07 90; *Open* Wed–Sat 9–8, Tue 3–8, Sun 9–2. *Admission charge, free for EU citizens*). Strikingly installed in the refurbished Convento de la Merced, this museum contains a magnificent collection of Sevilla school art.

Ceramic decoration on the Plaza de España, where the pond is spanned by a number of small bridges adorned with bright tiles. One series displays a different scene from each of Spain's provinces

A FLOWERING OF THE ARTS
In its heyday, Sevilla enjoyed a flowering of the arts. Diego Rodríguez de Silva y Velázquez (1599–1660) served his apprenticeship in the city, and many of his early works were painted here. Alonso Cano and the great sculptor Juan Martínez Montañés both worked in Sevilla. Last in the great line was Murillo, whose over-sweet scenes are redeemed by unrivalled draughtsmanship.

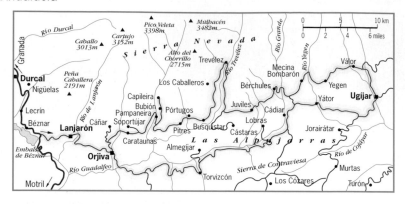

Drive

Alpujarras

Less a mountain range than a collection of fertile valley floors and steep slopes whose high ridges lean up hard against the Sierra Nevada to the north, the Alpujarras form an area of great physical beauty with impressive historical associations. It was here, after the fall of Granada, that the defeated Moorish ruler, Boabdil, was granted an estate. Here also the last surviving Moors, openly Muslim though technically now Christian, staged their last, desperate revolt. Defeated and dispersed, they were finally expelled in 1609.

Approach by the fast new main road "South from Granada" (the title of a classic book on the area by British author and Hispanophile, Gerald Brenan).

Turn east at Venta de las Angustias for Lanjarón.

As entry point to a thoroughly rustic area, **Lanjarón** may well surprise. It is a flourishing spa town with numerous hotels and restaurants. Patients are sent by their doctors to take the strong-tasting medicinal waters. They carry glasses of it up and down the streets in small baskets like candle-holders.

Continue to Orjiva, turn left, before entry to town, on local road 421.

There is a winding climb to **Pampaneira**, a beautiful Alpujarra village with striking architecture.

Above Pampaneira, turn left and ascend the Poqueira valley (with poplars, chestnuts, and abandoned terraces once worked by the Moors) to the touristy but lovely hilltop villages of **Bubión** and **Capileira**.

There are stunning views of the highest peaks in the Sierra Nevada.

Return to the 421 and continue north to Trevélez.

Spain's highest village, **Trevélez** is a focus now not only for mountain hams but for horse-riding, camping, hostels, and hotels.

The road loops to the south, soon much less frequented by tourists, passing via **Juviles** (unspoiled village architecture), **Mecina Bombarón** (magnificent views of the main Alpujarra valley), **Yegen** (one-time home of Gerald Brenan and his house is marked with a plaque), and finally rejoining the original, larger highway. At **Ugíjar**, turn right on a decidedly minor road, signposted Jorairátar and Murtas, and follow it round to the right for beautiful **Yátor** and **Cádiar**. Continue on this road through Torvizcón.

This stretch is fairly arduous driving. The road drops steeply to **Orjiva**, a little country town and capital of the Alpujarras, then out via Lanjarón for Granada or southwards to Motril.

Drive

White Towns

See map on pages 224–225.

This drive encompasses sea (both Mediterranean and Atlantic) and wild sierra. The route passes through some of the so-called Pueblos Blancos (White Towns), including Ronda, through cattle-raising ranchlands and the major port and town of Algeciras. In effect, it describes a wedge from the southerly point of San Roque north towards Ronda, then westwards to Arcos de la Frontera, south through Medina-Sidonia to Vejer de la Frontera. From there it follows the coast road along the Costa de la Luz to Tarifa before returning to San Roque. This is a two-day drive.

Leave San Roque by the C3331 in the direction of Jimena de la Frontera.

You drive through wooded country of cattle, cork-oak, and eucalyptus. **Jimena** has all the characteristics of a White Town. With pink-tiled roofs, wrought-iron balconies, and grilled windows, it climbs steeply through narrow cobbled streets, falling a little short of the towered Moorish castle on the top.

Follow signs to Ronda on C341.

The road goes through green, cultivated land climbing into sierra. This is the old tobacco smugglers' route from Gibraltar past lovely **Guacín** and **Algatocín**. Climb to the 715m (2,345ft) high Encinas Borrachas (Drunken Oaks) pass towards the town of **Ronda** high on its gorge.

Leave Ronda by the Sevilla road C339.

At about 26km (16mi) there is a diversion to **Cueva de la Pileta**, which has prehistoric paintings on its walls.

From the C339 take the turning for the picturesque town of **Grazalema**, and at El Bosque, turn left after the bullring in the direction of **Arcos de la Frontera**. Leave Arcos in the direction of Jerez, then turn south, following signs to Paterna and Vejer de la Frontera.

This is cotton, sunflower, and cereal country with signs off to sherry towns.

After Medina-Sidonia, continue southwards to **Véjer de la Frontera**, a lovely, classic-looking White Town. The coast road through Barbate de Franco leads to the small coastal resort of **Zahara de los Atunes**.

Cattle attended by egrets graze in fields hedged by prickly pear.

Return to the main N340 and head south to Tarifa with views of Africa. Then head northwards to Algeciras, and back to San Roque.

253

Precipitously placed Arcos de la Frontera, a challenge to drivers

Andalucía

Plaza Vázquez de Molina in Úbeda

ST. JOHN OF THE CROSS
The great mystical poet St. John of the Cross died in Úbeda and is commemorated there by a sentimental statue entirely unworthy of him. One of the great figures of Spanish literature, he celebrated ascetic notions in a passionate, sensual poetry more easily associated with physical love.

EUROPE'S WILD WEST
If there is something familiar about the parched landscapes around Tabernas it may be because they form the backdrop to a string of classic 1960s and '70s films, including *Lawrence of Arabia* and *A Fistful of Dollars*. Three former film sets are now run as mini-theme parks where stuntmen re-enact the clichés of the Wild West, such as gunfights and bank robberies. Another Almería landscape, a picturesque beach near the Cabo de Gata, turns up in *Indiana Jones and the Last Crusade*.

▶ **Sorbas and Tabernas**   *225E2*

These neighbouring towns lie amid dramatic landscape in the northern region of the Sierra Alhamilla, bristling with solar energy installations. Sorbas, known for ceramics, teeters on the edge of a grey stone cliff. Tabernas is a small flat-roofed town in gulch and canyon country, a perfect setting for the spaghetti (or paella) westerns once made there. Old film sets are now used for cowboy shows for visitors from coastal resorts (see panel).

▶▶ **Úbeda**   *225D3*

Ferdinand III captured this town definitively from the Moors in 1234. Aristocrats flocked here and built their mansions. A showpiece of Renaissance architecture, it owes the best part of its architectural glory, however, to three men: Francisco de los Cobos, who enriched himself fantastically as Charles V's secretary; his relative Juan Vázquez, who did the same in the same post; and the great local architect Andrés de Vandelvira.

The great set piece of Úbeda is the Plaza Vázquez de Molina, a perfect grouping of buildings around an L-shaped space. At one end is El Salvador, built as chapel to the now mostly vanished Cobos palace. This has a sculpted front by Diego de Siloé, while its interior was completed by Vandelvira (ring for entry at the side door of the church. The caretaker will show you around for a modest tip). Next to the chapel is the **Condestable Dávalos** parador, severe externally but with a lovely patio inside. Among other notable buildings in the square are the five-naved, eclectic church of **Santa María** and opposite it, immensely dignified, the Vázquez palace, known as the **Casa de las Cadenas** (House of Chains), built by Vandelvira. The town also produces a startlingly beautiful green-glazed pottery.

▶▶ **Véjer de la Frontera**   *224B1*

Véjer, south of Jerez and Cádiz, has a double claim to fame. It is one of the most enchanting of the White Towns (with crenellated walls and ancient whitewashed houses) and it is virtually on the coast, which means it can easily be combined with a visit to the growing resort of Conil de la Frontera or the wilder beaches of El Palmar and Los Caños de Meca.

Travel Facts

Arriving

All visitors to Spain need a valid passport while EU nationals (except those of the Republic of Ireland and Denmark) may use a national ID card. Passport-holders from the EU, Iceland, and Norway do not require visas, regardless of purpose and/or length of stay in Spain. Should the intended stay exceed 90 days, however, registration with the local police authorities is compulsory.

Passport-holders from the US, Japan, Australia, Canada, and New Zealand require a visa for stays exceeding 90 days.

For US citizens, more information on obtaining a passport can be found at the National Passport Information Center. Visit www.travel.state.gov or call 1-900-225-5674.

Always check with the consulate about entry regulations as they are liable to change, often at short notice. (see page 261).

By air The main airports for scheduled flights are Madrid, Barajas (tel: 913 05 83 43) and Barcelona, El Prat de Llobregat (tel: 932 98 38 38).

Iberia is Spain's national airline. Head office: Iberia, Velázquez 130, Madrid (tel: 902 40 05 00).

There are Iberia offices in many major cities including: Sydney (Australia), Toronto (Canada), Dublin (Republic of Ireland), London (UK), and Washington, New York, San Francisco, and Chicago (US).

By boat There are no scheduled boat connections between Spain and North America, although many cruise ships call in at Spanish ports.

Brittany Ferries (UK tel: 0870 536 0360) operates a ferry service between Plymouth (UK) and Santander (Spain). The ships sail twice a week from mid-Mar–Nov.

P&O European Ferries (UK tel: 0870 242 4999) sails twice weekly, year-round between Portsmouth (UK) and Bilbao.

Transmediterránea, Alcalá 61, 28014 Madrid (tel: 902 45 46 45) operates between the north of Africa and Spain, and between mainland Spain and the Canaries and the Balearics.

By car When considering the costs of driving to Spain from northern Europe, take into account road tolls, fuel, extra motor insurance cover, and overnight stops. An alternative to driving is to take the car with you on motor rail. Car sleeper trains operated by French National Railways (SNCF) run from northern France via Paris to the Spanish border. There is also a service from Paris (Austerlitz) to Madrid.

By train Spanish National Railways (RENFE) operate international inter-city Talgo (fast, luxury) trains

It is usually cheapest, and often most interesting, to get around by bus

between Paris (France) and Barcelona (11.5 hours) and Paris and Madrid (13 hours). Information can be obtained from the following numbers: RENFE international: 934 90 11 22; national: 902 24 02 02; or Renfe's website: www.renfe.es.

For non-Europeans, a Eurail pass is offered by the continental rail systems. You must buy it either in your country of origin or from an agent in Europe (providing you have not been more than six months in the country where you wish to purchase the pass).

Beaches
Spain's premier beaches have been awarded a Blue Flag by the Foundation for Environmental Education in Europe. Blue Flag requirements include the following:
• A high standard of water cleanliness
• Good facilities for bathers (toilets, first aid, life-saving equipment, etc)
• Daily cleaning of beaches during the busy season.

For a list of Blue Flag beaches, contact EU offices in member countries. Be careful of tidal and estuary currents when swimming from any beach; the Atlantic coast demands *great* respect.

Camping
There are over 400 authorized campsites throughout Spain, most along the coast or close to the main towns and cities. Advance bookings (advisable in summer) can be made directly with the site, or contact: Federación Española de Empresarios de Campings y CV, San Bernardo 97, 28015 Madrid (tel: 914 48 12 34).

Camping is prohibited in certain areas. Always check with the local authorities first, and if you are camping on private property make sure that you obtain the owner's permission. Tourist offices produce a *Mapa de Campings*, giving telephone numbers and locations for campsites throughout Spain.

Sites are divided into four grading categories, with facilities ranging from (at least) refreshments, running water, first aid, and postal services to the top Campings de Lujo category, including electricity, children's play area, telephone, laundry, car wash, etc.

Children
Children play a large role within the family and take part in all aspects of life in Spain, including outings to bars and restaurants.

Babysitting Ask for information about babysitters at the local tourist office or at your hotel. Babysitters sometimes advertise in local papers, but you should check their credentials very carefully.

Entertainment Madrid, Barcelona, the coastal resorts, and some other cities, have tailor-made entertainment for children in the form of zoos, aquaparks, and fun parks (such as Madrid's **Casa de Campo**, with a modern zoo, amusement park, and open-air entertainment during the summer). Many museums and other attractions offer reduced entrance rates for children; if you cannot see a price displayed, ask about a discount.

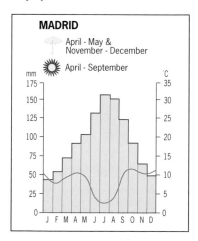

Climate
In northern Spain summers are warm with an average of eight hours' sunshine per day. Rainfall is highest in Galicia and the Cantabrian mountains. Central Spain experiences scorching summers

while the winters are usually bitter, with heavy snowfalls and biting winds coming off the sierras.

The Mediterranean coast in general has hot summers and mild, wet winters. In the north the summer heat is moderated by cool breezes off the sea and occasional thunderstorms. In the south, a hot, dry wind sometimes blows in from Africa.

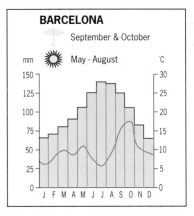

BARCELONA

September & October

mm   May - August   °C

Crime
In urban areas there is a growing problem of drug-related crime. It is becoming increasingly grave and obvious that tourists are, unfortunately, special targets. Below are a few points to remember:
• Avoid dark and lonely areas.
• Keep an eye on your luggage.
• Don't wear handbags, cameras, or anything with a shoulder strap over one shoulder. It is best to hold them against your chest.
• Carry wallets and purses in the front trouser pocket.
• If you can, put your valuables, travel tickets, and documents into a safety deposit box when not needed. If journeying by car:
• Make sure that you keep valuables out of sight.
• Always check, when you leave the car, that the doors are locked and that the keys are safe.
The chief problem for the visitor is the threat of petty crime in popular and crowded places, particularly in big cities, but the risk of violence or personal injury remains small.

Customs regulations
These are in line with those of other European Union countries. Visitors entering Spain from another EU country may bring in tax-paid goods for personal use (such as portable videos, camping equipment etc) without having to pay customs charges.

Upon request, Spanish customs can issue a receipt as proof of any goods brought into the country. For certain articles, however, maximum limits have been set, with customs duties leviable on amounts exceeding these. The following are guidance levels on tax-paid goods bought in the EU for your personal use and in brackets are limits for duty-free and tax-free shopping:

Tobacco	
cigarettes	800 (200)
or cigarillos	400 (100)
or cigars	200 (50)
or tobacco	1kg (250g)
Alcohol	
spirits	10l (1l)
wine	90l (2l still wine)
fortified wine	20l
(such as port or sherry)	(2l)
beer	110l
perfume	(60cc/ml)
toilet water	(250cc/ml)

There is no limit on the amount of foreign currency or euros you can take into Spain. However, it is best to declare any amount over 600 euros or the equivalent of 3,000 euros in foreign currency. You are allowed to take more than these amounts out of the country only if the excess was declared when you arrived.

The import of wildlife souvenirs from rare or endangered species may be either illegal or require a special permit. Before purchase check your home country's customs regulations.

Travellers with disabilities
Facilities are not widespread, but the situation is slowly changing.

The organization for the blind, **ONCE**, Calle Prado 24 (tel: 915 89 46 00), not only runs a national lottery, but is a strong pressure group for

Euro coins have a side dedicated to their country of origin, whereas euro notes are identical across the euro zone

259

people with disabilities. **COCEMFE**, Calle Eugenio Salazar 2, 28002 Madrid (tel: 914 13 80 01) has information on accessibility. It operates a travel agency, contact Rompiendo Barreras Travel, Calle Roncesvalles, 3, 28007 Madrid (tel: 915 52 84 07).

Brittany Ferries have specially adapted cabins on their ships to Santander: contact Brittany Ferries, Millbay Docks, Plymouth PL1 3EW (tel: 0870 536 0360). There are a number of international cruise lines from the US to Spain. For details contact the World Ocean and Cruise Linear Society, PO Box 92-B, Stamford CT 06904 (tel/fax: 203/329-2787).

For information on the accessibility of internal flights check with offices of Iberia (see **Arriving**).

RENFE (Spanish National Railways) has wheelchairs available for transfers at main stations.

In Spain If you use an automatic car, check first with the rental company that automatics are available.

There is no national parking scheme, however, several provinces allow parking in restricted areas, so check locally. As a general rule, newer buildings and museums are more likely to have ramps, plus wider doorways and cubicles.

ECOM, the federation of private organizations for the disabled. Contact ECOM, Avenida Gran Via de les Corts Catalanes 562, 08011 Barcelona, tel: 934 51 55 50, or Cruz Roja Española (the Red Cross), Rafael Villa s/n, 28023 Madrid, tel: 913 35 44 44.

Information General information can be obtained from:
Australia: The Disability Information and Resource Centre Inc, 195 Gilles Street, Adelaide SA 5000; tel: (08) 8223 7522; www.dircsa.org.au
Canada: The Easter Seals Society, 1185 Eglington Avenue East, Suite 800, Toronto, ON M3C 3C6; tel: 1-800-668-6252; www.easterseals.org
New Zealand: Disabled Persons Assembly (DPA), PO Box 27–524, Wellington 6035; tel: 644 801 9100; www.dpa.org.nz
UK: RADAR, 12 City Forum, 250 City Road, London, EC1V 8AF; tel: 020 7250 3222
US: SATH, 347 5th Avenue, Suite 610, New York City, NY 10016; tel: 212/447-7284; www.sath.org

Driving
You can bring your car into Spain duty free for up to six months a year as a tourist. For a longer stay, apply to the Spanish customs administration for an extension.

Documents You will need to be at least 18 years old and have with you the original vehicle log book (registration document), the "Green Card," motor insurance (a bail bond is also strongly advised in case of accident) and a valid driving licence.

Pink EU licences are acceptable, but national licences should be accompanied by either an official translation (from a Spanish consulate) or an international driving permit.

Rules and regulations Traffic in Spain travels on the right. Seat belts are compulsory and children under the age of 12 may not travel in the front seat unless the seat is fitted with a special harness.

The blood alcohol limit is 0.8 percent, but the best advice is not to drink and drive at all. In built-up areas the maximum speed is 50kph/30mph (local speed limits can be lower). Outside urban areas, the motorway speed limit is 120kph/75mph and 100kph/60mph or 90kph/55mph on other roads.

Accidents and breakdowns If you have an accident, your car and property could be impounded and you could be detained pending bail. Except in serious accidents a bail bond will usually be accepted by the police as a guarantee that you won't abscond and that you can meet any fines. Speak to your insurance company before taking a vehicle overseas, so ask them about a bail bond at the same time. For emergency services, see under **Emergency Telephone Numbers**.

You should carry two warning triangles in case of breakdown and a set of spare lightbulbs for the car.

Roads Some motorways (*autopistas*) are toll roads (*peaje*). Tickets are issued on entry; payment varies according to the distance travelled and class of vehicle. There is also a number of nonpaying *autovías*. The surfaces of main roads (*carreteras nacionales* prefix "N" and *carreteras comarcales* prefix "C") are on the whole good. Off the main roads, surfaces can be rough.

Parking Urban parking can be a problem. If you cannot find a car park (*aparcamiento*), you must not park on busy roads, within 5m (16.5ft) of the entrance to a public building, at a crossroads or intersection, on or near a tram line, or within 7m (23ft) of a tram or bus stop.

Garages are classified by the state into three categories according to the type of work they can deal with. They must display a blue sign giving their official rating and have set prices for common repairs.

Motoring associations The Spanish Motoring Club, Real Automóvil Club de España (RACE), has reciprocal agreements with the following associations:
Australia: Australian Automobile Association (AAA)
Canada: Canadian Automobile Association (CAA)
Republic of Ireland: AA Ireland Ltd
New Zealand: The New Zealand Automobile Association Inc (NZAA)
UK: Automobile Association (AA)
US: American Automobile Association (AAA).

RACE runs a 24-hour breakdown service from Madrid where there is an English-speaking service (tel: 915 93 33 33). If you have breakdown insurance or you are using a rental car, check on breakdown procedures before you start your journey.

Car rental If you are using one of the international companies (Avis, Budget, Hertz, Europcar, or Kemwell), it is usually cheaper to arrange (and pay for) a car before you leave home. If you hire when you get to Spain, look for local firms in the phone book under "Alquiler de Coches" (Car Hire) or ask at the tourist information office. These companies usually offer very competitive rates. Spain's leading car rental firm is ATESA (Paseo de la Castellana 130, Madrid; tel: 915 61 48 00). To rent a car you'll need your driver's licence, an international driver's permit is often more useful, and money for the deposit. There may be a minimum age (often 21,

sometimes higher) and a require-
ment that you've been driving for at
least a year. If you're using the car
for more than 21 days, it may be
cheaper to lease rather than rent;
your travel agent or the rental firm
can advise you on the best option.

Fuel Leaded petrol is still available in
Spain, known as Gasolina Super.
Unleaded petrol (ask for "*sin plomo*")
and diesel are available everywhere.

Electricity
The electricity system runs on 220
and 225 volts. In some older
buildings, the voltage is still 110 or
125 volts. Plugs have two round
pins, so you may need to buy an
adaptor to use your own electrical
equipment in Spain.

Embassies and consulates in Spain
Most countries have an embassy in
Madrid, and many also operate
consulates in major cities and tourist
resorts. Embassies in Madrid
include:
Australia: Plaza del Descubridor,
Diego de Ordás 3 (tel: 914 41 93 00)
Canada: Nuñez de Balboa 35
(tel: 914 31 43 00)
Republic of Ireland: Paseo de la
Castellana 46 (tel: 914 36 40 93)
New Zealand: 3rd Floor, Plaza de la
Lealtad 2 (tel: 915 23 02 26)
UK: Fernando el Santo 16
(tel: 913 19 02 00–02 12)
US: Serrano 75 28006 (tel:
915 87 22 00).
Abroad
Australia and New Zealand: 15
Arkana Street, Yarralumia, ACT 2600
Canberra (tel: 273 3555).
Canada: 74 Stanley Avenue, Ottawa,
Ontario KIM 1P4 (tel: 613 747 2252).
Republic of Ireland: 17a Merlyn
Park, Ballsbridge, Dublin 4
(tel: 3531 269 1640).
UK: 20 Draycott Place, London SW3
2RZ (tel: 020 7594 0128).
US: *Washington*: 2375 Pennsylvania
Avenue, NW Washington DC 20037
(tel: 202/728-2330).
Chicago: Consulate General, 180 N
Michigan Avenue, Suite 1500,
Chicago, Ill (tel: 312/782-4588);

Los Angeles: 5055 Wilshire Boulevard,
Suite 960, Los Angeles, Cal
(tel: 323/938-0158);
New York: 150 E 58th Street, New
York City, NY (tel: 212/355-4080).

Emergency telephone numbers
• **Fire** *(bomberos)*: in major cities 080,
otherwise phone the operator.
• **Police**: in all cities 091, in other
towns call the operator.
• **Ambulance**: contact the operator.

Etiquette
Remember that any attempt to
communicate in the host
country's language is always
appreciated, even if it is only to
apologize for not understanding.

Attitudes Spain embraces the whole
gamut of political opinion; and many
are prepared to give a free rein to
their views. For the visitor, the trick
is to understand what kind of
behaviour is the most appropriate to
the circumstance. Beach and
nightclubs may be free and easy, but
the remote Castilian villages less so.

*Traditional harvesting methods can still
be seen in the country*

261

Dress The Spanish in general dress well and appreciate it when others pay attention to their appearance. Formality of dress is rarely expected and "smart casual" is always the best policy. Even in beach resorts, people with naked torsos are not too popular in supermarkets, and though a woman may enter a church in jeans, many places will be covertly disapproving. Businesspeople are judged on the smartness of their clothes. In cities, Spanish women tend to dress "up" rather than down.

Church behaviour When visiting churches (or other religious buildings), remember that they are, first and foremost, places of worship and not tourist attractions; show respect for worshippers, and ask permission before taking pictures.

Regional differences Rural areas tend to be more conservative than towns, which in turn can seem staid compared with the cosmopolitanism of Madrid and Barcelona. Regional differences are also an important part of Spanish life and should be kept in mind. Some Catalans, for instance, see themselves as the commercial and industrial powerhouse of Spain, and look disparagingly on the more relaxed and perhaps less materialistic (certainly poorer) Andalucians.

A little understanding of Spain's highly regional nature—how and why each place differs to the rest, and an appreciation of local customs—will go a long way in getting you accepted and making you friends.

Health
Generally no inoculations are necessary to visit Spain, but an up-to-date tetanus jab is a good idea. If you need special medical treatment or diets you should take your own supply, or carry a letter, in Spanish, from your doctor explaining the condition and the treatments required. Buy travel insurance that includes medical cover, so that you can take advantage of private health care. (If you have medical insurance check that you are covered while travelling.) Residents of the EU are entitled to reciprocal care from the Spanish state health service. They should take with them a completed form (E111 in the UK, obtainable from post offices or local Health Authorities). The state service is quite limited; you must get treatment from a state hospital, state health centre, or a doctor who does work for the state health scheme. You will still have to pay for any prescribed medicines and for dental treatment.

In Washington, the State Department Citizens Emergency Center (tel: 202/647-5225) provides information on health conditions in other nations and

Rural life is a world away from the cosmopolitan cities and costas

on what US citizens can do in the event of an emergency overseas.

Be aware that the sun can be dangerous.

- Use plenty of protection, checking that you have the correct oil or cream for your skin type
- Cover your head
- Drink plenty of nonalcoholic drinks
- Take a tip from the locals, who avoid venturing out at midday.

Hitchhiking

As in any country, hitchhiking carries a risk and is ill-advised for anyone. If you *do* hitch, there is the additional problem that in the Basque and Catalan provinces, separatist violence can make drivers suspicious and lifts scarce. Motorway hiking is illegal and you can be fined on the spot. If you don't have the cash on you, your rucksack can be impounded or you could be imprisoned.

Language

Castilian Spanish (Castellano) is understood throughout the country. But there are important regional languages which are used in local government and everyday life and are in fact "official" in their own areas. The major regional languages are Catalan, Galician, and Basque. **Catalan**, which is closely related to Occitan/Provençal, is spoken in Catalonia and Valencia. **Basque**, the official language of the Basque Country in northern Spain, is intriguing in having no connection with any other modern European tongue. **Galician**, spoken in northwest Spain, is influenced by Portuguese.

Castilian Spanish belongs to the Romance family of languages, and is closely related to French and Italian.

As for the pronunciation of Castilian, there are, of course, regional variations. In the south, for instance, a "c" or a "z" is pronounced "s," rather than the more usual lisping "th." However, as a general rule every letter is pronounced, and the sounds are as follows (all vowels short):

A as in "bar"
E as in "let"
I as in "marina"
O as in "lot"
U as in "rule"
B as in "boom"
C before an "e" or an "i," a lisping "th"; otherwise as in cattle
G before an "e" or an "i" as "ch" in the Scottish "loch," otherwise as "g" in get
J as "ch" in Scottish "loch"
LL as "li" in "familiar"
Ñ as "ni" in "onion"
R always roll; "rr" doubly so
Z as "th" in "thin."

The emphasis in Spanish is on the last syllable, except when a vowel is accented for stress, or if the word ends in "n," "s," or a vowel, when the stress falls on the penultimate syllable.

Days of the week
Sunday domingo
Monday lunes
Tuesday martes
Wednesday miércoles
Thursday jueves
Friday viernes
Saturday sábado

Months of the year
January enero
February febrero
March marzo
April abril
May mayo
June junio
July julio
August agosto
September septiembre
October octubre
November noviembre
December diciembre

Numbers
one uno
two dos
three tres
four cuatro
five cinco
six seis
seven siete
eight ocho
nine nueve
ten diez
11 once
12 doce
13 trece
14 catorce

Goats at a waterhole, an unchanging scene in rural Spain

15 quince
16 dieciséis
17 diecisiete
18 dieciocho
19 diecinueve
20 veinte
30 treinta
40 cuarenta
50 cincuenta
60 sesenta
70 setenta
80 ochenta
90 noventa
100 cien
one hundred and... ciento...
500 quinientos
1,000 mil

how? ¿cómo?
what? ¿qué?
what time is it? ¿qué hora es?
where (is)? ¿dónde (está)?
with/without con/sin
go slowly despacio
do you have...? ¿tiene...?
how much is it? ¿cuánto es?
I do not understand no comprendo
I do not speak Spanish no hablo
español
Do you speak English? ¿habla usted
inglés?
excuse me (to attract attention)
¡por favor!
(to apologise) ¡perdón!
help! (call for) ¡socorro!

Basic words and phrases
good afternoon/early evening
buenas tardes
good morning buenos días
good night/evening buenas noches
hello hola
goodbye adiós
yes/no sí/no
please por favor
thank you gracias
here aquí
there allí
and y
today hoy
tomorrow mañana

Travel and sightseeing
airport aeropuerto
bus stop la parada de autobuses
train station la estación
de trenes
fast/slow rápido/despacio
up/down arriba/abajo
entrance entrada
exit salida
push/pull empujar/tirar
timetable el horario
opening times horas de oficina
beach playa
left/right izquierda/derecha
straight on (todo) derecho

Eating and drinking
beer cerveza
bill la cuenta
breakfast el desayuno
lunch la comida
dinner la cena
waiter/waitress el/la camarero/a
bread pan
set menu el menú del día
cheese queso
coffee café
cold frío
hot caliente
fish pescado
fruit fruta
meat carne
milk leche
vegetables verduras
wine, red/white vino tinto/blanco
water (mineral) agua mineral
water (drinking) agua potable

Lost property
Report any losses to the local police; you usually need to tell the police to make an insurance claim. If you lose any official travel documents, advise the police and your embassy or consulate. If your travellers' cheques are lost or stolen, let the issuing company know, as well as the police (always keep a separate record of your cheques' numbers).

Maps
The Spanish National Tourist Office offers a useful free map of road, rail, and air communications in Spain: *Mapa de Comunicaciones*. It gives information on road rescue, local railway stations, airport telephone numbers, and border crossings, and also has city road maps of Bilbao, Barcelona, Madrid, Sevilla, Valencia, and Zaragoza. For driving you will need a proper road map, such as Michelin Spain and Portugal 1:1,000,000. ASETA, Estébanez Calderón 3, 28020 Madrid (tel: 915 71 62 58), produces a free map to motorways, *Mapa de Autopistas de Peaje*. Local tourist offices can usually provide town maps. Walking maps can be obtained from Servicio de Publicaciones del Instituto Geográfico Nacional, General Ibáñez de Ibero 3, 28003 Madrid. Bookshops also stock them.

CONVERSION CHARTS

FROM	TO	MULTIPLY BY
Inches	Centimetres	2.54
Centimetres	Inches	0.3937
Feet	Metres	0.3048
Metres	Feet	3.2810
Yards	Metres	0.9144
Metres	Yards	1.0940
Miles	Kilometres	1.6090
Kilometres	Miles	0.6214
Acres	Hectares	0.4047
Hectares	Acres	2.4710
Gallons	Litres	4.5460
Litres	Gallons	0.2200
Ounces	Grams	28.35
Grams	Ounces	0.0353
Pounds	Grams	453.6
Grams	Pounds	0.0022
Pounds	Kilograms	0.4536
Kilograms	Pounds	2.205
Tons	Tonnes	1.0160
Tonnes	Tons	0.9842

MEN'S SUITS

UK	36	38	40	42	44	46	48
Rest of Europe	46	48	50	52	54	56	58
US	36	38	40	42	44	46	48

DRESS SIZES

UK	8	10	12	14	16	18
France	36	38	40	42	44	46
Italy	38	40	42	44	46	48
Rest of Europe	34	36	38	40	42	44
US	6	8	10	12	14	16

MEN'S SHIRTS

UK	14	14.5	15	15.5	16	16.5	17
Rest of Europe	36	37	38	39/40	41	42	43
US	14	14.5	15	15.5	16	16.5	17

MEN'S SHOES

UK	7	7.5	8.5	9.5	10.5	11
Rest of Europe	41	42	43	44	45	46
US	8	8.5	9.5	10.5	11.5	12

WOMEN'S SHOES

UK	4.5	5	5.5	6	6.5	7
Rest of Europe	38	38	39	39	40	41
US	6	6.5	7	7.5	8	8.5

265

A hop field

Media
Major European and American newspapers are usually available in Madrid, Barcelona, and the bigger resorts on the afternoon of their day of publication. The two national state-run television channels are TVE1 and TVE2. Regional authorities also run local stations, such as Canal Sur in Andalucía. There are also a number of private TV companies, for instance Tele 5, A 3 TV, and Canal Plus (subscription). Spanish radio broadcasts regular tourist emergency information.

Money matters
The unit of currency is the euro. Throughout the euro zone, euro bank notes are issued in denominations of 5, 10, 20, 50, 100, 200, and 500; coins in denominations of 1, 2, 5, 10, 20, and 50 centimes, 1 and 2 euros.

Admission charges Many sites charge admission fees, but these are generally moderate or inexpensive (under 5 euros), and often there is a free day for EU citizens. The more expensive sites (over 5 euros) tend to be the large, privately owned attractions, such as the Guggenheim in Bilbao, or theme parks.

Banks are generally open Monday to Friday 9.30–2, Saturday 9.30–1. In major cities, they may open all day until 4.30 or 5. It is often quicker to

withdraw and change money at ATMs, common throughout Spain and most often found outside banks. Most hotels and major stores accept credit cards. IVA, a value-added sales tax, is levied on most items. Tax refunds are usually available on large purchases (refunds for EU nationals are restricted). Ask in the shop for information or contact the commercial office of the Spanish Embassy before you leave home (see page 261).

National holidays
1 January (New Year); 6 January (Day of the Three Kings); 1 May (Labour Day); 15 August (Assumption); 12 October (celebrating the first voyage to America); 1 November (All Saints); 8 December (Immaculate Conception); 25 December (Christmas). The movable feasts of Good Friday and Corpus Christi are also national holidays. There are also four holidays established by local authorities which vary between regions. Local tourist offices can provide information on these.

Opening times
Shops usually open between 9.30 and 10AM, close for lunch from 1.30 or 2PM until 4.30 or 5PM and then stay open till 8PM. Most close on Saturday afternoons and Sundays, although in major resorts in summer, shops may stay open seven days a week. The larger department stores do not usually close for lunch.

Museums Opening times vary throughout the country and from summer to winter, so check locally. They can also change for no apparent reason. There are often reductions for students and those over 60 or 65 and occasional free entry for citizens of EU countries. The opening times of the national museums are given below.
Museo Arqueológico Nacional (Madrid): Tue–Sat 9.30–8.30, Sun 9.30–2.30; closed Mon.
Museu Nacional d'Art de Catalunya (Barcelona): Tue–Sat 10–7, Sun 10–2.30; closed Mon.

Museo Nacional de Escultura
(Valladolid): Tue–Sat 10–2 and 4–6,
Sun 10–2; closed Mon.
Museo del Prado (Madrid): Tue–Sat
9–7, Sun 9–2; closed Mon.
Centro de Arte Reina Sofia (Madrid):
Mon, Wed–Sat 10–9, Sun 10–2.30;
closed Tue.
Museu Picasso (Barcelona): Tue–Sat
10–8, Sun 10–2.30; closed Mon.
Museo de Santa Cruz (Toledo).
Tue–Sat 10–6.30, Mon 10–2 and
4–6.30, Sun 10–2.
Museo Nacional de Arte Romano
(Mérida): Tue–Sat 10–2 and 4–6 (in
summer 5–7); Sun 10–2; closed Mon.
Museu Dalí (Figueres): Tue–Sun
10.30–5.15 in winter; daily 9–8
in summer.

Organized tours

Package tours can give you the
benefit of expert couriers and guides
with knowledge of the country
and language, while taking the
burden of planning and organization
from your shoulders. It is in
specialist holidays (art, walking,
sports, etc) that organized packages
really come into their own.

The Spanish National Tourist
Office produces a regularly updated
list of operators in Spain, plus those
dealing in specialist holidays.

Pharmacies

These usually display a white sign
with a green cross. Their opening
hours are generally the same as those
of shops, but check locally. Outside
shop hours the name of the duty
pharmacist (*farmacia de guardia*) is
displayed on pharmacies' doors
and published in the local paper.
Pharmacies sell a wide range of
drugs and medicines, some of which
are only available on prescription
elsewhere in Europe.

Places of worship

Tourist offices can give information
on local places of worship and
service times. The following are
churches and religious centres for
visitors to Madrid.
Anglican: St. George British Chapel,
Nuñez de Balboa 43
(tel: 915 76 51 09).

Baptist Church: Hernández de
Tejada 4 (tel: 914 07 43 47).
Islamic Centre, Arab Mosque:
Salvador de Madariaga 4
(tel: 913 26 26 10).
Jewish: Balmes 3 (tel: 914 45 98 35)
Mormon Church: San Telmo 26
(tel: 913 59 26 34).
North American Catholic Church:
Avenida Alfonso XIII 165
(tel: 912 59 30 10).

Police

There are three different police
organizations in Spain dealing with
different aspects of public order.
• **Policía Municipal**, whose main
responsibility is urban traffic, are the
local police. They are identifiable by
their blue uniforms and the white
checked bands on their vehicles.
• **Policía Nacional**, who wear brown
uniforms and berets, deal with law
and order and national security.
Report crimes to the police station
(*comisaría*).
• **Guardia Civil**, who are responsible
for border posts, policing country
areas, highways and the coast, wear
olive green. There are also Basque
police in the Basque Country, who
wear red berets. Catalunya has its
own police force, too.

The Prado in Madrid

Post offices

Opening times of post offices (*correos*) vary depending on whether they are in a big city, a provincial town, or a village. But most of them are open 8.30–2, Monday to Saturday. It is quicker to buy stamps (*sellos*) from a tobacconist, or *estanco* (marked with a "T"). Spain's postal service is not fast. Post boxes are yellow.

Public transportation

Air Iberia and its subsidiary airline Aviaco operate an extensive network of domestic flights. Major cities are within easy reach of Madrid: Barcelona 55 minutes; Valencia 30 minutes; Bilbao 50 minutes; and Sevilla 50 minutes. Note that demand for seats is very high in summer.

Bus Spain has a good system of buses between major cities. The Spanish National Tourist Office produces a guide to domestic bus services. Check with local tourist information offices for details.

Taxis Although taxi fares differ between areas they are usually charged in the same way. An initial charge is made, plus mileage and surcharges for

Some people prefer to keep to the old modes of transportation

weekends, public holidays, and nights. Taxi drivers have a schedule of approved fares for journeys between cities and to airports and stations. City taxis are metered.

Rail The 3,000km (1,865mi) of railway in Spain are run by the state-owned RENFE. The main types of trains which are operated on the rail system are:
• EuroCity (EC): international express train
• algo, InterCity, Electrotren, Ter and Tres Estrellas: luxury inter-city trains
• Expreso and Rápido: fast, long-distance, stopping at main stations
• AVE and TALGO 200v: high-speed services (from Madrid to Sevilla and Málaga respectively)
• Tourist trains: Alandalus Express (Andalucía); Transcantábrico (northern Spain)
• Omnibús, Tranvía, Automotor: local stopping trains.

Fares are very reasonable by European standards, and are available for first- and second-class travel. There are discounted fares on Blue Days (*días azules*), which avoid the holiday periods. RENFE offers visitors from outside Spain a tourist card (*tarjeta turística*) for first- and second-class travel. Different rail passes exist, like Inter-Rail or Eurail, for travelling in Spain and the rest of Europe. There are no reductions on an AVE ticket and limited reductions on TALGOs. RENFE operates a 24-hour telephone railway information service (tel: 902 24 02 02).

Subways Madrid, Barcelona, Bilbao, and Valencia have modern and efficient subway systems. The Madrid subway runs from 6AM to 1.30AM. A metro tour card is on sale for unlimited travel for three or five days. The Barcelona subway runs from 5AM to 11PM on weekdays and from 5AM to 1AM at weekends and on holidays. For cheaper travel buy a book of 10 tickets: *Tarjeta T-2*.

Senior citizens

Saga is the leading international travel company organizing package tours for people over 60.

Saga International Holidays, 222 Berkeley Street, Boston, MA 02116, USA (tel: toll-free 800/343-0273; www.sagaholidays.com).

Saga Holidays Ltd, The Saga Building, Middleburg Square, Folkstone, Kent, CT20 1AZ, UK (tel: freefone 0800 300 500; www.saga.co.uk).

Information You can also get information and advice from the following national organizations:
Australia: Australian Retired Persons Association, 84 Archer Street, North Adelaide, SA 5006 (tel: 08 82 67 57 11; www.arpasa.asn.au).
Canada: Canadian Association of Retired Persons, 27 Queen Street East, Suite 1304, Toronto, Ontario M5C 2M6 (tel: 416/363-8748; www.50plus.com/carp).
Ireland: National Council on Ageing and Older People, 22 Clanwilliam Square, Grand Canal Quay, Dublin 2 (tel: 01 676 6484; www.ncop.ie).
New Zealand: Senior Citizens Unit, Ministry of Social Development, Private Bag 39993, Wellington (tel: 04 916 3738; www.mosp.govt.nz).
UK: Age Concern
England: Astral House, 1268 London Road, Norbury, London, SW16 4ER (tel: 020 8679 8000).
Scotland: 113 Rose Street, Edinburgh, EH2 3DT (tel: 0131 220 3345).
Wales: 4th Floor, 1 Cathedral Road, Cardiff, CF1 9SD (tel: 029 2037 1566).
Northern Ireland: 3 Lower Crescent, Belfast, BT7 1NR (tel: 01232 245 729).
US: Alliance for Retired Americans,

888 16th Street, NW Washington DC 20006 (tel: 888/373-6497; www.retiredamericans.org).

Sport

Aeroclubs There are plenty of aeroclubs in Spain, covering gliding, ultralights, sports planes, ballooning, and parachuting: government permits are needed for aero sports. Information can be obtained from the Spanish Aerial Sports Federation (FENDA), Carretera de la Fortuna s/n, 28044 Madrid (tel: 915 08 54 80).

Fishing There is deep-sea fishing in the Atlantic or Mediterranean, or underwater fishing in the Mediterranean, on the Costa Brava and around Almería. There are also over 120,000km (74,500mi) of rivers and streams. Information about fishing in Spain is available from the Spanish Fishing Federation, Navas de Tolosa 3, 28013 Madrid (tel: 915 32 83 53).

Golf New courses appear each year throughout Spain, many of them along the Mediterranean coast. Most golf clubs are members of the Royal Spanish Golf Federation, Capitán Haya 9, 28020 Madrid (tel: 915 55 26 82 or 915 55 27 57). Joining the federation gives access to courses.

Riding The Spanish Riding Federation, Plaza del Marqués de Salamanca 2, 28006 Madrid (tel: 914 36 42 00) can give information about riding, and also issues a membership

269

There are good long-distance bus services throughout Spain

Taking a taxi in Barcelona. A green light means "available for hire"

card for tourists. This gives access to race meetings without charge, and allows use of local riding club facilities.

Sailing Information on marinas, landing stages, and official sailing competitions can be obtained from the Spanish Motor Boat Federation, Avenida de América 33–4 B, 28002 Madrid (tel: 914 15 37 69). For further information on facilities and local clubs, contact the Spanish Sailing Federation, Luis de Salazar 9, Bajo 28002 Madrid (tel: 915 19 50 08).

Skiing The Pyrenees and Cantabrian ranges have a wide choice of ski resorts in the north. In central Spain, there are three resorts close to Madrid: Navacerrada, Valdesquí, and Valcotos; and in the south, there is Solynieve in the Sierra Nevada. The season is usually November to May. For information on skiing resorts contact ATUDEM (Tourist Association of Skiing and Mountain Resorts) in Madrid (tel: 913 59 15 57); or the Spanish Winter Sports Federation, Arroyo Fresno 3A, 28035 Madrid (tel: 913 76 99 30).

Tennis The Royal Spanish Tennis Federation is based at Avinguda

Diagonal 618, 08021 Barcelona (tel: 932 01 08 44/00 53 55/01 55 86), and can provide information on tournaments and local tennis clubs. Many tennis clubs are for members only, but you may be able to get day membership. Large hotels often have courts for rent, and municipal sports centres also provide tennis courts, often cheaper than hotels.

Student and youth travel
Enjoying yourself can be expensive, but the International Student Identification Card and, for people under 26 the International Youth Card, will help you to cut costs. They entitle you to discounts on museum and gallery entrance, transportation, and accommodation. Other hints:
• Students can get information about the Student Identification Card from their school or college student body.
• Contact the Youth Hostel Association of England and Wales, Dimple Road, Matlock, Derbyshire DE4 3YH (tel: 0870 870 8808) for details of membership, which gains you access to hostels worldwide.
• In the US, contact Hosteling International, American Youth Hostels at 733 15th Street NW, Suite 840, Washington DC 20005 (tel: 202/783-6161).

• The Spanish Youth Hostel Organization (Red Española de Albergues Juveniles) gives priority at its hostels to travellers under 26. Contact the youth hostel organization and the young people's travel information body, TIVE, at Fernando el Católico 88, 28015 Madrid (tel: 915 43 02 08).

Telephones
The telephone system is fast and efficient. Call boxes are blue, plentiful, and easy to use, for both domestic and international calls. Look for the Teléfono signs; they use 5, 10, 20, 50 centimes and 1 and 2 euro coins, or phone cards of 6 and 12 euros (available at post offices and *estancos*). Some phones accept credit cards. Cheap rate operates between 10PM and 8AM from Monday to Saturday, and all day on Sunday. Provincial area codes have to be dialled even for local calls. To make an international call, dial 00 then wait for a high-pitched continuous tone; then dial the country and area codes (omit the initial "0" of the area code) and the number itself. International codes from Spain are: Australia 61, Republic of Ireland 353, New Zealand 64, UK 44, US and Canada 1. To dial Spain from abroad the country code is 34.

Help They are being phased out, but most major towns still have telephone bureaux (*Locutorios Telefónicos*) where help is at hand if you need it and you don't have to struggle with change; just pay after you've made the call. In Spain, for information about making domestic calls dial 1003; for international information dial 025; for technical assistance dial 1002.

Time
Daylight Saving Time, when the clocks move forward one hour, is from the morning of the last Sunday in March to the first Sunday in September. Spain is one hour ahead of Greenwich Mean Time; two hours ahead during Daylight Saving Time. Clock times compared with Spain (Standard Time) are as follows:

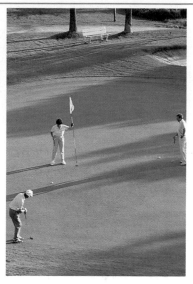

Golf is increasing along the coast

Australia: 7–9 hours ahead
Canada: 4.5–9 hours behind
New Zealand: 11 hours ahead
UK and Republic of Ireland: 1 hour behind
US: 6–9 hours behind.

Tipping
Most hotel and restaurant bills now include a service charge, but it is still customary to leave a tip of between 5 and 10 percent. Small tips are usually given in bars and to taxi drivers. Parking attendants, doormen, hairdressers, lavatory attendants, shoe shines, and tour guides generally receive small tips.

Toilets
Public toilets are pretty thin on the ground. The best places to look for toilets (*los servicios*) are in large department stores, some museums, and places of interest. Bars and restaurants have facilities for their customers. If you go into a bar to use the toilet it is probably a good idea to buy something.

Tourist offices
Spanish tourist offices abroad (see page 272) can provide you with information and advice on holidays, but they are not travel agencies and

On court at Los Monteros tennis centre in Málaga province

do not book or arrange holidays. Visit www.tourspain.es for general tourist information.

Canada: 34th Floor Bloor Street West, Toronto, Ontario M4W 3E2 (tel: 416 961 3131)

UK and Republic of Ireland: 22–33 Manchester Square, London, WIV 3PX (tel: 020 7486 8077)

US: *Chicago*: Water Tower Place, Suite 915 East, 845 N Michigan Avenue, Chicago, I1 60611 (tel: 312/642-1992)

Los Angeles: 8383 Wilshire Boulevard, Suite 960, Beverly Hills, CA 90211 (tel: 323/658-7188)

Miami: 1221 Brickell Avenue, Miami, FL 33131 (tel: 305/358-1992)

New York: 666 Fifth Avenue, New York 10103 (tel: 212/265-8822).

The following are the tourist information offices in the principal regional towns throughout Spain:

Barcelona: Passeig de Gràcia 107 (tel: 932 38 40 00)

Bilbao: Paseo del Arenal 1 (tel: 944 79 57 60)

Iruñea (Pamplona): Calle Eslava 1 (tel: 948 20 65 40)

Logroño: Paseo del Espolón s/n (tel: 941 29 12 60)

Madrid: Puerta de Toledo (tel: 913 64 18 76)

Mérida: José Álvarez de Buruaga (tel: 924 31 53 53)

Murcia: Calle Plano de San Francisco 5 (tel: 968 35 87 20)

Oviedo: Plaza de Alfonso II El Casto 6 (tel: 985 21 33 85)

Santiago de Compostela: Rúa do Vilar 43 (tel: 981 58 40 81)

Santander: Plaza de Velarde 5 (tel: 942 31 07 80)

Seville: Avda de la Constitución 21 (tel: 954 22 14 04)

Toledo: Puerta de Bisagra (tel: 925 22 08 43)

Valencia: Calle de la Paz 48 (tel: 963 98 64 22)

Valladolid: Calle Santiago 19 (tel: 983 35 18 01)

Zaragoza (Saragossa): Plaza del Pilar s/n (tel: 976 39 35 37).

Valeting and laundry
Hotels will deal with these, but they can charge more than local laundries and dry-cleaners.

Walking and hiking
Popular walking areas in Spain are the Sierra Nevada range, the historic Pilgrims' Way of St. James (see pages 168–169), running through the Cantabrian mountains, and the Picos de Europa, in the Cantabrian range, which has spectacular treks.

Many national parks, such as the Ordesa Park in the Aragonese Pyrenees (see page 111), have signposted walks and trails for the serious and not so serious walker.

Serviceable walking maps can be bought locally, but to plan routes beforehand, obtain walking maps from the **Instituto Geográfico Nacional** (see **Maps**, pages 265) and from the **Federación Española de Montañismo**. When walking in Spain, follow the usual advice:

• Wear comfortable walking boots and casual, comfortable clothing, remembering to take suitable clothes for cold and wet weather.

• Be prepared for emergencies, with a torch, whistle, and some energy-giving food such as chocolate.

• Also check with your insurance company that you are covered in case of accident.

Websites
There is a huge range of websites carrying information on Spain and its regions. The following are just a few; more can be found through any search engine.

• www.andalucia.org (Andalucia)
• www.barcelonaturisme.com (Barcelona)
• www.turgalicia.es (Galicia)
• www.comadrid.es (Madrid)
• www.euskadi.net (Pais Vasco)

Hotels in Spain are government-regulated

273

Hotels and Restaurants

Many of the hotels in the listings below are paradors. Originally a parador was an inn for the gentry. Today the state-run paradors still have an exclusive image. Many are in historic or beautiful old buildings; others are in particularly fine positions; all give a guarantee of good standards of service and accommodation.

All hotels in Spain are government-regulated and classified according to facilities. In addition to full hotels, there are *hotel residencias* (usually without a restaurant), and the more basic but reliable *hostales* and *pensiones*. The latter provide full board.

For Parador Central Reservations visit www.parador.es or tel: 915 16 66 66.

HOTELS

The hotels listed below are grouped into three price categories based on a nightly rate for double room with breakfast:
• **Expensive** (€€€): over €120
• **Moderate** (€€): €60–120
• **Inexpensive** (€): under €60

Madrid *See also page 69*
Emperador (€€€)
Gran Vía 53 tel: 915 47 28 00
Excellent for summer visitors, this hotel also has a roof-top swimming pool.
Galiano (€€)
Alcalá Galiano 6 tel: 913 19 20 00
Small but smart hotel that was once a private house and still feels like one.
Hotel Bauzá (€€€)
Goya 79 tel: 914 357 545,
fax: 914 31 09 43, www.hotelbauza.com
On a par with the best in contemporary design and decor with lots of soft grey and white, internet access, and play stations in every rooms.
Hotel Inglés (€€)
Calle Echegaray 8 tel: 914 29 65 51
A lovely hotel with airy rooms and Victorian lobby. The breakfast room is pleasant and spacious.
Hotel Santander (€€)
Calle Echegaray 1 tel: 914 29 95 51
Comfortable old-fashioned hotel with spacious bathrooms and all mod cons.
Palace (€€€)
Plaza de las Cortes 7 tel: 913 60 80 00,
www.palacehotel.com
This large sumptuous hotel has survived refurbishment. You are likely to glimpse politicians under the stained-glass rotunda.
Tryp Reina Victoria (€€€)
Plaza Santa Ana 14 tel: 915 31 45 00
This 1900s hotel is well-placed for old Madrid. Bullfighters stay here on fight nights. Bed and breakfast only.

Galicia
Araguaney (€€€)
Alfredo Branas 5, Santiago de Compostela, A Coruña tel: 981 59 59 00, www.araguaney.com
Smart hotel, part of the Meliá chain, with pool and disco in the newer part of town.

Convento de San Benito (€€)
Praza de San Benito, La Guardia, Pontevedra
tel: 986 61 11 66, fax: 986 61 15 17
A former Benedictine convent, now a comfortable hotel near the port.
Finisterre (€€€)
Paseo del Parrote 2, A Coruña
tel: 981 20 54 00, www.hotelfinisterre.com
Modern hotel with its own sports complex and views of the Atlantic.
Gran (€€€)
Isla de la Toja, El Grove, Pontevedra
tel: 986 73 00 25, fax: 986 73 00 26
This turn-of-the-20th-century hotel is set in an attractive pine wood.
Hostal Candído (€)
Rúa dos Hermanos Villar 25, Ourense
tel: 988 22 96 07, fax: 988 24 21 97
This cheerful, clean establishment is a pleasant place to stay near the cathedral.
Hostal Mar (€)
Playa Arena Grande, La Guardia, Pontevedra
tel: 986 61 02 08
An inexpensive family hotel set on a small bay.
Hostal Suso (€)
Rúa del Vilar 65, Santiago de Compostela
tel: 981 58 66 11
Right in the old town with a lively bar downstairs, often full of pilgrims, the Hostal is good-value.
Hotel Louxo (€€)
Isla de la Toja, El Grove, Pontevedra
tel: 986 73 02 00, www.louxolatoja.com
Resort hotel with good *ría* views from glass balconies and dining room.
Hotel Pazo O'Rial (€€)
El Rial 1, Vilagarcía de Arousa, Pontevedra
tel: 986 50 70 11, www.pazorial.com
This is a comfortable hotel in a converted manor house; good restaurant.
Parador de Vilalba (€€€)
Valeriano Valdesuso, Villalba, Lugo
tel: 982 51 00 11, email: vilalba@parador.es
Only six rooms in this fortified octagonal tower, so book ahead.
Parador de Verín (€€)
Verín, Ourense tel: 988 41 00 75
Modern parador in fortified manor style, looking across at Galicia's finest castle.
Parador de Pontevedra (€€)
Barón 19, Pontevedra tel: 986 85 58 00
An 18th-century *pazo* (unfortified manor house), well placed for the town and for touring the *rías*.
Parador Los Reyes Catolicos (€€€)
Plaza del Obradoiro, Santiago de Compostela, A Coruña tel: 981 58 22 00,
email: santiago@parador.es
Founded as a pilgrims' hospital by Ferdinand and Isabella in 1499, this is one of the grandest in the parador chain. Deeply memorable.
Parador de Ribadeo (€€)
Amador Fernández 7, Ribadeo, Lugo
tel: 982 12 88 25, email: ribadeo@parador.es
There are excellent views of the Eo *ría* from this modern parador.
Pazo Cibrän (€€)
San Xulián de Sales tel/fax: 981 51 15 15
Delightful 18th-century renovated farm surrounded by countryside.

Hotels and Restaurants

Hotels and Restaurants

The North Coast

Altamira (€€)
*Cantón 1, Santillana del Mar, Cantabria
tel: 942 81 80 25, www.hotelaltamira.com*
This 17th-century mansion in the middle of
the village has comfortable rooms and a good
restaurant. It is a well-priced alternative to the
local parador.

Arocena (€€)
*San Juan 12, Cestona, Guipúzcoa
tel: 943 14 70 40, www.hotelarocena.com*
Refurbished large "Belle Epoque" hotel with
swimming pool and tennis courts.

Bahía (€€)
*San Martín 54 Bis, San Sebastián, Guipúzcoa
tel: 943 46 92 11*
A stone's throw from the beach, this small hotel
has a pleasant, friendly atmosphere and offers
clean, modern rooms.

Las Brisas (€€)
La Braña 14, Santander tel: 942 27 50 11
A quirky but comfortable family-run hotel virtually
on Sardinero beach.

Carlton (€€€)
*Plaza F Moyúa 2, Bilbao, Vizcaya
tel: 944 16 22 00, www.aranzazu-hoteles.com*
This grand old hotel was a haunt of Basque
republicans in the Civil War.

Clarín (€€)
*Caveda 23, Oviedo, Asturias
tel: 985 22 72 72, www. hotelclarin.es*
Central, attractive hotel, with a restaurant.
Car parking in garage opposite, but it can be a
struggle. Disabled access.

Don Paco (€€)
*Posada Herrera 1, Llanes, Asturias
tel: 985 40 01 50, fax: 985 40 26 81*
A town hotel in a former mansion, which has an
excellent fish restaurant on the premises.

Gayoso (€€)
*Paseo de Gómez 4, Luarca, Asturias
tel: 985 64 00 50, fax: 985 47 02 71*
This comfortable small hotel has been family-run
for over a hundred years.

Hotel Asturias (€€)
*Plaza Mayor 11, Gijón, Asturias
tel: 985 35 06 00,
www.hotelesasturianos.com*
Comfortable hotel in a charming, quiet square.

Hotel Ego (€€)
*Playa de Area, Viveiro tel: 982 56 09 87,
fax: 982 56 17 62*
Enjoy fabulous sea views from all the rooms,
the excellent restaurant, and the nearby
private beach.

Hotel Ercilla (€€€)
Ercilla 37–9, Bilbao tel: 944 70 57 00
Within easy walking distance of the Guggenheim
Museum, bullfighters as well as businessmen stay
here. The Bermeo restaurant on the ground floor
serves good Basque food.

De Londres y de Inglaterra (€€€)
*Zubieta 2, San Sebastián, Guipúzcoa
tel: 943 42 69 89, fax: 943 44 04 90,
www.hlondres.com*
An elegant hotel right on La Concha beach. This
popular town rendezvous point has a casino and
restaurant.

NH Deusto (€€)
*Francisco Macia 8, Bilbao tel: 944 76 00 06,
fax: 944 76 21 99*
In a prime position across from the Guggenheim,
this hotel has 71 rooms and conference facilities
are available.

Pampinot (€€)
*Calle Mayor 5, Fuenterrabía, Guipúzcoa
tel: 943 64 06 00*
Small, charming town hotel in converted mansion.
Closed in Nov.

Parador de Fuente Dé (€€)
*Fuente Dé, Cantabria tel: 942 73 66 51,
email: fuentede@parador.es*
A magnificently sited parador, under a rock wall
on the side of Picos de Europa near the ascending
cable car.

Parador de Gijón (€€€)
*Parque Isabel la Católica, Gijón, Asturias
tel: 985 37 05 11, email: gijon@parador.es*
Attractively sited by the park, this modern
parador's bar and restaurant are popular with
locals. Pleasant garden.

Parador de Hondarribia (€€)
*Plaza de Armas 14, Fuenterrabía, Guipúzcoa
tel: 943 64 55 00,
email: hondarribia@parador.es*
This small parador was once associated with
Charles V. It is in a splendid position and good
decor, but no restaurant.

Parador de Santillana del Mar (€€)
*Plaza Ramón Pelayo 11, Santillana del Mar,
Cantabria tel: 942 81 80 00,
email: santillana@parador.es*
This parador is a mixture of old (15th- to 16th-cen-
tury) and new sections, both of which are pleasant.
There is also a good restaurant.

La Perla (€)
*Loyola 10, San Sebastián, Guipúzcoa
tel: 943 42 81 23*
Well positioned with simple, pleasant rooms.

Real (€€€)
*Paseo Pérez Galdós 28, Santander
tel: 942 27 25 50, www.hotelreal.es*
The town's grandest hotel, built high over the bay
at the end of the 19th century for visiting royalty.

Reconquista (€€€)
*Gil de Jaz 16, Oviedo, Asturias
tel: 985 24 11 00,
www.hoteldelareconquista.com*
Asturias' leading hotel, host to royalty, is a converted 18th-century orphanage.

La Rectoral (€€€)
Taramundi, Asturias tel: 985 64 67 67
Outstanding hotel in a converted rectory and
is dedicated to "green tourism" in this beautiful
hill district.

Sardinero (€€)
*Plaza Italia 1, Santander, Cantabria
tel: 942 27 11 00, www.grupossardinero.com*
In a pleasant building close to the beach.

Zubieta (€€)
*Portal de Atea, Lekeitio, Vizcaya
tel: 946 84 30 30, www.hotelzubieta.com*
Only five minutes' walk from the harbour and town,
this excellent family-run hotel is rustically decorated. On the edge of a small fishing resort, it has
views of green hills.

Aragón and Navarra
This area has plenty of self-catering houses and apartments in country areas. Ask in tourist offices for *Guía de Casas Rurales*.

Albarracín (€€)
Azagra, Albarracín, Teruel
tel: 978 71 00 11, www.gargallo-hotels.com
Converted 16th-century palace on hillside.

Conde Aznar (€)
Paseo Constitución 3, Jaca, Huesca
tel: 974 36 10 50, fax: 974 36 07 97
Agreeable small hotel, with antlers and beams providing a mountain feel. Good Aragonese food.

Hospedería de Leyre (€€)
Monasterio de Leyre, Yesa, Navarra
tel: 948 88 41 00,
email: hotel@monasterio-de-leyre.com
The 30-room traditional *hospedería* is run by monks.

Iruña Palace-Tres Reyes (€€€)
Jardines de la Taconera, Iruñea, Navarra
tel: 948 22 66 00, www.hotel3reyes.com
Modern hotel with good service and comfortable rooms, most of which have an attractive view over the gardens.

Lleida (€)
Glorieta Joaquín Costa, Graus, Huesca
tel: 974 54 09 25, www.icg.es/hlleida
Adequate overnight stopping point for motorists. Friendly service and a restaurant.

Maisonnave (€€€)
Nueva 20, Iruñea, Navarra
tel: 948 22 26 00, www.hotelmaisonnave.es
Big business hotel in the middle of town with garage and restaurant.

Monasterio de Piedra (€€)
50210 Nuévalos, Zaragoza tel: 976 84 90 11, www.monasteriopiedra.com
The bedrooms are not as impressive as the public areas in this 12th-century Cistercian monastery set in a lovely park.

NH Gran Hotel (€€)
Joaquín Costa 5, Zaragoza
tel: 976 22 19 01, www.nh-hoteles.es
An elegant hotel in the city centre with royal connections; King Alfonso XIII opened it in 1929.

Parador de Alcañiz (€€)
Castillo de los Calatravos, Alcañiz, Teruel
tel: 978 83 04 00, email: alcañiz@parador.es
This 12-room parador occupies part of the castle dating from 1728. Aragonese food in restaurant.

Parador de Olite (€€)
Plaza de los Teobaldos 2, Olite, Navarra
tel: 948 74 00 00, email: olite@parador.es
Stay in the castle of the kings of Navarre, with suitably medieval decor. Centrally placed but with fine country views from the castle.

Parador de Sos del Rey Católico (€€)
Sos del Rey Católico, Zaragoza
tel: 948 88 80 11, email: sos@parador.es
This parador, though modern, successfully evokes old Aragón. Good dining.

Parador de Teruel (€€)
Carretera Sagunto – Burgos N234 Teruel
tel: 978 60 18 00, email: teruel@parador.es
Modern parador 2km (1mi) out of town on the Zaragoza road. Pleasant gardens and agreeable dining room serving local cuisine.

Pedro I de Aragón (€€)
Avenida del Parque 34, Huesca
tel: 974 22 03 00, fax: 974 22 00 94
This is Huesca's best hotel and is set just outside the centre.

Ramiro 1 (€€)
Coso 123, Zaragoza tel: 976 29 82 00
Traditional hotel, with simple, comfortable rooms; good value for money.

Sant Antón (€€)
Carretera de Francia, Benasque, Huesca
tel: 974 55 16 11, fax: 974 55 16 21
Comfortable modern hotel on the southern side of town, with popular Don Pedro restaurant. Closed 2 weeks in Nov and May.

Santa Cristina de Somport (€€)
Carretera de Francia N330, Canfranc-Estación
tel: 974 37 33 00, www.santacristina.com
A good resting place across the Spanish border on the pilgrimage route. The scenery is impressive and the hotel provides facilities for hikers and skiers.

Tudela (€€)
Avenida de Zaragoza 60, Tudela, Navarra
tel: 948 41 08 02, www.tudelabardenas.com
Modest small hotel with restaurant.

Barcelona See also page 127
Gran Hotel Havana (€€)
Hotel Suizo, Plaça del Angel 12
tel: 933 10 61 08, fax: 932 68 90 62,
email: reserve@gargallo-hotels.com
Request a room overlooking the pretty side street at this intimate hotel with an old-fashioned feel. It is a good base for exploring the Gothic quarter.

Hotel Rialto (€€)
Ferran 42 tel: 933 18 52 12,
fax: 933 18 53 12
Agreeably refurbished, this hotel, just off Plaça Sant Jaume, is a good option for anyone wanting to be in the very heart of the Gothic Quarter.

Triunfo (€)
Passeig de Picasso, 22 tel: 933 15 08 60
Within staggering distance of the vibrant night scene in the nearby Born district, the real coup in this simple pension is booking the one room that overlooks the Parc de la Ciutadella.

Catalonia
Casamar (€)
Nero 3, Llafranc, Girona tel: 972 30 01 04
A small but nonetheless very charming establishment. The rooms have attractive views over the delightful bay of Llafranc. Open from spring to autumn.

Balneario Vichy Catalán (€€)
Avenida Furest 32, Caldas de Malavella, Girona tel: 972 47 00 00,
www.balnearivichycatalan.com
This is one of the region's most agreeable spa hotels.

Capri Veracruz (€€)
Avinguda de Sofía 13–15, Sitges, Barcelona
tel: 938 11 02 67, fax: 938 94 51 88
Away from the hubbub but still close to the beach, this hotel is quietly comfortable. Price includes breakfast.

277

Hotels and Restaurants

Carlemany (€€)
Plaça Miquel Santaló, Girona
tel: 972 21 12 12, www.carlemany.es
Stylish, modern building, full of sculptures and works of art, with a reputable restaurant.

Edelweiss (€)
Carretera Baqueira-Beret 7, Artiés, Lleida
tel: 973 64 44 23, fax: 973 64 44 28
This straightforward and welcoming hotel is convenient for seeing the sights.

Hotel Marsol (€€)
Passeig Jacint Verdaguer 7, Lloret de Mar
tel: 972 36 57 54, fax: 972 37 22 05
A beachfront hotel with good service and excellent facilities, including a roof-top pool.

Imperial Tarraco (€€)
Paseo Palmeras, Tarragona
tel: 977 23 30 40, www.husa.es
Comfortable large hotel overlooking the sea, with pool and tennis court.

Llevant (€€)
Francisco de Blanes 5, Llafranc, Girona
tel: 972 30 03 66, email: hllevant@arrakis.es
A pleasant small hotel on the main promenade, which boasts a good restaurant serving French-influenced Catalan food.

Parador de Aiguablava (€€€)
Aigua Blava, Girona tel: 972 62 21 62,
email: aiguablava@parador.es
Beautifully set among pines near one of the Costa Brava's most dramatic rockscapes, this is a modern parador.

Parador de Artíes (€€)
Carretera Baqueira-Beret, Artiés, Lleida
tel: 973 64 08 01, email: arties@parador.es
This is a very comfortable, modern parador, but it is rather basic.

Parador de Cardona (€€)
Castillo, Cardona, Barcelona
tel: 938 69 12 75, email: cardona@parador.es
Stay in one of Spain's most impressive hilltop castles, with medieval decor including four-poster beds. The restaurant is well reputed.

Port Lligat (€€)
Salvador Dalí, Cadaqués, Girona
tel: 972 25 81 62,
email: vbald@hgintercom.es
Fairly simple hotel near Dalí's home with good views. Open weekends only in Oct–Apr.

Romantic (€€)
San Isidro 33, Sitges, Barcelona
tel: 938 94 83 75, www.hotelromantic.com
Conversion of three 19th-century villas in the town and a large garden. Bed and breakfast only.

Castilla-León and La Rioja

Amefa (€)
Pozo Amarillo 18, Salamanca
tel: 923 21 81 89, fax: 923 26 02 00
A modern block near the old part of town with quiet, comfortable rooms.

Caserío de Lobones (€€€)
Valverde de Majano, Segovia
tel: 921 12 84 08,
www.terra.es/personal3/caserio-lobones
An ancient, renovated aristocratic farm house furnished in elegant style, set in peaceful countryside very close to Segovia.

Gran Hotel (€)
Plaza Poeta Iglesias 3, Salamanca
tel: 923 21 35 00, www.helcom.es/granhotel
At one end of the grand Plaza Mayor, this prestigious hotel is an institution, frequented by bull-breeders and country estate-owners.

Hostal Alcántera (€€)
Estéban Domingo 11, Avila tel: 920 22 50 03
A small and pleasant hotel close to the cathedral.

Hostería Real de Zamora (€€)
Cuesta de Pizarro 7, Zamora tel: 980 53 45 45
The (alleged) former home of the *conquistador* Pizarro, this hotel retains 15th-century walls and a charming patio, while having all modern comforts.

Hotel Gaudí (€€)
Plaza Eduardo de Castro 6, Astorga, León
tel: 987 61 56 54, fax: 987 61 50 40
Pleasant modern hotel.

Hotel Juan II (€)
Paseo del Espolón, Toro, Zamora
tel: 980 69 03 00, www.hoteljuan11.com
In the centre of Toro (33km/20mi from Zamora), this has basic rooms and public areas and good views over the Duero River. A surprisingly good, if simple, stopover.

Infanta Isabel (€€)
Plaza Mayor, Segovia tel: 921 46 13 00
A small but comfortable hotel in the Plaza Mayor, the heart of the old city.

Landa Palace (€€€)
Carretera de Madrid-Irún, Burgos
tel: 947 25 77 77, www.landapalace.es
Fanciful architecture distinguishes this modern hotel in the Relais and Châteaux chain. Good restaurant serving Castilian roasts, etc.

Palacio Valderrábanos (€€)
Plaza Catedral 9, Avila tel: 920 21 10 23
Slightly gloomy hotel in a 15th-century bishop's palace, but is within 50m (165ft) of the cathedral.

Parador de Ciudad Rodrigo (€€)
Plaza del Castillo 1, Ciudad-Rodrigo, Salamanca tel: 923 46 01 50,
email: ciudadrodrigo@parador.es
Though comfortable and well modernized, the castle building is still redolent of medieval Spain.

Parador de Gredos (€€)
Carretera Barraco-Béjar, KM 43, Gredos, Avila
tel: 920 34 80 48, email: gredos@parador.es
Built in 1928 on a site chosen personally by King Alfonso XIII, this was the first-ever parador. Views of Circo de Gredos.

Parador San Marcos (€€€)
Plaza San Marcos, León tel: 987 23 73 00,
email: leon@parador.es
One of the great hotels of Spain, this parador was once a monastery and is graced with a magnificent facade, staircase, and patio.

Parador de Segovia (€€€)
Carretera de Valladolid, Segovia
tel: 921 44 37 37, email: segovia@parador.es
Elegant, brick-built modern parador. Great floodlit views at night. Good restaurant.

Parador de Tordesillas (€€)
Carretera de Salamanca, Tordesillas, Valladolid tel: 983 77 00 51,
email: tordesillas@parador.es
Stately modern parador, very comfortable and convenient for visiting Tordesillas.

Parador de Villafranca del Bierzo (€€)
*Avenida de Calvo Sotelo, Villafranca del Bierzo,
León tel: 987 54 01 75,
email: villafranca@parador.es*
Modern parador on the Camino de Santiago.
Good atmosphere, with a restaurant that serves
local produce.
Parador de Zamora (€€)
*Plaza Viriato 5, Zamora tel: 980 51 44 97,
email: zamora@parador.es*
Set in a Renaissance palace, this parador is more
welcoming than grand. It has a fine patio and stair-
case. Swimming pool in the garden.
San Polo (€€)
*Arroyo de Santo Domingo 1–3, Salamanca
tel: 923 21 11 77, www.hotelsanpolo@terra.es*
At the ancient gates of the city, and a short walk
from its historical heart, this family-run hotel is
reasonably priced.

Extremadura
Hospedería del Real Monasterio (€)
*Plaza Juan Carlos I, Guadalupe, Cáceres
tel: 927 36 70 00, fax: 927 36 71 77*
Simple and peaceful in a still-functioning
monastery, gathered around one of Spain's most
beautiful cloisters, this is superb. There is also a
restaurant serving local food.
Meliá Cáceres (€€€)
*Plaza de San Juan 1, Cáceres
tel: 927 21 58 00, www.solmelia.com*
Luxury hotel in the old town, with a lovely feeling of
space and light.
Nueva España (€)
*Avda de Extremadura 6, Mérida
tel: 924 31 33 56, fax: 924 31 32 11*
This is a simple, family-run hostel with private
baths and TV.
Parador de Cáceres (€€€)
*Ancha 6, Cáceres tel: 927 21 17 59,
email: caceres@parador.es*
The hotel, in a 15th-century palace, is wonderfully
atmospheric.
Parador de Jarandilla de la Vera (€€)
*Carretera Plasencia, Jarandilla de la Vera,
Cáceres tel: 927 56 01 17,
email: jarandilla@parador.es*
A castle once used by Charles V, this is an elegant
stopover in the beautiful Tiétar Valley.
Parador de Mérida (€€)
*Plaza de la Constitución 3, Mérida, Badajoz
tel: 924 31 38 00, email: merida@parador.es*
In the heart of town but quiet, this parador
is well run and friendly, and most attractive in its
convent setting.
Parador de Trujillo (€€)
*Santa Beatriz de Silva 1, Trujillo, Cáceres
tel: 927 32 13 50, email: trujillo@parador.es*
In a former convent of the Poor Clares.
Parador de Zafra (€€)
*Plaza Corazón María 7, Zafra, Badajoz
tel: 924 55 45 40, email: zafra@parador.es*
This hotel in a 15th-century castle once used by
Cortés has an elegant Renaissance patio.
Plaza Mayor Pension (€)
6 Plaza Mayor, Trujillo tel: 619 54 46 56
Excellent value small hostal with TV and private
bathrooms. Ask for room 1 overlooking the plaza.

Castilla-La Mancha and the Madrid Region
Hotel Alfonso VI (€€€)
*General Moscardó 2, Toledo
tel: 925 22 26 00, fax: 925 21 44 58,
www.hotelalfonsovi.com*
Comfortable hotel with rooms overlooking the city,
a restaurant serving a high standard of food, and
typical tapas bar.
Hostal El Doncel (€)
*General Mola 1, Sigüenza, Guadalajara
tel: 949 39 00 01, www.doncel.com*
At the bottom of town, where the evening *paseo*
takes place.
Hotel Santa Isabel (€€)
*Santa Isabel 24, Toledo
tel: 925 25 31 36, www.santa-isabel.com*
Comfortable and moderately priced hotel, within
easy reach of all sights.
Leonor de Aquitánia (€€)
*San Pedro 60, Cuenca tel: 969 23 10 00,
www.hotelleonordeaquitania.com*
Opened in 1991, this is a comfortable, friendly hotel
in the high town and close to main monuments.
Parador del Alarcón (€€€)
*Alarcón, Cuenca tel: 969 33 03 15,
email: alarcon@parador.es*
In a spectacular castle setting on a rocky promon-
tory above a gorge. Handsome bar/lounge and
popular restaurant.
Parador de Almagro (€€)
*Ronda de San Francisco 31, Almagro, Ciudad
Real tel: 926 86 01 00,
email: almagro@parador.es*
Charming parador in an old convent with patios and
lovely tile work. An easy walk to the middle of town.
Parador de Sigüenza (€€)
*Plaza del Castillo, Sigüenza, Guadalajara
tel: 949 39 01 00, email: siguenza@parador.es*
Castle overlooking the town which has played host
to royalty. Today it is a sumptuous hotel. Many
rooms open on to central Patio de las Armas. Early
booking essential.
Parador de Toledo (€€€)
*Cerro del Emperador, Toledo
tel: 925 22 18 50, email: toledo@parador.es*
Modern comfortable parador with view of the city
very much as painted by El Greco.
Pensión La Tabanqueta (€)
*Calle de Trabuco 13, Cuenca
tel: 969 21 12 90*
The best budget option in town, mainly for its position overlooking the Júcar gorge with its rock face
surrounds. Rooms are basic and bathrooms are
shared, but the views help to compensate.
Posada de San José (€€)
*Julián Romero 4, Cuenca tel: 969 21 13 00,
email: psanjose@arrakis.es*
Set in an ancient convent/inn of medieval aspect,
this is a delightful and restful place to stay. Good
views over the gorge.
Santa María del Paular (€€€)
*Carretera M-604, KM 26, Rascafría, Madrid
tel: 918 69 10 11,
www.sierranorte.com/paular*
There are beautiful views from this luxury hotel
which is set in a former monastery. The adjoining
monastery is still in use.

279

Hotels and Restaurants

Levante

Ad Hoc (€€)
Boix 4, Valencia tel: 963 91 91 40,
fax: 963 91 36 67, www.sercotel.es
Ad Hoc is set in the old quarter and surrounded by some of the best bar life in Spain. The owner is an antiquarian and art enthusiast, which is reflected through the decor. Meals are available in an intimate dining room.

Hotel Mediterranea Plaza (€€€)
Plaza del Ayuntamiento 6, Alacant
tel: 965 21 01 88, fax: 965 20 67 50
In a fabulous position on the beautiful plaza near the shops and main promenade, this tastefully decorated hotel has a quality restaurant.

Huerto del Cura (€€€)
Porta de la Morera 14, Elx, Alacant
tel: 966 61 00 11, email: h.huertocura@alc.es
The accommodation is in bungalows in the extensive gardens. Lovely swimming pool under palms, tennis court, plus a good restaurant.

Meliá Alicante (€€€)
Playa del Postiguet, Alacant
tel: 965 20 50 00, www.solmelia.com
Although this is a very large block of a hotel, it is set at the end of the town beach, thereby having fine views.

Meliá Confort Inglés (€€€)
Marqués de Dos Aguas 6, Valencia
tel: 963 51 64 26, fax: 963 94 02 51
Opposite the Ceramics Museum, this is an intriguing mixture of Spanish and English decor. Bar serves good tapas.

La Muralla (€)
Calle Muralla 12, Morella Castelló de la Plana
tel: 964 16 02 43, fax: 964 16 02 43
In the heart of town, with breakfast included in the price of the room.

Parador de Jávea (€€€)
Avenida del Mediterráneo 7, Jávea, Alacant
tel: 965 79 02 00, email: javea@parador.es
This comfortable purpose-built parador looks over a hoop of excellent town beach.

Principe Felipe (€€€)
Hyatt La Manga Club, Murcia tel: 968 13 72 72
A sports resort complex (three golf courses, four swimming pools) set around a luxury hotel and apartment accommodation.

Sidi San Juan (€€€)
Playa San Juan, Alacant tel: 965 16 13 00
On the beach, some 3km (2mi) north of Alicante, this hotel has a luxurious feel, and includes two swimming pools (indoor and outdoor) and tennis courts.

Andalucía

Alfonso XIII (€€€)
San Fernando 2, Sevilla tel: 954 91 70 00
This is the top hotel in town with livery-clad staff, Edwardian/Moorish splendour, and huge bedrooms.

Atlántico (€€)
Duque de Nájera 9, Cádiz
tel: 956 22 69 05, email: cadiz@parador.es
This spacious hotel virtually on the edge of the Old Town at Cadiz is enlivened by local people who dine and dance here at weekends. There is a swimming pool in the garden.

La Bobadilla (€€€)
Finca La Bobadilla, Loja, Granada
tel: 958 32 18 61, www.la-bobadilla.com
Probably Spain's most spectacular country hotel. Purpose-built to resemble an Andalucian village, it is true *grande luxe* with every facility, including riding on the estate through beautiful sweeping countryside.

Casa del Aljarife (€€)
Placeta de la Cruz Verde 2, Albaicin, Granada
tel: 958 22 24 25, email: most@wanadoo.es
This has only four rooms, but is in the heart of the Albaicin with stunning views of the surrounding rooftops, 9th-century city walls, and the Alhambra.

Casas de la Judería (€€)
Callejón Dos Hermanos 7, Sevilla
tel: 954 41 51 50, www.casasypalacios.com
A small group of ancient houses converted into serviced apartments, which are well furnished with antique decor.

El Castillo de Monda (€€€)
Monda, Málaga tel: 952 457 142,
fax: 952 45 73 36, email: mondas@spa.es
Moorish castle tastefully restored into a 23-room hotel.

Cervantes (€€)
Cervantes 10, Sevilla tel: 954 90 02 80
This is a hotel in a quiet street that is patioed, small, and intimate.

Colón (€€€)
Canalejas 1, Sevilla tel: 954 50 55 99
Bullfighters dress for the ring in the luxurious surroundings here, then hold court after the fight. Rooms slightly small for the five-star prices, but has a satisfyingly Spanish feel.

Cónquistador (€€)
Magistral González Francés 15–17, Córdoba
tel: 957 48 11 02, www.otusa.com
This hotel, with a typical Cordoban patio and comfortable rooms, has a privileged spot right opposite the mosque.

Cuevas Pedro Antonio de Alarcón (€€)
Barriada San Torcuato, Guadix, Granada
tel: 958 66 49 86, fax: 958 66 17 21
Well-decorated cave apartments scooped out of the hillside. You will cater for yourself, but complete with all modern amenities. Each cave has a terrace with barbecue area, access to swimming pool, and opportunities for walking or horse-riding.

La Fonda (€€)
Santo Domingo 7, Benalmádena
tel: 952 56 82 73, fax: 952 56 82 73
In the heart of this pretty mountain village, this hotel is typically *andaluz*: white, patioed, and shady, with flowers, fountains, and fine views.

Gran Hotel Almería (€€€)
Avenida Reina Regente 8, Almería
tel: 950 23 80 11, www.granhotelalmeria.com
Functional rather than luxurious, the hotel has views of the bay and harbour.

Hostel and Hotel Maestre (€€)
Calle Romero Barros 4 & 6, Córdoba
tel: 957 47 24 10, fax: 957 47 53 95
There is little difference between the choice of hotel or hostel, apart from a slight increase in the price of the hotel. Both are furnished in terracotta tiles and marble and they are very central, just a five-minute walk from the Mesquita.

Hotel Doña Maria (€€€)
Don Remondo 19, Sevilla tel: 954 22 49 90
You can't get closer to Seville's old quarter; the rooftop swimming pool looks onto the cathedral.
Lis (€)
Calle Córdoba 7, Málaga tel: 952 22 73 00
Comfortable, simple hotel with some apartments, but no dining room.
Madrid (€€)
San Pedro Mártír 22, Sevilla tel: 954 21 43 07
Small (21 rooms), basic but clean hotel.
Meliá Don Pepe (€€€)
José Meliá, Marbella, Málaga tel: 952 77 03 00
Prestigious town hotel with good access to golf and tennis.
Parador de Arcos de la Frontera (€€€)
Plaza del Cabildo, Arcos de la Frontera, Cádiz tel: 956 70 05 00, email: arcos@parador.es
In the main square of this White Town, spectacularly perched on top of a cliff, the parador has superb views over the Guadalete Valley.
Parador de Carmona (€€€)
Alcázar, Carmona, Sevilla tel: 954 14 10 10, email: carmona@parador.es
A modern structure within fortress walls that once belonged to Pedro I of Castile (the Cruel). Old-fashioned rooms with fine views.
Parador Castillo de Santa Catalina (€€€)
Jaén tel: 953 23 00 00, email: jaen@parador.es
A visit to this historic crag, if only for a coffee, is essential to the Jaén experience. Its capture in 1246 was the key to the Christian conquest of western Andalucía.
Parador Cristóbal Colón (€€€)
Playa de Mazagón, Mazagón, Huelva tel: 959 53 63 00, email: mazagon@parador.es
Well placed for visiting Columbus sites, the parador is on a clifftop above the sea.
Parador de Nerja (€€€)
Almuñécar 8, Nerja, Málaga tel: 952 52 00 50, email: nerja@parador.es
This is one of the more functional-style paradors, but with good decor, a wonderful position, and views. There is a lift down to the beach.
Parador de Ronda (€€€)
Plaza España, Ronda, Málaga tel: 952 87 75 00, email: ronda@parador.es
A modern parador with a fine spot right beside the bridge on the tip of the gorge, with glorious views.
Parador de San Francisco (€€€)
Real de la Alhambra, Granada tel: 958 22 14 40
A former convent built right inside the Alhambra. Must be booked months in advance.
Parador de Úbeda (€€€)
Plaza de Vázquez de Molina, Úbeda, Jáen tel: 953 75 03 45, email: ubeda@parador.es
Small in scale (only 31 rooms), this is nevertheless one of the great places to stay. It is housed in a 16th-century palace on the town square.
Puente Romano (€€€)
Carretera N340, 3.5km (2mi) west of Marbella tel: 952 82 09 00, email: hotel@puenteromano.com
This elegant complex of white Andalucían buildings, developed as a village, is set in lush tropical gardens by the beach, with waterfalls and a small Roman bridge.

Reina Cristina (€€€)
Paseo de la Conferencia, Algeciras, Cádiz tel: 956 60 26 22; www.reinacristina.com
Despite the growth of industrial Algeciras, this remains a charming hotel.
Reina Victoria (€€)
Jerez 25, Ronda, Málaga tel: 952 87 12 40, email: reinavictoriaronda@husa.es
Charming turn-of-the-20th-century hotel. Comfortable, with fine views.

RESTAURANTS

The restaurants below have also been grouped into three price categories, based on a three-course meal with house wine:
• **Expensive** (€€€): over €36
• **Moderate** (€€): €18–36
• **Inexpensive** (€): under €18

Madrid   *See also page 67*
Asia Society (€€–€€€)
Calle Lope de Vega 37 tel: 914 299 292
Popular restaurant serving pan-Asian cuisine presided over by former New York chef Jamie Downing with a choice of Chinese, Thai, and Indian dishes. Booking is recommended.
Casa Paco (€€)
Puerta Cerrada 11 tel: 913 66 31 66
Steaks come on sizzling platters and go well with lashings of red wine. Must reserve. Closed Sun and Aug.
Elqui (€–€€)
Calle Buenavista 18 tel: 914 680 462
Handy for the post-Reina Sofia visit, this vegetarian self-service has a range of interesting and inventive dishes. Most of the wines are organic and ginger ale and cider are available.
La Gran Tasca (€€)
Santa Engracia 24 tel: 914 48 77 79
Not in the most salubrious area, but good Castilian food as grandmother made it. Closed Sun, holidays, and throughout Aug.
Gure-Etxea (€€€)
Plaza de la Paja 12 tel: 913 65 61 49
Basque cuisine is served in an atmosphere of 18th-century Madrid. Closed Sun and Aug.
La Trucha (€€)
Calle Manuel Fernández y Gonzáles 3 tel: 914 29 58 33
Popular, cheerful, and reasonably priced restaurant well-known for its fish; not just trout (*trucha*), but seafood and hearty meat stews as well.

Galicia
Anexo Vilas (€€€)
Avenida de Villagarcia 21, Santiago de Compostela, A Coruña tel: 981 59 86 37
This very Galician seafood restaurant, within walking distance of the middle of the city, has been run by the same family for generations.
Casa Solla (€€€)
Carretera El Grove, Pontevedra tel: 986 87 28 84
Serves excellent seafood, but reservations are usually needed. Closed Thu and Sun evenings.

281

Hotels and Restaurants

Chocolate (€€€)
Vilaxoán, Pontevedra tel: 986 50 11 99
Two kilometres (1mi) from Villagarcia de Arosa,
this is one of Galicia's top restaurants. Particularly
strong on seafood. Closed Sun evenings.

Coral (€€)
*Callejón de la Estacada 9, A Coruña
tel: 981 20 05 69*
Serves excellent fish and seafood near the port.
Closed Sun in winter.

Mar y Cielo (€)
*Monte de Santa Tecla, La Guardia, Pontevedra
tel: 986 61 11 64*
You get tapas on the first floor of this restaurant
perched on a crag above the River Miño and
the Atlantic; fish and meat restaurant on
second floor.

Posada del Mar (€€)
*Castelao 202, El Grove, Pontevedra
tel: 986 73 01 06*
Seafood delicacies include scallop pie. Busy
at weekends. Closed Sun evenings and
mid-Dec to Jan.

San Clemente (€€)
*San Clemente 6, Santiago de Compostela,
A Coruña tel: 981 56 54 26*
Nonstop, reasonably priced seafood from 8AM
to 2AM.

San Miguel (€€€)
San Miguel 12–14, Ourense tel: 988 22 12 45
This restaurant has a high reputation in Galicia,
using first-class ingredients. Closed Jan.

The North Coast

Akelaré (€€€)
*Paseo Padre Orcolaga 56, San Sebastián,
Guipúzcoa tel: 943 21 20 52*
This top restaurant in a town which rates cooking
as an art form offers excellent food in elegant sur-
roundings as well as brilliant views from Monte
Igueldo. Closed Feb and Mon.

Arzak (€€€)
*Alto de Miracruz 21, Donostia, Guipúzcoa
tel: 943 27 84 65*
Celebrated for its Basque cuisine and well-known
throughout Spain.

Casa Victor (€€)
*Carmen 11, Xixon, Asturias
tel: 985 34 83 10*
Seafood and traditional cuisine are on offer here,
as well as good wines. Closed Nov, Sun evenings,
and Thu.

Dos Hermanas (€€€)
*Madre Vedruna 10, Vitoria, Alava
tel: 945 13 29 34*
Over 100 years old and popular with Basque
parliamentarians. Classic Basque cooking.
Good local wines. Closed Sun and Wed
evenings.

Gatz (€€)
Santa Maria 10, Bilbao tel: 944 15 08 71
This lively, local haunt is well-known for its seafood
and *txarri* (pork). Closed Mon.

Goizeko-Kabi (€€€)
*Particular de Estraunza 4, Bilbao, Vizcaya
tel: 944 41 50 04*
Basque nouveau-cuisine served at this excellent
restaurant. Closed Sun.

El Raitan (€€)
*Plaza Trascorrales 6, Oriedo, Asturias
tel: 985 21 42 18*
Fixed Asturian menu for lunch, which is excellent
and hearty. *Á la carte* in the evenings.
Closed Sun.

Ramon Roteta (€€€)
*Villa Ainara, Irún s/n, Hondarribia, Guipúzcoa
tel: 943 64 16 93*
Great food in an old villa. Closed Feb and Sun
evenings.

Retolaza (€€)
*Tendería 1, Bilbao, Vizcaya
tel: 944 15 06 43*
Wonderful Old Town restaurant offering classic
Vizcayan cuisine. Closed late Jul to mid-Aug,
Easter, and Sun and Mon.

Aragón and Navarra

Alhambra (€€€)
*Bergamín 7, Iruñea, Navarra
tel: 948 24 50 07*
Traditional Navarrese food with an emphasis on
fresh local produce is served here. Truffles and
mushrooms are widely used. Closed Sun.

Erburu (€)
*San Lorenzo 19–21, Iruñea, Navarra
tel: 948 22 51 69*
This inexpensive restaurant in Iruñea's nightlife
district is popular with locals.

Meseguer (€€)
*Avenida del Maestrazgo 9, Alcañiz, Teruel
tel: 978 83 10 02*
This is a good-value restaurant that is well-liked by
locals. Closed Sun, holiday evenings, and late
Sep.

Las Torres (€€)
*María Auxiliadora 3, Huesca
tel: 974 22 82 13*
A family-run restaurant with an inventive menu, a
good choice of wines, and friendly service. Closed
Sun and Easter.

Barcelona   *See also page 125*

Agut (€)
Gignàs 16 tel: 933 15 17 09
Classic Catalan cooking in the Barri Gòtic.
Closed Aug.

Buenas Migas (€)
*Plaça Bonsuccés 6
tel: 934 12 16 86*
Hot tasty Italian focaccias, spinach tarts, and
the only apple crumble you're likely to find in
Barcelona in this friendly Anglo-Italian café with
urban terrace, just off La Rambla, on the way to
the Contemporary Art Museum.

Can Costa (€€)
Passeig Nacional 70 tel: 932 21 95 11
Excellent seafood restaurant in the Barceloneta
district, where fish restaurants abound. Closed
Sun evenings.

Can Lluis (€)
Calle Cera 49 tel: 934 41 11 87
This family-run restaurant serves dishes boasting
the typical Catalan combination of sweet and
savoury, for example pork and plums, or chicken
stuffed with prunes. The fixed lunch menu is a
bargain. Closed end Aug.

Casa Leopoldo (€€)
Sant Rafael 24 tel: 93 441 3014
You can be sure of excellent fish in this restaurant, found down a back street in El Raval, loved by the literati, and now run by the granddaughter of the founder.

La Dama (€€€)
Avinguda Diagonal 423 tel: 932 02 06 86
On the first floor of a Modernista house, this is a Michelin-star restaurant. The creative Catalan food is beautifully cooked and elegantly served.

Catalonia

Albatros (€€€)
Bruselas 60, Salou, Tarragona
tel: 977 38 50 70
Well-known for its seafood. Closed Sun evenings, Mon, and 7–31 Jan.

El Bulli (€€€)
Cala Montjoi, Apartado 30, Roses, Girona
tel: 972 15 04 57
A fine restaurant overlooking the Bay of Montjoi, accessible by road or sea. Closed mid-Sep to mid-Apr.

Cal Ros (€€€)
C. Cort Reial 9 tel: 972 21 73 79
Wonderful historic building in the middle of town; the house specials are game dishes and delicious desserts.

Can Llesques (€)
Calle Natzaret 6, Tarragona tel: 977 22 29 06
Popular, often crowded, restaurant serving traditional Catalan food. Closed Tue.

Casa Hidalgo (€€)
Sant Pau 12, Sitges, Barcelona
tel: 938 94 38 95
An intimate restaurant serving well-presented Catalan food.

Casa Irene (€€€)
Calle Mayor 3, Artíes, Lleida tel: 973 64 43 64
Enjoy a gastronomic blow-out, French and Pyrenean style. Good value. Closed Nov.

Garreta (€)
Platja d'Aiguablava, Aigua Blava, Girona
tel: 972 62 30 33
Agreeable fish restaurant, just behind the beach.

Joan Gatell-Casa Gatell (€€€)
Paseo Miramar 26, Cambrils de Mar,
Tarragona tel: 977 36 00 57
Known for its excellent cuisine, in particular fresh fish dishes. Closed Sun evenings, Mon, and Jan.

La Masía (€€)
Paseo Vilanova 164, Sitges, Barcelona
tel: 938 94 10 76
A typical Catalan cuisine is served here, for example rabbit stew with snails and peppers in piquant sauce.

Mas Pau (€€)
Carretera de Olot, Figueres, Girona
tel: 972 54 61 54
Specializes in game dishes. Closed 8 Jan to 15 Mar.

El Pescador (€)
Nemesio Llorens, Cadaqués, Girona
tel: 972 25 88 59
Seafront, seafood restaurant on two floors. Closed Nov and Jan.

Sol-Ric (€€)
Vía Augusta 227, Tarragona tel: 977 23 20 32
Varied menu, but best at Catalan dishes; accompanied by a good wine list. Closed Sun evenings, Mon, and 15 Dec–15 Jan.

Castilla-León and La Rioja

Adonías (€€)
Santa Noria 16, León tel: 987 20 67 68
Lively ceramic decorations and good regional cuisine. Closed Sun.

Casa Ojeda (€€€)
Vitoria 5, Burgos tel: 947 20 90 52
Serves classic Castilian cuisine, such as suckling lamb roast in a wood-fired oven, accompanied by wines from the Rioja or Ribera del Duero. Closed Sun evenings.

Fernán González (€€)
Calera 17, Burgos tel: 947 20 94 41
Interesting menu in this hotel restaurant. Wines are from the proprietor's own vineyard.

La Fragua (€€€)
Paseo de Zorrilla 10, Valladolid
tel: 983 33 87 85
Much of the cooking at this convivial restaurant is carried out in general view. The quality of the food is excellent. Closed Sun evenings and Aug.

Maroto (€€)
Paseo del Espolón 20, Soria tel: 975 22 40 86
Named after its proprietor, this is the most popular of Soria's better restaurants. It serves a good regional menu with some twists. Closed Mon.

Mesón de Cándido (€€)
Plaza del Azoguejo 5, Segovia
tel: 921 42 59 11
One of the best suckling pig eateries in Spain, but it can get very busy.

Mesón del Rastro (€€)
Plaza Rastro 1, Avila tel: 920 21 12 18
Hearty Castilian cooking, in a medieval setting.

El Molino de la Losa (€€)
Bajada de la Losa 12, Avila tel: 920 21 11 01
Set in a 15th-century mill; good for families as there is a garden with play area. Closed Mon.

La Oficina (€€)
Calle Cronita Lecea 10, Segovia
tel: 921 46 02 83
The dining room is attractively decorated with Castilian tiles; the restaurant has good cooking including suckling pig, known here as *toston*, a delicacy of Segovia.

Río de la Plata (€€)
Plaza del Peso 1, Salamanca
tel: 923 21 90 05
Charming family-run restaurant serving wonderful Castilian sausages and roast meat. Closed Jul and Mon.

Extremadura

Aldebarán (€€€)
Avenida de Elvas, Urbanización Guadiana,
Badajoz tel: 924 27 42 61
Famous for Spanish and Portuguese dishes, and offering wine from both countries. Closed Sun.

El Figón de Eustaquio (€€)
Plaza San Juan 12, Cáceres tel: 927 24 81 94
This place is good fun, with a real sense of gastronomic regionalism.

283

Accommodations and Restaurants

Castilla-La Mancha and the Madrid Region

Asador Adolfo (€€€)
La Granada 6 and Hombre de Palo 7, Toledo tel: 925 22 73 21
Set in an old house in the middle of town, this restaurant serves good local cuisine. Closed Sun evenings.

El Corregidor (€€)
Plaza Fray Fernández de Córdoba 2, Almagro, Ciudad Real tel: 926 86 06 48
This town centre restaurant serves Manchegan cooking, such as stuffed partridge and fresh sheep's cheese. Closed Mon.

Figón de Pedro (€€)
Cervantes 13, Cuenca tel: 969 22 68 21
Good local cuisine in one of Cuenca's best restaurants. Closed Sun evenings.

Hierbabuena (€€)
Cristo de la Luz 9, Toledo tel: 925 22 34 63
In the historical heart of the city, this is one of two high-quality restaurants with the same name run by two brothers. Closed Sun evenings, Jun, and Aug.

Mesón Casas Colgadas (€€)
Canónigas, Cuenca tel: 969 22 35 09
Great position and excellent local food. Closed Mon evenings.

Venta del Quixote (€€€)
El Molino 4, Puerto Lápice, tel: 926 57 61 10
An old inn built round a courtyard of the kind from which Don Quixote set off on his adventures.

Levante

Cándido (€)
Santo Domingo 13, Lorca, Murcia tel: 968 46 69 07
Cooking inspired by regional dishes from the surrounding area. Closed Sun in summer.

Gargantua (€€)
Navarro Reventer 18, Valencia tel: 963 34 68 49
Serves Valencian cuisine. Closed Sun evenings and Mon.

Girasol (€€€)
Carretera Moraira-Calpe 1.5km (1mi), Alacant tel: 965 74 43 73
This seaside villa furnished with antiques is renowned for its Mediterranean cooking and has French, German, and Spanish wines. Closed Nov and Mon, except during summer.

Mesón el Granaíno (€€)
José María Buch 40, Elx, Alacant tel: 966 66 40 80
Good regional food. Closed Sun and late Aug.

Oscar Torrijos (€€€)
Doctor Sumsi 4, Valencia tel: 963 73 29 49
Serves creative rice dishes plus fish and seafood. Closed Mon, Sun, and Aug.

Andalucía

El Caballo Rojo (€€€)
Cardenal Herrero 28, Córdoba tel: 957 47 53 75
One of the city's top restaurants serving Andalus dishes (lamb with honey and pine nuts) recalling the region's Moorish past. A roof-top patio overlooks the Mezquita.

Casa Pedro (€€)
Quitapeñas 121, El Palo, Málaga tel: 952 29 00 13
Large, popular restaurant, where sardines and paella are particularly good. Closed Mon evenings.

Casa Robles (€€)
Álvarez Quintero 58, Seville tel: 954 56 32 72
Close to the cathedral, this is popular with both locals and visitors.

Chiquito (€€)
Plaza del Campillo 9, Granada tel: 958 22 33 64
Lively atmosphere and excellent food keep this restaurant as popular as it was in the days when the poet García Lorca and his friends met here. Closed Wed.

El Churrasco (€€€)
Romero 16, Córdoba tel: 957 29 08 19
Restaurant in the Judería serving Andalucían cuisine and meat dishes. Closed Aug.

El Figón de Bonilla (€€)
Cervantes, Edificio Horizonte, Málaga tel: 952 22 31 23
Fish and local dishes; good tapas. Closed Sun.

La Hacienda (€€€)
Urbanización Hacienda Las Chapas, N340, Marbella, Málaga tel: 952 83 12 67
The chef's personal version of French/Spanish cuisine is served in a villa-like ambience. Five-course gastronomic menu available. Closed Mon and Tue.

La Langosta (€€)
Francisco Cano 1, Los Boliches, Fuengirola, Málaga tel: 952 47 50 49
Well-established town restaurant; international menu with the emphasis on seafood. Closed Sun and Dec.

Pedro Romero (€€)
Virgen de la Paz 18, Ronda, Málaga tel: 952 87 11 10
Opposite Ronda's famous bullring, the restaurant is predictably rich in bullfighting paraphernalia.

La Posada (€)
San Juan de Dios 4, Marbella, Málaga.
Local food in a characterful setting.

Rió Grande (€€)
Betis, Sevilla tel: 954 27 39 56
Wonderfully positioned, with a terrace on the river looking across at the Torre del Oro and the Giralda.

El Roqueo (€€)
La Carihuela, Torremolinos, Málaga tel: 952 38 49 46
One of the many restaurants in the Carihuela, known for its fresh seafood. Popular with the locals; pleasant, casual atmosphere and good seafood dishes. Closed Tue and Nov.

Ruta del Veleta (€€€)
Carretera de la Sierra Nevada N-136, KM 5.4, Granada tel: 958 48 61 34
This mountain restaurant, 5km (3mi) out of Granada, provides the best cooking in and around the city. Closed Sun evenings.

Santiago (€€€)
Paseo Marítimo 5, Marbella tel: 952 77 00 78
The seafood here is wonderful, and the grilled meat is a close second. A great position on the sea front. Closed Nov.

Index

288

Acknowledgments

The Automobile Association would like to thank the following photographers, libraries and associations for their assistance in the preparation of this book.

J ALLAN CASH PHOTOLIBRARY 211 La Albufera; **ANCIENT ART & ARCHITECTURE COLLECTION** 88 Hunters, Altamira cave painting, 89 Hand of palaeolithic man; **ANDALUCIA SLIDE LIBRARY** 230, 244/5; **ADAM HOPKINS** 15 Picos de Europa, 16 Oviedo, 18 San Sebastián, 23 Mountain folk, 73 Galicia, 87 Veigas, 92 Picos de Europa, 97 Bridge, Alto Campoo, 110 Ordesa, 114 & 115 Barcelona, Las Ramblas, 160 Coca Castle, 162 León, San Isidoro, 164 León, San Isidoro, 197 Cuenca, 199 Statue, 200 Sigüenza fiesta; **CORBIS** 27(M Everton), 162 (N Wheeler), 169 (M Busselle), 176 (K Schafer); **DIAF 123** (J-P Garcia), 170/1 (R Mazin); **EYE UBIQUITOUS** Front cover (a); **FMGB GUGGENHEIM BILBA MUSEO** 83; **IMAGES COLOUR LIBRARY** Front cover (d); **MARY EVANS PICTURE LIBRARY** 32 Alfonso VI, 34 Isabella I, 35 Ferdinand II, 37 Philip II, 38 Diego Velázquez de Silva, 40 Siege of Barcelona, 41 Naval Victory at Viego, 42 Isabella II, 44 Primo de Rivera, 45 Civil War, 46 Franco, 48 'La Falange', 168 & 169 Pilgrims, 218 Knights Templar; **NATURE PHOTOGRAPHERS LTD** 104 White stork (A D Schilling), 105 Tongue orchid (P R Sterry); **NICK INMAN** 181; **PICTURES COLOUR LIBRARY** 83, 163; **POWERSTOCK/ZEFA** Front cover (b); **REX FEATURES LTD** 49 King Juan Carlos; **SPECTRUM COLOUR LIBRARY** 24/5 San Sebastián, 30/1 San Juan de los Reyes, 94 San Sebastián, 140 Riders, 141 God's Day Festival, 205 New Bisagra Gate, 207 Wine tasting, 212/3 Valencia, 216 Elche; **THE IMAGE BANK** Front cover (c); **THE MANSELL COLLECTION** 36 Charles V, 188/9 Spanish ships; **THE PHOTOGRAPHERS LIBRARY** Spine Flamenco dancers; **WORLD PICTURES** 95; www.euro.ecb.int 259.

All remaining pictures are held in the Association's own library (AA PHOTO LIBRARY) with contributions from: M CHAPLOW, S DAY, J EDMANSON, P ENTICKNAP, A MOLYNEUX, T OLIVER, J POULSEN, D ROBERTSON, R STRANGE, J TIMS, P WILSON.

Contributors

Original copy editor: Audrey Horne
Revision verifiers: Nick Inman, Clara Villanueva, and Josephine Hodgson